EUCHARISTIC RECIPROCITY

EUCHARISTIC RECIPROCITY

A PRACTICAL THEOLOGICAL INQUIRY INTO THE VIRTUE OF GRATITUDE

A. William DeJong

☙PICKWICK *Publications* · Eugene, Oregon

EUCHARISTIC RECIPROCITY
A Practical Theological Inquiry into the Virtue of Gratitude

Copyright © 2019 A. William DeJong. All rights reserved. Except for brief quotations in critical publications or reviews, no part of this book may be reproduced in any manner without prior written permission from the publisher. Write: Permissions, Wipf and Stock Publishers, 199 W. 8th Ave., Suite 3, Eugene, OR 97401.

Pickwick Publications
An Imprint of Wipf and Stock Publishers
199 W. 8th Ave., Suite 3
Eugene, OR 97401

www.wipfandstock.com

PAPERBACK ISBN: 978-1-5326-7253-8
HARDCOVER ISBN: 978-1-5326-7254-5
EBOOK ISBN: 978-1-5326-7255-2

Cataloguing-in-Publication data:

Names: DeJong, A. William, author.

Title: Eucharistic reciprocity : a practical theological inquiry into the virtue of gratitude / by A. William DeJong.

Description: Eugene, OR : Pickwick Publications, 2019 | Includes bibliographical references.

Identifiers: ISBN 978-1-5326-7253-8 (paperback) | ISBN 978-1-5326-7254-5 (hardcover) | ISBN 978-1-5326-7255-2 (ebook)

Subjects: LCSH: Gratitude. | Theology, Practical.

Classification: BJ1533.G8 D44 2019 (paperback) | BJ1533.G8 D44 (ebook)

Manufactured in the U.S.A.   04/18/19

Contents

Acknowledgments | vii

CHAPTER 1: INTRODUCTION | 1
Research Question | 3
The Method for Researching Gratitude | 6
Thesis Statement | 27
Entering the Conversation | 28
Gratitude in Different Narratives | 35
Conclusion | 54

CHAPTER 2: MORAL SABOTEURS OF GRATITUDE | 56
An Anthropology of Desire | 57
A Phenomenology of Habits | 63
Coming to Terms with Sin and Vice | 68
The Seven Deadly Sins | 73
Conclusion | 113

CHAPTER 3: PHILOSOPHICAL REDUCTIONS OF GRATITUDE | 115
Gifts Require Returns: Gratitude as Inferiority | 116
Gifts Must Not Require Returns: Gratitude as Poison | 125
Positive Psychology: Gratitude as Advantageous | 136
Conclusion: A Preliminary Profile of Gratitude | 145

CHAPTER 4: A THEOLOGICAL PROFILE OF GRATITUDE | 153
Gratitude in the Narrative of Scripture | 155
Theologians of Gratitude | 182
Conclusion: A Theologically Reflective Profile of Gratitude | 201

CHAPTER 5: GRATITUDE RITUALIZED AND PRACTICED | 205
Deficiencies of Law-Ethics in Relation to Ingratitude | 208
Redressing Ingratitude | 215

Eucharist: Paradigm for Transformation | 220
Practices of Gratitude | 243
Conclusion | 248

Bibliography | 251

ACKNOWLEDGMENTS

THE PHD DISSERTATION FROM which this book originated commenced just under a decade ago, and little in my life is still the same. Our family relocated within the city we live, two foster daughters and two foster sons passed through our home, and I became the pastor of a new congregation that was launched out of the church I previously pastored. Most significantly, my father passed away in April 23, 2014, and his steadfast interest in and support for all of my endeavors, academic and otherwise, must be acknowledged as they are missed.

The congregations of Cornerstone Canadian Reformed Church and Blessings Christian Church, both in Hamilton, Ontario, are to be thanked for affording me time to read and write and for supporting this inquiry. Allard Gunnink prodded me regularly and helped me to discipline myself at times when the project seemed larger than life. Dr. Steve Foster provided meaningful friendship, philosophical engagement, and pastoral encouragement along the way. Francine van Woudenberg-Sikkema graciously and capably provided careful editing for some of the chapters. As of October 2016, Hilmer Jagersma became my associate and I want to thank him for carrying many pastoral responsibilities while I was consumed by the work of completing this book.

Two creative and wise entrepreneurial friends, Dick Barendregt and Rob Wildeboer, supported me through their generosity and counsel. Drs. Gerhard Visscher and John Smith of the Canadian Reformed Theological Seminary offered unwavering encouragement from the sidelines. Drs. Craig Bartholomew and David Beldman of Redeemer University College provided stimulating and visionary collegiality.

Through the generosity of the Theological University in Kampen, NL, I was able to participate in the Advanced Theological Studies Fellowship in the summer of 2015 and there completed parts of chapters 3 and 4. I am grateful for the friendships that were forged with Dr. Burger and others, and for the peer scrutiny of Dr. Harm Goris of Tilburg University. Dr. Arnold Sikkema and the Geneva Society invited me to deliver a lecture at Trinity Western University in Langley, BC, in which some of the claims of chapter 5 were tested.

McMaster Divinity College proved to be an extraordinarily stimulating and supportive community for academic inquiry. Nina Thomas reminded me of obligations (e.g., deadlines) with unusual kindness and grace. Drs. Phil Zylla and Michael Knowles should be rewarded for their patience in working with me and for overseeing this project when, all too frequently, nothing was forthcoming. I benefited from Dr. Knowles's sharp mind and was sanctified both by his effortless and astute deconstructions of my arguments and by his pastoral encouragement. Dr. Zylla's perception and profundity pushed me to think deeper and with more creativity than comes naturally. Having enjoyed his lectures, I feel privileged to have received his personal attention and counsel. Dr. Jonathan Wilson of Carey Theological Seminary also provided invaluable feedback.

As was true of my father, my mother has been unwavering in her interest and support, and I want to thank her for her love. My four sons, now tall and imposing, are the source of immense joy in my life and I hope my delight in them is not vulnerable to the critique of pride I render in chapter 2. To Calvin, Alex, Jacob, and Ian, thank you so much!!! I so look forward to having more time to spend with you.

Especially to my dear wife Kim, I want to express my gratitude. Happy to work in the shadows, she has been my faithful and loyal companion through my married life. Far more than an encourager, she contributed to the completion of this book in numerous ways, both significant and trivial. To her especially I want to express my deep love and gratitude. Now that the seven years are completed, the sabbatical begins.

CHAPTER 1

INTRODUCTION

On September 17, 2011, a protest movement was launched by a Canadian magazine that attracted followers from across North America and garnered widespread media attention.[1] Dubbed "Occupy Wall Street," this movement was occasioned by resistance to social and economic inequality and opposition to greed, corruption, and the unfair influence of the financial sector in government affairs. Whatever assessment one has of the movement, one fact is indisputable—greed is widespread and increasing. Apparent among those with both high and modest incomes, greed is evident in Canada especially in terms of growing household debt, i.e., people spending more than they earn.[2]

Simultaneous with rampant overspending in Canadian culture is the widespread embrace of gratitude as something virtuous. Though there have always existed cultures, both ancient and non-Western, in which expressions of gratitude are deemed unnecessary or unwelcome, the absence of gratitude seems intolerable, if not immoral, for Canadians.[3] From the mo-

---

1. An anti-consumerist magazine, *Adbusters*, first promoted an occupation in Lower Manhattan on its website on February 2, 2011, momentum for which grew by subsequent emails to its subscribers.

2. The debt-to-income ratio of Canadian households has been steadily climbing now for 30 years (Wong, "Household Debt in Canada"; Crawford, "What Explains Trends"). Household debt in Canada is approaching two trillion dollars and Canadian households "owe about $1.68 in credit market debt for every dollar of disposable income" (Wong, "Household Debt in Canada"). See Kirby, "Canada's Fatal Attraction to Debt".

3. Margaret Visser indicates that the early European explorers, for example, were shocked to discover that in some foreign lands no gratitude was returned for gifts.

ment they can speak, children are taught to say, "thank you." It is easy to say, offends no one, and can be used even to discourage certain behaviors in advance (as in, "Thank you for not smoking."). Gratitude is regarded as a necessary expression of appreciation for a gift received, "one of the building blocks of a civil and humane society."[4] Thanksgiving Day, in Canada and the United States, remains a popular civic holiday and the occasion when many happily take inventory of what they have and enumerate the items for which, and the people for whom, they are grateful.

Many will argue that saying "thank you" for many Westerners is merely reflexive and instinctive, the product of an etiquette indelibly etched into one's subconscious by parents and teachers and thus often spoken thoughtlessly. To conclude that reflexive and instinctive behaviors are meaningless is reductionistic, however, and fails to acknowledge the power embedded in the ordinary. Cultural anthropologists increasingly recognize that common rituals do not merely represent power; they are powerful.[5] To forego an expected ritual is to slight it, thereby threatening social equilibrium and provoking angst, if not anger.

It is the simultaneity of a widespread cultural problem with greed and an equally widespread cultural esteem of gratitude that first occasioned my interest in gratitude. Is there perhaps something in our understanding of gratitude that still leaves us vulnerable to greed? In what follows, therefore,

---

Moreover, some cultures lack vocabulary for "thanks" while others find the practice rude and offensive. An Inuit hunter who shared with friends the meat of the seal he harpooned, for example, was applauded for his skill, but not thanked. The seal, though killed by the hunter, belonged to the community, and thus the hunter was obligated to share it. In similar tribal societies, attempts on the part of guests to return gifts for hospitality, for instance, can cause offence to the host, who might say, "Do I sell food?" (Visser, *Gift of Thanks*, 20–30). On the other hand, "gratitude is one of those responses which seems essential to and among civilized human beings" (Solomon, *Defense of Sentimentality*, 102).

4. Harpham, "History of Ideas," 21. The United Nations, in fact, has proclaimed that "thanksgiving is basic in human nature and is observed worldwide" (Emmons, *Thanks*, 118).

5. Victor Turner, a theoretician of ritual theory whose contribution dominates the field, proposes, for example, that the metaphor of social drama or dramatic interaction (i.e., the reality of people interacting) is a far more effective key to understanding social reality than "either the mechanistic metaphor of behaviorists or the organic metaphor of evolutionists" (Collins, "Ritual Symbols and the Ritual Process," 341). Compare with Elizabeth Collins, who writes, "Rituals do structure human behavior. However, precisely because social relations are ritualized and therefore relatively predictable, people can be effective agents. They can use the medium of ritual to pursue both conscious and unconscious aims. And they may be able to act collectively to change cultural patterns by creating new rituals and giving new meaning to old ones" (Collins, "Reflections on Ritual," 4).

I launch a theological inquiry to probe the nature of gratitude as a virtue. The moral saboteurs of gratitude are considered in chapter 2, and its philosophical detractors are addressed in chapter 3. Chapter 4 offers a theological profile of gratitude which amounts to a modest apologia for gratitude as a virtue in response to the issues raised in chapter 3, and chapter 5 recommends practices to reduce the sabotage identified in chapter 2. Because there is, so far as I know, no book-length treatment of the theology of gratitude this venture has a particularly vulnerable character.[6]

RESEARCH QUESTION

The subject of gratitude is especially fascinating to me as a pastor in a confessionally Reformed church because gratitude is situated at the very heart of the Reformed construal of the Christian life. The Heidelberg Catechism (1563), widely embraced as a doctrinal standard in confessional Reformed churches, views the Christian life under the rubric of the Ten Commandments, but treats the Ten Commandments themselves under the motif of gratitude. "In this frame of reference," Stob writes, "morality loses all its hardness and harshness. Duties are no longer onerous."[7] The law is "contemplated as a gracious prescription supplying a happy and thankful man with helpful directives concerning how to satisfy someone whom it is his deepest desire to please."[8]

Stob's favorable perspective notwithstanding, literature produced by Reformed ethicists tends to focus on moral quandaries, dilemmas, and pressing contemporary ethical issues.[9] The insights generated by this approach are certainly instructive for assessing ethical problems and helpful in sharpening one's conscience, though the underlying assumption seems to be that ethical problems are best resolved by clear thinking, i.e., knowing how to apply rightly biblical norms, principles, patterns, etc.[10] Such

---

6. One of the challenges this inquiry faced was the absence of a standard theological treatment against which to compare one's ideas. The theological profile of gratitude offered in this inquiry, therefore, is somewhat of a pioneering contribution. In such cases, gaps will become apparent, rendering the overall contribution to be quite modest in the end, however important the pioneering venture is.

7. Stob, "Heidelberg Catechism," 8.

8. Stob, "Heidelberg Catechism," 8.

9. One thinks of Douma, *Ten Commandments*; Frame, *Doctrine of the Christian Life*; Murray, *Principles of Conduct*; Smedes, *Mere Morality*. Even Douma's book, *Responsible Conduct*, pays scant attention to virtue and character formation.

10. By all accounts the Protestant Reformation was predominantly an ideological movement, i.e., a movement of ideas, whose rapid expansion is largely attributable to

literature, therefore, is not always particularly useful in ministry because the moral problems pastors encounter often fall beyond its scope. Most people do not lie awake at night grappling with the ethics of euthanasia, abortion, or military drones, etc. This is not to say that they always think clearly about these issues; it is to say that their lives are not unsettled by questions of their morality. On the other hand, many are racked with fear, shame, guilt, and powerlessness because of sinful urges and impulses which threaten and often subdue them. The ethical challenges most face, in other words, belong to a category I would designate as sins of desire rather than simply sins of thought. In many instances, in fact, the sin of desire is problematic to someone precisely because he or she is thinking clearly.

How should one respond pastorally to the problem of sinful desires? For some, it is to recall and then recite a Bible verse in which the sin is denounced under the assumption that a fresh conviction of the sin will drive the person to Christ for forgiveness and renewal. For others, it might be to recommend a book or pamphlet in which the particular sin is addressed. Many pastors feel unable to do little more than identify the sin (of which the person is often keenly aware), urge repentance and seeking forgiveness in Christ. How should one respond to relapses in these struggles? To repeat the cycle of sin-repentance-forgiveness again and again reduces life to a frustrating moral treadmill on which one goes nowhere fast.

Christian discipleship, however, is a journey—a pilgrim's progress. For progress to be experienced, therefore, something must be done with the sins of desire. Among Protestant thinkers who have reckoned with the moral force of desire, C. S. Lewis is particularly insightful. In his masterful

---

the spread of literature (e.g., pamphlets, sermons, treatises, etc.). Colloquies were held, ideas were debated, letters were written, and those convinced by the logic of the Protestant cause joined her ranks. Perhaps not surprisingly, the Protestantism that evolved out of the Reformation has had a decidedly rational bent. This remains evident today in, for example, the worship of confessionally Reformed churches, including both the continental Reformed (i.e., Dutch and German Reformed churches) as well as the offspring of the Scottish Reformation (i.e., Presbyterian churches). Dating back to the Reformation liturgies of Geneva, Strasbourg, and Zurich, the sermon, as a largely intellectual exposition of the text, is the centerpiece. Other liturgical components, such as fellowship, prayers, songs, and the sacraments, are often secondary and peripheral. Between 1523 and 1598, singing in services following Zwingli's liturgy was forbidden in Zurich, whose city council ordered the destruction of pipe organs in 1527. Further, Zwingli's 1525 liturgy envisioned the Lord's Supper being celebrated only four times a year. Preaching, on the other hand, "formed a major item in all worship" (White, *Protestant Worship*, 63). "So great was the imperative to teach," White says of Calvin's Genevan worship, "that each service contains a condensed course in theology and ethics. This became a lasting characteristic of Reformed worship, contributing to its *overwhelmingly cerebral character*" (White, *Protestant Worship*, 65 [emphasis added]). See also Macquarrie, *Guide to the Sacraments*, 26.

Screwtape Letters, Lewis speculates about the dynamics of temptation. Uncle Screwtape advises Wormwood regarding how to sabotage the Christian faith:

> It is far better to make them live in the Future. Biological necessity makes all their passions point in that direction already, so that thought about the Future inflames hope and fear.... Hence nearly all vices are rooted in the future. Gratitude looks to the past and love to the present; fear, avarice, lust, and ambition look ahead.[11]

The moral inhibitors to sins of desire, for Lewis, are love and gratitude—the very two virtues celebrated in Reformed ethics.[12] Gratitude in particular is highlighted in Reformed ethics as the primary moral incentive to living a God-pleasing life.

To probe the moral nature and function of gratitude, therefore, is a wonderful avenue for recalibrating the regnant Reformed ethical paradigm. More importantly, such an inquiry would avail pastors with ministerial resources to help those burdened by sins of desire. The world approximates a spiritual minefield in which moral vigilance is constantly required. One wrong move and a person's life, moral and otherwise, can rapidly spiral. Though our minds are darkened by sin and our consciences sometimes seared, we still often have sufficient mental clarity to identify the moral saboteurs in our lives. Knowledge of the threat, however, is insufficient to repel it. Something else must change.

Throughout history, Christians especially have identified seven sins as particularly "deadly." What is remarkably distinct about the so-called "seven deadly sins" if one thinks of all the possible sins to identify as deadly is that they are all desires. When we scan the list even superficially the validity of this ancient taxonomy seems immediately apparent. Few can ever admit to being immune to pride, envy, anger, sloth, greed, gluttony, and/or lust. The seven deadly sins, however, do not feature prominently in the moral tradition of Reformed Protestantism. One does not find them discussed, for example, in the Reformation catechisms, as one does in the Catechism of the Catholic church, or in the standard books of Reformed ethics, as one does in comparable Catholic books.

Whereas sins of desire "look forward," gratitude "looks back." That occasions such questions as: How does gratitude function morally in relation

---

11. Lewis, *Screwtape Letters*, 77.

12. The Heidelberg Catechism, for instance, wastes no time in underscoring love as the essence of what God requires of us (Lord's Day 2) and then later presents instruction on the Christian life under the rubric of gratitude.

to sins of desire, and the seven deadly sins in particular? How is gratitude virtuous? What moral power does gratitude embody? The central goal of this book is to address the question: *To what extent can gratitude, freshly understood, theologically articulated, and thoughtfully practiced, protect individuals, relationships, and communities from the destructive power of disoriented desire and rehabilitate those who have been ensnared?*

THE METHOD FOR RESEARCHING GRATITUDE

In order to address the above question, I will undertake a practical theological investigation of the subject of gratitude. The term "practical theology" has its origin in the theological encyclopedic tradition in Germany which transformed theologia into theological disciplines, thereby dispersing theology into "a multiplicity of sciences."[13] That history begins in the Protestantism that immediately followed the Reformation, when theology was taught at "schools" but in the context of prayer and spiritual formation. The primary inquiry then was the study of Scripture, of which doctrinal articulation was a part, and its relevance was seen largely in terms of understanding the true doctrine and refuting the bad (e.g., *theologia elenctica*, *theologia polemica*).[14] Attention was also paid to the acquisition of skills and knowledge necessary for the proper understanding of Scripture (or what later was called propaedeutics). Many distinctions were made (e.g., between archetypal and ectypal theology or between thetic and polemical theology), but none of them constituted "proposals for distinct theological sciences."[15]

Theologia, Edward Farley claims, was dismantled under multiple influences, not least the ideals of German Pietism.[16] Theology was reconfigured by the Pietists to have as its objective holy living, and thus the study of interpretation and dogmatics, for instance, were means to that end. What emerged was a new term for theology—namely, *Gottesgelahrtheit*, to denote theology as divine truths.[17] Beyond this, one must discern practical objectives and ways to attain those objectives. "With this shift," Farley claims, "theory-practice in the modern sense is born."[18] What earlier theologians embraced as theological distinctions, the pietist theologians (e.g., Gundling, Walch, and Mosheim) began to call "theological disciplines" (e.g., *theologia*

---

13. Farley, *Theologia*, 49.
14. Farley, *Theologia*, 52. See also Bavinck, *Reformed Dogmatics* 1:208ff.
15. Farley, *Theologia*, 54.
16. Farley, *Theologia*, 59. See also Purvis, *Theology and University*, 41.
17. Purvis, *Theology and University*, 63.
18. Farley, *Theologia*, 61.

theoretica, catechetica, practica, etc.), each with their own objectives and their own literature.[19] Gundling in particular distinguished between theoretical sciences and practical sciences, arguing that *Gottesgelahrtheit* includes both *Glaubenslehren* (doctrines of faith) and *Lebens-regeln* (rules for living).[20]

Theologia as a unifying enterprise also suffered, Farley claims, under the influence of the German *Aufklärung* with its extensive critique of supernaturalist theology and its advance of historical criticism.[21] What was lost was the unifying text of Scripture and the specifically Christian context for doing theology. Out of this emerged the German theological encyclopedic movement in which the study of theology was engaged as an "encyclopedic" quandary. The Pietist Gundling's two-fold distinction between theory and practice became the origin of the fourfold distinction in which Scripture, church history, and dogmatics were seen as theoretical sciences and practical theology as applied science.[22] Though dogmatics and exegesis were distinguished by earlier Protestant theologians, they became separate disciplines under the influence of the historical methods of the Enlightenment. Church history was included among the theoretical sciences as having equal importance to the Bible and dogmatics because of, among other things, the polemics between Protestants and Catholics.[23]

A key figure in the establishment of the fourfold paradigm is Friedrich Schleiermacher. Schleiermacher was engaged with others in the faculty of the University of Halle regarding how theology related to the other faculties of philosophy, medicine, and law and whether theology should be taught at the university.[24] Schleiermacher argued that theology was not "pure" science (i.e., universal), as was philosophy, but a "positive" science (i.e., cultural and historical) like medicine and law.[25] Further, theology functioned like medicine and law in the sense that it provides knowledge necessary for the leadership to govern and order the religious community. Edward Farley appropriately calls this "the clerical paradigm."[26] In Schleiermacher's

---

19. Farley, *Theologia*, 62. See also Purvis, *Theology and University*, 50.
20. Purvis, *Theology and the University*, 51.
21. Farley, *Theologia*, 64.
22. Farley, *Theologia*, 78.
23. Farley, *Theologia*, 79.
24. 1914 was the first year a German university (Frankfurt) was founded without a theological faculty (Grethlein, *Practical Theology*, 13).
25. Farley, Theologia, 86–87. See also Miller-McLemore, *Christian Theology*, 168.
26. Farley, *Theologia*, 87.

scheme, theology could be organized into three disciplines: practical theology, historical theology, and philosophical theology.[27]

Practical theology, for Schleiermacher, is a normative discipline which "assesses the activities, procedures, and operations of the church's ministry," including preaching, pastoral care, church education, and administration.[28] Historical theology helps appraise, in terms of the essence of Christianity, the health of the faith community as an historical phenomenon and includes the traditional theoretical disciplines of exegesis, church history, and dogmatics. Philosophical theology, lastly, investigates the distinctive essence of Christianity—namely, piety—and includes apologetics and polemics.[29] Yet Schleiermacher rejected a theory-practice encyclopedia, arguing that all three disciplines were cognitions required by healthy praxis.[30] Schleiermacher's view dominated throughout the nineteenth century. The prevailing view was that "theology is a science (a systematizing of data yielding knowledge) of the Christian religion for the special purpose of educating the leadership of the church."[31] Yet in the nineteenth century, Schleiermacher's "attempt to identify a theological subject matter for practical theology" is abandoned.[32]

A comparable practical theology did not surface in the United States until the mid-twentieth century. The seeds were thrown by William James (d.1910) and his thick descriptions of individual experiences. Anton Boisen (d.1965) followed in this tradition by regarding people as "living human documents" requiring study and interpretation.[33] There was mutual interpretation between pastoral theology and psychology and between pastor and parishioner. Building on Boisen, Seward Hiltner (d.1984) distinguished between "logic-centered fields" such as historical theology and dogmatics and "operation-centered fields" such as pastoral theology, educational theology, and ecclesiastical theology.[34] Until the second half of the twentieth century, therefore, practical theology was construed either as "functional skill," whereby attention was paid to the techniques necessary for the successful exercises of the church's ministry, or "applied theology" whereby the

---

27. Purvis, *Theology and University*, 150; Bavinck, *Reformed Dogmatics* 1:47.
28. Farley, *Theologia*, 91.
29. Purvis, *Theology and University*, 156.
30. Farley, *Theologia*, 93.
31. Farley, *Theologia*, 104. "Right from the start, the chief concerns of Practical Theology were the church and its praxis" (Grethlein, *Practical Theology*, 12).
32. Farley, *Theologia*, 106.
33. See Gerkin, *Living Human Document*, 37.
34. See the seminal Hiltner, *Preface to Pastoral Theology*, 20.

fruit of systematic theology (i.e., "real" theology), was harvested for use in ministry.[35] In the former, the theological component of the discipline was limited; in the latter, it was nearly absent.[36] Especially toward the end of the twentieth century, a shift was made in the discipline of practical theology "from a *therapeutic* to a *hermeneutic* model of pastoral engagement in which the activity of *theological reflection* assumes center stage."[37]

Practical theology is increasingly seen by practitioners today, not as a subset of the theological enterprise or as a rival to systematic theology, but as a comprehensive method for doing theology in general.[38] If systematic theology typically begins from above, with the Scriptures and the Christian tradition, practical theology begins from below, with human situations that require interpretation and invite theological reflection and thoughtful response.[39] This approach is not meant to devalue Scripture or the Christian tradition, but to ensure that theology is always contextual and dynamic and never timeless and static. Theologians have a responsibility not only to speak, but to listen, to be attentive to the cultural contexts in which they speak. Perhaps because of the influence of theologies of liberation, practical theology shifted from what Edward Farley called "the clerical paradigm" to a more democratized discipline in which formerly neglected voices of the people were heard.[40]

As part of its renewal and renovation, and through the trailblazing endeavors of scholars like David Tracy and Don Browning, practical theology

---

35. An example of the latter approach is Eduard Thurneysen, a friend of Karl Barth and a pastoral theologian heavily influenced by him (See Thurneysen, *Theology of Pastoral Care*). Gerald Hawkes alleges that for Thurneysen, "all that practical theology can say . . . must be deduced from theology" (Hawkes, "Role of Theology," 40). The danger of the functional approach is that it easily generates pragmatism and the shortcoming in the applied approach is its tendency to traditionalism (See Schuringa, "Wagging the Dog," 155).

36. Cf. Kromminga, *Pastoral Genius*, 6.

37. Graham et al., *Theological Reflection*, 2–3.

38. This is Farley's thesis in *Theologia*. One finds a discussion of this approach in Lartey, "Practical Theology."

39. An example of systematic theology from above is Karl Barth who regarded theology as God's self-disclosure and, as such, saw "no role for human understanding, action, or practice in the construal of God's self-disclosure" (Browning, *Fundamental Practical Theology*, 5). Theology, as such, is "practical only by applying God's revelation as directly and purely as possible to the concrete situations of life" (Browning, *Fundamental Practical Theology*, 5). "In distinction from exegetical theology, historical theology, and systematic theology, *practical* theology has *the praxis* for its *locus theologicus*" (Schuringa, "Wagging the Dog," 156). Cf. Heitink, *Pastoraat Als Hulpverlening*, 18.

40. Graham et al., *Theological Reflection*, 3.

began to envisage the wider society as its "primary audience."[41] There were, according to Bonnie Miller-McLemore, two motivations for this "public" turn—namely, "concern about the public silence of mainstream Christianity on key social issues, and awareness of the serious limitations of the pastoral focus on the individual alone."[42] Practical theology, therefore, has become public theology, whose objective is not just "to state the norms . . . for the faithful (although certainly for them), but also to determine whether these norms have general significance even for those who are not explicitly Christian."[43] Practical theology recommends ways to renew and reconstruct the praxis it has observed, interpreted, and scrutinized. As such, it might be dubbed "everyday theology," theology concerned with "the embodiment of religious belief in the day-to-day lives of individuals and communities."[44] It is theology for public well-being and public welfare.

Practical theology is sometimes distinguished from pastoral theology—namely, "that branch of practical theology focused on pastoral care and counseling."[45] If practical theology envisions the world both as its realm of inquiry and the arena in which it pursues human flourishing, then pastoral theology has its eye especially on the church. The line between the two, however, is sometimes too heavily demarcated as if practical theology and pastoral theology are driven by independent, if not contradictory objectives and invoke alternative theological methods. What is good for the church, however, is good for the world and vice versa. It seems impossible, in other words, to produce theology that is good for the world that is not simultaneously good for the church. In this vein, Elaine Graham et al. identify among the tasks of practical theological reflection both "building and sustaining the community of faith" and "communicating the faith to a wider culture."[46] Because this study envisions issues that concern humanity and not just Christian believers, this book will embrace the category of practical theology, but this should not be construed to mean that the church is beyond the purview of this inquiry. Rather, this book will argue that the church has potential to be a model community, embodying gratitude and fostering its

---

41. Miller-McLemore, *Christian Theology*, 71. See, for example, Browning, *Moral Context of Pastoral Care*; *Religious Ethics and Pastoral Care*; Tracy, *Analogical Imagination*.

42. Miller-McLemore, *Christian Theology*, 86.

43. Browning, "Pastoral Theology," 194–95.

44. Miller-McLemore, *Christian Theology*, 103. According to David Tracy, "practical theology is the most concrete exemplification of all theology" (Tracy, "Practical Theology," 142).

45. Miller-McLemore, *Christian Theology*, 100.

46. Graham et al., *Theological Reflection*, 10.

practice not just for the church's benefit, but for human flourishing more generally.

Phenomenological

The method of practical theology, therefore, is initially inductive, descriptive, empirical, and hermeneutical.[47] This involves paying attention to a particular situation in order to understand it.[48] John Patton termed this exercise "existential phenomenology," by which he means "an intentional, rational effort to allow phenomena to be experienced without my conventional ways of seeing and understanding getting in the way of that experience."[49] With indebtedness to Husserl's philosophical phenomenology, Patton urges the practical theologian to bracket attempts to classify and categorize in order to permit the situation to speak for itself. The initial text under scrutiny, therefore, is the human text. Human texts, however, are always located in the midst of specific and complex contexts thereby inviting not simply a hermeneutic of the human document, but of the situation in which the human text is located. Bonnie Miller-McLemore, for this reason, prefers the language of "the human web," to account for the social systems in which people operate and to rectify the individualistic implications assumed by the language of "the human document."[50]

Why do practical theologians study and interpret situations? "Situations or their elements," writes Edward Farley, "get our attention when they become problematic, pose crises, require decision."[51] Practical theology, however, should not be consumed exclusively by perceived challenges and problems, but by opportunities to contribute to increased knowledge and to human flourishing. What, then, are some of the ways in which phenomena can be studied? Richard Osmer helpfully presents a spectrum of observation, with informal attending on one side and formal attending on the other.[52] Informal attending is openness to what we see in our everyday life. Formal attending involves studying certain situations through empirical research,

---

47. "While both induction and deduction can form part of the practical theological process, induction has a particularly important place" (Pattison and Woodward, "Introduction," 10).
48. See Farley, "Interpreting Situations."
49. Patton, *From Ministry to Theology*, 36.
50. Miller-McLemore, *Christian Theology in Practice*, 42.
51. Farley, "Interpreting Situations," 10.
52. Osmer, *Practical Theology*, 38.

either quantitative or qualitative or both. This work, as John Swinton and Harriet Mowat allege, is comparable to the work of a detective:

> It involves the painstaking and complex process of unpicking the detail of who did what, when, and why with particular situations and formulating this into evidence which will enable a fair judgment to be made.... However, unlike the detective the qualitative researcher does not seek to solve the problem or 'crack the case.' She is very much aware that neither is possible.[53]

This book will attend, both formally and informally, not simply to gratitude, but to the desires that threaten it. In chapter 1, for instance, I will attend to different cultural practices of gratitude, and in chapter 2, I will investigate the seven deadly sins and especially their potential as saboteurs of gratitude. I will argue that the seven deadly sins are all distortions of desires for good things: pride is the distorted desire for acceptance, envy for equality, anger for justice, sloth for rest, greed for provision, gluttony for pleasure, and lust for relationship.

Correlational

The practical theologian then brings the situation, phenomenologically interpreted, into a broader discussion, inviting the interpretations of both theological and non-theological (often social-scientific) disciplines. This phase is often called "correlation" with deference to Paul Tillich who endeavored "to correlate existential questions that were drawn from human experience with theological answers offered by the Christian tradition."[54] Tillich averred that an analysis of human experience should bring questions to the theological table and that these questions, in turn, should be answered out of Scripture and the Christian tradition.[55]

David Tracy became a key figure in development of this method when he revised Tillich's model to include a dialectical element which enabled the conversation partners, e.g., psychology and the Christian tradition, to be mutually correlative and critical. Tracy explicates his model, now widely embraced, in terms of five proposals, the first of which is that Christian texts and common human experience form the two principal texts for theology:

---

53. Swinton and Mowat, *Practical Theology*, 36.

54. Swinton and Mowat, *Practical Theology*, 77. Tillich exemplified this approach in his sermons where he correlated the message of the gospel with, for example, the psychological concept of unconditional acceptance (See, e.g., Tillich, *Courage to Be*).

55. See Tillich, *Systematic Theology*, 64; Swinton and Mowat, *Practical Theology*, 78.

"Insofar as the scriptures claim that the Christian self-understanding does, in fact, express an understanding of authentic human existence as such, the Christian theologian is impelled to test precisely that universalist claim."[56] Moreover, the theologian is compelled to show the adequacy of theological categories for all human experience.

The second proposal is that the theological task involves a *critical correlation* of the results of the investigations of the two sources of theology. Here Tracy finds Tillich's version of correlation unacceptable because, though it involves questions from one source and answers from another, it does not make provision for the answers to be investigated critically: "Tillich's method of correlation does not actually correlate; it juxtaposes questions from the 'situation' with answers from the 'message.'"[57]

Tracy's third proposal is that the method of investigating common human experience can be described as a *phenomenology* of the religious dimension. If theology involves "a claim to universal existential relevance," we need a methodology to "explicate the religious dimension of our common experience and language" and the philosophical discipline of phenomenology, initiated by Husserl and refined by, inter alia, Merleau-Ponty, Heidegger, and Ricoeur, seems best suited for it.[58]

His fourth proposal is that the principal method for investigating the Christian tradition can be described as an *historical and hermeneutical* investigation of classical Christian texts. By historical, Tracy means, "the theologian as historian pays heed to those historical reconstructions of Christian events and texts which modern historical scholarship has made available."[59] Beyond that, the theologian must utilize a hermeneutic that enables him or her to determine the meanings of the metaphors and symbols of the texts in order to express the religious significance of the embedded claims.

Tracy's final proposal is that to determine the truth-status of one's investigations of the two sources, the theologian should employ an explicitly metaphysical mode of *reflection*. Since comparative analysis cannot of itself resolve the question of the truth-status, we need a discipline that can. Such a discipline must be reflective and capable of articulating conceptual

---

56. Tracy, *Blessed Rage*, 44.

57. Tracy, *Blessed Rage*, 46. Incidentally, Thomas Oden faults Tillich for the exact opposite problem—namely, recommending a theological method that was heavily weighted in favor of psychology. The supposed conversation between human experience and theology was reduced, in Oden's understanding to a monologue in which theology was largely silent (See Oden, *Contemporary Theology*, 59).

58. Tracy, *Blessed Rage*, 47–48.

59. Tracy, *Blessed Rage*, 49.

categories in a way that will be able to account "not merely for some particular dimension of experience but for *all experience* as such."[60]

Combining into one sentence the pivotal words italicized above, we could define David Tracy's revised correlation methodology as the endeavour to correlate, in a mutually *corrective* manner, two *principal texts*, human experience and Scripture, the former accessed through *phenomenology* and the latter probed through a *historical and hermeneutical* investigation, thus equipping the theologian to *reflect* on a situation so as to account for its experience.

Stephen Pattison helpfully describes the enterprise of correlation as a mutual critical conversation. Invoking the metaphor of friends, Pattison describes a dialogue between two parties who have much in common and much to learn from one another. This mutually critical conversation, according to Pattison, is designed to make scholars "conscious of their own presuppositions, the resources of the Christian tradition and the realities of a practical situation in such a way that each modifies and learns from the others in a dynamic interaction."[61] The line between the two texts for practical theology—namely, the Scriptures, as interpreted and understood in the theological tradition and the human situation, as observed and interpreted by philosophers, psychologists, and other social scientists—is porous, and the one can inform the other without confusing the two. In a similar vein, Swinton and Mowatt write, "Mutual critical correlation sees the practical-theological task as bringing situations into dialectical conversation with insights from the Christian tradition and perspectives drawn from other sources of knowledge (primarily the social sciences)."[62]

Correlation Challenged

Though adherents of the revised critical correlation theory see Scripture/the Christian tradition on par with voices from other disciplines, others wonder whether Christian theology and the human situation *should* be correlated and, even prior, whether they can be correlated. Among the contemporary

---

60. Tracy, *Blessed Rage*, 55.

61. Pattison, "Some Straw for Bricks," 136. According to Thomas Long, "Practical Theology . . . seeks after and generates knowledge rather than merely applying knowledge acquired elsewhere. Practical theology draws wisdom from the findings of other fields, but it also has a word to speak in a larger conversation that other fields do not have, and its insights are potentially useful to those fields, including those beyond the circle of theology" (Long, "Practical Theology on the Quad," 250).

62. Swinton and Mowat, "Practical Theology," 77.

critics are John Milbank, Andrew Purves, and Oliver O'Donovan, each of whose critiques will be summarized and assessed below.

John Milbank, first, is the Cambridge theologian who launched, along with Graham Ward and Catherine Pickstock, what is termed Radical Orthodoxy, an anglo-catholic movement with an explicitly socialist-pacifist-anarchist political agenda and, for our purposes, a deliberate privileging of theology as a meta-discourse or, to invoke an older phrase, as "the queen of the sciences."[63] The backdrop for Radical Orthodoxy is the postmodern assertion that all Cartesian claims to knowledge only serve to subject adherents to self-imposed ethical rules and exclude, if not harm, others. Postmodern Christian theorists argue similarly for "religion without religion," an indeterminate faith not circumscribed by creed or denomination.[64] Radical Orthodoxy endeavors to recover an Augustinian account of knowledge which, while lacking pretensions to absolute certainty or objectivity, is derived from revelation, remains a matter of interpretation, and requires the Spirit's illumination. Far from denying the possibility of revelation, as do other postmodern theorists, Radical Orthodoxy affirms its primacy. "Either the entire Christian narrative tells us how things truly are," Milbank writes, "or it does not. If it does, we have no other access to how things truly are, nor any additional means of determining the question."[65] Instead of seeing the social sciences, for instance, as an ingredient in theology, therefore, Milbank insists that classical orthodoxy formulates its own social and political theory.

In his book *Theology and Social Theory*, Milbank argues that secular (as supposedly neutral) theory must be understood in religious terms, either as heretical or pagan, either as modifying orthodox Christian views or rejecting them.[66] "Everywhere on earth Christ is typologically foreshadowed," Milbank writes, "and all are faced with the choice whether to accept or refuse Jesus—as he himself told us."[67] Scientific social theories are therefore either theologies or anti-theologies. Christian theorizing of any

---

63. To be sure, Milbank's understanding of theology is sometimes more akin to what might be termed "Christian philosophy" or, as Milbank himself says, "Christian sociology" (See Milbank, *Theology and Social Theory*, 382).

64. See Caputo, *Prayers and Tears*.

65. Milbank, *Word Made Strange*, 250.

66. Milbank, *Theology and Social Theory*, 1.

67. Milbank, "Introduction," 18; cf. Milbank, *Theology and Social Theory*, 25. For Milbank "correlationist" theologies seem like "a bizarre academic twilight zone inhabited by the intellectually craven and impotent" (See Milbank, "Introduction," 12). Milbank is rightly critiqued here by those who point out that, notwithstanding his promotion of an ontology of peace, his rhetoric of demolishing secular reason and rooting out violence is itself violent (See Boersma, "Being Reconciled," 197).

sort must be self-consciously and self-admittedly Christian such that "every discipline must be framed by a theological perspective."[68] The problem with modern theology is its "false humility"—namely, the surrender of its claim to be a "metadiscourse."[69] Since the gospel is not up for negotiation, "the task of such a theology is not apologetics, nor even simply argument. Rather it is to tell again the Christian *mythos*, pronounce again the Christian *logos*, and call again for Christian *praxis* in a manner that restores their freshness and originality. It must articulate Christian difference in such a fashion as to make it strange."[70] "If theology no longer seeks to position, qualify or criticize other discourses," Milbank elsewhere asserts, "then it is inevitable that these discourses will position theology."[71]

Influenced by the *nouvelle theologie* of Henri de Lubac, Yves Congar, and others, Radical Orthodoxy rejects the dualism of scholastic Thomism in which, alongside of grace, there is an autonomous realm of pure nature or *saeculum*.[72] For Milbank, this coalesces with his presentation of the church, in Augustinian terms, as the *civitas Dei* and realm of peace and forgiveness and the *altera civitas* to all other public spaces denoted by the *civitas terrena* and characterized by "self-love and self-assertion; an enjoyment of arbitrary, and therefore violent power over others—the *libido dominandi*."[73] This illustrates how Milbank is excessively and unjustifiably antithetical in his formulations. Not only is it possible to speak of redemptive violence within the *civitas Dei* (the cross assumes violence), it also possible to speak of pagan peace within the *civitas terrena*. We should not deny, as Hans Boersma alleges, that in the created order beyond the confines of the church there are still "grace-filled spaces of nature, reason, and metaphysics."[74] Theological theorizing ought to have theo-logical priority, but to insist that all secular thought is heretical or pagan hinges on one of two unacceptable assumptions—either that nothing is left of God's good creation or that God's grace is limited only to the church.

A second critic is Andrew Purves, among those pastoral theologians in the Barthian tradition who reject correlation wholesale.[75] A native of Scot-

68. Milbank et al., "Introduction," 3.
69. Milbank, *Theology and Social Theory*, 1.
70. Milbank, *Theology and Social Theory*, 383.
71. Milbank, *Theology and Social Theory*, 1.
72. See Smith, *Introducing Radical Orthodoxy*, 44.
73. Milbank, *Theology and Social Theory*, 194.
74. Boersma, "Being Reconciled," 201. This point is expressed, Boersma suggests, by the Reformed theology of common grace.
75. Karl Barth eschewed the possibility of correspondence between the Christian message and secular knowledge. "The Gospel is not a truth among other truths. Rather

land who obtained his doctorate from the University of Edinburgh where he studied under Thomas F. Torrance, Purves betrays a theological commitment to the Christocentricity of Karl Barth, as mediated through the Torrance brothers, Thomas and James. For Purves, the notion of correlation is based on "an a priori, immanent, and panentheistic view of God that assumes God and humankind are in some kind of relationship of mutuality—a pleasant thought, but one that quite neglects the sovereignty and holiness of the Lord God."[76] Furthermore, if one does not affirm as its "principal task" the doctrine of the practice of God, and ministerial participation in it, the theology of pastoral care will ultimately be "effectively controlled by something other than the church's Trinitarian knowledge of the practice or mission of God."[77] Thus, "the doctrine of the Trinity is the basis for Christian practical theology."[78]

Purves insists that if pastoral theology is not first and foremost Christology, it is inherently misguided and erroneous and must be reappraised. Such a pastoral theology "stands over and against the more recent perspectives in pastoral theology that begin with human experience on its own terms."[79] One of his central claims, in this connection, is that Jesus Christ is the primary minister and that ministers today do not imitate or derive skills from his ministry so much as participate in it.[80] There is not only good news in salvation (i.e., Jesus died and rose for us), there is good news in ministry, (i.e., Jesus ministers for us). By virtue of our union with Him, "we share in Christ's competence and thus in his ministry."[81] Participation in the priesthood, for Purves, is the "foundation of practical theology."[82] We must learn to speak not only of the vicarious humanity of Christ, but of his vicarious ministry: he prays, teaches, and ministers for us. "Let us look at Christ,"

---

it sets a question mark against all truths. . . . The Gospel does not expound or recommend itself. It does not negotiate or plead, threaten or make promises" (Barth, *Epistle to the Romans*, 35; cf. 38–39). Less polemically, Deborah Hunsinger writes, "The disciplines that describe creaturely reality logically function at a different level because they are not trying to make the kind of claims about ultimate reality that Christian theology makes" (Hunsinger, *Theology and Pastoral Counseling*, 93). Miller-McLemore gives a nod in this direction in arguing that since the disciplines of theology and science operate in distinct spheres, employ unique methods, and are concerned with different questions, one should not prejudice the other (Miller-McLemore, "Cognitive Science," 76).

76. Purves, *Reconstructing Pastoral Theology*, 5.
77. Purves, *Reconstructing Pastoral Theology*, xxii.
78. Purves, *Reconstructing Pastoral Theology*, xxv.
79. Purves, *Reconstructing Pastoral Theology*, 1.
80. Purves, *Reconstructing Pastoral Theology*, 44.
81. Purves, *Reconstructing Pastoral Theology*, 208.
82. Purves, *Reconstructing Pastoral Theology*, 61.

Purves insists, "as the one who leads our worship and proclaims the Word of God, who teaches us the things of God and who acts in the freedom of his love for us and for our salvation."[83]

What does the vicarious ministry of Christ mean, for instance, in relation to preaching? The sermon, Purves suggests, is an instance of incarnation, of Jesus Christ appearing enfleshed in speech.[84] The power of preaching, therefore, is not to be located in "homiletical techniques, rhetorical strategies, or even theological acuity" but in attesting to "the reality, truth, and power of the Word of God."[85] Those who strive endlessly for sermonic relevance need to be reminded that Christ "is practical, relevant, and significant."[86] Not only is this homiletic faithful to Jesus Christ, it spares the minister from "a kind of ministerial Pelagianism," the fruitless pursuit of acquiring skills or the burden of having to convince or convert people.[87] What does the vicarious ministry of Christ mean for pastoral care? Purves claims that Seward Hiltner and other pastoral theologians, borrowing from Carl Rogers, alleged that the resources for healing "lie latently within a person, to be drawn out by the good work of the counselor."[88] Purves demurs, holding the conviction of Eduard Thurneysen, for whom "pastoral work happens in the form of a conversation in which both parties listen to and respond to the Word of God, for it is God's Word alone that ultimately interprets and heals the human situation."[89] "The pastoral conversation," Purves writes, "will seek to allow and enable a person to examine and reflect on his or her life circumstances in the light of the gospel, to gain deeper insight into the truth of his or her life in Christ, as it touches this presenting life event."[90]

The significance of Jesus's ministry for pastoral theology is not limited to the past or the present, however, but includes the future. Here Purves is especially dependent on Jürgen Moltmann's theology of hope and specifically his conviction that the cross must be "seen to be the cross of the risen Christ" such that the cross is "the present form of the resurrection."[91] This has immense significance for pastoral theology because the cross makes the meaning of Christ's resurrection "manifest for those who suffer under their

---

83. Purves, *Crucifixion of Ministry*, 87.
84. Purves, *Reconstructing Pastoral Theology*, 157.
85. Purves, *Reconstructing Pastoral Theology*, 156.
86. Purves, *Crucifixion of Ministry*, 90.
87. Purves, *Reconstructing Pastoral Theology*, 159.
88. Purves, *Reconstructing Pastoral Theology*, 161.
89. Purves, *Reconstructing Pastoral Theology*, 162.
90. Purves, *Crucifixion of Ministry*, 136.
91. Purves, *Reconstructing Pastoral Theology*, 135.

own unrighteousness and who live in the shadow of death."[92] "In Christ's death," Purves writes, "we find the significance of his resurrection, for there Christ is in solidarity with the human plight, and from this atonement means that the coming God is one in Christ with all humankind in life unto death, giving all a future that humankind would not have otherwise."[93] In Purves's thinking this has tremendous implications for pastoral theology. Without Moltmann's eschatology of the cross, as "God's own protest against death and deadliness in the world," pastoral work will degenerate into "a generalized Docetism—a lack of concern for the physical, political, and economic side of suffering."[94]

Purves's reconstruction of pastoral theology, however, is not without problems. His Christology is so dominant that it nearly eclipses other important doctrines such as protology, or the doctrine of creation.[95] While Purves faults Seward Hiltner for assuming continuity between creation and redemption such that health and salvation get blurred, he fails to advance any theology of creation.[96] If we profess that God speaks to us in Christ, must we conclude that he is silent everywhere else? If one accepts the claim that God speaks in and through the created order, as do Christians of various theological traditions both Protestant and Catholic, one's esteem for the claims of the scientific enterprise, including psychology, immediately increases. Though his accent on the peculiar features of Christian theology as Trinitarian and Christocentric is welcome, the antithesis that Purves draws between theology and the social sciences seems overstated.

The third critic, the British evangelical theologian Oliver O'Donovan, provides a happy balance between correlationists and Barthians/Radical Orthodoxy theorists by rejecting the neutrality of secular thought (à la the Radical Orthodox), advancing a Christocentric theology (à la the Barthians) and affirming both natural revelation and a Christocentric theology. In his book *Resurrection and Moral Order*, he sets forth the claim that Christian ethics, for example, "depends upon the resurrection of Jesus Christ from the dead."[97] Not only does the claim that Scripture is divine revelation rest on the historicity of Christ's resurrection, but the resurrection implies an

---

92. Purves, *Reconstructing Pastoral Theology*, 136.
93. Purves, *Reconstructing Pastoral Theology*, 136.
94. Purves, *Reconstructing Pastoral Theology*, 146.
95. Oliver O'Donovan alleges, analogously, that Barth's doctrine of creation was "subordinated ontologically to Christology" (O'Donovan, *Resurrection and Moral Order*, 87).
96. Purves, *Reconstructing Pastoral Theology*, xxxiii.
97. O'Donovan, *Resurrection and Moral Order*, 13.

affirmation of creation and of humanity.[98] The Christian faith, as such, affirms the objectivity of a divine order in creation generally and in human nature specifically. The way the universe objectively is, O'Donovan argues, determines how humanity ought to conduct itself.[99] The knowledge of the natural order, therefore, is moral knowledge to which one is either obedient or disobedient, and much of it does not require revelation and is thus widely accessible. On these grounds, the notion of correlation is acceptable and the pursuit of correlation possible.

O'Donovan is not content, however, simply to affirm an ontological ground for an objective order to which ethical appeal can be made. Our knowledge of the natural order is incomplete without knowing the whole created order, not least its relations to the uncreated. "If the Creator is not known," O'Donovan writes, "then the creation is not known as *creation*; for the relation of the creation to its Creator is the ground of its intelligibility as a created universe."[100] Moreover, because of the primeval fall into sin, humanity is inclined to misinterpret, if not reject the created order. Though the order is observed, fallen humanity "misconstrues that order and constructs false and terrifying worldviews" expressed in Scripture "by the sin of idolatry."[101] While there is an *ontological* ground for affirming an objective moral order in creation, there is insufficient *epistemological* warrant for confidence regarding whether it can be properly known. This leads O'Donovan to insist that only in the sphere of revelation "can we see the natural order as it really is and overcome the epistemological barriers to an ethic that conforms to nature."[102] This should not be misconstrued to mean that revelation confers on a person a knowledge one could not otherwise have. Christian thinkers should not "proceed in a totalitarian way, denying the importance and relevance of all that he [sic] finds valued as moral conviction in the various cultures and traditions of the world (whether these be 'Christian,' non-Christian,' or 'post-Christian')."[103] On the other hand, one must approach such "phenomena critically, evaluating them and interpreting their significance from the place where true knowledge of the moral order is given, under the authority of the gospel."[104] More specifically, "only in Christ do we apprehend that order in which we stand and that knowledge

---

98. O'Donovan, *Resurrection and Moral Order*, 15.
99. O'Donovan, *Resurrection and Moral Order*, 17.
100. O'Donovan, *Resurrection and Moral Order*, 88.
101. O'Donovan, *Resurrection and Moral Order*, 82.
102. O'Donovan, *Resurrection and Moral Order*, 20.
103. O'Donovan, *Resurrection and Moral Order*, 89.
104. O'Donovan, *Resurrection and Moral Order*, 90.

of it with which we have been endowed."[105] Without recognition that theological authority is located solely in Christ, the project of correlation simply becomes "a work of ideology, in which the gospel is proved to be 'at home' in our favored cultural setting, whatever it may be."[106]

In conclusion, O'Donovan's distinction between the ontological reality of an objective moral order and our epistemological inability to discern it rightly deserves much consideration among practical theologians.

Correlation Refined

Correlation as method in practical theology is acceptable, therefore, so long as O'Donovan's distinction between the ontological existence of natural order and the epistemological difficulty of apprehending it is affirmed. Not only are doubt and suspicion justified because of the epistemological uncertainty involved in apprehending the natural order, they are powerful methodological stances since doubt makes room for learning and suspicion for criticism.[107] In this connection, the practical theologian should retain a *prophetic* or *deconstructive* stance in view of theo-logical priority.[108] As Kuitert observes, "Theology does not have a current market value, dependent on whether it gives a good answer to the problems of the time: it also has an intrinsic value by virtue of its reflections on God and his salvation for human beings and the world."[109] David Schuringa elaborates: "The priority of theological theory forming is based not only on an intrinsic value of reflecting upon God, but it is also founded on the priority of the existence of God and his self-revelation with respect to created reality. In other words, it is more than a mere logical priority. It is a 'theo-logical' priority of theology over praxis."[110] Theology as such, Miller-McLemore insists, should not shrink from its explanatory power that derives from what it regards as empirical realities such as creation, sin, idolatry, and grace.[111] Acknowledging

---

105. O'Donovan, *Resurrection and Moral Order*, 20. "Such knowledge, according to the Christian gospel, is given to us as we participate in the life of Jesus Christ. He is the point from which the whole is discerned, 'in whom are hid all the treasures of wisdom and knowledge' (Col 2:3)" (O'Donovan, *Resurrection and Moral Order*, 85).

106. O'Donovan, *Resurrection and Moral Order*, 90.

107. Miller-McLemore, *Cognitive Science*, 78.

108. Similarly, Miller-McLemore recommends "*receptivity* rather than religious assurance, on the one hand, and *measured proclamation* of particular theological truths rather than modesty or relativism, on the other" ("Cognitive Science," 80).

109. Kuitert, *Everything is Politics*, 19.

110. Schuringa, "Wagging the Dog," 159.

111. Miller-McLemore, "Cognitive Science," 79.

the uniqueness of theological claims, Swinton and Mowat recommend the notion of "critical faithfulness," which "acknowledges the divine givenness of Scripture and the genuine working of the Holy Spirit in the interpretation of what is given, while at the same time taking seriously the interpretive dimensions of the process of understanding and ensuring the faithful practices of individuals and communities."[112] This is a critical discipline, Swinton and Mowat aver, "because it approaches both the world and our interpretations of the Christian tradition with a hermeneutic of suspicion, always aware of the reality of human fallenness."[113]

Admitting the power of suspicion and deconstruction, Miller-McLemore rightly insists that the practical theologian also ought to be *hospitable* to the claims of non-theological disciplines, inviting into our theorizing as we would a stranger into our home even those claims that unsettle us.[114] To paraphrase the apostle John, "perfect love casts out intellectual fear."[115] Hospitality for Miller-McLemore nowhere implies intimate fellowship or agreement, but receptivity.[116] "In being hospitable to other forms of knowledge and alternative approaches to the world," Swinton and Mowat concur, one can "create a context wherein the voice of qualitative research can be heard, respected, taken seriously, but with no a-priori assumption that theology needs to merge, follow, or fully accept the perspective on the world that is offered to it by qualitative research."[117] None of this, however, is meant to bypass Tracy's mutual critical approach in order to return to Tillich's essentially unidirectional approach. Both theological theorizing and the interpreted situation can and ought to inform and chastise one another in a circular manner, though the former retains theo-logical priority.[118]

This book will engage especially philosophy and psychology as conversation partners. In the orbit of philosophy, a significant conversation partner will be the ancient Greek philosopher Aristotle, who advocated a helpful anthropology of desire (chapter 2) and a deficient view of gratitude (chapter 3). Because Aristotle regarded self-sufficiency as a characteristic

---

112. Swinton and Mowat, *Practical Theology*, 93.

113. Swinton and Mowat, *Practical Theology*, 76.

114. Miller-McLemore, "Cognitive Science," 78.

115. This paraphrase is from Ben Faber, English professor at Redeemer University College.

116. Miller-McLemore, "Cognitive Science," 80.

117. Swinton and Mowat, *Practical Theology*, 91.

118. Granting theological theorizing logical priority ought never to imply that it is beyond critique. To allege that is to open the door to a kind of traditionalism in which received theology can never be revised. The human situation should at times invite a reassessment of cherished theological views.

of the virtuous man, one should not need or desire gifts (making gratitude unnecessary). Another significant conversation partner is the postmodern philosopher Jacques Derrida, who insisted that because it is against the nature of gifts to solicit returns, gratitude nullifies the "giftedness" of gifts. Further, in chapter 3 I will engage theorists with more positive construals of gratitudeespecially Robert Emmons, a psychologist, and Terence McConnell, a philosopher.

Theological

The turn in practical theology from a therapeutic to a hermeneutic model also implied a turn from a technical to a theological model. Here practical theologians prefer the language of "reflection" because it lacks dogmatic overtones of a Cartesian rationalistic mindset and suggests that theology is a process and not a product, an expedition in which one explores rather than arrives. Rather than a determinative project, theological reflection is open-ended, involving "a critical, interrogative enquiry into the process of relating the resources of faith to the issues of life."[119] Practical theologians quickly realized that this project of theological reflection was under-resourced and that expecting especially novices to engage theological reflection was analogous to requiring, in Stephen Pattison's memorable phrase, the construction of "bricks without straw."[120] Among the deficiencies immediately apparent was a neglect of the Bible. "There is," Pattison bemoaned, "an almost absolute and embarrassing silence about the Bible in pastoral care."[121] Similarly Roger Walton observed a "paucity or complete absence of guidelines on how the Bible and Christian tradition are to be used in theological reflection."[122]

The dearth of resources for those wanting to practice theological reflection, however, is being addressed. Graham et al., in particular, have demonstrated the variety of possibilities in identifying seven types of theological reflection. Two of these are oriented especially to the *experience* of the believer or the believing community. The first is "theology by heart" in which encounters with God in the interiority of human experience are interpreted as texts and then reflected on theologically. Having an antecedent in some biblical psalms and in Augustine's *Confessions*, for example, and John Wesley's journals, this type became popular especially through the rise of the depth psychologies of Freud and Jung, the interrogation of religious

---

119. Graham et al., *Theological Reflection*, 6.
120. Pattison, "Straw for Bricks," 136.
121. Pattison, *Critique of Pastoral Care*, 106.
122. Walton, "Bible and Tradition," 135.

experience by William James, and the verbatim chronicles of pastoral encounters recommended by Anton Boisen. Theological reflection here includes "reflexivity" defined as "the acknowledgement of the significance of self in forming an understanding of the world."[123] This approach in particular gives women a voice in a theological orbit dominated by men and masculine construals of reality.[124] A similar approach, "Writing the Body of Christ," widens the lens of theological reflection in the recognition that entire communities of faith are living and dynamic entities and as such have narratives (e.g., tragic, comic, ironic, etc.) that can be interpreted theologically—a notion widely embraced by ethnographers.[125] An instance of this approach is Don Browning's *A Fundamental Practical Theology* which, investigating the extent to which congregations are "communities of memory and communities of practical reason," examines three churches in particular in terms of their vision, obligations, needs, environments, etc.[126]

Three other approaches identified by Graham et al. are culturally oriented. One such approach, dubbed "Speaking of God in Public," encourages conversation between revelation and culture, albeit with two complementary dimensions: the apologetic and the dialectical. The apologetic shows Christian answers to human questions, and the dialectic illumines the possibility of embryonic theological truths from secular thought.[127] This approach, essentially Thomistic in orientation, regards the created order as a source of revelation and attributes value to everyday experience. A second cultural approach, "Theology-in-Action" assumes the inseparability of theory and practice and thus regards theology as "performative knowledge." Theological reflection here is not speculation about timeless truths, but consideration of present responsibilities (e.g., toward poverty, racism, oppression). A product of liberation theology, though anticipated by the Quaker movement, this approach regards salvation as empowering the marginalized and endeavors to discern God's eschatological activity in movements for social justice, to reinterpret Scripture anew, and to recast theology as a transformative discipline.[128] The final approach, "theology in the vernacular," endeavors to locate resources for theological reflection in the embodied expressions of particular cultures. Assuming that the gospel is never timeless, but always embodied in a particular time and place, this

123. Graham et al., *Theological Reflection*, 20.
124. Graham et al., *Theological Reflection*, 41.
125. Graham et al., *Theological Reflection*, 122.
126. Browning, *Fundamental Practical Theology*, 3.
127. Graham et al., *Theological Reflection*, 139.
128. Graham et al., *Theological Reflection*, 170–98.

essentially anthropological model locates signs of God's grace in the midst of cultural activities and institutions.[129]

There are, finally, two approaches that seek especially to integrate Scripture. The first such approach, "Speaking in Parables," engages in theological reflection as informed by the parabolic character of story in Scripture and by life stories. The divine and human narratives can be interwoven in generative ways to challenge and to renew the church. Herbert Anderson and James Foley, for instance, have presented the notion that church members are not merely objects of the story of redemption, but participants, "sacramental agents," through whom Jesus works.[130]

Not all of these types of theological reflection are equally promising for evangelicals. "Speaking of God in public" and "theology in the vernacular" are too heavily weighted in the direction of an unnuanced correlation and therefore cannot escape the criticisms of O'Donovan and Milbank. "Writing the body of Christ" and "theology by heart" generate ambiguity by their subjectivity. How can one determine whether individual feelings or communal experiences have a divine source? "Theology-in-action" intends to track with God's eschatological and redemptive purposes but, apart from a hermeneutic that objectively grounds these purposes in Scripture, is too easily confused with (or hijacked by) the progressivism and idealism of liberal Western thought. "Speaking in parables" is itself chastised by the final approach Graham et al. propose, and the one that holds the most promise—namely, "telling God's story."

This final approach, used in this book, views the story of Scripture as a meta-narrative, an over-arching story in which Christians can locate themselves and from which they can derive their identity. The story of Scripture narrates God's redemptive movement to reclaim the fallen world and to mend its brokenness, and Christians are to see themselves as part of the new Israel through whom God works in the world today. Adherents of this approach are generally convinced that the Christian story subverts all other stories and that the community this story generates forms an alternative to all other communities. Though it is anticipated by Francis of Assisi and Ignatius, both of whom advocated a way of life patterned after the life of Jesus, this approach was inspired especially by Karl Barth and developed significantly by Hans Frei and George Lindbeck, the Yale post-liberals. Frei and Lindbeck recommended a process of intratextuality, of relating to what is beyond the Church only on the basis of internal self-understanding.[131] The

---

129. Graham et al., *Theological Reflection*, 200–229.
130. Graham et al., *Theological Reflection*, 69.
131. Graham et al., *Theological Reflection*, 99.

story of Scripture, interpreted with the grammar of the church's theological formulations, becomes the cultural framework through which the world is perceived. Stanley Hauerwas teased out some ethical implications of this canonical narrative theology by emphasizing that Christians make the kingdom of Christ visible by living out the narrative of God. The story of Jesus in particular gives the church a cruciform shape.[132]

An advocate of the latter method (though not to exclusion of others), Charles Gerkin suggests that "the Bible provides us with an overarching narrative in which all other narratives of the world are nested."[133] In such a scenario, the narrative of the human situation must be interpreted in terms of the overarching story of Scripture. If this is so, it is impossible, as "speaking in parables" endeavors, to correlate a Scripture-as-metanarrative with other narratives, including the narrative of the human situation, without Scripture-as-metanarrative losing its meta-nature.[134]

After attending to gratitude in philosophy and psychology (chapter 3), chapter 4 of this book will probe gratitude first in terms of the progression of the narrative of Scripture from creation to fall to Israel to Jesus and beyond and then in the theologizing of significant theologians—notably Thomas Aquinas, John Calvin, and Karl Barth. Correlating the contributions of philosophy, psychology, and theology, chapter 4 will conclude with a robust profile of gratitude as virtue.

Practical

Practical theology always begins where it ends—on the ground, with praxis. Renewal of practice, in fact, is an essential objective of the practical theologian's reflection. This practical theological investigation, therefore, will conclude with recommendations about the practice of gratitude. In recognition that a traditional Protestant ethics of law offers little other than judgement to those plagued by sins of desire, this inquiry finds promise in virtue ethics,

---

132. Graham et al., *Theological Reflection*, 101.

133. Gerkin, *Widening the Horizons*, 48. Notwithstanding postmodern incredulity, seeing Scripture as metanarrative is helpful. "The whole point of Christianity," N.T. Wright avers, "is that it offers a story which is the story of the whole world. It is public truth" (Wright, *New Testament*, 41–42). James K. A. Smith argues that Scripture-as-metanarrative ought not to be subject to Lyotard's "incredulity to metanarratives" since Lyotard envisioned "distinctively modern systems of legitimation that appeal to (illusory) universal human reason as the ground of their legitimation" (Smith, *Introducing Radical Orthodoxy*, 60). For many, an affirmation of Scripture-as-metanarrative does not exclude Lyotard's critique of universal secular reason.

134. Bartholomew, "In Front of the Text," 145.

which is concerned with one's identity and character and the possibility of living well. Whereas the former renders a judgement, the latter provides a recipe; whereas the former involves a static assessment, the latter orients one on a dynamic journey.

Contributing to a growing initiative among contemporary Protestants of retrieving and renewing virtue ethics, chapter 5 will argue that within a slightly chastised version of ancient virtue ethics there are resources for addressing and mitigating sins of ingratitude. In identifying and distinguishing the roles of the Holy Spirit and the church, virtue and practice in shaping grateful lives and character, chapter 5 will argue that the Eucharist, as the ritual embodiment of gratitude in the kingdom of Jesus, has potential to re-socialize people by cultivating gratitude and so displacing idols of desire. This final chapter will conclude with some suggestive explorations of the implications of the Eucharist for the practices of hospitality, prayer, and community.

THESIS STATEMENT

Contributing to the emerging academic discourse on gratitude, this practical theological inquiry utilizes a methodology of mutual critical correlation in which philosophical and psychological claims about gratitude are brought into a conversation with the Christian tradition. Nested in the overarching drama of Scripture, this conversation will engage in theological reflection in order to generate a renewed and thick profile of gratitude as a responsive virtue in which one, seeing oneself as a recipient of a gift, freely and joyfully salutes the giver in order to perpetuate a personal and peaceable relationship. Against the detractors of gratitude, such as Aristotle and Jacques Derrida, this inquiry proposes seeing gratitude, on the basis of an ontology of communion in which humans are inextricably situated in giving-and-receiving relationships with God, others, and the world, as asymmetrical, agapic reciprocity. Furthermore, this book argues that gratitude—embodied, practiced, and ritualized especially, though not exclusively, in the Eucharist—has potential to repel the destructive idolatries generated by the seven deadly sins[135] and thus function as a crucial ingredient in human social flourishing.[136]

---

135. Pride is regarded as a distorted desire for acceptance, envy for equality, anger for justice, sloth for rest, greed for provision, gluttony for pleasure, and lust for relationship.

136. As a social ritual, the Eucharist celebrates acceptance and inhibits pride; as an inclusive ritual, it celebrates equality and inhibits envy; as a peaceable ritual, it

ENTERING THE CONVERSATION

Perhaps surprisingly, given its widespread acclaim and celebrated status in contemporary Western society, gratitude has rarely been the subject of academic inquiry. Twenty years ago, philosopher Terence McConnell wrote of his guild, "Twentieth-century philosophers have had comparatively little to say about gratitude."[137] Similarly, historian Peter Leithart, in a seminal book published recently, observed: "As I searched index after index for substantive discussions of gratitude, however, I largely came up empty."[138] Robert Emmons indicates that in terms of the complexities of emotions and the ability of psychologists to unravel them, there is a gap—namely, the psychology of gratitude.[139]

The lacuna of academic inquiry into gratitude is being filled, however, and in recent years four scholarly books on gratitude have been published, all of which deserve consideration and interaction. In 2002, in the wake of 9/11, Mary Jo Leddy penned *Radical Gratitude*, in which she reflects on gratitude in terms of contrasting economies of consumerism/greed and of grace/gift. In order to rebuild our world—Leddy is thinking of the social and economic collapse, especially in the wake of 9/11—one must return to root (radical) questions, she argues, and to thinking in a more foundational way: "We must begin by becoming grateful."[140] Leddy argues that we are in a captivity of consumerism, funded by a profound sense of powerlessness, emptiness, and disorientation, along the lines of the Jewish experience of Babylonian captivity.[141]

Leddy finds existing political options to resolve social ills unpromising. The conservative option to bring back order, meaning, and traditional (family) values, is doomed because social conservatism contradicts economic conservatism (e.g., free markets destroy traditional institutions like

---

celebrates justice and inhibits anger; as a gratuitous ritual, it celebrates rest and inhibits sloth; as a purposeful ritual, it celebrates provision and inhibits greed; as a joyful ritual, it celebrates pleasure and inhibits gluttony, and as a personal ritual, it celebrates relationship and inhibits lust.

137. McConnell, *Gratitude*, vii.

138. Leithart, *Gratitude*, 1. Similarly, "I also found it odd that our intellectuals give so little attention to gratitude at a *theoretical* level in a culture that clearly puts a premium on gratitude" (Leithart, *Gratitude*, 2).

139. Emmons, "Psychology of Gratitude," 3.

140. Leddy, *Radical Gratitude*, 3.

141. "We are in captivity because we have made a god out of an economic system" to whom our allegiance is so strong we even sacrifice young people by insisting, for instance, that they get a job rather than pursue a calling (Leddy, *Radical Gratitude*, 34).

family businesses) and because social meaning cannot be forced.[142] Liberalism, on the other hand, assumes that the individual is the base point for all arrangements, social and economic, and that common good results from self-actualization.[143] Recommending pluralism and tolerance, liberalism has yielded good fruit in terms of the freedom of speech and freedom of conscience, etc., but it has reached its limits because it cannot deal with the reality of limits.[144] Its vocabulary being devoid of words like sacrifice and commitment, liberalism is unable to respond to the human need for meaning and vision.[145]

We are helped, Leddy suggests, by reflecting on creation, on God as creator and on ourselves as creatures. Through our bond to him, we share in God's creative power which is exercised in new beginnings and enacted ultimately to resurrect the dead. As we reflect on the powerlessness of life's entrances and exits, we are invited to experience the power of God to create.[146] "The liberation of gratitude," Leddy argues, "begins when we stop taking life for granted."[147] When we say that the most important things in life cannot be taken for granted though they are free, gifts from God issued in love, we are talking about the economy of grace.[148] At the Eucharist, "we enter into the imagination of the great economy of grace" to see love and life freely offered.[149] This grace in turn generates giving, and "the craving that holds us captive begins to loosen its grip."[150] To dwell in the mystery of creation in gratitude is to discover identity and purpose and thereby to live in time and not be consumed by it.[151]

The contribution of this book dovetails with Leddy's in several ways, not least by invoking the category of idolatry and recommending gratitude

142. Leddy, *Radical Gratitude*, 121.

143. Leddy, *Radical Gratitude*, 122.

144. It assumes economic growth, flounders without it, and has no social vision beyond self-interest (Leddy, *Radical Gratitude*, 123).

145. Leddy, *Radical Gratitude*, 123.

146. "Rebirth is a possibility every day" (Leddy, *Radical Gratitude*, 97).

147. Leddy, *Radical Gratitude*, 40.

148. Leddy, *Radical Gratitude*, 56. The economy of grace is not founded on the law of scarcity, but in the "mystery of superabundance" (Leddy, *Radical Gratitude*, 57). "On the way to get something more, we fail to see what we have (Leddy, *Radical Gratitude*, 59). Tanner uses this language in reconfiguring gift-giving in terms of the pooling of resources in Tanner, *Economy of Grace*.

149. Leddy, *Radical Gratitude*, 65.

150. Leddy, *Radical Gratitude*, 66.

151. Leddy, *Radical Gratitude*, 138. In gratitude, we see the past for its power and can savor the present. In gratitude, acknowledging a purpose for history, the episodes of life are connected, and our lives point even beyond death.

as an idol breaker. Rather than focus on a consumeristic economy per se, and the psychological and theological account of emptiness beneath its veneer, this book attends to the seven deadly sins as sins of desire and therefore saboteurs of gratitude (chapter 2). Moreover, this inquiry will engage prominent detractors of gratitude, especially Aristotle and Jacques Derrida (chapter 3) and offer a more substantial theology of gratitude, incorporating biblical material from the Old and New Testaments and including insights from prominent theologians (chapter 4).

Seven years later, in 2009, Margaret Visser yielded *The Gift of Thanks: The Roots and Rituals of Gratitude*, the most significant contribution to the emerging scholarship on gratitude. Examining gratitude in the light of different cultures and through the lens of diverse disciplines, including linguistic theory, cultural anthropology, philosophy, and psychology, Visser regards gratitude as irreducibly complex, both free and socially demanded. Not purely spontaneous, gratitude must be taught, and though it arises in a moment, it depends upon one's whole life, unlike the surge of energy characteristic of anger.[152] "Gratitude," Visser writes, "is easily felt by people for whom thankfulness has become part of their emotional landscape, their 'repertoire.'"[153] To function well, Visser claims, gratitude "cannot stand on its own, but needs to grow from other virtues, principally love and justice, that must come first."[154] Gifts and gratitude do not yield profits; they bear fruit.[155] "Gratitude," Visser writes, "replacing selfishness, greed, and disregard, will in my opinion be called upon to help us surmount the ecological crisis that now threatens our very existence."[156] Moreover, gratitude situates people in narratives of interpersonal relationship which, having been formed by memory, ensure memory persists.[157] Without memory, one does not know who he or she is. "Being able to be grateful," Visser writes, "is an early sign of the possibility of deliverance when we have lost our way, when

---

152. Visser, *Gift of Thanks*, 345.

153. Visser, *Gift of Thanks*, 355.

154. Visser, *Gift of Thanks*, 417.

155. Visser, *Gift of Thanks*, 454. Gift-giving is absent, Visser argues, when orchestrated by manipulation and coercion (and often blackmail) rather than by freedom and equality, when the goal is money rather than friendship, when the exchanges are secret rather than open, when the goal is to profit the giver rather than the receiver, when repayment happens quickly rather than slowly and when accountability is private rather than public (Visser, *Gift of Thanks*, 414–16).

156. Visser, *Gift of Thanks*, 434.

157. Visser, *Gift of Thanks*, 289.

our very identity is under threat: gratitude points forward."[158] "We begin to see," she writes, "how desirable a virtue it is."[159]

Visser's book is an enormous resource for understanding the cultural dynamics of gratitude both historically and globally. This book will probe many of the same dynamics but from a uniquely theological perspective. In agreement with Visser, this inquiry recommends gratitude as a social virtue. The social dimension of gratitude is probed, however, especially in terms of our being God's creatures and the recipients of his gifts.

In 2012, Mark T. Mitchell's *The Politics of Gratitude* was published, an innovative, though distinctively American proposal to bring closer together the disparate political impulses of Republicans and Democrats and to generate "an account of politics and culture rooted in gratitude."[160] Unhappy that gratitude is often misconstrued as a mere feeling of appreciation which, without an object, translates into self-satisfaction, Mitchell proposes instead that gratitude be understood as relational, "a disposition to the world that reminds us that we are not alone."[161]

Mitchell envisions the natural world as the orbit we inhabit and, with insight from Wendell Berry, critiques the modern industrial economy as an anti-human, unsustainable mechanism by which people delegate responsibility to provide for their needs to organizations with no commitment to individual or community health.[162] As an alternative to industrialism, Mitchell recommends an agrarian economy in which small owners of small properties care for their land and are integrated in their communities.[163] Agrarians begin with gratitude to God, and a strong conviction that the natural world is a gift.[164] Their work is done with tools, not machines, by the light of the sun, not artificial light, and in the silence of the rural, not the cacophony of the urban.[165] Mitchell does not endorse urban flight, but does recommend "urban homesteading, the pursuit of an agrarian lifestyle within the

---

158. Visser, *Gift of Thanks*, 299.

159. Visser, *Gift of Thanks*, 441. The morality of gratitude is especially evident when we see ingratitude, which Visser regards as not merely the abdication of duty but a moral shortcoming which speaks to a person's character (Visser, *Gift of Thanks*, 352). Cf. Visser's claim that ingratitude is not so much immoral as it is a closure to people, a failure to grow (Visser, *Gift of Thanks*, 454).

160. Mitchell, *Politics of Gratitude*, xv.

161. Mitchell, *Politics of Gratitude*, 18.

162. Mitchell, *Politics of Gratitude*, 129–35.

163. Mitchell, *Politics of Gratitude*, 133–34.

164. Mitchell, *Politics of Gratitude*, 134.

165. Mitchell, *Politics of Gratitude*, 139.

city."[166] Gratitude is economically powerful for Mitchell because it "begets satisfaction, and satisfaction is a strong barrier against greed, avarice, and consumerism. An economy of gratitude is an economy of responsibility."[167]

Another significant component to Mitchell's economic vision of gratitude is the centrality and importance of private property.[168] Private property encourages virtue because property owners have reason to be responsible, to protect their property by living within their means, and therefore to exercise self-control.[169] Furthermore, ownership of property forges relationships between neighbors who cooperate in caring for each other's properties.[170] Private property is essential to freedom, and therefore should be encouraged by supporting local producers and patronizing locally owned stores.[171]

Home is the metaphor Mitchell embraces to represent a human scale appropriate both to creatureliness and the practice of gratitude.[172] Yet in today's global and mobile culture, Mitchell observes, people lack roots and suffer a kind of homelessness geographically, culturally, and spiritually. Transportation technologies enable us to relocate for work all over the world, and communication technologies unhinge us from the world of physical constraints and we slowly shift to a view of reality with little use for embodied existence in a geographical locale.[173] Similarly, the shift towards centralization disrespects the hallmarks of community—namely, local culture and history, but also meaningful relationships.[174] "In the process," Mitchell writes, "love itself becomes an abstraction."[175] Local communities respect human scale and give individuals access to the power brokers and foster a culture of accountability. "Home" is also undermined by the contemporary denigration of tradition both as a bank of resources and a conceptual framework through which we see the world and from which we

---

166. Mitchell, *Politics of Gratitude*, 144.

167. Mitchell, *Politics of Gratitude*, 127.

168. Conversely, Kathryn Tanner is critical of the notion of private property on the grounds that "a theological economy of grace is a fundamentally noncompetitive economy" in which one should not regard what we have "simply as our own, as our exclusive possession" (Tanner, "Economy of Grace," 177, 180). Mitchell sees personal ownership of property as a form of stewardship before God and requisite for responsibility towards others.

169. Mitchell, *Politics of Gratitude*, 120–22.

170. Mitchell, *Politics of Gratitude*, 123.

171. Mitchell, *Politics of Gratitude*, 124.

172. Mitchell, *Politics of Gratitude*, 57.

173. Mitchell, *Politics of Gratitude*, 60.

174. Mitchell, *Politics of Gratitude*, 66.

175. Mitchell, *Politics of Gratitude*, 67.

derive the language to describe it.¹⁷⁶ A casualty of this disregard of tradition is the rise of the autonomous individual who, resisting any restraint, lacks commitment to both authority and place.¹⁷⁷

Gratitude is the mother of stewardship, Mitchell claims, and without stewardship, concern for the world, place, and the past evaporate until nothing is left but concern for self.¹⁷⁸ Under the rubric of stewardship, he recommends five aspects of renewed education: participation, by which he understands reading books in particular; memorization, whereby to create mental furniture; imitation, and learning from the masters; instantiation, and finding ways to implement the abstract and; transmission, and cultivating respect for tradition.¹⁷⁹

Mitchell sees the family as the cradle of gratitude.¹⁸⁰ Choosing to have a child, Mitchell argues, is an expression of hope because it implies that life is worth living and that the world is worth preserving.¹⁸¹ When the birthrate of a country plummets below the replacement level, Mitchell indicates, there is often a corresponding surge in consumerism.¹⁸² In North America, for instance, people live with far fewer children in much bigger homes than they did 50 years ago. The space to be alone, in one's own bedroom with one's own TV and gadgets only occasions greater narcissism.¹⁸³ In the face of increasing mobility and fragmentation, Mitchell sees advantages in an agrarian culture where a family settles in one locale and operates a business, thereby creating an environment in which generational ties are forged, skills are acquired, and healthy work habits are imparted.¹⁸⁴ Lastly, Mitchell recommends what he terms "the neighborly arts," virtues that prize people and community over efficiency and productivity and that spawn cultures in which people bake bread together, for example, rather than purchase it in the store.¹⁸⁵

Mitchell's thesis is provocative and has many commendable features, not least the recognition of the social and civic value of gratitude.

---

176. Mitchell, *Politics of Gratitude*, 62–64.
177. Mitchell, *Politics of Gratitude*, 63.
178. Mitchell, *Politics of Gratitude*, 99.
179. Mitchell, *Politics of Gratitude*, 181–90.
180. Mitchell, *Politics of Gratitude*, 149.
181. Mitchell, *Politics of Gratitude*, 153.
182. Mitchell, *Politics of Gratitude*, 161.
183. Mitchell, *Politics of Gratitude*, 162–63.
184. Mitchell, *Politics of Gratitude*, 166–70. Cavanaugh agrees: "The first step toward overcoming our detachment is to turn our homes into sites of production, not just consumption" (Cavanaugh, *Being Consumed*, 57).
185. Mitchell, *Politics of Gratitude*, 197.

His preference for agrarianism as the antidote, however, to the "giantism" and autonomy of an increasingly secular society has the marks of a Luddite worldview and betrays a questionable resistance to technological progress and urbanization. Unlike Mitchell's book, this book will unveil, in light of philosophical reductions, a theological profile of gratitude and then recommend practices to reduce the ways in which it can be sabotaged.

Most recently, in 2014, Peter Leithart wrote *Gratitude: An Intellectual History*, a veritable *tour de force* of historical scholarship, beginning with ancients and ending with contemporary theorists, but stopping along the way to listen to poets, philosophers, and theologians. Especially Western thinkers and European intellectuals are engaged as Leithart helpfully traces the multiple ways gratitude has been understood, and many of his insights are harvested in this book. Leithart conceives of gift-giving in terms of lines and circles: whereas in circular conceptions, gifts are given with the expectation of return (e.g., Aristotle), in linear concepts, they are given without the expectation of return (e.g., Derrida). Leithart's claim about Christian gratitude is particularly interesting—namely, that it is neither linear nor circular, but both. On the one hand, Christians are summoned to give without the expectation of return and on the other, Christians believe that God will reward them if they give. The line of giving, for Leithart, is circumscribed by an infinite circle.[186] Instructed by the Old Testament and shaped by the teaching and example of Jesus, early Christians, Leithart claims, rejected the logic that the reception of gifts incurred debts or that the donation of gifts imposed debts. As such they broke "the snares of Greco-Roman reciprocity" and were therefore accused of subverting Roman order and challenging fixed hierarchies through ingratitude.[187] The fourth-century, early-medieval writer Lactantius perpetuated the Christian ethic that charity be demonstrated to the sick and destitute with no expectation of return other than the Lord's reward.[188] Unlike pagan Rome, which took no interest in burying the poor, Christians anticipate a reward from the God who raises the dead, Lactantius argued, so their charity extends beyond the grave.[189]

In the Middle Ages, the church, Leithart argues, began to look like a Greco-Roman culture in which the bishops were the wealthy patrons dispensing charitable benefits to those whose allegiance was expected.[190] The

---

186. Leithart, *Gratitude*, 7.

187. Leithart, *Gratitude*, 76. "Judged by the standards of the ancient world, Christianity introduced the possibility of holy *in*gratitude, and thus sowed seeds of a new form of social life in Greco-Roman soil" (Leithart, *Gratitude*, 59).

188. Leithart, *Gratitude*, 80.

189. Leithart, *Gratitude*, 80.

190. Leithart, *Gratitude*, 83.

medieval church was initially accustomed to seeing the Mass as a eucharistic sacrifice, a gift for which they expected a divine benefit.[191] Over time the Mass became less a gift and more a commodity priests would sell. In lieu of suffering through twelve days of penitential fasting, wealthy church members, Leithart illustrates, could purchase twenty masses to be chanted by monks.[192] Martin Luther railed against the presentation of the Mass as a gift exchange, i.e., human work for divine grace, and preached a gospel of sheer gift to be received with faith and gratitude.[193] Unlike Luther, who saw the reception of the Eucharist largely as a display of gratitude, John Calvin argued that grateful reception requires the dissemination of love and kindness.[194] William Tyndale operated with a purely linear conception of grace, as did later Reformed theologians for whom the affirmations of sola gratia and the doctrine of election minimized both the notion of divine reward and that of grateful reception implying a return gift.[195]

In the course of his argument, Leithart insists that Christian gratitude is not a "return," but "the right use of the gift."[196] He argues further that "human givers give, but recipients owe thanks and grateful service not to the giver but to God."[197] This book will regard claims of this sort as a mistaken implication of Jesus's exhortation to give without the expectation of a return (e.g., Luke 6:30–36). To argue that because one should not seek a return, a return is therefore improper, impious, or worse, is a *non sequitur*. For this reason, I will argue that gratitude exhibits the reciprocity of a healthy return.

GRATITUDE IN DIFFERENT NARRATIVES

Gratitude has been variously understood throughout history, and the differences can often be attributed to the diverse narratives in which its advocates or detractors are located. In ancient and medieval civilizations, for example, society was glued together by a variety of reciprocal relationships in which goods were exchanged. Giving and receiving initially occurred in the context of hierarchical relationships such that what a person gave or received

---

191. Leithart, *Gratitude*, 99.
192. Leithart, *Gratitude*, 100.
193. Leithart, *Gratitude*, 101.
194. Leithart, *Gratitude*, 103.
195. Leithart, *Gratitude*, 104–05.
196. Leithart, *Gratitude*, 7.
197. Leithart, *Gratitude*, 7. "Christian recipients acknowledge no debts, except to love" and the gifts of Christians "evoked returns not from earth but from heaven, not in time but in eternity" (Leithart, *Gratitude*, 7–8).

was often reflective of his or her status or power. With the progress of time and the development of new ideas, the individual in Western civilization became disengaged from others and gratitude increasingly lost its social nature, thereby denying something that is important for the thesis of this book—namely, an ontology of communion, of being-in-communion. In the Enlightenment, for example, when individual feelings become paramount, gratitude was cordoned off (horizontally) from others in the public square and privatized. With the rise of existentialism, when many chose to embrace life without God, gratitude was cordoned off (vertically) from God. "In modernity individual self-fulfillment has displaced God from the centre of the world," Colin Gunton writes, and "it makes itself the centre of things, and so uses both person and world as means to its ends."[198] Ultimately and recently, in postmodernism, gratitude requires the exclusion not just of others and God, but of oneself so that there is no gratitude. The significance of this historical trajectory is immense. The emergence in Western civilization of dualisms that pit human nature against society, or mind against spirit, alienated people from the world, each other, and even themselves. Here already there is a hint regarding the importance of the Eucharist in a worldview of gratitude: the Eucharist, by refusing to separate the natural from the spiritual, protests the dualisms that have corroded Western civilization.[199] The next section freshly and uniquely presents a vast amount of data, especially from Visser and Leithart, in terms of dominant historical narratives.

Ancient Gratitude: The Narrative of Hierarchical Relations

One of the dominant narratives in the Greco-Roman world (until circa 400 CE) is that society is ordered hierarchically. The cosmos has an order, in which human beings have a particularly important place. Similarly, within humanity there is order and those who exercise reason well are (or at least should be) higher than others. Even within a person, for Plato at least, there is a hierarchy between higher and lower parts of the soul.[200] That the

198. Gunton, *One, Three, and Many*, 226–27.

199. See Macquarrie, *Guide to the Sacraments*, 32–33.

200. Taylor, *Sources of Self*, 115, 125. Even though the cosmic order and social hierarchy were affirmed, there is within the ontology of Greek philosophy, because it was predicated on reason (i.e., man is a rational animal), an individualistic dimension. For Plato, for example, morality required self-mastery in which reason ruled desires. This is what Taylor dubs Plato's "warrior ethic" in which the soul wars against the body, and the eternal against the transient. Not until Augustine is this dualism formulated in terms of "inner" and "outer" (Taylor, *Sources of Self*, 120–21). Not identically but similarly Aristotle recommended φρόνησις to determine how to conduct oneself in certain circumstances (Taylor, *Sources of Self*, 124–25).

cosmos has an order, however, was apparent in the hierarchy of reciprocal relationships in which goods were typically exchanged. In heroic Greece, for instance, victorious warriors were rewarded by chiefs and rulers with goods and relationships, though they were expected to be generous in turn.[201] Similarly, in political Greece, citizens accepted debts of service or loyalty to the polis/ruler, their benefactor, and attempted to curry favor through service or liturgies of civic donations; the ruler in turn would reward such devotion.[202] In attempt to extricate itself from such mutual obligations and the bribery they implied, Athens experimented with democracy, the "victory of community over hero," and implemented a system in which public officials were paid from a public treasury.[203] Reciprocity thus persisted in political Greece, though those who were bound together were no longer rulers and heroes, but rulers and people. Such reciprocity is also apparent in Greco-Roman religion in which one, by offering sacrificial gifts and performing rituals, could purchase favors from the gods which, when bestowed, elicited more prayer.[204] Gifts were returned to those who give.[205] Though the context of these social, political, and religious exchanges was often relational (rather than commercial), returns were often given without feeling.[206]

Functioning in many ways as a societal hinge, the return of gratitude was not always viewed positively. The Greek philosopher Aristotle, whose views will receive substantial scrutiny in chapter 3, valued giving much more than thanksgiving and prized liberality over gratitude.[207] In Aristotle's ethics, in which independence is idealized, gratitude is an undesirable virtue because it assumes the reception of a good one needed and did not have. Centuries later, Seneca contested Aristotle's views in an entire treatise dedicated to the subject, titled *De Beneficiis*, in which he advocated for an

---

201. The exchange of gifts implied "an ongoing circle of mutual service" (Leithart, *Gratitude*, 27).

202. Leithart, *Gratitude*, 30–31.

203. Leithart, *Gratitude*, 33.

204. Leithart, *Gratitude*, 21.

205. Leithart, *Gratitude*, 24. The exception would be Epicureans who held that the gods were disinterested in human affairs.

206. The prototype of grateful feelings, Margaret Visser argues, lies in ancient votive offerings which also feature the circle of reciprocity, though the movement heads in the opposite direction (See Visser, *Gift of Thanks*, 176). With the logic, "If you give, then I will give such in return," worshippers would dedicate objects to fulfill vows in response to supernatural favors (Visser, *Gift of Thanks*, 178–79, 185). Though the vow was often spoken in private, the votive offering (e.g., a shrine, statute, painting) was displayed in public to express gratitude and encourage it in others (Visser, *Gift of Thanks*, 186–87).

207. Leithart, *Gratitude*, 35–37.

ethics not of independence but of mutual dependence and social cohesion.[208] According to Seneca, the shrine of *The Three Graces* in ancient Rome (sculptures of three beautiful girls) represented the obligations of giving, receiving, and returning gifts.[209] Whereas Aristotle regarded the sisters as equal in the sense that we have duties to give and to repay, Seneca alleged that the first, who gives freely, is so honorable that the second, who repays out of indebtedness, can never match her virtue.[210] Though he celebrated gratitude, encouraged its publicity, and redefined benefits to include attitudes, intentions, and other immaterial aspects, enabling even the poor to repay gifts, Seneca was still unable to extricate himself, Leithart argues, from the totalitarian impulses of Greco-Roman political theory by insisting that the emperor transcended the exchange system as one who could impose debts, but could never incur them.[211]

Ancient society was inextricably embedded in a system of exchanges, and in that system gratitude was an obligatory reciprocation. This obligatory reciprocation, characteristic in this narrative of hierarchical relationships, also surfaces in other non-Western hierarchical relationships which situate gratitude in what Visser terms "the web of obligation."[212] Those who acquire

208. Seneca's contribution had a uniquely Stoic flavor by privileging manner over content in both giving and repayment since for Stoics all things are *animus* ("spirit" rather than *res* "thing") and the goal in giving and repayment is internal virtue (i.e., gratitude) (Barclay, *Paul and the Gift*, 48). See Seneca, *Ben.* 2.31.1.

209. "Seneca *never* idealizes the one-way unreciprocated gift . . . [retaining] the unanimous ancient assumption that the point of gifts is to create social ties" (Barclay, *Paul and the Gift*, 50; cf. Visser, *Gift of Thanks*, 103). *The Three Graces* have been represented often and variously in sculptures and paintings and are sometimes depicted in a circle holding hands as if dancing, possibly implying that one must participate to benefit from the circle or that the sequence means continual motion or that giving moves circularly so that those who give also receive (See Visser, *Gift of Thanks*, 115–16).

210. See Visser, *Gift of Thanks*, 107.

211. Leithart, *Gratitude*, 54–55. See also Harpham, "History of Ideas," 25.

212. Visser, *Gift of Thanks*, 30. Among the most puzzling traditions involving reciprocal gift-giving is the *kula* traded practiced by the Trobriand Islanders. *Soulava* (red shell necklaces) and *mwali* (white shell bracelets), precious but impractical objects, are transported in canoes around the islands in opposite direction, the *soulava* moving clockwise and the *mwali* counterclockwise. The recipient might retain such a gift for a year, but would eventually trade it to another chieftain. Though having economic value, the gifts were indicative of power relations among the aristocratic islanders (Leithart, *Gratitude*, 165; cf. Visser, *Gift of Thanks*, 119–20). Receiving the gift indicated one's importance and donors displayed excessive modesty in giving in spite of the disinterest recipients often feigned in receiving (Visser, *Gift of Thanks*, 89). Equally puzzling is the potlatch institution among Kwakiutl Indians in British Columbia during which one would donate or recklessly destroy possessions (e.g., burn blankets) and challenge rivals to surpass them (Visser, *Gift of Thanks*, 121). Those who donated or destroyed excessively demonstrated their high rank in the tribal social scale. Here honor does

something ought to give, because those who give will one day need to obtain from those who acquired.[213] The response to a cup of tea for the Japanese, for instance, is not "thank you," but *sumimasen*, meaning literally, "I'm sorry" (you had to go through this trouble for me).[214] The Japanese might also say *doomo sumimasen* which means "oh this does not end!" or *arigato*, meaning "how dreadful."[215] For the Japanese, therefore, gifts are obligations indebting recipients who often feel unable to repay. Grateful expressions are admissions of inferiority, reducing the recipient's honor and elevating that of the donor, thereby offering a kind of compensation.[216] In short, the Japanese focus is not the delight the recipient experiences in receiving but in the trouble the donor took to give.

Visser also indicates that in most cultures, Japanese or otherwise, gratitude adheres to the principle that receivers are "lower" than givers.[217] Non-verbal submissions are expressed by bowing and prostration, kissing the dirt (humility derives from *humus*, earth).[218] Rigid rules apply to gift-giving depending on the occasion or the status of the recipient.[219] Though

---

reside in things, but in readiness to divest oneself of things. In some cultures, admiration of a particular possession requires the owner to give it immediately to the admirer, again suggesting the honour of detachment (Visser, *Gift of Thanks*, 122).

213. Visser, *Gift of Thanks*, 30. As such, giving functioned as a kind of insurance for individual and communal stability and those who received were expected to help in the future. You gave to friends because they had potential to be your helpers and you gave to strangers because they had potential to be your enemies (Visser, *Gift of Thanks*, 28–29).

214. Visser, *Gift of Thanks*, 44.

215. Visser, *Gift of Thanks*, 45.

216. Visser, *Gift of Thanks*, 45. Those who give often sense that it implies an imposition, forcing the recipient to do something. Japanese donors diminish the gift by saying *Tsumaranai mono desuga*, "It's not worth having, but . . ." (Visser, *Gift of Thanks*, 106). Similarly, Western givers sometimes respond to expressions of gratitude by saying, "It's nothing" or "don't mention it" or "no strings attached" (Visser, *Gift of Thanks*, 106).

217. Visser, *Gift of Thanks*, 265.

218. Visser, *Gift of Thanks*, 266. The Gonja people of north Ghana, according to Visser, express gratitude through a greeting in which juniors approach seniors, crouching at their open doors, and say *"Me choro,"* meaning "I greet you!" Other ways of expressing gratitude include removing the hat, kneeling, and softly clapping hands (Visser, *Gift of Thanks*, 268). Without any feeling, the Tamil people of South India enact a ritual to show deference (e.g., touch feet and lower eyes) before praising the benefactor if hierarchy is permanent or the benefit, if the hierarchy is temporary (Visser, *Gift of Thanks*, 255–56).

219. Visser, *Gift of Thanks*, 97. The gift for an engagement in Japan is tea in a decorated box, for example, and gifts of condolence have paper printed with different symbols (such as lotus flowers) such that wrappings of at least formal gifts do not conceal the gift, but proclaim it (Visser, *Gift of Thanks*, 97).

Japanese gifts demand a response, emotional reactions are beside the point, and presents are not opened until after the donor leaves.[220]

In the narrative of hierarchical relations, the return gift (of gratitude) functions as a social hinge, is obligatory, and given without feeling. This book affirms that gratitude is social and reciprocal, but argues that as a response it is fitting without being obligatory and is ordinarily characterized by joy. Furthermore, return gifts in this narrative were often necessary for the relationships (e.g., patron-clients) to continue, regardless of whether the relationships were desirable. This book argues that gratitude to donors is conveyed in the interest of perpetuating a relationship.

Medieval Gratitude: The Narrative of Feudal Responsibility

Medieval civilization (from circa 400 to 1500 CE) evolved out of ancient societies in an organic way. Reciprocal relationships continued between, for instance, rulers and citizens, but the nature of gifts and their returns varied. What is especially significant is the bestowal of land to individuals in return for outstanding service.[221] This consisted initially of kings rewarding nobles with land and distinguishing them with titles such as "duke/duchess" and "count/countess" that were then passed down through the generations. Subsequently, lords rewarded followers with allotments of land on which they could look after, among other things, horses that could be used in battle. "This system of mutual obligation and reward of contractual service, of rewarding the warrior with land," Lopez writes, "is known as feudalism."[222]

The medieval realignment of societal life in terms of feudal arrangements had implications for how one understood and practiced gratitude. Unlike in Seneca, for example, gratitude became associated especially with one's responsibilities in the social hierarchy.[223] "Loyalty," in fact, nearly

---

220. Visser, *Gift of Thanks*, 99. Even in cultures in which hierarchical relations are not as dominant, many gestures of gratitude still communicate respect. Gratefulness among Arabs, Visser indicates, is conveyed by kissing the back of the right hand, then lifting it with the palm facing upward (Visser, *Gift of Thanks*, 276). In our culture, it is generally assumed that one should not stretch out one's hand to receive a gift. In the Catholic church, one receives communion by extending both hands (Visser, *Gift of Thanks*, 277). We show gratitude sometimes by bowing, nodding, embracing, shaking hands, applauding (e.g., at a concert, after a speech), etc. Shaking hands is historically disarming because it negates any intention to seize a weapon (Visser, *Gift of Thanks*, 278). Applause combines praise and gratitude, and often today performers will applaud in response to audience applause (Visser, *Gift of Thanks*, 281).

221. Lopez, "Carolingian Prelude," 6.

222. Lopez, "Carolingian Prelude," 6.

223. Harpham, "History of Ideas," 26.

eclipsed the concept of gratitude and "gratitude" was at times reduced to mere signs.[224] The generosity of the lord in feudal systems obliged reciprocity from the vassal, as it did for subjects in relation to princes, who were obliged, in less contractual terms than vassals, to honour their protectors.[225] The word *gratitudo*, created out of the Latin *gratia* and used frequently by Thomas Aquinas (1266–1273), first appeared in the thirteenth century as replacement of sorts for feudal loyalty and to distinguish human gratitude from divine *gratia* (grace).[226] Though gratitude approximates loyalty in awareness (gratitude emerges by thought) and partiality (only to some is gratitude owed), the two words must be distinguished, Visser argues, because, unlike gratitude, loyalty exists without feeling.[227]

Relatedly, in the late Middle Ages, a parallel emerges between ingratitude and treason.[228] Ingratitude is depicted as political evil in, for instance, Shakespeare's *King Lear*, where Dante's claim that treachery is a political version of ingratitude is affirmed.[229] Similarly, Shakespeare's Coriolanus illumines the individual and political implications of ingratitude.[230] Himself ungrateful to Rome, Coriolanus idealizes Aristotle's magnanimous man rather than Seneca's grateful man, and aspires after independence, forgetting

---

224. Visser, *Gift of Thanks*, 212.

225. Visser, *Gift of Thanks*, 213.

226. Visser, *Gift of Thanks*, 215–16. The Latin term *gratitudo* is missing in Augustine whose use of *gratia* is almost always connected to divine favor than human obligation (See Harpham, "History of Ideas," 25). The one who showed benevolence in thirteenth-century England was said to be *kynde*. This word, derived from "kin" and assuming filial piety, was used to translate the Latin *gratus* "grateful" (Visser, *Gift of Thanks*, 217). The English word gratitude derives from the Latin *gratia* and ultimately from Sanskrit *gurtih* and *gurtah*, meaning "praise" (Visser, *Gift of Thanks*, 201). The Latin distinguished praise (*laus*) from gratitude (*gratia*), which in Latin is only a noun and therefore only something you did, had, brought, or gave (Visser, *Gift of Thanks*, 202). The English obtained its verb "to thank" from Germanic roots and *danken* is related to *denken*, because gratitude is never simply emotion, but also thoughtfulness, as is also apparent in the French word for gratitude—*reconnaissance*, or re-cognition (Visser, *Gift of Thanks*, 208; cf. 469ff.). The Old English noun for thought is *thanc* or *thonc*.

227. Visser, *Gift of Thanks*, 210.

228. Harpham, "History of Ideas," 26.

229. Leithart, *Gratitude*, 114.

230. Leithart, *Gratitude*, 115–16. In the first scene, the patrician Menenius tells a parable to assembled plebs about the rebellion of the body's organs against the rather idle stomach which receives the food first. The stomach replies it is the source of the health and vitality of the organs; the organs of the body should be grateful to the stomach. The Roman plebs, and later the patricians, do not acknowledge Coriolanus's heroic service and so by their ingratitude become "monstrous," i.e., unnatural (Leithart, *Gratitude*, 116).

how Roman society has underwritten his successes.²³¹ Towards the end, however, his "experiment in (un)natural individualism and independent freedom collapses" and Coriolanus acknowledges his debt of political gratitude to Rome, saving her by his death.²³²

In the medieval world, however, this reciprocity was understood especially in terms of loyalty to one's lord, duke, or king. As such, gratitude was largely public, if not political. The political debt of gratitude, however, can be very problematic. The "generous" Soviet system under Lenin manipulated the people, Visser argues, "to say what the regime wanted to hear" and Stalin's "gifts" manipulated the people to show gratitude in spite of his cruelties and failures.²³³ In fact, the State sanctioned civic rituals of gratitude to Stalin, and Stalin invoked filial gratitude by presenting himself as "the Little Father of the Peoples."²³⁴

Whereas the return gift in the narrative of hierarchical relations was obligatory, imposed from the outside, and often unwelcome, the return gift in the narrative of feudal responsibility was regarded as a duty, but an honorable one. Whether the medieval lord was more benevolent than the Greek patron is uncertain, but the medieval vassal was seemingly more willing (perhaps even with some emotion) than the Greek clients to honor those above in the hierarchy. This book will argue that gratitude, as in this medieval narrative, involves reciprocity, though the freedom with which it is given transcends not simply the obligation of the Greek client, but the responsibility of the medieval vassal.

Enlightenment Gratitude: The Narrative of Social Detachment

Towards the end of the seventeenth century, the social hierarchies once so prominent began to be displaced. Once viewed as "a derogation of aristocratic status," trade was embraced and the "locus of the good life" was displaced from some "special range of higher activities" and positioned "within 'life' itself."²³⁵ With the displacement of social hierarchies there was a parallel displacement of traditional views about the cosmos.

---

231. Leithart, *Gratitude*, 119.

232. Leithart, *Gratitude*, 119.

233. Visser, *Gift of Thanks*, 406. Visser recognizes gratitude "is not a good thing in itself," but can be vitiated by a bad reason (*Gift of Thanks*, 405).

234. Visser, *Gift of Thanks*, 408.

235. Taylor, *Sources of Self*, 213. Eventually, "what was previously stigmatized as lower is now exalted as the standard, and the previously higher is convicted of presumption and vanity. And this involved a revaluation of professions as well. The lowly

INTRODUCTION

Though the Enlightenment had English and German counterparts, it was primarily the product of the *philosophes*, French intellectuals such as Montesquieu and Voltaire. With indebtedness to the science of Bacon and Newton, intellectuals increasingly perceived nature as self-sustaining and independent, governed by laws and not the capricious intervention of a god or gods. What enabled one to recognize the nature of these laws and derive implications from them was reason. Reason became the new "revelation," the basis upon which human morality could now be established. What became central in the minds of the *philosophes* was individual freedom.[236]

The philosophy of Rene Descartes (1596–1650), in particular, represented a shift of concern that amounted to "a retreat into the individual self-consciousness as the one sure starting point in philosophy."[237] Descartes is therefore representative of the Enlightenment thinkers who follow, all of whom deny the innate social nature of humanity.[238] Unlike Plato, for whom the self-mastery of reason meant being attuned to an existing order, the self-mastery of reason for Descartes involved constructing an order amenable to standards demanded by knowledge or certainty.[239] The hegemony of reason "disenchants" the world for Descartes, "because the cosmos is no longer seen as the embodiment of meaningful order which defines the good for us. And this move is brought about by our coming to grasp the world as mechanism."[240] For Descartes, therefore, passions were "functional devices" or "emotions of the soul" to strengthen one's survival response.[241] One such passion was gratitude, which Descartes regarded as something aroused

---

artisan and the artificer turn out to have contributed more to the advance of science than the leisured philosopher" (Taylor, *Sources of Self*, 213–14).

236. Marsak, "Introduction," 3–9.

237. Brown, *Philosophy*, 52. Taylor argues that Descartes's self-reflective disposition is inherited ultimately from Augustine for whom "inward," unlike Descartes, was the "the road to God" (Taylor, *Sources of Self*, 129). "Descartes gives Augustinian inwardness a radical twist and takes it in a new direction" (Taylor, *Sources of Self*, 143). For Descartes, "God's existence is a theorem in *my* system of a perfect science," Taylor writes. "The center of gravity has decisively shifted" (Taylor, *Sources of Self*, 157).

238. Colin Gunton argues that both Hobbes and Locke "found their concepts of the social contract on a deficient sociality, a failure to consider the essentially social nature of human being" (Gunton, *One, Three, and Many*, 220).

239. Taylor, *Sources of Self*, 147.

240. Taylor, *Sources of Self*, 149. The hegemony of reason has power to objectify body, world, and passions.

241. Taylor, *Sources of Self*, 150. "Reason rules the passions when it can hold them to their normal instrumental function" (Taylor, *Sources of Self*, 150). Taylor calls them "warrior-aristocratic virtues, now internalized" (Taylor, *Sources of Self*, 153).

by something good or done for one's good.²⁴² Exceeding mere approval, gratitude is strengthened for Descartes by the desire for reciprocation.²⁴³ Its opposite is anger which, like gratitude, has a personal object.²⁴⁴ Whereas gratitude, for Descartes, is love demonstrated towards something good done to a person, anger is hate expressed towards something evil.²⁴⁵

In writing *Leviathan*, Thomas Hobbes (1588–1679) endeavored to formulate a political theory with mathematical precision.²⁴⁶ From a starting point of fear of death, the greatest evil, Hobbes hypothesized that the greatest good is self-preservation and then proceeded to identify eighteen laws of nature which essentially forbid a person from self-destruction.²⁴⁷ Hobbes has "an ontology of human fallenness or sin, saying that certain forms of anti-social behaviour reveal us as what we are essentially are."²⁴⁸ Given Hobbes's conviction that the state of nature is war of all against all, he postulated first that one should strive for peace and secondly, that one should be content with as much liberty against others as one would permit against oneself.²⁴⁹ Justice is his third law of nature, and gratitude his fourth.²⁵⁰ Ethics for Hobbes involves identifying and recommending those actions that will produce the society most want.²⁵¹ Assuming universal human egotism, Hobbes alleged that gifts are necessarily self-interested and that gratitude makes for peace.²⁵² If there is nothing to get, no one would give, and if no one is thanked, no one would give. Gratitude is necessary because it encourages otherwise selfish people "to act in disinterested ways for the benefit of

---

242. Leithart, *Gratitude*, 146. "Gratitude is also a kind of love aroused in us by some action of the person to whom we are grateful" (Descartes, *Passions of the Soul*, para. 193).

243. Leithart, *Gratitude*, 146.

244. Descartes, *Passions of the Soul*, para. 199.

245. Leithart, *Gratitude*, 146.

246. Leithart, *Gratitude*, 122. Hobbes followed what he regarded as Galileo's method in studying physical nature that involved reconstructing "complexity out of simplicity" and located as "fundamental human motives" both "the desire to dominate and the desire to avoid death" (See MacIntryre, *Short History of Ethics*, 132).

247. Leithart, *Gratitude*, 124.

248. Gunton, *One, Three, and Many*, 220.

249. Leithart, *Gratitude*, 124.

250. Hobbes, *Leviathan*, 93.

251. MacIntyre, *Short History of Ethics*, 148.

252. Leithart, *Gratitude*, 124.

others and for society in general."²⁵³ Gratitude thus oils the machinery of giving, and that is socially beneficial.²⁵⁴

John Locke (1632–1704) continued in Descartes's trajectory. His theory, Taylor writes, "generates and also reflects an ideal of independence and self-responsibility, a notion of reason as free from established custom and locally dominant authority."²⁵⁵ In Locke's view, society is best off entrusting civil power—and one that can be trusted—with authority to protect natural rights, especially life, liberty, and property.²⁵⁶ These rights derive from a moral law accessible through reason. If a government fails to defend individual rights, its citizens are no longer obligated to submit.²⁵⁷ Authority, in other words, is legitimate only on the basis of the consent of those under it.²⁵⁸ Compared to Hobbes, Locke's view is slightly more optimistic, though still strongly individualistic.²⁵⁹ "Social existence," says Gunton, summarizing Hobbes's and Locke's views, "is not essential to our being as humans, but a more or less unfortunate necessity."²⁶⁰ Locke's views on authority did not apply to the family, however, because there the right to command is issued on the basis of benefits, not the consent of a civil contract.²⁶¹ In this way, Locke distinguished from the public and political realm a private social life governed by its own norms.²⁶² For Locke, gratitude, for instance, is foundational only for the family as a realm in which charity is expected, but not for the state, whose concerns were with ownership and justice.²⁶³

Following Locke's lead in political theory, Adam Smith (1723–1790) in his economic theory distinguished from the world of commerce and industry a private sphere for gratitude.²⁶⁴ The thesis of *The Wealth of Nations* is that the basis of a vibrant economy is not benevolence, but self-interest.

---

253. Harpham, "History of Ideas," 27.

254. Leithart, *Gratitude*, 126. If children did not feel obligations to parents, Hobbes argued, people would stop procreating and humanity would end (See Visser, *Gift of Thanks*, 233).

255. Taylor, *Sources of Self*, 167.

256. MacIntyre, *Short History of Ethics*, 157. See also Koyzis, *Political Visions*, 130.

257. Koyzis, *Political Visions*, 130.

258. Koyzis, *Political Visions*, 131.

259. "Locke had certainly shed the belief in original sin in anything like its orthodox sense . . . but he substituted a naturalized variant, an inherent penchant of human beings to egocentricity and personal power" (Taylor, *Sources of Self*, 240).

260. Gunton, *One, Three, and Many*, 220.

261. Leithart, *Gratitude*, 132–33.

262. Leithart, *Gratitude*, 134.

263. Leithart, *Gratitude*, 130–31.

264. Leithart, *Gratitude*, 135.

Whereas benevolence is occasional, Smith surmised, human self-interest is unrelenting, and its constancy makes economic progress calculable and predictable.[265] Secondly, Smith contended that self-interest underscored a person's dignity and ability, whereas benevolence assumed a beggar and a culture of need and dependence.[266] Self-interest assumed autonomy to enter into commercial relationships, whereas benevolence assumed obligations.[267] Because failure to be grateful is not injurious to people and therefore not punishable, gratitude is good for society, but not essential.[268] Justice, on the other hand, is essential to society because its violations injure people and therefore are punishable.[269] Smith therefore implicitly rejects the theorizing of both Seneca and Aquinas who subsumed gratitude under justice.[270]

To conclude from this that Smith had no place in his outlook for benevolence is understandable, but fundamentally mistaken. To obtain Smith's views on benevolence, one has to move beyond *The Wealth of Nations* (1776) and his economic theory to his earlier book, *Theory of Moral Sentiments* (1759), where he underscores the importance of moral capital. Though autonomy was especially prized by Smith, social virtues such as honesty, compassion, and gratitude were required for humanity to flourish.[271] Along with David Hume and others, Smith belonged to a philosophical school of thought for whom morality was derived more from emotion than reason.[272] To understand moral norms, one must grasp moral sentiments. Because Smith insisted, albeit without evidence, that sympathy was a universal human experience, it (and not reason, as Locke argued) was foundational for moral life as the expression of moral approbation. Smith identifies sympathy as the motivator of human action (inclusive of what today we call empathy) and not, as Locke had, reason or egotism.[273] To sympathize was to approve.

---

265. Harpham, "History of Ideas," 20.

266. Harpham, "History of Ideas," 20.

267. Harpham, "History of Ideas," 20. Smith engaged the challenge of how cooperation among autonomous individuals could be fostered in the economic realm without coercion. The answer, for Smith, was located in mutually beneficial exchanges (Cavanaugh, *Being Consumed*, 2).

268. Leithart, *Gratitude*, 139.

269. Leithart, *Gratitude*, 139.

270. Leithart, *Gratitude*, 139.

271. Leithart, *Gratitude*, 135.

272. Sometimes called "the British Enlightenment" in distinction from "the French Enlightenment." It gave birth to Romanticism and the greater validation of emotions.

273. Leithart, *Gratitude*, 135.

For Smith, sympathy is exhibited by two sentiments in particular: gratitude and resentment.[274] Judging them to be universal human responses to the actions of others, Smith presented them as the standard by which all actions are judged and thus the basis of his moral theory.[275] An action that excites sympathetic gratitude is meritorious and ought to be rewarded, whereas an action that invites sympathetic resentment is injurious and ought to be disapproved.[276] Further, if we cannot sympathize with gratitude for a gift, we are disapproving, and something, perhaps the motivations of the benefactor, is wrong.[277] Interestingly, to assess the appropriateness of a grateful response, one must be a third-party impartial spectator.[278] "His view is therefore heavily relativist," Visser writes. "Everything depends on what a particular society deems 'proper.' The ancient 'shame culture' component of this view of morality is evident."[279] "Gratitude," Leithart writes of Smith's view, "is a soft virtue reserved to drawing rooms, dance halls, romances, and novels of manner . . . a sentiment rather than a Senecan return gift."[280] Excluding any notion of doing, gratitude was merely "the passion or sentiment that prompts us to reward others for the good that they have done us."[281]

In the modern era, far removed from the Greco-Roman world in time, Jean-Jacques Rousseau (1712–1778) celebrated independence much like Aristotle and thus also regarded the reciprocity implied in gratitude as unwanted indebtedness. Because he viewed constraints as irksome, Rousseau resisted the sense of duty implied in both gratitude and generosity.[282] Unlike those who recognized something natural about gratitude, as did Locke and Hobbes, Rousseau regarded independent autonomy as the essence of humanity, and thus gratitude, implying indebtedness, is unnatural.[283] Whereas

274. Leithart, *Gratitude*, 136.
275. Leithart, *Gratitude*, 136.
276. Leithart, *Gratitude*, 136.
277. Leithart, *Gratitude*, 137.
278. Harpham, "History of Ideas," 30. Smith "elevated human sensitivity to the opinions of others into a total explanation of how and why morality works" (Visser, *Gift of Thanks*, 328).
279. Visser, *Gift of Thanks*, 328.
280. Leithart, *Gratitude*, 11.
281. Harpham, "History of Ideas," 28.
282. Leithart, *Gratitude*, 149. "He came to believe that the bonds of dependency that were being forged were more dangerous to the individual in the modern world than connections that were being established" (Harpham, "History of Ideas," 34).
283. Leithart, *Gratitude*, 150. The one exception, for Leithart, to Rousseau's otherwise independent and autonomous natural man is the experience of pity, and pity therefore is the source of all social virtues, including generosity (Leithart, *Gratitude*, 152). In seems Rousseau's views on human independence might be more complex.

for Hobbes, human nature was broken, for Rousseau, human society was distorted. Rousseau romanticized nature: humanity is happy in nature, but society makes him miserable.[284]

Moral conduct for Immanuel Kant (1724–1804) is conducting oneself according to a maxim one wishes were universal.[285] Moral duties, in other words, are those which would make fitting universal laws.[286] Kant therefore follows in the tradition of Rousseau whose "inner self" becomes for Kant the "noumenal self," which is in touch with the absolute morality and leads to the displacement of God.[287] Since it is inconceivable that rational people would want a rule universalized that one should neglect to show gratitude, one should respond to favors with gratitude. Beneficence is obliged because we should promote the happiness of others—a theme that becomes prominent towards the end of Kant's life.[288] If an action imposes an obligation, Kant reasons more specifically, as beneficence does, it is a duty of love, and if it does not, it is a duty of respect.[289] The duty of love includes the obligation to cultivate sentiments (which themselves cannot be commanded) such that those who have received benefits, for instance, are obliged to nurture feelings of gratitude towards their benefactors.[290] As such, gratitude consists of respect and honor which a beneficiary owes a benefactor for her kindness.[291] Such respect, however, should only be given in scenarios where there is true beneficence, i.e., where there is no intent to humble, for example, or indebt a beneficiary, and where the beneficiary welcomes the beneficence.[292] In fact, Kant designates gratitude as a sacred duty because (a) failure to be grateful compromises the main duty of love, which is beneficence, and (b) the obligation of gratitude is never fully satisfied. The recipient of beneficence, in

---

"Rousseau sees that what men aim at for themselves is a certain kind of life lived in a certain type of relationship with others. True self-love, our primitive passion, provides the notion of a reciprocal relationship of the self to others and so a basis for an appreciation of justice" (MacIntyre, *Short History of Ethics*, 186).

284. Gunton, *One, Three, and Many*, 224.

285. Leithart, *Gratitude*, 156.

286. "There is therefore but one categorical imperative, namely, this: 'Act only on that maxim whereby thou canst at the same time will that it should become a universal law'" (Kant, "Fundamental Principles," 98). Kant's position "requires an absolute distinction of duty from desire" (Hart, *Beauty of Infinite*, 262).

287. Gunton, *One, Three, and Many*, 224.

288. Leithart, *Gratitude*, 157.

289. Leithart, *Gratitude*, 157.

290. Leithart, *Gratitude*, 157.

291. Leithart, *Gratitude*, 157.

292. Leithart, *Gratitude*, 157.

other words, never fully discharges the duty of gratitude or else gift-giving is no different from a loan. The original gift, freely given, establishes a relationship between donor and recipient that cannot be severed.[293]

What Gunton says of Rousseau and Kant applies to a degree to Hobbes and Locke as well: "Their approaches are two sides of the same dualism of spirit and nature, mind and thing, that alienates person and world."[294] The individual Descartes isolated, Hobbes categorizes as innately combatant and anti-social. Locke and Smith assess human nature more positively and see individualism and even selfishness, for example, as advantageous, but they cordon off a private social life subject to norms distinct from the public realm. Rousseau goes farther, romanticizing human nature and making human society culpable for the ills of life.

In the narrative of social detachment, gratitude suffers. The hegemony of reason, for Descartes, disenchanted the world and severed it from God's generous providence and subjected the cosmos to the individual mind. Hobbes's ontology of fallenness regarded the social nature of humanity as something essentially evil. Locke perpetuated Descartes's trajectory towards independence and self-responsibility and Smith cordoned off gratitude as a wonderful sentiment for the private sphere, thereby diminishing the social nature of gratitude. Rousseau shares Hobbes's concern about society. Unlike Hobbes who blamed human nature, however, Rousseau saw society as something miserable. This book presents gratitude as fundamentally a social virtue which acknowledges and affirms an ontology of communion with God, self, and others. Further, though emotion is a constituent part of gratitude—a notion foreign to both Cicero and Seneca, Visser points out, for whom gratitude is an action—this book will argue that gratitude cannot be reduced to mere emotion.[295]

---

293. "The original, uncoerced act forever obligates the receiver" even if the beneficiary repays the benefactor (Mitchell, *Politics of Gratitude*, 20). How does one reconcile Kant's stress on moral autonomy with his emphasis on duty of gratitude? Kant distinguished perfect from imperfect duties. Whereas *perfect* duties require only the right sort of action, *imperfect* duties can be wrong even when performed rightly (Visser, *Gift of Thanks*, 254). Killing an enemy of a friend to show gratitude is wrong because the imperfect duty (rightly returning gratitude) is performed while transgressing the perfect duty (not killing) (Visser, *Gift of Thanks*, 254). Furthermore, gratitude is a *narrow* imperfect duty, distinguished from a *wide* imperfect duty, because when the opportunity avails, the beneficiary *must* be grateful (provided she doesn't violate a perfect duty) (Visser, *Gift of Thanks*, 255).

294. Gunton, *One, Three, and Many*, 228.

295. Visser, *Gift of Thanks*, 326. In the orbit of politeness, as is true of "shame cultures," it is only the action that counts: social propriety matters more than sincerity or morality (Visser, *Gift of Thanks*, 329).

Existential Gratitude: The Narrative of Divine Displacement

Existential philosophy has its roots in two prolific individuals who were not academic philosophersnamely, Sören Kierkegaard (1813–55) and Friedrich Nietzsche (1844–1900). According to William Barrett, what distinguished these two thinkers as philosophers (and what introduced a revolution in philosophy) was their subject matter: not ideas so much as "the unique experience of the single one, the individual, who chooses to place himself [sic] on trial before the gravest question of his [sic] civilization."[296] Whereas Kierkegaard was determined to see whether Christianity was still livable, Nietzsche pronounced God dead and envisioned life without him. Pace Kierkegaard's embrace of Christ, Existentialism signaled the entrance of Western society into a secular phase of history in which humanity found itself "for the first time *homeless*."[297]

What the Enlightenment funded, for Mitchell, was a denial of limits. He argues that though modern science, and the promises of technology, pushed back the limits of space and time, they did nothing to overcome them.[298] Ancient cosmologies and religious claims were judged to be unscientific and therefore inadequate and unhelpful and so the philosophical world we inhabit today opposes limits and advocates independence, self-assertion, and autonomy.[299] Only by embracing the concept of creaturehood can we attain contentment with the mystery of human existence.[300] Mitchell argues further that modern secularism, having rejected the heavenly home, is left only with an elusive earthly home, with no meaningful history or future.[301] One narrative that still orients people, Leddy argues, is the myth of progress.[302] But the myth of progress assumes dissatisfaction with the past and obsesses over the future. It seems like heresy, Leddy suggests, but many are acknowledging: it is not working anymore; we do not know what to do.[303]

---

296. Barrett, *Irrational Man*, 13.

297. Barrett, *Existential Philosophy*, 35.

298. Mitchell, *Politics of Gratitude*, 11.

299. Mitchell, *Politics of Gratitude*, 16.

300. Mitchell, *Politics of Gratitude*, 9–10.

301. Mitchell, *Politics of Gratitude*, 64.

302. Discernible in the popularity of how-to books (e.g., how to make friends, how to cook, how to pray, etc.). Assuming its existence, we pursue the know-how, the technology, to see it happen.

303. Leddy, *Radical Gratitude*, 111. When dissatisfaction in the myth of progress mixes with dissatisfaction generated by consumerism, a potent cocktail is created, pushing people even faster to perpetual and now pointless consumption. The despair over the myth of progress is comparable to the fading of an imperial vision, which historically parallels the dissolution of the social institutions the empire once embodied and induces social despair and apocalyptic dreams (Leddy, *Radical Gratitude*, 118–19).

The absence of a compelling narrative funds, for Leddy, a cultural captivity and sense of powerlessness.[304] Power today is often conceived in terms of the acquisition of knowledge which, for Enlightenment thinkers, displaced tradition, authority, and community and was viewed as a way to predict and control the machine-like world. Control, however, is illusory, and we must learn, Leddy says, "to live with mysterious realities that are beyond our control."[305] Yet powerlessness is enchanting to some, giving victims, for example, high moral ground, and the feeling of innocence, quickly embraced in a culture where people struggle with a vague sense of guilt.[306] Victimization, however, is sometimes quantified, Leddy argues, and sadly used as a scorecard to diminish the offences others feel, or worse, license the abdication of responsibility.[307]

This has implications for how one perceives gratitude. For Nietzsche, for instance, gratitude is a way to pay back the unwanted indebtedness. When a benefactor intrudes into another's realm by providing a gift, the recipient can and should show resistance with gratitude—something Nietzsche regarded as a milder form of revenge.[308] As such, "gratitude is not an acknowledgment of dependence, but an affirmation of autonomy."[309] He opposed Christian gratitude, Leithart avers, because it negates what should be affirmed—namely, moral autonomy. As such, Christian gratitude is "slave

---

304. Experiences of meaning are episodic for us, as are our commitments, even to health and spirituality. Without conviction about how it all interrelates, we experience fatigue (Leddy, *Radical Gratitude*, 106).

305. Leddy, *Radical Gratitude*, 79. Sensing a lack of control and desperately wanting it, some resort to violence, especially common in communities where adult men in particular feel powerless. What often characterizes mass murderers is lack of control. "Those who have little or no control over their own existence can be driven to take ultimate control over their own lives and the lives of others" (Leddy, *Radical Gratitude*, 84).

306. Leddy, *Radical Gratitude*, 84–85.

307. Leddy, *Radical Gratitude*, 86–87. Leddy demurs from the impulse of victims to assert moral rights because of their victimhood; rights are the property of human beings, victims or not. In bureaucratic organizations, no one is really sure where responsibility lies, at the upper, middle, or lower tiers. Everyone feels vaguely guilty and vaguely responsible (Leddy, *Radical Gratitude*, 87).

308. Leithart, *Gratitude*, 183. See also Visser, *Gift of Thanks*, 423. Nietzsche's view of gratitude is striking since both gratitude and revenge involve memory and a kind of repayment and yield satisfaction (Visser, *Gift of Thanks*, 427, 439). Whereas vengeance seeks the same for the offender, gratitude seeks something different, and whereas vengeance endeavors to teach a lesson, gratitude does not. Vengeance seeks justice, but gratitude fairness—a response, not a requital. In pre-modern societies gift-giving was chosen to substitute peace for hostility, but once hostility resumed, it was hard to attain peace (Visser, *Gift of Thanks*, 431).

309. Leithart, *Gratitude*, 185.

morality" or *ressentiment*, the revenge of the weak against a hostile world.[310] True gratitude, for Nietzsche, is revenge of the strong and an affirmation of autonomy.[311] Nietzsche, Gunton argues, was correct to associate Christianity with sacrifice, though he was wrong to associate sacrifice with suffering. If there had been no Fall, gifts and sacrifices would still be given, but without suffering.[312]

The sense of estrangement from being one discerns in both Nietzsche and Kierkegaard becomes the theme for Martin Heidegger (1889–1976), an academic philosopher. Whereas Nietzsche saw gratitude as moral revenge for the intrusion of a gift, Heidegger redefined it to allow for an impersonal and non-social function. In his monumental *Sein und Zeit*, Heidegger questioned the relation between knowing, subject, and object and endeavored to transcend the dualisms of subject and object, self and world, knower and known. Leithart argues that for Heidegger the knower, for instance, is not a disinterested subject as above and outside, but embedded in the world; not simply *Sein*, "being," but *Da-Sein*, "being there."[313] Similarly for Heidegger, objects are never abstracted in life, but experienced first in terms of their use. "The first human stance is one of reception rather than domination," Leithart summarizes, "and reception is a hairbreadth away from gratitude."[314]

---

310. Leithart, *Gratitude*, 184.

311. Leithart, *Gratitude*, 185. Many sociobiologists insist, proposing unwittingly a scientific basis for Nietzsche's views, that gratitude is genetically determined and is ultimately performed, as is the case with all altruistic behavior, out of self-interest (Visser, *Gift of Thanks*, 32–34). Visser is not so convinced, and underscores how humans, in distinction from animals, "resist evolution" by protecting the disabled, for instance, and helping them to survive against nature (Visser, *Gift of Thanks*, 40). Respecting the brain's plasticity and the distinctively human impulse to learn, rehearse, and refine, Visser alleges that human gratitude seems to transcend mere self-interest (Visser, *Gift of Thanks*, 41).

312. Gunton, *One, Three, and Many*, 226.

313. Leithart, *Gratitude*, 185. "*Dasein* is a being that does not simply occur among other beings. Rather, it is ontically distinguished by the fact that in its being this being is concerned about its very being. Thus it is constitute of the being of *Dasein* to have, in its very being, a relation of being to this being" (Heidegger, *Being and Time*, 11).

314. Leithart, *Gratitude*, 186. Heidegger made a "turn" after the writing of *Sein und Zeit* from the traditional philosophical concepts to very creative philosophizing on the function of language and the nature of particular German words. *Wesen* as a noun, for instance, means "essence" and as an archaic verb connotes how things work (Leithart, *Gratitude*, 187). For Heidegger, *Wesen* does not happen to individual things; beings simply "are," but they unfold (Leithart, *Gratitude*, 188). *Es gibt* means "there is," but literally, "it gives," and what it gives is *Ereignis*, appropriation, Being's way of happening, and through it something enters the mind (Leithart, *Gratitude*, 188; see also Visser, *Gift of Thanks*, 283). More a matter of reception than discovery, thinking for Heidegger is revelation of what is there. Thinking is responding to what is, and memory is awareness

Noting the Old English noun for thought, *thanc* (or *thonc*), Heidegger argues that thanking implies thinking, but a thinking as a concentrated abiding with something, to what is thought-provoking, to what "gives" us to think, a gift.[315] The thought of existence, for Heidegger, provokes the thought of the givenness of Being.[316] In the end, such thought for Heidegger, possibly fearing unwanted indebtedness, Leithart argues, "does not need to repay, nor be deserved, in order to give thanks. Such thanks is not recompense; it remains an offering."[317] No gift is appropriated, so no-thing must be returned. Thought as response to Being's advent easily becomes acquiescence in whatever is with no space at all for ingratitude. "It seems no accident," Leithart provocatively concludes, "that the greatest modern philosopher of gratitude is also the philosopher of fascism."[318]

In the narrative of divine displacement, gratitude towards God becomes difficult or impossible. If God is excised from the picture, gratitude must be redefined as awareness or acknowledgment. This book argues that not only is gratitude social, it is personal, and that, as such, gratitude should never be confused with mere appreciation.

Postmodern Gratitude: The Narrative of Self-forgetfulness

Jacques Derrida, the French postmodern philosopher, devalued gratitude on the grounds that gifts do not require returns and thus the return of gratitude poisons the gift. Derrida, whose views will be considered at length in chapter 3, engaged Marcel Mauss's scholarship in *The Gift*, demurring from any configuration of gift-giving that involves a circle or a return gift. He insists that for a beneficiary simply to acknowledge a gift is to annul it: a gift must not appear as a gift.[319] Both beneficiary and benefactor must absolutely forget the gift for it to be a gift. The gift renounces self-interest,

---

of what has been and is, and therefore thanking is especially thinking about the gift of being. It works in reverse too: *Es gibt*, Being seizes us with the wonder that there is something rather than nothing. "If Being unfolds in the self-giving of Being, then we should receive," Leithart writes, and "our primary stance in the world is one of receptive gratitude" (Leithart, *Gratitude*, 188). In this connection, Heidegger repeats the Pietist motto, *denken ist Danken*, "to think is to thank" (Leithart, *Gratitude*, 188).

315. Leithart, *Gratitude*, 190.
316. Leithart, *Gratitude*, 191.
317. Leithart, *Gratitude*, 192.
318. Leithart, *Gratitude*, 193.
319. Leithart, *Gratitude*, 197–99. "The only gift, for Derrida, that can be given is no gift at all: given without intention to no one whom it can oblige, it must be the gift of nothing" (Hart, *Beauty of Infinite*, 261).

refuses calculation, denies reason, and seeks no return. "The gift," for Derrida, "is the effaced gesture of being's absence or lack, devoid of generosity, remembrance, or gratitude, and is so the purest forgetfulness and purest donation."[320] In Derrida's philosophy, we discover something very different from the philosophies of Descartes, Locke, Smith, and Rousseau. Instead of self-affirmation, there is value in self-forgetfulness and a willingness, as in Existentialism, to embrace nothingness.[321] The self does not escape Derrida's radical project of deconstruction and is exposed as ignoble and unstable, polluted by destructive motives. Without God in the picture—the fruit of the Enlightenment as much as of Existentialism—the self becomes transcendent. In postmodernism, however, the transcendent self turns on itself, deconstructs itself, and dissolves. This book defends the possibility of gift-giving and therefore of gratitude and argues, relatedly, that gratitude is the fitting response to a gift and one that contributes to peaceable relationships.

CONCLUSION

Gratitude has been conceived of in various ways throughout history, largely on account of the narrative in which it is situated. In the narrative of hierarchical relations, for example, the return gift (of gratitude) functioned as a social hinge, was obligatory, and was given without feeling. In the narrative of feudal responsibility, gratitude becomes warmer, still regarded as a duty, but a welcome and honorable duty. In the narrative of social detachment, as rationalism, individualism, and a mechanistic view of the universe gained momentum, gratitude is excised from the public square and is reduced to a helpful sentiment in private relationships. In the narrative of divine displacement, God is excised from the picture, requiring gratitude to be redefined as mere awareness or acknowledgment. Finally, in the narrative of self-forgetfulness, the self itself is deconstructed and its value is diminished.

---

320. Hart, *Beauty of Infinite*, 262. Further, in Derrida's scheme, "talk of a God who creates from the beneficence of his love is a self-defeating metaphor" (Hart, *Beauty of Infinite*, 262).

321. For Mary Jo Leddy, this explains what lies beneath the veneer of consumerism. The dissatisfaction produced by consumerism shifts to the very core of one's being: "I don't have enough becomes I am not enough becomes I am not good enough" (Leddy, *Radical Gratitude*, 25). Leddy thus profoundly conjectures a link between "outer" economic and "inner" psychological dynamics to account for why North Americans, in the wealthiest nations, feel vaguely powerless (e.g., nothing I say will make a difference), vaguely guilty (e.g., I'm not good enough), and vaguely responsible for what's wrong in the world. See Leddy, *Radical Gratitude*, 26.

Hardly noble, one's gesture of gratitude, in fact, is simply an attempt to "pay" for a gift, rendering the gift null and void.

On the basis of an ontology of communion in which one is inextricably joined to God, others, and the world in relationships which should neither be denied nor resisted, this book defines gratitude as a responsive virtue in which one, seeing oneself as the recipient of a gift, freely and joyfully salutes the giver in order to perpetuate a personal and peaceable relationship.

CHAPTER 2

MORAL SABOTEURS OF GRATITUDE

In his masterful *Screwtape Letters*, C. S. Lewis depicts an old and wise devil, Screwtape, advising his nephew Wormwood, a junior devil, on the tactics of sabotaging Christian professions. One ploy he recommends to Wormwood is to lure Christians away either from eternity or the present and get them to fixate on "the Future" because the Future, he alleges, is the most temporal aspect of time and the least like eternity. The pleasure inherent in much sin is actually from God and is enjoyed in the present. "The sin, which is our contribution," Screwtape writes, "looked forward."[1] He continues,

> We want a man [sic] hag-ridden by the Future—haunted by visions of an imminent heaven or hell upon earth—ready to break the Enemy's commands in the present if by so doing we make him think he can attain the one or avert the other—dependent for his faith on the success or failure of schemes whose end he will not live to see. We want a whole race perpetually in pursuit of the rainbow's end, never honest, nor kind, nor happy now, but always using as mere fuel wherewith to heap the altar of the future every real gift which is offered them in the present.[2]

An obsession with the future can easily result in a devaluation of the present and the past. This chapter will argue that sinful desires have potential to sabotage gratitude and thereby derail the enjoyment of life. For centuries Christians have identified seven sinful desires as particularly

---

1. Lewis, *Screwtape Letters*, 78.
2. Lewis, *Screwtape Letters*, 78–79.

deadlythe so-called "seven deadly sins." In this chapter, I will describe and reflect on the seven deadly sins as saboteurs of gratitude, highlighting their capacity to devalue God, things, self, and others and so poison the soil in which gratitude ordinarily grows. I will begin, however, by probing the nature and function of desire in terms of anthropology before offering a phenomenological account for the habituation of desire and reflecting on how sin might twist desire. In so doing, I will correlate philosophical, phenomenological, and psychological accounts of desire, habit, and vice with theological depictions.

AN ANTHROPOLOGY OF DESIRE

What essentially constitutes a human being? The notion that humans are essentially thinking creatures received substantial backing from Rene Descartes. Descartes discovered that he could doubt the certainty of just about anything until he was left with nothing to believe but the certainty of his doubting existence, leading him to voice his famous maxim, "I think, therefore I am."[3] Subsequent and prominent philosophers, including Kant and Hegel, embraced this essentially rationalistic anthropology, albeit in different ways, and funded its persistence throughout modernism. Perhaps unintentionally, Protestant theology absorbed this anthropology in several ways, not least by underwriting a rationalist apologetics in which secular and Christian worldviews were reduced to competing sets of beliefs and by recommending an ethics of law in which the moral life is largely a matter of decision and rightness, rather than vision and character.[4] Roman Catholicism did not fall prey to the temptations of Cartesianism to the degree Protestantism did because of its inherited fondness, dating back at least to Thomas Aquinas, for the anthropology of Aristotelian philosophy.

This chapter will advocate generally for an anthropology of desire and, relatedly, for an assessment of human unhappiness and discontentment that locates the problem in distorted desire. I will begin with a consideration of the views of Aristotle, from whom we obtain our grammar for an anthropology of desire, followed by those of Augustine, the first significant Christian thinker to invoke Aristotelian categories and then substantially modify them along Christian ideals.

---

3. Descartes, *Discourse and Meditations*, 18.
4. See Lee, *Against the Protestant Gnostics*; cf. Hauerwas, *Vision and Virtue*, 29.

Aristotle

One way to access an Aristotelian anthropology is to see it against the foil of its ancient rivals—namely, Epicureanism, which came before Aristotle, and Stoicism, which came after. Together with Aristotelianism, Epicureanism and Stoicism were oriented by eudaimonianism, the ancient conviction that there is an end we pursue for the sake of nothing elsenamely, εὐδαιμονία, the happy life.[5] Advocated by Epicurus and centuries later modified by Lucretius, Epicureanism (third century BCE) approaches the contemporary secular view in recommending the pursuit of pleasure for its own sake. Convinced that the gods needed nothing beyond themselves to fulfill their desires, Epicurus argued that they were aloof to human concerns and untroubled by events on earth.[6] To live in fear of divine punishment, therefore, is a meaningless waste of time. Since the immortality of the soul, reincarnation, and resurrection were disavowed and annihilation affirmed, living in fear of death was equally futile. "The Epicurean prescription for a happy life," Charry writes, "is to eradicate irrational fear of things that cannot really cause pain or distress in order to be free to enjoy the pleasures of life that reward one's efforts."[7] The pleasures of life for Epicurus were the sole arbitrators of morality. One should pursue justice, in other words, only because injustice causes one too much anxiety.[8] As such, virtue is a means to pleasure, though pleasure for Epicurus was not, as conventionally argued, sensual indulgences, but tranquility, and the absence of anxiety and desire.[9] The Epicurean fixation on pleasure was individualist and thus neglected communal and societal duties.

The main rival of Epicureanism, Stoicism originated shortly after Aristotle's death and famously insisted that happiness derives only from virtue, not pleasure. Having more or less health, wealth, beauty, fame and so forth is irrelevant to virtue and therefore to happiness.[10] The Stoics advocated exercising reason to control irrational impulses in the wake of turbulent events in order to conduct oneself appropriately in any and every circumstance. The virtuous life, in which happiness is exclusively located, is generated by

---

5. The root of εὐδαιμονία is δαιμον, originally meaning, "the god who dispenses goods." The εὐδαιμον is the one who receives gifts dispensed by a good (εὐ-) spirit (δαιμον). Originally with passive connotations, εὐδαιμονία eventually assumed activity (Vanier, *Happiness*, 31).

6. Schoch, *Secrets of Happiness*, 52.
7. Charry, *God and the Art of Happiness*, 9.
8. Kamtekar, "Ancient Virtue Ethics," 42.
9. Schoch, *Secrets of Happiness*, 6.
10. Kamtekar, "Ancient Virtue Ethics," 42.

ἀπάθεια, the inability for one's rational control to be derailed by tragic or unsettling events. Charry dubs stoicism "rationalist cognitive therapy."[11]

How does Aristotelianism differ from Epicureanism and Stoicism? Whereas Epicureanism eschews virtue by locating happiness in the eradication of pain-producing, irrational fear, and the pursuit of pleasure, Stoicism eschews pleasure by locating happiness in the control of morality-defying irrational impulses and enduring whatever comes to pass. Unlike Epicureanism, Aristotle affirms the importance of virtue, and unlike Stoicism, he affirms the goodness of desire, of pleasure, and of material things. By arguing that the greatest pleasure is located in the most virtuous life, Aristotle unites in his anthropology the two variables Epicureanism and Stoicism respectively deny—namely, virtue and pleasure.

For Aristotle, as for Epicureans and Stoics, humans are beings of desire, inclined towards something and attracted to some good.[12] The question that captivated Aristotle, therefore, was not, *what ought we to do*, but rather, *what do we really want*?[13] "We human beings are drawn to ends," Jean Vanier writes, nodding his head to Aristotle. "We desire them, we want to possess them, consume them, be one with them; we want to look at them, contemplate them, take delight in them. That is the experience of desire."[14] The highest end of our desires, because it is sufficient in itself, is not pursued for the sake of anything else and, unlike an object, cannot be removed from us.[15] For Aristotle, the great desire and most profound motivator of all people is, as it was for the Epicureans and Stoics, εὐδαιμονία. For us happiness is subjective, associated with the feeling of pleasure, but for Aristotle it was the subjective satisfaction of objectively living morally and productively.[16] For Aristotle, therefore, εὐδαιμονία "seems to be a good life that involves both *human* fulfillment and *individual* fulfillment."[17]

Virtue, for Aristotle, is not simply about fulfilling desire, but about making choices. As such it required φρόνησις or practical wisdom, a distinctive human ability to think rationally about how to live, to act with rationally trained emotions, and in so doing to change the way things are.[18]

11. Charry, *God and the Art of Happiness*, 10.
12. Vanier, *Happiness*, 3.
13. Vanier, *Happiness*, xi
14. Vanier, *Happiness*, 6.
15. Vanier, *Happiness*, 13–14.
16. Charry, *God and the Art of Happiness*, 3.
17. Russell, "Virtue Ethics," 11.
18. "Well, it is thought to be the mark of a prudent (φρόνησις) man to be able to deliberate rightly about what is good and advantageous for himself... what is conducive to the good life generally" (Aristotle, *Eth. nic.* 1140a15–20). As such, it is distinguished

Our practical reasoning, for example, about "how, whether, when, and what to eat" makes "human *dining* completely unlike animal *feeding*."[19] The implication is that virtue, for Aristotle, is not about simply fulfilling desire or about curbing it, but about pursuing the fulfillment of "deliberated desires."[20] Further, practical reasoning determines what else is essential to virtue—namely, the "mean" between excess and deficiency.

Aristotle did not try to prompt people to moral goodness by external forces but through the development and practice of habits "based on the relative calculus of pleasure and pain."[21] Aristotle regarded habituation as "the process by which performing acts of a certain kind produces in us dispositions of the corresponding kind."[22] Vanier writes,

> The aim of Aristotle's ethics is to help human beings choose the activity from which they will derive the greatest pleasure of joy, and thus become as happy as possible by divorcing themselves from activities that give them more superficial and temporary pleasure, but prevent them from progressing towards the finest activities and pleasures.[23]

The satisfaction we experience in being virtuous is a form of pleasure such that happiness is the province of those who acquired and practiced the virtues necessary to live well.

Aristotle's views are commendable for their recognition of the place of desire, but not without substantial liabilities. First, Aristotle's pagan philosophy discounted the presence of a personal God in whom true happiness should be sought. Secondly, Aristotle had no doctrine of original sin and therefore desire, though it could be deficient or excessive, could never be corrupt.[24] Thirdly, though Aristotle subsumed ethics under politics and conceived of ethics in the context of the πόλις or city-state, he distinguished ποίησις (i.e., making something external to oneself [production]) from

from scientific knowledge (of unchanging things) or the study of nature (where things change by nature, not decision) (Kamtekar, "Ancient Virtue Ethics," 36–37).

19. Russell, "Virtue Ethics," 13.

20. Kamtekar, "Ancient Virtue Ethics," 35. See Aristotle, *Eth. nic.* 1113a2–12. For Aristotle virtue, good reason in concert with one's desire, must be distinguished from mere continence, good reason opposed by one's desire.

21. Herman, *Cave and Light*, 55.

22. Kamtekar, "Ancient Virtue Ethics," 36. See Aristotle, *Eth. nic.* 1103a30–b25. Habit (ἕξις) for Aristotle is the acquisition of a kind of "second nature" (*Eth. nic.* 1152a31), a disposition that empowers one to act in a certain way.

23. Vanier, *Happiness*, 43–44.

24. "All appeals to Aristotelian moderation seem incongruent with the thought of Jesus" (Willimon, *Sinning Like a Christian*, 13).

πρᾶξις, (i.e., making oneself different [action]).[25] The public and economic realm, in other words, was beyond the realm of practice. Lastly, virtue for Aristotle is the victory of reason over passion and desire.[26] Needed chastisement for these views was provided by Augustine for whom ethics is pursued, not in the register of reason, but of love.[27]

Augustine

Much like Aristotle, Augustine, "the most influential theologian in the early church,"[28] theorized that human life is defined by desire and purpose and that what people especially crave is happiness. Right from the conception of his Christian life, Augustine was intrigued by the subject of happiness and penned *De Beata Vita* ('The Happy Life') in the fall of 387 while preparing for baptism the following Easter. He engaged pagan philosophy about εὐδαιμονία "not to endorse it so much as to *reconsider* it."[29] Unlike Aristotle, Augustine located happiness in being in the presence of the God who created us and enjoying as the object of our love him who is perfectly worthy of it.[30] God, therefore, should be desired because he alone can provide us happiness. Here we see Augustine's explicitly Christian (or at least theist) convictions. It might seem troublesome that God should be desired to provide us happiness as if this were God's *raison d'être*. This notion, however, becomes less objectionable when we see this desire as part of our human constitution by virtue of God's creation. God did not create us to be self-sufficient, but to exist in relationship with him and to delight in his presence. Human ontology, therefore, is an ontology of communion.

For Augustine, in sharp contrast to Aristotle, there is no human autonomy: to be independent of God "is to be cut off from being, and thus

---

25. See, e.g., Aristotle, *Eth. nic.* 1103a–1103b.

26. Ἀρετή (virtue) originally meant victory in conflict.

27. Leithart, *Against Christianity*, 101. What make virtue virtuous for Aristotle is φρόνησις; what made virtue virtuous for Augustine (and Aquinas) is love.

28. Lester, *Angry Christian*, 41.

29. Boone, *Conversion and Therapy*, 6. Boone identifies ways in which Augustine's *De Beata Vita* parallels Aristotle's *Nicomachean Ethics* (Boone, *Conversion and Therapy*, 74). Lester indicates that Augustine explicitly aligned himself with Aristotle (in contrast to the Stoic philosophers) on the need to moderate emotions rather than excise them (Lester, *Angry Christian*, 44).

30. Charry, *God and the Art of Happiness*, 37. For Augustine, happiness is "the spiritual benefit of knowing, loving, and enjoying God, and loving self and others in pursuit of that goal" (Charry, *God and the Art of Happiness*, 57).

to be nothing."[31] Furthermore, sin enslaves and the grace of God is needed to liberate one from false desires and so restore freedom of choice. True and false desires are distinguished by their *telos*.[32] "For Augustine," Cavanaugh writes, "the most important question is not whether the will has been moved externally or internally; rather, the most important question is to what end the will has been moved."[33] Understanding the teleology of desire provides tremendous insight into the nature of human liberty. Our contemporaries consider liberty in ways inconceivable for pre-moderns—namely, not simply as freedom from interference or intrusion, but as freedom from the ends to which our desires are directed. Once liberated from these ends, society is reduced to the dynamics of "the sheer arbitrary power of one will against another."[34] In an Augustinian framework, there is no autonomous being: "freedom is wrapped up in the will of God, who is the condition of human freedom."[35]

Further, Augustine increasingly realized, in contrast to Aristotle, that perfect happiness will elude us until the eschaton because we are never immune from suffering and distress.[36] Happiness brings healing, and our inability to experience full happiness in this life assumes an inability to be fully healed. Even so, some healing is located in the soul's rest in God. "Augustine experienced that rest and was inebriated by it," Charry writes, "yet he was unable to luxuriate in it continually, and thus he hoped for the time when he would be able to do so."[37] The implication here is that humanity, until the eschaton, will be characterized by a measure of sadness. "The God-shaped vacuum in us is infinite," Kreeft writes, "and cannot be filled with any finite objects or actions."[38] For Augustine, "the solution to our dissatisfaction is

---

31. Cavanaugh, *Being Consumed*, 8.

32. Though the language of "ends" hardly surfaces in Calvin's theology, it is apparent in his *Geneva Catechism* (1541), whose first question is, "what is the chief end of human life?" Happiness, for Calvin, was located in fulfilling the purpose for which humans were created—namely knowing God. As question 5 makes clear, "we see that nothing worse can happen to a man [sic] than to live without God" (Calvin, *Catechism of the Church of Geneva*). Gerrish observes that Calvin's "thoughts on the goal of human activity come closer to the Aristotelian-Thomistic notion of an appetitive drive than first appears" (Gerrish, *Grace and Gratitude*, 37).

33. Cavanaugh, *Being Consumed*, 11.

34. Cavanaugh, *Being Consumed*, 2. This is what Augustine termed the *libido dominandi*, the lust for power.

35. Cavanaugh, *Being Consumed*, 8.

36. This was always Augustine's Christian view (see Boone, *Conversion and Therapy*, 4).

37. Charry, *God and the Art of Happiness*, 61.

38. Kreeft, *Back to Virtue*, 157.

not the continuous search for new things but a turn toward the only One who can truly satisfy our desires."[39] The deprivation of spiritual joys, for Augustine, incites addiction to carnal pleasures.

Lastly, unlike Aristotle for whom desires had to be deliberated, Augustine argued with his robust view of original sin that sinful desires must be supplanted by pure desires. "Lust diminishes," Augustine wrote, "as love grows."[40] The problem with desire, therefore, is not that it is unformed, but that it is deformed and must therefore be reformed into the form of Christ. Our desires must be converted by the Trinitarian God whose grace enables us to cultivate new desires, specifically the so-called theological virtues of faith, hope, and love.[41] For Augustine, the soul could face two ways and these represented two directions of desire towards either concupiscence or charity.[42] Explaining Augustine's view, Charles Taylor writes, "In being turned towards God, our love for him goes beyond the measure of any order, however good."[43] "Vices in the soul are nothing but privations of the natural good," Augustine wrote.[44] "When they are cured," he continued, "they are not transferred elsewhere: when they cease to exist in the healthy soul, they cannot exist anywhere else."[45]

A PHENOMENOLOGY OF HABITS

The Aristotelian-Augustinian anthropology of desire influenced the phenomenology of Husserl and Heidegger, and generated some fruitful notions about habit in Merleau-Ponty in particular. What unites the phenomenologists is the refusal to analyze a subject in abstraction from lived experience.[46] Husserl, in particular, aspired to transcend Kant's phenomenal-noumenal dualism and other speculative dead-end streets and proposed that we "bracket" ("epoche" = bracketing) all questions about the true nature of

---

39. Cavanaugh, *Being Consumed*, 49.

40. Augustine, *Enchir.*, CXXI.

41. See Boone, *Conversion and Therapy*, 154–55.

42. Taylor, *Sources of Self*, 128, 137. For Augustine, the will is perverse and it acts against our insight, as it did, he alleged, for Paul in Romans 7 (Taylor, *Sources of Self*, 138–39).

43. Taylor, *Sources of Self*, 139. "So both for better and for worse, the will leaps beyond the desire appropriate to a cosmos ordered for the Good. There is something gratuitous in love as well as in the refusal of love" (Taylor, *Sources of Self*, 139).

44. Augustine, *Enchir.* XI.

45. Augustine, *Enchir.* XI.

46. Much of what follows is derived from Cox, *Guide to Phenomenology*, 9–33.

material realities "in themselves."[47] This involved the setting aside of the "natural attitude" we take toward the world in order to focus upon the phenomena—that is, the structure of consciousness, how things appear to us in consciousness, and how our consciousness "intends" them (i.e., directs itself to them as objects of consciousness).[48] We can describe and analyze the contents of consciousness against the backdrop of "intuition" and thereby describe the essential features of objects phenomenologically in a process Husserl denominates "reduction."[49] This phenomenological reduction, by allowing us to grasp the features of things, grants us a basis for scientific theory, but one which is rooted in empirical induction from the weight of evidence. The "objectivity" of the world, in other words, is constituted by inter-subjectivity.[50] Insisting that consciousness is necessarily intentional in the sense that consciousness is always consciousness of something, Husserl reduced experience to a kind of cognitive perception.[51]

Subsequent phenomenologists were not convinced. In distinction from Husserl, Heidegger viewed intentionality as non-cognitive participation, or what he termed "attunement."[52] For Heidegger, it was impossible for a subject to be a detached observer of intentional objects and to perceive only mentally; rather the subject intends in an involved manner through what he denominated "care" (*Sorge*).[53] Continuing in Heidegger's philosophical trajectory, Merleau-Ponty conceived of intentionality as largely corporal (and thus non-cognitive). He was convinced that Husserl was unable sufficiently to disentangle himself from the influence of Descartes, whose views on the body Merleau-Ponty found especially objectionable. Not only did Descartes analyze the body through conceptualization, in abstraction from its existential context, and thus wrongly assume one could conceptually extricate oneself from one's body and still be true to the body as a phenomenon, he denigrated the body precisely by objectifying it.

In contrast, Merleau-Ponty advocated the research of "the phenomenal body" (*le corps phénoménal*), the lived body, the body in its existential context, and underscored the indispensability of the body for perception. The body, he argued, was "the field of vision" (*champ de vision*) through which the world was knowable and therefore cannot be regarded as one

---

47. Cox, *Guide to Phenomenology*, 20.
48. Cox, *Guide to Phenomenology*, 20.
49. Cox, *Guide to Phenomenology*, 21.
50. Cox, *Guide to Phenomenology*, 28–30.
51. Cox, *Guide to Phenomenology*, 31.
52. Heidegger, *Being and Time*, 136–43.
53. Heidegger, *Being and Time*, 184–93.

object among many.⁵⁴ The body determines what comes into view and how it is perceived and thus assembles a world of meaning. "Without the body," Bennett says of Merleau-Ponty, "there is no experience of space and time and, therefore, no ability to have a concept of space and time."⁵⁵ Moreover, the body forms "intentional threads" (*fils intentionnels*) that determine a person's relationship to everything in the world.⁵⁶ "The body networks meaning and significance within its environment," Bennett writes, "and is, thereby, moved by 'attraction' to meaningful and significant things within this environment."⁵⁷

The body inhabits the world and begins to integrate itself with its environment, developing "sedimentations and habits" necessary to navigate successfully through it.⁵⁸ This structuring of behavior occurs at two levels, through the "habit body" (*corps habituel*) and the "moment-body" (*corps actuel*).⁵⁹ The "habit body" is thoroughly integrated into the environment and successfully maneuvers through it without deliberation. The "moment-body" relies on the "habit-body" to process experiences. Habit therefore is behavior solidified from sedimented meanings, and the means by which "the body comes to practice what it knows."⁶⁰ Merleau-Ponty is careful to distinguish habit from instinct since habit has meaning with established grounds, is intentional about what it pursues, and does not need stimuli to activate it.⁶¹ Even more importantly, habit is a necessary function for body, without which the world would remain forever strange and movement forever foreboding.⁶²

Merleau-Ponty specifically identifies three levels where habit emerges: perception, motor, and tactile. Perceptive habit concerns how one sees and understands objects in the world; motor habit involves how one postures and moves toward objects; and tactile habit concerns how one emotes and behaves in relation to these objects. The body modulates meanings at these three levels and then facilitates habits predicated on these meanings. Replacing or modifying habits in any one of these three spheres is difficult because each has been formed by deposits of meaning and sensation. On

---

54. Merleau-Ponty, *Phenomenology of Perception*, 152.
55. Bennett, *Involved Withdrawal*, 30.
56. Merleau-Ponty, *Phenomenology of Perception*, xiii, 72, 86, 106, 130.
57. Bennett, *Involved Withdrawal*, 36.
58. Bennett, *Involved Withdrawal*, 37.
59. Merleau-Ponty, *Phenomenology of Perception*, 82.
60. Bennett, *Involved Withdrawal*, 38.
61. Merleau-Ponty, *Phenomenology of Perception*, 146.
62. Merleau-Ponty, *Phenomenology of Perception*, 138.

the other hand, as one increasingly discovers the unwelcome fruit of a bad habit, one can begin to do things differently and that different behavior then becomes a deposit that forms a new habit. Meaning and identity, therefore, are never abstract, but always cultivated and habituated.[63]

In line with Aristotle and Augustine, contemporary philosopher James K. A. Smith claims that human desires are teleological, directed to a thing of ultimate concern. Further, in line with Merleau-Ponty, he argues that desires are inescapably embodied, practiced, and habituated. The implication of this is that desire is never purely private, internal, spiritual, or abstract, but always public, external, embodied, and situated. As embodied and public, desires are formative, having the capacity to transform social circumstances and communal environments. As habituated, desires shape, in Merleau-Ponty's categories, perceptual, motor, and tactile responses to one's environment.

These philosophical concepts have precipitated changes in cognitive science. The once dominant "cognitivist" model—in which the mind was seen as a kind of neural computer and all the dimensions of cognition, including memory, language, and emotion, as information processing—was judged to be too static and thus replaced with a "connectionist" model that was more dynamic, emergent, and holistic.[64] Furthermore, Merleau-Ponty's phenomenology coheres with recent studies in social psychology regarding "automaticity." In deference to recent research, Visser writes, "The human body creates, in the normal course of living, a kind of background set of familiar patterns, built up, maintained, and developed by experience."[65]

Because of the influence of Freud, who reduced the unconscious to primordial urges which could be accessed if repression and resistance were circumvented, social psychologists have been inclined to construe the non-conscious control of one's internal psychological processes negatively, as the source of aggression, for example, or discrimination.[66] The negative assessment of the unconscious, however, is being challenged by recent research which demonstrates that non-conscious processes often function positively, especially in the areas of self-regulation, evaluation, motivation, and social perception. Bargh and Chartrand write,

> Thus 'the automaticity of being' is far from the negative and maladaptive caricature drawn by humanistically oriented writers; rather, these processes are in our service and best interests—and

63. Bennett, *Involved Withdrawal*, 42.
64. Andresen, "Introduction," 5–6.
65. Visser, *Gift of Thanks*, 322.
66. Wilson, *Strangers to Ourselves*, 8.

in an intimate, knowing way at that. They are, if anything, "mental butlers" who know our tendencies and preferences so well that they anticipate and take care of them for us, without having to be asked.[67]

This assessment of non-cognitive processes is perhaps too positive. The auto-pilot of human processing can also be responsible for inhibiting change. Wilson writes,

> People are creatures of habit, and the more they have used a particular way of judging the world in the past, the more energized the concept will be. Our non-conscious minds develop chronic ways of interpreting information from our environments.[68]

Wilson argues, however, that it is possible to change non-conscious inclinations and the way to do so is to change one's behavior. By changing one's behavior, the adaptive unconscious is provided "with new 'data' from which to infer attitudes and feelings." Furthermore, Wilson writes, "one of the most enduring lessons of social psychology is that behavior change often precedes changes in our attitudes and feelings."[69]

This phenomenological account of habit must be correlated with a theological interpretation of habit in a mutually corrective conversation. Theological accounts of breaking from sinful habit, for example, must acknowledge that denying oneself, for instance, is not merely an intellectual act, but the surrender of oneself inclusive of one's body.[70] Yet a theological account of breaking a habit provides an answer to a question raised by Merleau-Ponty's phenomenology of habit—namely, if our habits are so deeply embodied, what real hope is there for those who want to change? Put differently, if my very identity is inseparable from my body, to whom can I look for help when my body has me seemingly trapped? "If I am nothing but self," Clare Carlisle astutely observes, "there is no way of transcending myself; if I am nothing but habit there is no way of liberation through my own actions."[71] Two options are foreseeable, the first of which is what Der-

---

67. Bargh and Chartrand, "Unbearable Automaticity of Being," 476. "The non-conscious nature of these judgment-and-behavior-guiding processes make them a boon to effective self-regulation, because of their immediacy, efficiency, and reliability" (Bargh and Williams, "Automaticity of Social Life," 3).

68. Wilson, *Strangers to Ourselves*, 37. This exposes the myth that one enjoys spontaneous autonomy; rather, we are shaped in the choices we make, so shaped that our choices rarely involve pure freedom.

69. Wilson, *Strangers to Ourselves*, 212.

70. See also Carlisle, "Creatures of Habit," 32.

71. Carlisle, "Creatures of Habit," 32.

COMING TO TERMS WITH SIN AND VICE

Sin as Shalom Vandalism

One might judge that the study of sin and vice is both depressing and unhelpful, but our motivation is not simply to understand delinquent behavior, but to locate antidotes and remedies.[73] "If we do not take seriously our capacity for evil," Henry Fairlie avers, "we are unable to take seriously our capacity for good."[74]

What is sin? Sin, first, is related to evil, but is not evil *per se*. In the biblical narrative of the Fall, the serpent, with intention to sabotage, appears prior to the first sin and thus evil predates sin. Evil was not created by God, and the Bible makes no attempt to explain its origin. "Evil just inexplicably is."[75] The precise identity of sin, on the other hand, has been hotly debated in history. Pantheistic philosophers, such as Spinoza, regarded sin as *negatio*, the negation of being, the mere opposite of good, and therefore non-being.[76] Similar construals surface in the history of theology among those, including Augustine, who reduce sin to *privatio* in which the act of sin is essentially a deprivation of obedience, faithfulness, love, etc.[77] In Augustine's case, the conception of sin as privation evolved in a polemic with Manichaeism, whose cosmology of moral dualism—good and evil are both independent and eternal—requires the conclusion that God created evil. While the notion of negation simply sees sin as the absence of goodness,

---

72. Carlisle, "Creatures of Habit," 32. See Derrida, *Gift of Death* (discussed in chapter 3 of this book).

73. "If we fear what the idea of sin tells us of ourselves, it is because we fear ourselves" (Fairlee, *Seven Deadly Sins*, 4).

74. Fairlee, *Seven Deadly Sins*, 15.

75. Volf, *Free of Charge*, 30. Cf. "Evil arises with the advent of humanity" (Willimon, *Sinning Like a Christian*, xix).

76. Berkhof, *Systematic Theology*, 228. See also Bavinck, *Reformed Dogmatics*, 3:137.

77. Augustine, *Confessions* 3.7.12. See also *Enchir.* IX. "Badness is only spoiled goodness. And there must be something good first before it can be spoiled" (Lewis, *Mere Christianity*, 46).

privation regards sin as lacking the essence of goodness.[78] As Herman Bavinck explains, limping is a privation of walking, but it is not nothing.[79]

Protestant theologians have generally insisted that sin is not simply *privatio*, a deficiency of goodness, but also *corruptio*, an assault on goodness. If shalom for Cornelius Plantinga represents the way things ought to be and thus the wholeness, justice, and harmony of the created order, then sin, because it invades and disrupts God's design, is "culpable shalom-breaking."[80] Following Bavinck, Plantinga depicts sin as a destructive parasite which cannot exist apart from good.[81] Colin Gunton argues that human ontology is an ontology of communion and, as such, we were created with relationality to the non-personal world and sociality with other persons.[82] If one grants that humanity is created in relationship with God and others and that such relationships are *constructed* rather than constructive, sin sabotages creation by breaking communion with God and others.[83] Put still differently, if humanity was created to be in relation with (and therefore responsible to) things and to exist socially and responsibly to each other and especially to God, then sin sabotages this responsibility at every turn. As such, sin displeases God not merely because he is assaulted, but because what he has designed and created is vandalized.[84] Sin is therefore anti-creation, blurring distinctions God has made and separating what God has joined.

How does sin relate to an anthropology of desire? Protestants and Catholics differ in their answers, and the divide is apparent in their contradictory conceptions of concupiscence—namely, the desire for evil, apparent in, for example, Eve's longing for the tree of the knowledge of good and evil (Gen 3).[85] Whereas Catholics believe that the Fall destroyed only the *donum superadditum*, the supernatural gifts, leaving human nature

---

78. Rejecting the claim of the Manichaeans that sin is a substance, Christian theologians have typically argued that sin is an ethical, not a physical phenomenon. See Berkouwer, *Sin*, 261–63; Bavinck, *Reformed Dogmatics*, 3:137.

79. Bavinck, *Reformed Dogmatics*, 3:137–38. Similarly, "No being can be spoken of as evil, formally as being, but only so far as it lacks being. Thus a man is said to be evil, because he lacks some virtue; and an eye is said to be evil, because it lacks the power to see well" (Aquinas, *Sum* 1.5.3.ad2).

80. Plantinga, *Not the Way*, 10–12.

81. "Sin is a parasite, an uninvited guest that keeps tapping its host for sustenance" (Plantinga, *Not the Way*, 89). Cf. Bavinck, *Reformed Dogmatics* 3:139.

82. Gunton, *One, Three, and Many*, 214, 229.

83. Gunton, *One, Three, and Many*, 216.

84. Plantinga, *Not the Way*, 16.

85. Early English translations of the Bible used concupiscence to translate ἐπιθυμία, a Greek term often used in the New Testament to denote sinful longings (e.g., 1 Pet 1:14; cf. Phil 1:23).

untouched, Protestants believe that human nature itself is corrupted.[86] For many Protestants, therefore, concupiscence is sin, whereas for Catholics it is merely "an inclination to evil" and not sin itself.[87] "Matters of the heart matter," Willimon writes. "Our dispositions and inclinations are, at least to Jesus, as significant as our actions."[88]

An Augustinian/Aristotelian anthropology of desire requires one to see desire itself as primordial and creational. The question is whether such purely creational desire can exist untainted by the Fall in postlapsarian humans. The Protestant reformers were convinced, in line with Augustine, that all desire has been corrupted so that apart from the grace of God, the sinner (in Augustine's phrase that Luther found so helpful: *incurvatus in se*) is turned in on him/herself and pursues satisfaction in created things. This is a significant demurral from Aristotle's anthropology of desire: since all desires are infected, they require eradication, not simply moderation.[89]

Catholics and Protestants agree, however, that humanity's teleological orientation is inviolable and ineradicable. The end pursued by fallen humanity, however, no longer conforms to that for which humanity was created—namely, happiness in intimate fellowship with God.[90] Moreover, such distorted desire: (a) pursues happiness in creation rather than the

---

86. This was a development in especially medieval Catholicism, dating back at least to Anselm (Bavinck, *Reformed Dogmatics*, 3:95). A natural law ethic of virtues and vices, for traditional Protestants, is objectionable for attributing too much value to unsanctified postlapsarian human wisdom and thus is generally regarded as humanistic and rationalistic at best, and pagan at worst. Calvin appeals to the apostle Paul's injunction to "make no provision for the flesh, to gratify its desires" (Rom 13:14) (Calvin, *Instit.* 3.10.3).

87. *Catechism of the Catholic Church*, para. 405. Speaking of the Catholic doctrine, Bavinck writes, "Concupiscence, which remains in the baptized, is not itself seen as sin, but only arises from sin and inclines to sin" (Bavinck, *Reformed Dogmatics*, 3:96). Distinguishing between entertaining sins in our thoughts and yielding to temptation, Catholic theologians conjectured that the commission of sin requires the consent of the will and/or an action and not simply a disposition or an unsavory attitude (Bavinck, *Reformed Dogmatics*, 3:96). In his Sermon on the Mount, however, Jesus condemns not just the action of murder, for example, but hateful desires. "Who on earth," Willimon asks, "would criticize us for merely thinking murderous thoughts, while successfully restraining ourselves from committing murder? Jesus, that's who" (Willimon, *Sinning Like a Christian*, 14).

88. Willimon, *Sinning Like a Christian*, 40.

89. See Willimon, *Sinning Like a Christian*, 13. Aristotle of course had no doctrine of original sin and reduced human fault to ignorance (Willimon, *Sinning Like a Christian*, 15).

90. The Geneva Catechism authored by John Calvin begins with the question, "what is the chief end of human life?" The answer is, "to know God" (Calvin, *Catechism of the Church of Geneva*).

Creator; (b) is necessarily insatiable because creation (finite) is not the Creator (infinite); and (c) distracts humanity from pursuing God as the intended object of desire.[91]

Robert C. Roberts has suggested, in reflecting on Augustine's anthropology, that it might be better to speak of a human need for God rather than a desire for him. Whereas the concept of desire assumes some sort of emotional awareness on our part, the concept of necessity assumes no such consciousness.[92] The human psyche, in Roberts's words, "needs a positive and happy relationship with God as a condition of its being mature and healthy."[93] Often what makes a person aware of such a need is a situation that provides "perceptual clarity."[94] For Roberts, this psychological need for God has multiple dimensions, including: (a) the need for something trustworthy beyond anything that can be trusted in finite life; (b) the need to be loved and valued by One who knows us perfectly; and (c) the need for orientation beyond any finite orientation we have (i.e., by someone absolute).[95]

Sin has unleashed a trajectory in human history that embraces self-fulfillment. "In modernity individual self-fulfillment has displaced God from the centre of the world," Colin Gunton writes, and "it makes itself the centre of things, and so uses both person and world as means to its ends."[96]

Vices as Idolatrous Habits of Sinful Desire

Though the words "sin" and "vice" are often used interchangeably, each has a specific nuance. If sin is defined as shalom vandalism, vices are far more comprehensive and cumulative and denote idolatrous habits of sinful desire. Vices are sinful by wanting the right thing in the wrong way.[97] They are all instances of concupiscencenone are actions; all are sinful desires. They

---

91. The pursuit of vices "diverts or hinders you from thought of the heavenly life and zeal to cultivate the soul" (Calvin, *Instit.* 3.10.4).

92. Roberts, *Spiritual Emotions*, 35.

93. Roberts, *Spiritual Emotions*, 36.

94. Roberts, *Spiritual Emotions*, 37.

95. Roberts, *Spiritual Emotions*, 37.

96. Gunton, *One, Three, and Many*, 226-27.

97. Many argue that vices can pursue either the wrong thing or the right thing in the wrong way (e.g., DeYoung, *Glittering Vices*, 66, 148). I want for the sake of simplicity to subordinate the former to the latter and argue that *all vices pursue the right thing in the wrong way* and that one such wrong way is to pursue an approximation of the right thing (and thus the wrong thing).

are not innocent desires for something bad, but perverted desires for something good, and the latter is far more destructive.[98] Vices can be distorted as:

a. *excessive* desires, in which one wants something good too much, too often, or for too long;

b. *deficient* desires, in which one wants something good too little, too infrequently, or too short a while.

Vices thus distort virtues, sabotaging them in opposite ways, by excess or deficiency.[99] As their distortions, vices sometimes masquerade as virtues (e.g., lust as love, anger as righteous indignation). Further, vices can be distorted as:

c. *superficial* desires, in which one wants something good for a shallow and unsatisfactory reason; and

d. *selfish* desires, in which one wants something good, but only for oneself.

These vices are habits in the sense that they are habituated desires shaped by perception, cognition, and action that emerge, like ruts that form on dirt roads, from the persistent traffic of delinquent behavior over time.[100]

They are idolatrous because they habituate desires for satisfaction in creation and form "spiritual addictions" for pleasures apart from God.[101]

---

98. Think of the ancient maxim *corruptio optimi pessima* (the corruption of the best is the worst).

99. Plantinga, *Not the Way*, 98. The virtue of courage, for example, i.e., fearing the right thing in the right way at the right time, is distorted by both rashness and cowardice: the former is overwhelmed by fear and the latter is underwhelmed. Similarly, liberality is distorted by greed and prodigality. This parallels Aristotle's conception of virtue as "the mean" between excess and deficiency. Courage is the mean between rashness and cowardice and liberality the mean between greed and prodigality.

100. This is not to deny that impulses towards these habits are inherent by "virtue" of inherited fallenness. Donald Capps describes sin as an "orientation" that is destructive to God's intentions for the world, to community and to oneself. In so doing "sin" includes dispositions, attitudes, and impulses and not just actions (Capps, *Deadly Sins*, 2). In Capps's view these impulses manifest in multidimensional ways through ordinary development such that at each of Erik Erikson's developmental life-stages one particular deadly sin has "special prominence" (Capps, *Depleted Self*, 47; cf. *Deadly Sins*, 3). The value of linking these sins with life-stages is one begins to see sins less as "discrete acts" and more as "enduring habits and traits, developed over time" (Capps, *Depleted Self*, 47). Rebecca Konyndyk DeYoung often refers to vices as "habits of the soul" (DeYoung, *Glittering Vices*, 15, 100).

101. Keller, *Counterfeit Gods*, xv. Calvin writes, "Many so enslave all their senses to delights that their mind lies overwhelmed" and "if we yield too much" to our desires "they boil up without measure or control" (*Instit.* 3.10.3). "Our hearts become factories

Idols are defined by Andrew Lester as "values that have gained prominence in our lives and detract from our commitment to the living God" and by Timothy Keller as "anything more important to you than God, anything that absorbs your heart and imagination more than God, anything you seek to give you what only God can give."[102] "Eluding God's attempt to get God's hands on us," Willimon writes, "we grab for every other false god."[103] In this way, the sin of idolatry "is the progenitor of the Seven."[104] Because habituation is largely corporal, supposing Merleau Ponty's phenomenology, liberation from habit must also be corporal. Without access to power beyond one's body, therefore, one finds oneself in a kind of self-bondage or body-bondage. The term "idol" is an explicitly theological term to describe something that captivates human loyalties. As habituated idolatrous desires, vices necessarily degrade, publicly and socially, humanity and all creational shalom.[105] Among the perversions I identify, vices:

a. *isolate*, separating people from others; thus anti-social
b. *antagonize*, turning people against others; thus anti-peace
c. *corrode*, tarnishing things; thus anti-justice
d. *depress*, producing sadness, if not despair; thus anti-joy
e. *enslave*, stealing their freedom by stealth; thus anti-freedom
f. *distract*, turning people from the divinely purposed ends, desensitizing them from recognizing and admiring true goodness; thus anti-purpose
g. *dehumanize*, devaluing and injuring; thus anti-personal

THE SEVEN DEADLY SINS

The list of vices, historians conjecture, was first compiled in writing by a desert father, Evagrius of Pontus (346–399 AD), a contemporary of

---

of idols in which we fashion and refashion God to fit our needs and desires" (Volf, *Free of Charge*, 22). The fallen human heart is "a perpetual factory of idols" (Calvin, *Instit.* 1.11.8).

102. Lester, *Angry Christian*, 201; Keller, *Counterfeit Gods*, xvii.
103. Willimon, *Sinning Like a Christian*, 40.
104. Willimon, *Sinning Like a Christian*, 8.
105. "When a creature is made into a god, it becomes a devil" (Kreeft, *Back to Virtue*, 109). Calvin argues that a distorted regard for God's gifts "robs man of all his senses and degrades him to a block" and that "excessive abundance into vile lust infects the mind with its impurity so that you cannot discern anything that is right and honorable" (Calvin, *Instit.* 3.10.3).

Augustine, who identified eight "thoughts" or "demons" that plagued the hermits—namely, gluttony, lust, covetousness (or greed), sadness (*tristitia*), anger, boredom (*acedia*, apathy), vainglory, and pride.[106] Their origin, therefore, is located in the Eastern monastic movement and they were identified particularly as a threat to monastic life.[107] The early monks did not see them as sins so much as "erupting temptations" that obscured devotion to God.[108]

Subsequent Western Christian leaders, notably Gregory the Great (540–604), reduced the eight vices to seven, the biblical number of completion, by combining sadness (*tristitia*) with apathy or sloth (*acedia*), combining vainglory with pride, and adding envy to the list.[109] Furthermore, he put them on a spectrum from spiritual to carnal—pride, envy, anger, sloth, avarice, gluttony and lust, anticipating Thomas Aquinas (1225–1274), who distinguished gluttony and lust as two "carnal" sins from the other five "spiritual" vices. The sins also inspired artists and writers, not least Dante, who depicted the Mount of Purgatory as having seven terraces for each of the seven deadly sins to be purged en route to heaven.[110]

Sometimes these vices are dubbed "capital" from the Latin *caput* (head) to accent their deep-rooted nature as the source of other sins. Such a perspective on sin inhibits the compartmentalization of our lives, much less our sins, and thus underwrites a holistic anthropology and incentivizes a wholesome life.[111] The descriptor "deadly" implies the Catholic distinction between mortal and venial sins though, for Aquinas and others, some vices (e.g., lust and gluttony) were more instances of weakness than expressions of mortal sins.[112] Capps suggests the adjective "deadly" also captures their likelihood to become ingrained, or what he terms "dispositional."[113] Rebecca DeYoung argues, with acknowledged indebtedness to Aquinas, that these seven vices "have such attractive power because they promise a good that seems like true human perfection and complete happiness."[114]

Moreover, the seven deadly sins are all, as indicated above, instances of concupiscence—privations of good desire or perverted desires for

---

106. A demon here denotes an evil power that could control people.

107. Fairlie speculates that the deep recognition of sin was funded for these hermits by their deep devotion to God (Fairlie, *Seven Deadly Sins*, 11).

108. Cunningham, *Seven Deadly Sins*, 63.

109. DeYoung, *Glittering Vices*, 28.

110. Cunningham, *Seven Deadly Sins*, 64.

111. Fairlie, *Seven Deadly Sins*, 15.

112. DeYoung, *Glittering Vices*, 35.

113. Capps, *Deadly Sins*, 2. See also Willimon, *Sinning Like a Christian*, 8.

114. DeYoung, *Glittering Vices*, 38.

something good.[115] What are the goods that the seven deadly sins desire in distorted ways?[116] One can conceive of multiple ways of construing these distortions.[117] I propose the following construal:

a. Pride distorts the desire for acceptance
b. Envy distorts the desire for equality
c. Anger distorts the desire for justice
d. Sloth distorts the desire for rest
e. Greed distorts the desire for provision
f. Gluttony distorts the desire for pleasure
g. Lust distorts the desire for relationship

The unsoiled created realm in which humanity was first placed was a home in which there was acceptance, equality, justice, rest, provision, pleasure, and relationship. By means of the seven deadly sins, fallen humanity pursues an illegitimate and superficial return home. In what follows I propose that the seven deadly sins, as idolatrous, habituated sinful desires, sow ingratitude by devaluing:

a. God (vices that distract from him)
b. oneself (vices that isolate, enslave and depress oneself)
c. things (vices that corrode things)
d. neighbors (vices that antagonize and dehumanize others)

Embodied and habituated, these desires alter, in Merleau-Ponty's categories, one's perceptual, motor, and tactile levels and thus are always public and socially destructive.

Redemption through Christ is comprehensive and initiates the restoration, through sanctification, of a broken humanity. To be restored includes a renewed view of God and one in which he is the centerpiece of one's life, the *sina qua non* of one's existence. "When the true God comes," Kreeft writes, "the false gods go."[118] With a renewed view of God, one further enjoys a re-

---

115. This is an Augustinian account of vice: "For in vice," Augustine wrote, "there lurks a counterfeit beauty" (Augustine, *Conf.* 2.6.13). I disagree therefore with Aquinas who argues that some sins, such as envy, desire only evil (Aquinas *Sum* 2-2.158.1).

116. Throughout this chapter the vices of sin are personified in a way analogous to how the apostle Paul personifies sin in Romans 5 and 6 (e.g., "you have been freed from sin and enslaved to God" [Rom 6:22]).

117. Pride, for instance, can also be depicted as the distorted desire for glory or honor; envy as the distorted desire for supremacy; sloth as the distorted desire for hope, etc.

118. Kreeft, *Back to Virtue*, 169.

newed view of oneself, things, and others. In such a renewed view, gratitude extends to God for oneself, things, and others. In chapter 4 of this book, I will set forth a seven-fold profile of renewed gratitude as social, peaceable, inclusive, joyful, free, purposeful, and personal.

Chapter 5 of this book will present gratitude as the firewall against and antidote to the seven deadly sins. I will argue specifically that, as a social virtue, gratitude celebrates acceptance and inhibits pride; as an inclusive virtue, it celebrates equality and inhibits envy; as a peaceable virtue, it celebrates justice and inhibits anger; as a gratuitous virtue, it celebrates rest and inhibits sloth; as a purposeful virtue, it celebrates provision and inhibits greed; as a joyful virtue it celebrates pleasure and inhibits gluttony; and as a personal virtue, it celebrates relationship and inhibits lust. In short, this book will unveil the potential gratitude embodies to redress and reverse, or as Augustine would say, "to heal" the destructive tendencies inherent in the seven deadly sins.

In what follows I will harvest the insights of others, in some cases correlating psychology with theology, in order to offer a distinctive profile of the seven deadly sins. In so doing I will situate the sins in narrative context of creation and redemption and highlight how in each instance the seven deadly sins devalue God, self, things, and others.

Pride (*Superbia*): The Distorted Desire for Acceptance

Humanity was ushered into existence, not out of divine need, but out of divine generosity. Created by the living breath of God who later raised Jesus from the dead, humanity was the object not just of God's generosity, but of his love. Moreover, humanity was created in communion with God, in a relationship of mutual love with the Trinity. To judge this communion as unimportant, unnecessary, or undesirable is to assault one's own ontology. If humanity is wired for the love of God, it needs it, will languish without it, and will presumably seek to find it, though not always in the right places. In the pristine Garden of Eden, sinless Adam enjoyed the generous affirmation of his Father in what might be termed sinless mirroring. Instigated by the serpent, Adam somehow dreamed of a different life, one without God's voice setting the perimeters of his conduct. He yearned for freedom, independence, autonomy, and self-sufficiency and consequently flouted God's authority by disobeying his clear command.[119] Sometimes attributed to the

---

119. Opposing authority and convention, pride embodies a spirit of rebellion that seeks to displace authorities, including God himself (Fairlie, *Seven Deadly Sins*, 48). "It is the sin of trying to be as God" (Sayers, *Creed or Chaos*, 150). Pride turns away

mutinous angel who in the narrative of Scripture becomes known as Satan, pride is alleged to be the original, paradigmatic sin of Adam and Eve in the garden, and the source of all other vices.[120] If the apostle Paul is recalling the Fall in Romans 1, as this book will later argue, one might say that although Adam knew God, he did not honor him as God or give thanks to him, but became futile in his thinking and his senseless mind was darkened.[121] He knew God as a generous giver, the source of life and love, but he did not honor him as such, but misrepresented him as stingy.

Sin separates what God has joined and devalues what God honors. Pride devalues God by seeking and locating value in one's own face rather than God's. Acceptance is a gift for which we should be thankful, but our gratitude is sabotaged by pride. Parasitic sin in humans seeks acceptance elsewhere and pride finds it in the mirror. As the distorted desire for acceptance, pride involves doubting God's generosity and affirmation and locating dignity and value only in oneself.[122] This is especially clear in terms of vainglory, a species of pride defined by Rebecca DeYoung as "the excessive and disordered desire for recognition and approval from others."[123] Whereas pride seeks value in oneself, vainglory seeks the *display* of one's apparent value in order to enjoy affirmation from others as well.[124] Because they see

---

from God by refusing to look up and by choosing to look instead at oneself. "Pride looks down, and no one can see God but by looking up" (Kreeft, *Back to Virtue*, 102). Pride confuses one's feelings, inaccessible to others, with genuine knowledge, and then appeals to that knowledge to justify saying or doing whatever one wants.

120. Fairlie, *Seven Deadly Sins*, 50. "Through pride the devil became the devil" (Lewis, *Mere Christianity* 106). "Pride is the queen and mother of all the vices" (Aquinas, *Sum* 2–2.132.4.ad1). The following biblical passages condemn pride: Prov 16:18–19; Luke 4:1–11; 18:9–14; Rom 5:6.

121. This is a paraphrase of the NRSV which, unless otherwise indicated, will be the translation used of all Bible citations in this work.

122. Donald Capps understood pride as a disposition prominent among adolescents. The adolescent stage of life (12–18) for Erik Erikson, whose life-cycle theory Capp embraced, features a crisis involving a negative pole (i.e., identity confusion) and a positive pole (i.e., identity). What is essential for identity to form in adolescents, in Erikson's mind, is self-esteem, the mean between an excessive endorsement of one's value and an unjustified denunciation (Capps, *Deadly Sins*, 46–48). While it is appropriate for adolescents to be curious about who they are, identity should not be pursued in excessively self-centered ways. The adolescent, for example, must embrace community values and roles, and the failure to do so will generate rebellion (Capps, *Deadly Sins*, 51).

123. DeYoung, *Glittering Vices*, 60. For Kreeft, vanity shows greater humility than pride. If I need your admiration, then I'm not totally independent or self-sufficient (Kreeft, *Back to Virtue*, 100).

124. Cf. DeYoung, *Glittering Vices*, 62. DeYoung uses "excellence" where I use "value."

themselves as holy and distinct from the world, Christians are especially susceptible to vainglory.[125] When the vainglorious covets admiration in the name of God, however, the charge of hypocrisy applies. Often mistakenly defined as doing what one does not feel like doing (which can in fact be a virtuous), biblical hypocrisy is practicing piety in public only to be seen by others (Matt 6:1–8).[126] While the Scriptures do enjoin believers to showcase their virtue and let their light shine (Matt 5:14–16), it is undoubtedly clear that divine and not human goodness must be illumined.[127]

Thomas Aquinas contrasted the vainglorious with the magnanimous, the latter caring more about truth than opinion and unpreoccupied with "the things that are sought for honor's sake, such as power and wealth."[128] The magnanimous reflect God's beauty and the admiration they invite brings glory to God, the acknowledged source of talent, skill, and beauty.[129] For Aquinas, the worst manifestation of vainglory is one that steals glory from God by attributing one's giftedness to oneself rather than to God.[130] As such, vainglory is a desire for one's own glory, and not God's.

Not only does pride devalue God, it devalues oneself. God created humanity in his own image, but pride resists believing it and the consequence is a distorted self-image and low self-esteem. The sense that one is not good enough to be someone can generate absorption in self-improvement in order to better one's image. So driven by a desire for acceptance, the vainglorious are prepared to abandon much along the way, perhaps even morality. The yearning for approval from parents or peers, for instance, could motivate a vainglorious student to cheat on a test.

---

125. Cf. Fairlie who argues that the virtuous are particularly susceptible candidates to the sin of pride, which attacks areas where people are strong (Fairlie, *Seven Deadly Sins*, 43).

126. See Wright, *Small Faith, Great God*, 89–101.

127. DeYoung, *Glittering Vices*, 72.

128. Aquinas, *Sum* 2-2.132.2.ad1.

129. "There is in man something great which he possesses through the gift of God; and something defective which accrues to him through the weakness of nature. Accordingly, magnanimity makes a man deem himself worthy of great things in consideration of the gifts he holds from God" (Aquinas, *Sum* 2-2.129.3.ad4).

130. "Yet as regards the love of God, [vainglory] it may be contrary to charity in two ways. In one way, by reason of the matter about which one glories: for instance when one glories in something false that is opposed to the reverence we owe God. . . . In another way vainglory may be contrary to charity, on the part of the one who glories, in that he refers his intention to glory as his last end: so that he directs even virtuous deeds thereto, and, in order to obtain it, forbears not from doing even that which is against God" (Aquinas, *Sum* 2-2.132.3). See also DeYoung, *Glittering Vices*, 67.

Pride, thirdly, can devalue things because the proud do not regard "things" apart from the tributes "things" invite nor celebrate skill apart from the recognition the skill produces. For this reason, the proud tend to gravitate towards "vain" goods (e.g., manicured lawns, fast cars, designer clothes, etc.).[131] The satisfaction lies not so much in the ownership or enjoyment of these things, but in the admiration they generate in others. The vainglorious, therefore, derive little enjoyment from an unobserved, unnoticed life.

Fourth, pride can devalue others because the autonomous impulses of the proud, for instance, often generate isolation and retreat from others. Proud intellectuals, for example, retreat from the general public, perceived to be simple and mediocre, into communities of "sophistication."[132] North Americans, in particular, often retreat into private life under the motto, "one is satisfied with oneself; only oneself is necessary."[133] With a measure of affluence and security, one can now enjoy life uninterrupted in the privacy of one's home.[134] Our consumeristic economy, in fact, markets many products precisely for this kind of enjoyment.[135] The wholesale embrace and celebration of self-sufficiency transforms an individual into a fortress of self-love that bars the admission to all others, including God.[136]

The isolating impulses of pride are ultimately enslaving. "The more desperately we struggle for self-sufficiency," Belliotti writes, "the emptier and more self-absorbed we become."[137] Morality is about choices, Fairlie argues, but if one's choices revolve only around oneself, "there is in fact no choice at all, but merely a submission to one or other whim or impulse."[138] Driven by the illusion that to be truly free one must be alone, without the possibility of interference from others, pride's quest concludes with having oneself as the only object of love devoid of the freedom to think of anything or anyone but oneself. This was the predicament of Narcissus, whom the gods, to chastise him for his vanity, incited to fall in love with his own image. He loved the image, not because it was beautiful, but because it was his, and he wasted away in self-love, loving himself to death.[139]

131. DeYoung, *Glittering Vices*, 64.
132. Fairlie, *Seven Deadly Sins*, 45.
133. Fairlie, *Seven Deadly Sins*, 42.
134. Fairlie, *Seven Deadly Sins*, 46.
135. Fairlie, *Seven Deadly Sins*, 51.
136. Cunningham, *Seven Deadly Sins*, 76.
137. Belliotti, *Dante's Deadly Sins*, 129.
138. Fairlie, *Seven Deadly Sins*, 53.

139. Fairlie, *Seven Deadly Sins*, 54. For the proud, the only person who is truly attractive is the one who completely shares one's view of life–namely, oneself. See Fairlie, *Seven Deadly Sins*, 52.

The proud person has difficulty sustaining relationships in which one's ego is not stroked. Applause is sought at the price of distancing oneself from people, others are denigrated to elicit laughter, and even crimes are committed to win approval. Relationships cannot succeed where people are duped or manipulated, but only in contexts of sincerity and humility.[140] "My Pride usually poses no real problem to you, as long as we remain strangers," Willimon writes.[141] "But if we should attempt to get together, to work on something in common, then Pride is a problem."[142]

Rarely today does pride today have negative connotations.[143] "Black pride" and "gay pride," for instance, are expressions designed to underscore the inherent value blacks and gays have in spite of being marginalized in society. Similarly, parents might scold their children for sloppy dress by urging them to take more pride in themselves. Even these instances of the word "pride," however, are not as innocuous as they first appear: they create welcome environs for the vice of pride. Feeling good about oneself, laudable on its own, easily morphs into a license for self-indulgence or outright wrongdoing. "The steps from a reasonable self-concern to an utter selfishness," Fairlie suggests, "are short and swift."[144]

Is there a sense, however, in which there is something healthy about pride? Heinz Kohut, a premier psychoanalytic theorist, provided some seminal ideas about narcissism, a close cousin of pride. If pride involves looking to oneself for value, then narcissism, understood as excessive self-interest, is a species of pride. The prevailing view within the psychoanalytic world of Kohut's day was that people are driven by instinctual desires to bond with other persons in order to satisfy those desires. Kohut altered this conception in a more favorable way. We attach in positive narcissistic ways, Kohut argued, to people we admire, to people who admire us, and to others with whom we feel a special kinship such that these people function within our psyches as if they were part of ourselves: they are what Kohut termed "self-objects."

For Kohut, this narcissistic impulse is deeply rooted in infant experience. The baby sees the mother as an extension of him/herself, and his/her cry means that he/she should receive the breast.[145] The mother approximates

---

140. DeYoung, *Glittering Vices*, 73.

141. Willimon, *Sinning Like a Christian*, 23.

142. Willimon, *Sinning Like a Christian*, 23.

143. "If one were not attempting to listen to and follow Jesus, I can't imagine why would know that Pride is a bad thing" (Willimon, *Sinning Like a Christian*, 19).

144. Fairlie, *Seven Deadly Sins*, 40.

145. Kohut, *Seminars*, 57.

an organ within the baby.[146] When the baby's needs are physically met, the experience is of what Kohut terms *narcissistic equilibrium*, the objective of all healthy humans. The self-object fulfills the narcissistic functions of the child. Eventually, the child discovers that the world does not exist to satisfy her needs and sustains "narcissistic injury."

> Anything that frustrates the physical and mental well-being of the child—any noise, any coldness, any wetness, any hunger, any delay—all this is a narcissistic disturbance. And then the child, recognizing that they are shortcomings in this narcissistic paradise, that it is not limitless, attempts to save it in some way.[147]

Those who experience disruptions or failures in self-esteem regulation are fragmented, lacking narcissistic equilibrium or self-cohesion. They exhibit a defense mechanism called "splitting" in which two selves emerge: a "grandiose" self (exaggerated self-importance) and a "depleted" self (feelings of shame, humiliation, worthlessness), which is largely an overreaction to the narcissistic injury.[148] This "secondary narcissism," in distinction from healthy narcissism, results in those who have suffered extraordinary narcissistic injury, likely on account of deficient parental attention.

Parental inattention represents inadequate "mirroring," the term Kohut used to describe the means by which a parent returns to the child positive, loving responses (e.g., smiles). Those guilty of parental inattention have themselves often suffered emotional depletion. Infants who sustain narcissistic injury, as all do, typically idealize those responsible for caring for them, and good parents will indulge this ideal during this early stage of the child's development. Secondary narcissism can birth great ambition in which a child who, responding to the reality that she is not the center of the world, makes that her goal. Good parenting mirrors the child's emotions and its absence produces self-depletion.

Kohut's psychological insights about narcissism inform a theological profile of pride in a couple of ways. First, the conduct of a proud person, i.e., reducing others to mirrors in which one's value can be affirmed, must be interpreted in terms of their backstory. Culpability for proud assertions vary given the amount of narcissistic injury one has sustained. Patience must be

---

146. Kohut, *Seminars*, 62. This point is made well by Margaret Klein: "The good breast is taken in and becomes part of his ego, and the infant who was at first inside the mother now has the mother inside himself" (Klein, *Envy and Gratitude*, 179).

147. Kohut, *Seminars*, 78.

148. This is discussed in Kohut, *Restoration of the Self*, 171–219. What further characterizes narcissists is not only a grandiose view of self, but an absence of empathy for others (Capps, *Depleted Self*, 14).

exercised with the narcissistic tendencies of those who experienced parental neglect and especially abandonment.[149] Second, Kohut's insights generate a new vista for understanding the fall of humanity especially if the relation of humanity to God is seen as analogous to the relation of infants to their mother. Humanity was created with positive mirroring from God in the Garden. The moment humanity became suspicious of God's benevolence—a thought instilled by the serpent—it sustained a kind of "narcissistic injury" in which it aspired to be like God (i.e., "grandiose self") and then felt deeply ashamed and sought covering (i.e., "depleted self"). Perhaps one can see pride today as born out of a kind of narcissistic injury in which one, suspicious of God's benevolence, asserts a grandiose self. As such, pride seeks a return home to the Garden of Eden and to the time before suspicions of God's benevolence first arose in the human mind.

In summary, pride is the distorted desire for acceptance, a frantic "looking forward" disposition to acquire the affirmation and sense of dignity only God provides. This distorted desire for acceptance sows ingratitude by devaluing God, self, things, and others. God is devalued through pride's distracting quality with which one seeks one's own face instead of God's. The self is devalued through the depressing quality of pride by which one fails to attain a satisfactory self-image and by its enslaving quality by which one is unable to think of others. Things are devalued through the corrosive quality of pride by which one manipulates one's possessions for the tributes they generate. Lastly, others are devalued by the isolating quality of pride by which one retreats into an exclusive fortress of self-love, by its antagonizing quality, by which those who do not mirror a favorable image are rejected and by its dehumanizing quality, by which the proud are often deficient in empathy.

The tendency to pride, I will argue, is potentially inhibited by gratitude which, as a social virtue, celebrates the acceptance of God and others and dependence on God and others. Furthermore, gratitude values dignity from God's greeting and celebrates "the joy and warmth of the glow of God's face that corresponds to our own."[150]

Envy (*Invidia*): The Distorted Desire for Equality

God created humanity, male and female, in his Trinitarian image. Just as Father, Son, and Holy Spirit are co-equal, so all humans, men and women,

---

149. As a foster parent to several infants over the years, I can attest to the immense psychological injury infants can experience through neglect and mistreatment.

150. Capps, *Depleted Self*, 68.

jointly share that image and thus are equal in dignity. Further, all are jointly invited into oneness in Christ (Gal 3:28) in whom all are jointly promised his inheritance (1 Pet 3:7). In the world before the Fall, when everything was right, there was peace and reciprocal love between God and humanity and within humanity, between men and women. Though there is a gradation in God's gifts to humanity, there is no gradation in one's dignity. Such equality in dignity is a gift, and one for which we should be grateful. In their ingratitude, Adam and Eve fell, and vertical shalom between Creator and creatures was distorted, as was horizontal shalom among creatures. Far from reciprocal love, Adam blamed Eve. Through the redemption of Christ, however, not only was the vertical barrier between God and humanity removed, represented by the tearing of the temple veil, so were the horizontal barriers dividing humanity. Christ brought humanity near to God by his blood, "for he is our peace" (Eph 2:14) and broke down "the dividing wall, that is, the hostility between us." Equality is a gift for which we should be thankful, but such gratitude is sabotaged by envy, the distorted desire for equality.[151]

Today, sensing the way it is supposed to be, humanity yearns for peace with God and equality with one other, but finds itself, by nature, estranged from God and envious of others. YHWH had regard for Abel's sacrifice, but not Cain's. Seeing Abel as a competitor who was succeeding in ways he was not, Cain interpreted the differences between them as inequality, and became envious. The notion of egalitarianism, the theory that all should be equal, is distorted by envy to mean that all should be identical.[152] Envy, in other words, views gradations in talents, gifts, and abilities as instances of inequality and thus supposes that an equitable world is one in which "everyone should be able to do and experience and enjoy everything that everyone else can do and experience and enjoy."[153] Envy seeks to level the playing field by bringing down the rival, and the ultimate form of such reduction is murder (e.g., Cain murdered Abel out of envy).

Envy must be distinguished from jealousy. Whereas envy involves a person lacking what another has (and thus assumes two individuals), jealousy involves a person "having" a relationship with another that is threatened by a rival (and thus assumes three individuals). Envy must also be distinguished from greed. Whereas greed seeks accumulation for oneself, envy is competitive with another. As such, "greed is mainly bound up with

---

151. "Envy is contentious over rank accorded to another" (Augustine, *Conf.* 2.6.13).

152. Fairlie, *Seven Deadly Sins*, 63.

153. Fairlie, *Seven Deadly Sins*, 62. Illustrated in the parable Jesus taught in Matthew 20 about workers who arrived at work at different times of the day.

introjection and envy with projection."[154] Envy must also be distinguished from covetousness. Whereas the covetous person wants what another has, the envier wants the other not to have what the envier wants. The envier experiences a kind of satisfaction in knowing that one's rival does not have the desired object.[155] Whereas covetousness and greed are attentive to things, envy is focused on a rival person and how he or she compares with the envier. What upsets the envier is not simply another's good, but the sense that this good diminishes one's own and brings disgrace upon oneself.[156]

Envy denies an ontology of communion and devalues God, self, things, and others. First, envy devalues God, the source of the gift of equality. Regarded early on in Christian reflection as an overestimation of oneself and thus a breach of humility, envy is an instance of pride.[157] Thomas Aquinas regarded envy as a mortal sin, worthy of damnation, because the unhappiness generated by envy is ultimately with God, the one responsible for the inequity apparent in the distributions of individual gifts and talents.[158] Since human life is finite, the world is full of half-full glasses which present the options of gratitude for the half-full or ingratitude for the half-empty, "and envy at those whose glass is fuller."[159] Anger with God is fueled by an "imaginary disadvantage," the conviction that one is worthy of the gifts or successes enjoyed (often undeservedly in the envier's mind) by another.[160]

Secondly, envy features, as Willimon avers, "a kind of diminishment of ourselves, which is one of those things that makes this sin so sad."[161] Assuming a competitive world of you-versus-me, envy is aroused by the perception of inferiority.[162] Beginning seemingly innocuously in one's mind and generated through comparison with others, envy produces not simply a sense of inferiority, but feelings of sadness, if not emotional distress.[163] For this reason Thomas Aquinas categorized envy as a species of *tristitia*, which,

154. Klein, *Envy and Gratitude*, 181.
155. DeYoung, *Glittering Vices*, 43.
156. Fairlie, *Seven Deadly Sins*, 64.
157. Cunningham, *Seven Deadly Sins*, 60.
158. "There is, however, a kind of envy which is accounted among the most grievous sins, viz. envy of another's spiritual good, which envy is a sorrow for the increase of God's grace, and not merely for our neighbor's good. Hence it is accounted a sin against the Holy Ghost, because thereby a man [sic] envies, as it were, the Holy Ghost Himself, Who is glorified in His works" (Aquinas, *Sum* 2–2.36.4.ad2).
159. Kreeft, *Back to Virtue*, 122.
160. Fairlie, *Seven Deadly Sins*, 65.
161. Willimon, *Sinning Like a Christian*, 42.
162. DeYoung, *Glittering Vices*, 45.
163. Cunningham, *Seven Deadly Sins*, 58.

originally a vice of its own and then later subsumed by Gregory the Great under sloth, included not just melancholy but resentment and "suppressed rage."[164] Moreover, whereas gluttony and lust enjoy an initial satisfaction, envy is always insatiable, perpetually oppressive, unrelenting in its torment.[165] As such, envy can produce a kind of immobility or impotency which sabotages true industry, transforming the envier into a victim of his or her own envy.[166]

Third, envy devalues things by preferring standards to be lowered and by rendering people unable to discern excellence. "Envy cannot bear to admire or respect," Sayers writes, "it cannot bear to be grateful."[167] Envy is evident among those who, unable to paint, for instance, want the standards of painting rescinded in what has been termed "the revenge of failure."[168] The envier can become equal with a gifted rival by redefining the categories by which the giftedness of the rival is acknowledged. This in turn produces a devaluation of anything for which a person might be regarded as gifted. "We seem no longer able to admire, respect, or be grateful for what is nobler or lovelier or greater than ourselves," Fairlie writes, "we must pull down—or put down—what is exceptional."[169]

Fourth, envy devalues others by reducing them to rivals in a competition. Whereas greed wants things, and lust can be nurtured in one's imaginations, and gluttony can be pursued on one's own, envy necessarily targets another.[170] "Trapped in self-centredness," Peskett and Ramachandra write, "we tend to see others as competitors to be feared, as means to further our own ends, or as threats to our well-being. We have an innate bias towards defending and advancing our own interests."[171] Generally, one envies only those with whom one realistically might be compared (i.e., an athlete will likely envy other athletes rather than, for instance, musicians).[172] "Envy, for

---

164. Cunningham, *Seven Deadly Sins*, 56. "Another's good may be reckoned as being one's own evil, in so far as it conduces to the lessening of one's own good name or excellence. It is in this way that envy *grieves* for another's good: and consequently men [sic] are envious of those goods in which a good name consists, and about which men [sic] like to be honored and esteemed (Aquinas, *Sum* 2-2.36.4 [emphasis added]).

165. Willimon, *Sinning Like a Christian*, 41.

166. Capps, *Deadly Sins*, 42.

167. Sayers, *Creed or Chaos*, 145.

168. "As long as no talent is required, no apprenticeship to a skill, everyone can do it, and we are all magically made equal" (Fairlie, *Seven Deadly Sins*, 63).

169. Fairlie, *Seven Deadly Sins*, 64.

170. Capps, *Deadly Sins*, 40.

171. Peskett and Ramachandra, *Message of Mission*, 169.

172. DeYoung, *Glittering Vices*, 49.

Willimon, "is a same-sex sin. Men tend to envy what men have or are, and women appear to do much the same regarding other women."[173]

Envy is not merely the sense of inferiority, however, but the determination to bring the envied down or the refusal to aspire for her proficiency. "If my neighbors are able to take pleasure in intellectual interests which are above my head," Sayers writes of the envious person, "I will sneer at them and call them derisive names, because they make me feel inferior, and that is a thing I cannot bear."[174] Fundamentally, the envious "hates to see other men [sic] happy."[175] Poison in one's life, the seepage of which harms others, envy precludes the possibility of love, inhibits kindness and generosity to others, and is deadly because it concludes with hatred, though its pathway there is shorter than it is for anger.[176] Nearly invariably, envy evolves from feelings to actions, from concealed thoughts to public behavior (often passive-aggressive).[177] Unbridled sadness-turned-rage can fuel a hatred that plots to sabotage, if not murder, the rival, or at least vandalize the rival's coveted possessions.

Grief over the success of a neighbor, Aquinas argued, gives birth to joy at his or her misfortune (what in German is called *Schadenfreude*).[178] Whereas in most cases of envy, the person asks, "Why not me?" in an instance of *Schadenfreude*, the envier says, "Thank God it's him."[179] The sense is captured by the French *ressentiment*, which has a stronger connotation than resentment, but is included under it. *Ressentiment* captures the envy for the qualities or possessions of another which, if not assuaged by inflicting injury on the object of envy, results in a persistent and volatile condition of poisonous and repressed emotions.[180] "The experience of powerlessness easily leads to an inner rage," Nouwen writes, "and when this becomes a lasting emotion it settles within us as resentment."[181] "Resentment," Nouwen continues, "is thus a sign of our having become victims of the darkness of this world and of having lost faith in the One who is the light."[182] What

---

173. Willimon, *Sinning Like a Christian*, 45.
174. Sayers, *Creed or Chaos*, 143.
175. Sayers, *Creed or Chaos*, 142.
176. Cunningham, *Seven Deadly Sins*, 60; Kreeft, *Back to Virtue*, 123.
177. Cunningham, *Seven Deadly Sins*, 61.
178. Aquinas, *Sum* 2–2.36.4.ad3.
179. Willimon, *Sinning Like a Christian*, 52. The protest of *ressentiment* is, "I am not you" (Schlossberg, *Idols for Destruction*, 52).
180. Schlossberg, *Idols for Destruction*, 51.
181. Nouwen, *Peacework*, 116.
182. Nouwen, *Peacework*, 116.

distinguishes *ressentiment* from mere resentment is "a festering quality that seeks outlet in doing harm to its object."[183] It is often the explanation behind violent crimes that are otherwise judged to be "senseless" because those who see and hear about it cannot identify any gain for the offender, though it is crystal clear in her mind. *Ressentiment* often uses third parties as foils so that by praising person A, person B is devalued.[184] In some cases, *ressentiment* motivates equality, but "the leveling movement has nothing to do with justice, because its impulse is not to raise those who are down, but to topple those who are up."[185] As such, envy is implicated for failure to love both God and neighbor.[186]

As with pride, the psychoanalytic tradition also accounts for the rise of envy. For Margaret Klein, the premier theorist in this area, an infant regards the mother's breast as the primal good object, the prototype of maternal goodness, everything desirable, the foundation of trust and hope, and thus the first object to be envied.[187] Envy is the angry feeling that another person possesses and enjoys something desirable and when infant is deprived of breast, he or she feels that breast has kept milk (love and gratification) for itself and thus is bad.[188] The mean and grudging breast is hated and envied.[189] Envy spoils the primal good object and gives impetus to sadistic attacks on the breast.[190]

Klein's insights do not yield the same fruit for theological reflection as Kohut's insights about narcissism. Whereas "secondary narcissism," for Kohut, occurs in the context of an inattentive parent, the rise of envy, in Klein's account, does not require an inattentive mother. Every child is weaned at some point and a mother is not negligent for withholding from the child the

183. Schlossberg, *Idols for Destruction*, 51.

184. Schlossberg, *Idols for Destruction*, 53.

185. Schlossberg, *Idols for Destruction*, 55.

186. DeYoung, *Glittering Vices*, 52.

187. Klein, *Envy and Gratitude*, 180. Donald Capps understood envy as a peculiar disposition of school age children. The school age stage of life (5–12) for Erik Erikson features a crisis involving a negative pole (i.e., inferiority) and a positive pole (i.e., industry). We grow tired of mere playing and strive for a measure of productivity. We discover here, however, that we are not the same as our classmates, that we differ in our abilities, and that in some areas we cannot succeed, and a sense of inferiority can arise. School age children want the skills of another for themselves. Furthermore, if the skills of another bring shame upon oneself, the envier attempts to equal the playing field by reducing the other in some form (Capps, *Deadly Sins*, 40).

188. Klein, *Envy and Gratitude*, 180.

189. Klein, *Envy and Gratitude*, 183.

190. A good relation to primal object is the source of gratitude (Klein, *Envy and Gratitude*, 188).

desired breast. On the other hand, Klein's insights inform a theological account of the Fall. Adam and Eve partook of the forbidden fruit the moment they perceived that something was being withheld from them—namely, that eating of the fruit would open their eyes and make them like God, knowing good and evil (Gen 3:4). In this construal, God was a rival and the world was a competitive realm and Adam and Eve sought equality with him. To partake of the forbidden fruit, in this sense, was a form of envy. Further, the relationship between infant and mother is analogous to person and God. One of the pictures of contentment in Scripture is a weaned child at his or her mother's breast. To be quiet and calm at the very place of (perceived) deprivation (Ps 131) is the opposite of envy. As such, envy seeks a return home to the Garden of Eden and to the time before the notion of a competitive world first arose in the human mind.

In summary, envy is the distorted desire for equality, a frantic "looking forward" disposition to enjoy one another without a worldview of competition and rivalry. This distorted desire devalues God through envy's distracting quality with which one seeks sameness instead of equality, thus objecting to God's distribution of gifts among people. Things are devalued through the corrosive quality of envy that vandalizes the standards of beauty. The self is devalued through the depressing quality of envy by which one adopts a self-image of inferiority, and by its enslaving quality by which one is driven by all-consuming impulse to equalize. Lastly, others are devalued by the isolating quality of envy by which one excludes others who are gifted in different ways; by its antagonizing quality, with which one displays hatred or resentment to others; and by its dehumanizing quality, by which the successful are resented simply because of their success.

The tendency to envy is potentially inhibited by gratitude which, as an inclusive virtue, celebrates equality among people. Gratitude, in other words, refuses to interpret differentness in terms of a competitive worldview in which those who have more are superior. As such, gratitude values all of God's gifts, even those given to others.

Anger (*Ira*): The Distorted Desire for Justice

God is a God of justice, and the world he created, untainted by sin, was a world in which justice and fairness prevailed. In this realm, there was gratitude for gifts and reciprocal love between God and humanity and among people. The promised new earth, again untainted by sin, will be a world in which evil is absent. Between creation and new creation, injustice persists, but not without God's determination to eradicate it. On the cross, Jesus dealt evil a debilitating blow, triumphing over powers and principalities that endeavored to sabotage justice (Col 2:17). Further, God dissuades us from taking revenge because vengeance is his (Rom 12:19) and he has appointed authorities to administer his justice until the new creation is consummated (Rom 13:1–4) and recommended ways for us to respond to injustice (Matt 5:38–39). We should receive with gratitude God's gift of justice, his determination to right injustices, and the tools he has given to uproot injustice. Such gratitude is sabotaged by anger, the distorted desire for justice.

The Fall is in the first instance unreciprocated love, and it generated God's anger. "The wrath of God is revealed from heaven against all ungodliness," Paul writes (Rom 1:18). As image-bearers, we are similarly provoked to anger by injustice and unreciprocated love. Our anger, however, is not always righteous anger. What we perceive as injustice is not always injustice, and our appropriate response to injustice is sometimes compromised by excess or prolongment. We can assume the role of judge to administer punishment ourselves. We discover anger in Peter when as Jesus is apprehended by the mob in Gethsemane he cuts off the ear of Malchus, the servant of the High Priest. He yearned for justice, but in a distorted way, by taking justice into his own hands.

As a deadly sin, anger is unique, warranting distinctions unnecessary for the six other deadly sins.[191] The ambiguity around anger is present in Scripture itself which teaches simultaneously that God is sometimes angry and that anger is something dangerous (e.g., Gal 5:20; Col 3:8).[192] Notwithstanding the objection of John Cassian, for whom it is always self-serving,

---

191. "Continuing to place anger on the list of Seven Deadly Sins," Andrew Lester warns, "is a costly mistake. Given what we have learned from the neurosciences, constructionist narrative theory, Scripture, and historical theology, the anger-is-sin tradition is no longer a viable belief. I hope that moral and systematic theologians attend to these alternative stories and work to remove anger from the list of deadly sins. Perhaps they could substitute hostility, hate, abuse, violence, or any other expression of anger that has become destructive. An effective case could be made for the inclusion of any of these, but to include anger on the list, without separating the capacity of anger from destructive expressions of anger, is unfair to this gift from God, denies its relationship to the *imago Dei*, and ignores the many positive contributions that anger makes to our life" (Lester, *Angry Christian*, 184–85).

192. Campbell argues that theologians have typically responded to texts about God's anger either by dismissing such portrayals as primitive or by regarding such anger as a dimension of his holiness held in tension with his love or by seeing it as a component of his passion for humanity (Campbell, *Gospel of Anger*, 5). Campbell inspires the thought that "perhaps the dark shadow of destructive aggression emanating from divine wrath is just our limited view of the brilliance of divine love" (Campbell, *Gospel of Anger*, 43). Further, "hidden in the terror of God's anger there is a love greater than any human love" (Campbell, *Gospel of Anger*, 44).

anger is a healthy emotion that, generated by injustice, yearns for justice.[193] Thomas Aquinas understood anger to arise when the pathway to the good was impeded. As such, anger is hostile towards the obstacle (injustice) and devoted to the good (the reestablishment of justice).[194] Andrew Lester further illumines our understanding by distinguishing between anger as an emotion and aggression as behavior and argues that not all aggression results from anger, and not all anger generates aggression.[195] Along similar lines, Alistair Campbell notes in terms of biblical Greek vocabulary (i.e., Septuagint and New Testament) the difference between θυμός, generally an emotional reaction, and ὀργή, the outbreaking of God's anger in punishment.[196]

There is even a sense, Campbell argues, that we must "use anger more creatively" in order to strengthen interpersonal relationships.[197] This includes, first, acknowledging the physiological reaction without morally assessing it in order to determine the true source of frustration.[198] Secondly, one must identify the trigger for the bodily arousal and ascertain why the situation or person is threatening.[199] Is the arousal better explained by anxiety, for instance, than anger? Thirdly, one must determine how anger should be expressed.[200] To refuse to show anger in some scenarios is sometimes, Campbell says, "to be lost in an apathy which diminishes us."[201] Anger right-

193. DeYoung, *Glittering Vices*, 119. Lester argues that Cassian also made room for a positive role for anger (Lester, *Angry Christian*, 125). Lester regards that the view that all anger is sinful as "the dominant belief about anger in the Christian tradition" (Lester, *Angry Christian*, 115).

194. Though envy, for Aquinas, always connotes sin, anger does not: "Now this does not apply to anger, which is the desire for revenge, since revenge may be desired both well and ill. Secondly, evil is found in a passion in respect of the passion's quantity, that is in respect of its excess or deficiency; and thus evil may be found in anger, when, to wit, one is angry, more or less than right reason demands. But if one is angry in accordance with right reason, one's anger is deserving of praise" (Aquinas, *Sum* 2–2.158.1). See DeYoung, *Glittering Vices*, 120.

195. Lester, *Angry Christian*, 67. Lester regards emotion as a strong feeling that "moves us to action." (Lester, *Angry Christian*, 20). Campbell similarly distinguishes between "feelings of anger and aggressive acts" (Campbell, *Gospel of Anger*, 17).

196. Campbell, *Gospel of Anger*, 18. When Jesus says, "if you are angry with a brother or sister, you will be liable to judgment," he uses the participle ὁ ὀργιζόμενος, "being angry with."

197. Campbell, *Gospel of Anger*, 68. Lester uses the exact same phrase (Lester, *Angry Christian*, 226).

198. Campbell, *Gospel of Anger*, 70.

199. Campbell, *Gospel of Anger*, 71.

200. Campbell, *Gospel of Anger*, 71.

201. Campbell, *Gospel of Anger*, 74. Similarly for Aquinas, the absence of anger can

fully expressed is "a sign of hope ... that one's fellow human beings can be made to listen."[202] As such the expression of anger at systemic injustice can prevent destructive violence by forcing authorities to rethink policies.[203] Similarly, Lester argues that because we are free to choose how to express anger (rather than it being something inevitable), we are responsible for such expression.[204]

Further, aggression itself, understood by Lester as "a primary expression of the life force," an aspect of the *imago Dei*, can either be positive or negative.[205] Anger is unlike hunger or sexual arousal because it is not biologically necessary but a capacity which is aroused only in certain circumstances.[206] Lester defines anger as "the physical, mental, and emotional pattern that occurs in response to a *perceived threat* to the self, characterized by the desire to attack or defend."[207] Campbell similarly regards anger as a particular fight/flight "arousal" to looming danger, threats, or frustrations which includes "physiological reaction, immediate feelings and cognitive interpretation."[208] The physiological reaction initiating this arousal, however, is not the emotion of anger itself, though it is often interpreted this way.[209] As such, anger is an acquired emotional reaction, rather than an inevitable instinctive one, though the physiological reaction provides "the feeling of a feeling."[210] Even more so, aggression is not the invariable outcome of anger, but can be denied even in extreme instances.[211] Anger certainly makes us "vulnerable to destructive behavior"[212] and therefore what must be severed

---

be sinful since it implies a disinterest in justice. "Lack of the passion of anger is also a vice, even as the lack of movement in the will directed to punishment by the judgment of reason" (Aquinas, *Sum* 2-2.158.8). Cf. "He that is entirely without anger when he ought to be angry, imitates God as to lack of passion, but not as to God's punishing by judgment" (Aquinas, *Sum* 2-2.158.8.ad1).

202. Campbell, *Gospel of Anger*, 79.

203. Campbell, *Gospel of Anger*, 80. See also Lester, *Angry Christian*, 216–18.

204. Lester, *Angry Christian*, 180.

205. Lester, *Angry Christian*, 74. Further, aggression can occur apart from anger. This is illustrated, Campbell argues, with "a war mentality" in which aggression is often impersonal (Campbell, *Gospel of Anger*, 26). Think too of those for whom the arousal of anger is absent and murder in "cold blood" (Campbell, *Gospel of Anger*, 63).

206. Lester, *Angry Christian*, 84.

207. Lester, *Angry Christian*, 85.

208. Campbell, *Gospel of Anger*, 51, 18, 24.

209. Campbell, *Gospel of Anger*, 19.

210. Campbell, *Gospel of Anger*, 19.

211. Campbell, *Gospel of Anger*, 27.

212. Lester, *Angry Christian*, 175.

from anger, Campbell argues, is destructiveness in particular.²¹³ Unless explicitly indicated, references to anger as a deadly sin in what follows exclude healthy instantiations and uniformly assume aggressive and destructive anger.

Such aggressive anger sows ingratitude, first, through its devaluation of God. This is evident when anger features self-aggrandizement and the insistence of one's own way to the exclusion of others.²¹⁴ Such self-aggrandizement is often apparent in scenarios where anger is easily provoked. This experience—one of the ways in which anger is disordered for Aquinas—exempts few and is easily, and often piously, rationalized in terms of one's rights. The implication, however, is that both the offence and one's importance are unduly magnified, and God is subsequently devalued.²¹⁵ In extreme cases, when God is blasphemed, anger can become a mortal sin.²¹⁶

Anger can also devalue oneself when subtly prolonged and unrelenting—the second way anger is disordered for Aquinas.²¹⁷ Since rage was easily recognized and condemned, early Christian writers especially feared internalized anger (*indignatio*) or what we would characterize as "bitterness."²¹⁸ Not always discernible to others, such bitterness often surfaces in scenarios of injury and disappointment (e.g., where one's love is rebuffed) and features deep sorrow, dark thoughts, and discontentment that easily become all-consuming and thus self-destructive.²¹⁹ In this connection Lawrence Cun-

---

213. Campbell, *Gospel of Anger*, 31. Anger, for Donald Capps, is the peculiar temptation of those in early childhood who seek resolution between, to think of Erikson's categories, the poles of autonomy and shame/doubt. Often toddlers are perceived to be stubborn, but in their resistance, there is a development from an aggressive to a more relaxed and genuine autonomy (Capps, *Deadly Sins*, 29). Failure to complete tasks successfully results in shame, and shame often produces doubt as we discover bodies less reliable and people less sympathetic than imagined. These feelings generate anger in young boys and girls and this anger becomes sinful, for Capps, "when it leads to erecting barriers between ourselves and others" (Capps, *Deadly Sins*, 31).

214. DeYoung, *Glittering Vices*, 122.

215. This is anger "in relation to the desired object, as when one desires to be avenged in a *trifling* matter, which should be deemed of no account, so that even if one proceeded to action, it would not be a mortal sin, for instance by pulling a child slightly by the hair, or by some other like action" (Aquinas, *Sum* 2-2.158.3 [emphasis added]). See also, DeYoung, *Glittering Vices*, 124.

216. Aquinas, *Sum* 2-2.158.3.ad1.

217. This occurs "if one be too fiercely angry *inwardly*" (Aquinas, *Sum* 2-2.158.3 [emphasis added]).

218. Cunningham, *Seven Deadly Sins*, 67.

219. DeYoung, *Glittering Vices*, 125; Capps, *Deadly Sins*, 31; Cunningham, *Seven Deadly Sins*, 67.

ningham distinguishes between getting angry and being an angry person.[220] Whereas it is entirely appropriate, in some instances, to react to injustice with anger (as did Jesus and countless other biblical characters), one's life should never be defined by anger.

Third, the anger that devalues things is not so much *indignatio*, but *ira*, the destructive eruption of anger which we often call "rage."[221] For Aquinas, such an excessive display of anger is the third way anger can be disordered.[222] We imagine a person "blowing his lid" or "flying off the handle," kicking over chairs and throwing things against the wall. Ira can be generated by accumulating indignatio or resentment and manifests itself in road rage, murder, terrorism, spousal abuse, etc.

Fourth, anger devalues others when it spawns harmful words and actions. Ira can be mistakenly justified as an instance of "righteous anger," as in the claim that "anybody who tortures a helpless animal should be flogged till he shrieks for mercy."[223] The form of anger most liable to injure others, however, is unrelenting anger or bitterness because it can cement unwillingness to forgive and sometimes even spark a determination to retaliate.[224] The angry impulse to avenge, much like envy, is an equalizing disposition, motivated by a pursuit of justice and intent on making one's offender feel one's pain. In some cases, the angry person's "lust of wrath cannot be sated unless somebody is hounded down, beaten, trampled on, and a savage war dance executed upon the body."[225] But anger can devalue one's neighbor in other ways, not least by scapegoating, for example, in which anger is unleashed against innocent third parties.

In this connection, one should be wary of recommendations to "let off steam" or vent one's anger. Not only is there some evidence that the euphoria of this experience can incite the desire for more, such counsel fails to acknowledge that "anger" is not always justified.[226] We should not assume, Lester rightly argues, that "*experiences* of anger are morally neutral."[227] Anger can be generated by an insult, for instance, intended as a joke. To vent

---

220. Cunningham, *Seven Deadly Sins*, 65. Roberts distinguishes "episodes" of gratitude from the "disposition of gratitude" (Roberts, "Blessings of Gratitude," 61).

221. Cunningham, *Seven Deadly Sins*, 66.

222. This occurs "if one exceed in the *outward* signs of anger" (Aquinas, *Sum* 2-2.158.3 [emphasis added]).

223. Sayers, *Creed or Chaos*, 124.

224. DeYoung, *Glittering Vices*, 125.

225. Sayers, *Creed of Chaos*, 125.

226. Campbell, *Gospel of Anger*, 28.

227. Lester, *Angry Christian*, 17. The capacity for anger is a morally neutral physiological given; the experience is not. See Lester, *Angry Christian*, 179.

one's anger in such a scenario is to privilege "feeling" over reflection and self-control without demonstrating sufficient concern for people who could get hurt or relationships that could be hindered.[228] The opposite counsel of "bottling up" one's anger, more common in Christian circles, is equally deficient. Anger has close affinity to justice and love, and to suppress anger is to refuse to challenge others "in the name of love to take notice of us."[229]

In summary, anger is the distorted desire for justice, a frantic "looking forward" disposition to make things right, albeit through aggression and destructive behavior. Anger devalues God, first of all, by its distracting quality by which one pursues revenge instead of justice, taking matters into one's own hand and ignoring God's wisdom. Things are devalued through the corrosive quality of anger by which property is often thoughtlessly destroyed. The self is devalued through the depressing quality of anger by which the bitterness of unrelenting angst eats away at one's peace and through the enslaving quality of anger by its occasional unrelenting persistence. Lastly, others are devalued through the isolating quality of anger by which others are driven away through unreasonable responses to injustice, through the antagonizing quality of anger by responding to real or perceived offences rashly or excessively and through the dehumanizing quality of anger by which scapegoats are selected to absorb one's pain.

The tendency to anger, I will argue, is potentially inhibited by gratitude which, as a peaceable virtue, celebrates God's promise and provision of justice. Gratitude, in other words, celebrates Christ's victory over evil and God's promise to eradicate evil.

Sloth (*Acedia*): The Distorted Desire for Rest

After creating the heavens and the earth, YHWH rested. He also made provision for rest and worship in the Sabbath institution in the Torah. In their Sabbath day worship at the central sanctuary, Israel would offer sacrifices of thanksgiving to acknowledge his pardon. Such thanksgiving was often accompanied by joy, song, and music. As a weekly festival in which Israel rested and worshipped, praised God and thanked him, it was a microcosm of the great annual festivals God prescribed in the Torah, such as the Festival of Weeks and the Festival of Booths, both of which celebrated the gift of harvest in grateful praise and rest. The rest Israel enjoyed was a reminder that the created world is God's and that its wellbeing did not hinge ultimately on

---

228. Campbell, *Gospel of Anger*, 29.

229. Campbell, *Gospel of Anger*, 30. Campbell also highlights the health implications of bottling up one's anger in Campbell, *Gospel of Anger*, 53.

human work. Analogously, the redemptive project of restoring people and creation is also God's and its success does not ultimately hinge on human work. In this connection, in the context of a Sabbath controversy with the Pharisees (Matt 12:1–8), Jesus promises rest to the weary and heavy laden (Matt 11:28–30).

Sloth is generated by a misunderstanding of vocation and responsibility that assumes a power to change things that ultimately belongs only to God. Refusing to rest in God's provision, the slothful person endeavors to accomplish things on his or her own. The inertia of sloth arises from a sense of powerlessness, a recognition that one is unable sufficiently to fulfill one's vocation or engage one's responsibility. As such, sloth is a failure to trust in God's power and his promises. Refusing to accept and enjoy the provision of rest, sloth seek reprieve not just from work, but from responsibility.[230] Sloth is a sin of omission in which "we neglect what we ought to do, and especially we neglect our neighbors."[231] Sloth, for Dorothy Sayers, "believes in nothing, cares for nothing, seeks to know nothing, interferes with nothing, enjoys nothing, loves nothing, hates nothing, finds purpose in nothing, lives for nothing, and only remains alive because there is nothing that it would die for."[232]

Rebecca DeYoung helpfully distinguishes what we typically understand as sloth today from what the desert fathers envisioned. "Sloth has more to do with being lazy about love," she writes, "than lazy about our work."[233] Throughout much of early history, sloth was therefore categorized as a spiritual and not a carnal vice. It resists one's spiritual vocation, reacts to it with disgust and restlessness, and thus threatens one's fundamental loyalties and commitments.[234] According to DeYoung, John Cassian modified the conception of sloth by describing it in terms like "sluggishness" and "laziness" and by recommending manual labor as the antidote to sloth.[235] Sloth, therefore, should not be equated with laziness because one can avoid one's spiritual vocation precisely by investing oneself completely in one's work.

---

230. Similarly, "Sloth pretends to aspire to rest" (Augustine, *Conf.* 2.16.13).

231. Fairlie, *Seven Deadly Sins*, 129.

232. Sayers, *Creed or Chaos*, 148.

233. DeYoung, *Glittering Vices*, 82. The word *acedia* (from ἀκηδία) means literally "lack of care." "When the Christian tradition talks about the deadly sin of sloth, it has in mind more than a bit of neglectful goofing off" (Cunningham, *Seven Deadly Sins*, 47).

234. DeYoung, *Glittering Vices*, 84. Sloth creates resistance to those people and places where there is confrontation with one's identity in Christ—namely, worship services and prayer times (DeYoung, *Glittering Vices*, 93).

235. DeYoung, *Glittering Vices*, 84.

How sloth devalues God is apparent in Thomas Aquinas's depiction of sloth as an aversion to God's work in us and a resistance to the work of sanctification.[236] Sloth shuns the calling to deepen one's love for God and his ways and to be transformed into new people. Adherents of easy-believism, the practitioners of sloth find the demands of discipleship too costly, selfish impulses too difficult to overcome, and the cross of Christ is so uninviting that alternative, less-demanding pathways are pursued. The slothful person, in other words, is unwilling to surrender his or her life, convinced that the "easy" yoke of Christ is in fact "burdensome" (Matt 11:28–30). Sloth robs us of "our appetite for God, our zest for God, our interest and enjoyment in God."[237]

Sloth can also devalue oneself. For Aquinas, it is an "oppressive sorrow, which, to wit, so weighs upon man's [sic] mind, that he wants to do nothing."[238] For Kreeft, it is the most depressing thing in the world because it "finds our very highest joy—God himself—joyless."[239] Karl Barth offers a similar assessment:

> We can regard life as such a solemn matter that there is no desire for celebration. We can upon an icy seriousness as the highest duty and virtue. On the basis of experienced disappointments we can try to establish that our only right is to bitterness.... But the fact that we actually become joyless is only a symptom that in self-embitterment we do violence to life and to God as its Creator.[240]

There is an analogous version of sloth for secularists in which one responds to the demands of life with apathy, if not despair. Fairlie regards sloth as "a state of dejection that gives rise to torpor of mind and feeling and spirit ... a lack of real desire for anything, even for what is good."[241] The boredom of life and the despair of the future generate temptations to fantasize about, for instance, life on the beach.[242] For Fairlie, sloth is also apparent

---

236. Sloth is a mortal sin when it "consents in the dislike, horror and detestation of the Divine good, on account of the flesh utterly prevailing over the spirit" (Aquinas, *Sum* 2-2.35.3).

237. Kreeft, *Back to Virtue*, 153.

238. Aquinas, *Sum* 2-2.35.1.

239. Kreeft, *Back to Virtue*, 154. "If we are bored with God, we will be bored with everything.... Modern man is ... a cosmic orphan. Nothing can take the place of his dead Father; all idols fail, and bore. When God is dead, it is the time of the twilight of the gods as well" (Kreeft, *Back to Virtue*, 157).

240. Barth, *CD* 3/4:378.

241. Fairlie, *Seven Deadly Sins*, 113.

242. Cunningham, *Seven Deadly Sins*, 50.

in self-help and self-actualization movements because they purport to treat a "meaningless" life with superficial and trivial strategies to avoid difficulty and pain, if not life itself.[243] Implied in guidelines, available through books and conferences, about how to transform one's life simply by setting aside an hour a day for some discipline is slothful apathy.[244] "All of this slackness and self-excusing, slovenliness and lack of endeavor, one finds in today's prescriptions for feeling good about oneself."[245]

Third, sloth has capacity to devalue things. Mental sloth is apparent in the elevated status of mere physical activity. When the game of golf or the practice of jogging is regarded as a kind of "strenuous spirituality," Fairlie argues, it is because of the embrace of sloth.[246] There is also an academic sloth in which history is trivialized, grammar is minimized, and experience is celebrated.[247] This reflects, for Fairlie, a Manichaean perspective in which creation is despaired, in which art emphasizes what is ugly, in which invitations to contemplate the good are rejected.[248] Sloth, therefore, should not be confused with leisure. In freedom from the busyness of life, music is composed, plays are written, and philosophy is produced.[249] It is important in this connection to distinguish leisure from vacation. Today's family vacations frequently include full agendas of activities and often at a high price. According to Cunningham, Thomas Merton often complained that his monastery was "a beehive of work and labor" and thus not fitting for the contemplative life.[250] We fill our emptiness, our need for meaning, with busyness. "It is our very sloth," Kreeft writes, "that produces our frantic activism."[251]

---

243. Fairlie, *Seven Deadly Sins*, 114.

244. Fairlie, *Seven Deadly Sins*, 122.

245. Fairlie, *Seven Deadly Sins*, 123. Relatedly, Donald Capps argues that mature adults are vulnerable candidates for melancholy because in the eighth and final stage of life cycle, they vacillate between Erikson's poles of integrity and despair. Integrity is a holistic worldview in which one accepts her place not just in one's family or even in humanity, but in world at large. Despair is regret with life as it ebbs to its close. Unlike mourning, in which one accepts loss, melancholy wants to avenge it. See Capps, *Deadly Sins*, 65–67. The melancholy of the older generation is related not just to regret, but to losses, of autonomy, for example, intimacy. "Of all the deadly sins," Capps avers, "melancholy exacts its own punishment" (*Deadly Sins*, 68).

246. Fairlie, *Seven Deadly Sins*, 121.

247. Fairlie, *Seven Deadly Sins*, 128.

248. Fairlie, *Seven Deadly Sins*, 126.

249. Cunningham, *Seven Deadly Sins*, 47.

250. Cunningham, *Seven Deadly Sins*, 48.

251. Kreeft, *Back to Virtue*, 156.

Fourth, sloth devalues others when it emerges out of a conviction that "the evil of the world and of our societies is so great that there is little we can do to combat it."[252] Sloth becomes unhappy "about the gift of love" and wants to keep it at arm's length.[253] Unable to escape the truth of responsibility, the slothful person finds it unbearable and copes by checking out. Convinced of personal shortcomings, but not enough to fight them, the slothful person fills life with superficial pleasures, mindless work, and sometimes even religious activities.[254] In its active manifestations, sloth is apparent in boredom and restlessness which spawns meddling, thus making life troublesome for others.[255] One sees this in "social apathy" generated by a complacency in which one locates the meaning of life within oneself and thus rejects solidarity with others—in which the obligations one has within society, and the institutions that embody them, are dismissed.[256] Love requires effort, and serious relationships, in particular, require tremendous sacrifices, and the person who is unwilling to invest daily in the relationship in order to keep it strong and well is slothful.[257] Sloth reduces marriage to the honeymoon or the perks of companionship.

In summary, sloth is the distorted desire for rest, a frantic "looking forward" disposition to enjoy reprieve from the burdens and responsibilities of life apart from the rest God provides. Sloth devalues God, first of all, through its distracting quality by which one seeks the abdication of God-given responsibilities instead of true rest. Things are devalued through the corrosive quality of sloth by which material goods spoil from neglect. The

---

252. Fairlie, *Seven Deadly Sins*, 124.

253. DeYoung, *Glittering Vices*, 89.

254. DeYoung, *Glittering Vices*, 95. For Donald Capps, sloth is better represented by "apathy" and "indifference." Whereas the word "indifference" envisions especially the implications for victims of lack of interest, apathy describes the psychological condition of those who cannot develop an interest (Capps, *Deadly Sins*, 60). Apathy denotes withdrawal from caring for others and even ourselves. "If *acedia* in its passive form is the absence of desire," Capps alleges, "*acedia* in its active form is the distortion of desires" (Capps, *Deadly Sins*, 62). The former is captured by apathy; the latter by indifference. In its passive manifestations, sloth is discernible in lethargy and lifelessness, problems that emerged among Christian monks because of their overvaluing of the life hereafter (Capps, *Deadly Sins*, 61). As such, sloth is the peculiar temptation, Capps argues, for middle-aged adults who vacillate between Erikson's poles of generativity and stagnation. The sin of *acedia* is a preoccupation with oneself and a lack of interest in those entrusted to our care, the chief concern of generativity. *Acedia* and stagnation are therefore nearly synonymous, and "stagnant adults are apathetic" (Capps, *Deadly Sins*, 63).

255. Capps, *Deadly Sins*, 62.

256. Fairlie, *Seven Deadly Sins*, 123, 118.

257. DeYoung, *Glittering Vices*, 87.

self is devalued by the depressing quality of sloth by which boredom results from the inability to find joy in one's vocation and by the enslaving quality of sloth by which one readily concedes defeat in the battle against sin. Lastly, others are devalued by the isolating quality of sloth by which the rejection of responsibility denies solidarity with others, by the antagonizing quality of sloth by which the calling to love and care for others is denied, and by the dehumanizing quality of sloth by which others do not have sufficient value to motivate one to love or care for them.

The impulse to sloth is potentially inhibited by gratitude which, as a gratuitous virtue, celebrates God's liberating power in the face of human limitations and the sense of powerlessness. Further gratitude celebrates what God has commanded, the grace with which he commands, and the provisions he has made for our obedience and rest.

Greed (*Avaritia*): The Distorted Desire for Provision

As the owner of this world (Ps 24), God created humanity to be his viceregents, to have dominion over the earth and to subdue it (Gen 1:26–28).[258] Everything in the world and in life is a gift, and God intends humanity to steward his gifts in service to him and to others, to use and enjoy what he has given for his purposes and his glory. Humanity must recognize that it brings nothing into the world and removes nothing from the world (1 Tim 6:7). What is true of humanity as a whole is also true of individual people. God supplies each person with gifts he intends to be used in loving service to him and to others. When humanity fell into sin, God did not rescind his gifts or his mandate to humans to care for the world. Jesus was sent to redeem both the world (so that it could be renovated at his return) and its inhabitants (so that humanity could be restored and reequipped to fulfill the calling of stewardship). The divine gifts of the postlapsarian world flow through Christ and those gifts today must be stewarded and enjoyed with contentment. Contentment is even within reach of those with only food and clothing (1 Tim 6:8). The desire for provision is motivated by greed, by the impulse to acquire possessions beyond necessity.[259] Like lust and gluttony, greed is typically understood as a sin of excess. One requires money and needs possessions to live, but greed is an inordinate desire.[260]

---

258. The military language of "subdue" does not connote "exploit" but either (a) domesticate the wild for service to God (e.g., bridle an untamed horse) or (b) fight the presence of evil (i.e., step on the serpent and destroy forces of evil).

259. Capps, *Deadly Sins*, 35.

260. The traditional term for this vice, avarice, derives from the Latin (*aveo, avare*),

First, greed devalues God when it yearns for things beyond what God has provided or when it substitutes money's promise of self-sufficiency for God's promise, and thereby incites one to deny one's need for God.[261] Greed is therefore rooted in pride, which led Aquinas and others to categorize it as a spiritual rather than a carnal vice.[262] The greedy person sees things as ends in themselves, as the legitimate object of her desires, and thus privileges temporal goods over eternal goods.[263] Greed is deadly because it distracts from what is truly important.[264] Because they can never fulfill the role of God, "things" are necessarily unsatisfying and enslaving. "Once the shopper purchases the thing," Cavanaugh writes, "it turns into a nothing, and she has to head back to the mall to continue the search. With no objective ends to guide the search, her search is literally endless."[265] Spiritual values have no monetary value and when attempts are made to assign such value to them, Sayers alleges, "they softly and suddenly vanish away."[266] Jesus taught, "For where your treasure is, there your heart will be also" (Luke 12:33–34). True

---

meaning "to crave" and the Anglo-Saxon word "greed" originally denoted something close to hunger.

261. "Riches give great promise of self-sufficiency" (Aquinas, *Sum* 2-2.118.7). "Greed for any temporal good is the bane of charity, inasmuch as a man turns away from the Divine good through cleaving to a temporal good" (Aquinas, *Sum* 2-2.118.5.ad2). The miser views his gold as his god (Fairlie, *Seven Deadly Sins*, 134). See also Kreeft, *Back to Virtue*, 109; DeYoung, *Glittering Vices*, 111.

262. "Spiritual sins are consummated in pleasures of the spirit without pleasure of the flesh. Such is covetousness: for the covetous man takes pleasure in the consideration of himself as a possessor of riches. Therefore covetousness is a spiritual sin" (Aquinas, *Sum* 2-2.118.6).

263. "As a consequence, however, it is a sin against God, just as all mortal sins, inasmuch as man contemns things eternal for the sake of temporal things" (Aquinas, *Sum* 2-2.118.1.ad2). See also Cunningham, *Seven Deadly Sins*, 37.

264. Capps, *Deadly Sins*, 36. The sin to which especially those in Erikson's "play age" (3–5) are susceptible, Capps argues, greed is a temptation for young children as they begin to enjoy mobility and through emerging communication skills are exposed to more information, all of which prompts colorful imagination. This is the seedbed for both initiative, the positive pole, which includes vitality and a cooperative spirit in constructing things, and guilt, the negative pole, as mobility enables traversing space and language boundaries into forbidden territory. The growing "radius of goals" enabled by mobility can produce "the false impression that there is no limit to what we may desire to do or to have" (Capps, *Deadly Sins*, 37). The excess of curiosity, talk, and movement are often coupled with the denial of the rights and privileges of others, i.e., the invasion of their quiet time or privacy. Furthermore, the imagination which develops at this stage sometimes confuses appearance and reality (i.e., true boundaries), as does greed (Capps, *Deadly Sins*, 38).

265. Cavanaugh, *Being Consumed*, 15.

266. Sayers, *Creed and Chaos*, 141.

contentment is enjoyed only when we recognize the "ephemeral nature of earthly goods."[267]

One must be careful in this connection, however, not to create a dualism between spiritual and material because God came in the flesh, and the material world is sacramental, charged with spiritual significance.[268] Further, consumerism is not a rejection of materialism in favor of spirituality, but an embrace of materialism as a component of spirituality.[269] "Things and brands must be invested with mythologies," Cavanaugh writes, "with spiritual aspirations; things come to represent freedom, status, and love. Above all, they represent the aspiration to escape time and death by constantly seeking renewal in created things."[270] Because of its capacity to incite other sins, Thomas Aquinas regarded greed as a deadly sin.[271] "Greed turns love into lust," James Ogilvy explains, "leisure into sloth, hunger into gluttony, honor into pride, righteous indignation into anger, and admiration into envy. If it weren't for greed, we'd suffer fewer of the other vices."[272] By means of avarice one can obtain the means to commit any sin and satisfy any sinful desire.[273]

Greed also has the capacity to devalue things. Not so much love of possessions, Fairlie avers, greed is love of possessing, since people so often purchase things they do not need or use or appreciate.[274] Consider the person who buys a shirt for its brand name label or a car for its make and model. The enjoyment of having the shirt or car transcends the enjoyment of the shirt or car. The sin here is not so far from that of the miser who hoards money or things. The miser is chastised for belittling money by hoarding it, but money is also belittled through carelessly spending.[275]

Greed can also devalue things by distorting their purposes. In a consumeristic culture, labor is often seen as a means to a paycheck rather than a vocation from God. Labor itself can become a commodity, and the

267. DeYoung, *Glittering Vices*, 113.

268. Cavanaugh, *Being Consumed*, 36; cf. Calvin, *Instit.* 3.10.3.

269. Cavanaugh, *Being Consumed*, 36.

270. Cavanaugh, *Being Consumed*, 48.

271. The daughters of greed are "treachery, fraud, falsehood, perjury, restlessness, violence, and insensibility to mercy (Aquinas, *Sum* 2–2.118.8).

272. Ogilvy, "Greed," 87.

273. Fairlie, *Seven Deadly Sins*, 144.

274. Fairlie, *Seven Deadly Sins*, 135. While purchase things we don't need, we sometimes say, "I must have that" (Fairlie, *Seven Deadly Sins*, 136). "At the heart of Avarice is the evil of waste" (Fairlie, *Seven Deadly Sins*, 149).

275. Fairlie, *Seven Deadly Sins*, 134. "Scrooge gave nothing to anybody for Christmas, but we go on an orgy of spending" (Fairlie, *Seven Deadly Sins*, 135).

production of products can be seen exclusively as a means to profit, rather than the manufacturing of quality items for human use and enjoyment. As such, the consumer culture is characterized more by detachment from things, than attachment (e.g., the miser).[276] For Christians, however, there is a legitimate detachment in which we view "things" not as ends, but as means to a greater end—namely attachment to God and to others.[277]

Greed also has capacity to devalue oneself and is apparent in those, for example, who are possessed by their possessions.[278] Such people trust their things to speak for them and to speak well, so they polish them far beyond necessity.[279] Even divesting oneself of one's riches, as one does in making a substantial donation, does not necessarily eliminate avarice, especially if one wishes to be remembered for the donation.[280] What remains in the tomb of Tutankhamen is not the body which is decomposed but the gold—objects and not the person.[281] Greed can produce a "total atrophying" of imagination, evident both in the embrace of get-rich-quick schemes and in the inability to see how some goods might improve the lives of others.[282] This atrophying therefore depersonalizes and dehumanizes ourselves and others.[283]

Greed strengthens its hold on one's life through possessiveness of goods (for which we worked hard) and by fear. In Scripture, warnings against greed are often coupled with exhortations not to fear (e.g., Luke 12:32–34). Fear of not having enough gripped those in the Great Depression and motivates the miser for whom "the pile of gold on the table is a wall against the world."[284] It is fitting that the word "miser" derives from the same Latin root as "miserable." Previously valued as "honest thrift," the sin of miser-y is unromantic and unspectacular and opposed to gluttony for its

---

276. Cavanaugh, *Being Consumed*, 34. For which reason, shopping and not simply buying, lies at the heart of consumerism. "Pleasure is not so much in the possession of things as in their pursuit. . . . The consumerist spirit is a restless spirit, typified by detachment, because desire must be constantly kept on the move" (Cavanaugh, *Being Consumed*, 47).

277. Cavanaugh, *Being Consumed*, 52.

278. Fairlie, *Seven Deadly Sins*, 137.

279. Fairlie, *Seven Deadly Sins*, 137.

280. Fairlie, *Seven Deadly Sins*, 141.

281. Fairlie, *Seven Deadly Sins*, 152.

282. The phrase "total atrophying" is Kenneth Slack's, quoted in Capps, *Deadly Sins*, 36.

283. Fairlie, *Seven Deadly Sins*, 140.

284. Fairlie, *Seven Deadly Sins*, 133.

extravagance.[285] In spite of assigning excessive value to wealth, the miser has poor self-image and deprives him/herself of enjoyment.[286]

Lastly, greed can devalue others. "Greed corrodes the virtue of generosity" and violates justice by depriving others.[287] Greed for fast cars, for instance, involves excessive consumption of fossil fuels, and our penchant for cheap products ignores the poor labor conditions of those who produced them.[288] In the parable Jesus taught about the rich man and Lazarus in Luke 16, the problem is not that one was rich and the other poor, but that the rich man was self-sufficient and therefore the poor man was deprived. Avarice, therefore, includes sins of omission, including the neglect of the poor. Deeply-rooted greed is willing to use people for the love of money rather than use money for the love of people.[289] "Every time a man expects . . . his money to work for him," Sayers alleges, "he is expecting other people to work for him."[290] The value of improving human well-being, individually and communally, must transcend the value of increasing wealth.[291]

In summary, greed is the distorted desire for provision, a frantic "looking forward" disposition to acquire more than God has already amply provided. Greed devalues God through its distracting quality by which one seeks ownership of what is God's instead of stewardship. Things are devalued by the corrosive quality of greed by which possessions are reduced to avenues for self-indulgence. The self is devalued by the depressing quality of greed which gives the miser his misery and by the enslaving quality of greed by the persistent inability to secure enough to be happy. Lastly, others are devalued by the isolating quality of greed, by which one's self-indulgence excludes others; by the antagonizing quality of greed by which wealthy employers, for instance, deny their employees a share in profits; and by the dehumanizing quality of greed, by which the value of people is subordinated to the value of material things.

285. Sayers, *Creed of Chaos*, 134.
286. Fairlie, *Seven Deadly Sins*, 134.
287. DeYoung, *Glittering Vices*, 101.
288. Cunningham, *Seven Deadly Sins*, 40.
289. DeYoung, *Glittering Vices*, 109. "Do we never choose our acquaintances with the idea that they are useful people to know, or keep in with people in the hope that there is something to be got out of them?" (Sayers, *Creed or Chaos*, 137).
290. Sayers, *Creed or Chaos*, 138–39.
291. Cunningham, *Seven Deadly Sins*, 41. Sayers faults the church for its readiness to address sexual immorality but reluctance to speak to financial immorality. "Do officials stationed at church doors in Italy to exclude women with bare arms," she asks, "turn anybody away on the grounds that they are too well dressed to be honest?" Would Divesname assigned to rich man in Luke 16be refused the sacrament the way Magdalene, the supposed prostitute, would be? (Sayers, *Creed or Chaos*, 136).

The disposition to greed is potentially inhibited by gratitude which, as a purposeful virtue, celebrates God's ample provision and recognizes the purposes for which God has given us things—namely, for our use and for our enjoyment. Gratitude celebrates God's gifts by dignifying them, stewarding them well, and enjoying them.

Gluttony (*Gula*): The Distorted Desire for Pleasure

Central among God's gifts are his provision of food and drink for our health (necessity) and for our enjoyment (pleasure). Already in the Garden of Eden, God provided Adam and Eve a menu with numerous possibilities. As with acquiring possessions, enjoying food and drink is both natural and necessary. Not surprisingly, much of human culture revolves around food and meals. "We are," Leon Kass writes, "only because we eat."[292] So much of human life and culture revolves around eating, from the nurture of farmers, for instance, to the production of butchers, the logistical dimensions of distribution and transportation, the stocking of grocery shelves, the manufacturing of tables and chairs, the development of kitchen implements, the management of bakeries and restaurants, etc. A purely scientific account of eating reduces it to biochemistry, physiology, and molecular biology, all of which are happily set aside when scientists meet for a meal. Kass writes,

> They choose when and what to eat and they do so quite purposively; hunger or appetite prompts them; gustatory preference guides their choices. They eat sitting down, at a table, where they notice temperatures and textures, enjoy seasonings and spices, and take pleasure in the abatement of their hunger and in the sequences of courses and tastes. . . . They converse while eating, taking as much pleasure in the company and the conversation as in their food.[293]

The gifts of food and drink are not purely material gifts. Food and drink have a sacramental quality, and through their use God enables people to live. The possibility of life, in other words, is not inherent in the food and drink, but in the way that God uses them to sustain life. To reduce the activity of eating and drinking to ingesting materials, therefore, is to ignore the dynamic way in which God uses food and drink. In both the temptations of Adam and of Christ, the devil appealed to the human desire for food in

---

292. Kass, *Hungry Soul*, 2.
293. Kass, *Hungry Soul*, 10.

reductionistic ways. In repelling the temptation, a famished Jesus reminded the devil that "one does not live by bread alone" (Matt 4:4).

Gluttony is typically defined as "an *inordinate* appetite for food."[294] Comparable to greed in terms of its insatiable desire for more, gluttony distinctively yearns for an internal and bodily euphoria. Like greed, in other words, gluttony yearns for satisfaction, though the satisfaction it craves involves biology and physiology in a way greed does not. In this sense, gluttony devalues God because it looks to food for pleasure rather than to God, forgetting that the satisfaction of bodily desires is always temporary and that material enjoyment is always partial and can never fully satisfy the human constitution.[295] The satisfaction promised by food is far more elusive than the satisfaction promised by greed. Food dissolves quickly whereas things deteriorate slowly. The glutton confuses appetite for food with spiritual hunger and then must reckon with an escalating and futile craving. In fact, in the enjoyment of food the glutton often becomes immune to meaningful spiritual joy and pleasure, seemingly unaware of their potential to satisfy.[296] "Never forget," Screwtape reminded Wormwood, "that when we are dealing with any pleasure in its healthy and normal and satisfying form, we are, in a sense, on the Enemy's ground."[297] Thus the glutton's pursuit of material pleasures, induced by the "illusion that we can be made happy by cramming our inner emptiness, of body as of soul, full of the things of this world" necessarily generates discontentment.[298] "Only a knowledge of God's love for me," Kreeft writes, "can fill that emptiness, make me a solid self, give me ultimate worth."[299]

---

294. Cunningham, *Seven Deadly Sins*, 12. See also DeYoung, *Glittering Vices*, 140. Aquinas writes, "Gluttony denotes, not any desire of eating and drinking, but an inordinate desire" (Aquinas, *Sum* 2–2.148.1). For Donald Capps, gluttony is the peculiar sin of infants who vacillate between the poles of trust and distrust. The glutton suffers either from excessive trust in the pleasures the world offers or from a distrust/fear regarding whether the one responsible for our welfare will be able to provide in the future. This in turn isolates us from them such that "our demands for physical nurturance, love, and affection can destroy the very companionship we need to sustain our trust in the world and in ourselves" (Capps, *Deadly Sins*, 27).

295. Kreeft regards drunkenness as a subspecies of gluttony because it idolizes alcohol (Kreeft, *Back to Virtue*, 178). See also DeYoung, *Glittering Vices*, 146.

296. DeYoung, *Glittering Vices*, 146. "The smell of the kitchen or the sweetness of its odors so stupefies other that they are unable to smell anything spiritual" (Calvin, *Instit.* 3.10.3).

297. Lewis, *Screwtape Letters*, 87.

298. Kreeft, *Back to Virtue*, 179.

299. Kreeft, *Back to Virtue*, 180.

Second, gluttony devalues oneself when it reduces the gluttons to "mere pleasure-seekers."[300] As such one's own satisfaction and pleasure transcend other good things, and one begins to rely "on the pleasure of food to compensate for the lack of rest, relaxation, and joy in an overstressed life."[301] Further, as Calvin argues, gorging oneself or excessive alcohol consumption renders one "stupid" or "useless for the duties of piety and of your calling."[302]

Gluttony, thirdly, has capacity to devalue things. "It is the great curse of Gluttony," Sayers wrote, "that it ends by destroying all sense of the precious, the unique, the irreplaceable."[303] This is apparent through the acronym FRESH, a contemporary version of a medieval ditty which captures the dimensions of gluttony, all of which have potential to dominate the consumer—namely, "eating fastidiously, ravenously, excessively, sumptuously, hastily."[304] Along with eating sumptuously, eating fastidiously focuses on the object or what we eat, whereas the remaining variables relate to the manner or how we eat. Think of the picky eater whose tastes are so peculiar, whose standards are so high, and whose preferences are so discriminatory that few items on the menu ever suffice. Insistence on having the perfect meal betrays excessive interest in the food.[305] The sumptuous glutton craves expensive foods, finding pleasure not necessarily in the taste of the food itself, but in the satisfaction the food brings.[306] The remaining three forms of gluttony all involve an excessive desire for pleasure in the manner of consumption. Eating too hastily envisions taking a second helping while the first remains in one's mouth.[307] Eating too greedily implies an inordinate desire for consumption, sometimes driven by the fear that it will soon be

---

300. DeYoung, *Glittering Vices*, 141.

301. DeYoung, *Glittering Vices*, 145.

302. Calvin, *Instit.* 3.10.3.

303. Sayers, *Creed or Chaos*, 132.

304. DeYoung, *Glittering Vices*, 141.

305. The glutton is culpable here, Aquinas argues, in terms of how food is viewed: "As regards its quality, he [sic] seeks food prepared too nicely—i.e., 'daintily'" (Aquinas, *Sum* 2–2.148.4).

306. The glutton is culpable here, Aquinas argues, in terms of how expensive the food is: "As regards the substance or species of food a man [sic] seeks "sumptuous"—i.e., costly food" (Aquinas, *Sum* 2–2.148.4). See also DeYoung, *Glittering Vices*, 143. The glutton only devours and never savors. If the enjoyment of food existed only in taste, we could always spit out after tasting. In decadent ancient Rome, one could find *vomitoria*, small rooms adjoining banquet halls where nobility could disgorge their first course in order to make room for the second.

307. "One forestalls the proper time for eating, which is to eat "hastily" (Aquinas, *Sum* 2–2.148.4).

gone and enjoyed by others.³⁰⁸ Gluttony, however, can be difficult to recognize because it is sometimes masked by the semblance of temperance. Those who ask for modest amounts, who recoil at generous allotments, are sometimes masking their desires for more. "Because what she wants is smaller and less costly than what has been set before her," C. S. Lewis writes, "she never recognizes as gluttony her determination to get what she wants, however troublesome it may be to others."³⁰⁹

Technological progress has made the mass-production of food possible and funded the multiplication of fast-food restaurants. "As the necessity to sell goods in quantity becomes more desperate," Sayers writes, "the people's appreciation of quality is violently discouraged and suppressed."³¹⁰ Sayers argues further that this push for mass production (I would add "fast food") "could not be kept up for a single moment without the cooperative gluttony of the consumer."³¹¹ The irony is that gluttonous consumption diminishes the enjoyment of food and devalues those with whom we eat and the divine source of the food.³¹² Barth comments,

> Man [sic] can very quickly become trivial. Or rather, the deep triviality which is to be found in every man can very rapidly rise to the surface if he allows himself to veer or to be steered in this direction, i.e., that of the plate and the bottle. . . . We can deepen, develop, and educate and train our receptiveness and taste in this field, and if we do we shall never be at a loss for causes and objects of joy.³¹³

Gluttony distorts the enjoyment of food either by idolizing or by marginalizing it, even abasing it.³¹⁴ For Donald Capps, the sinfulness of gluttony lies not so much in excess, but in the attitudes behind the excess which betray carelessness towards life and beauty and a dearth of "aesthetic appreciation for the created world."³¹⁵

---

308. "One fails to observe the due manner of eating, by eating "greedily" (Aquinas, *Sum* 2–2.148.4).

309. Lewis, *Screwtape Letters*, 76.

310. Sayers, *Creed or Chaos*, 129.

311. Sayers, *Creed or Chaos*, 130. "The sin of Gluttony . . . of overmuch stuffing of ourselves, is the sin that has delivered us over into the power of the machine" (Sayers, *Creed or Chaos*, 131).

312. DeYoung, *Glittering Vices*, 141.

313. Barth, *CD* 3/4:381.

314. Cunningham, *Seven Deadly Sins*, 12.

315. Capps, *Seven Deadly Sins*, 26.

Lastly, gluttony devalues others when, like greed, one's self-indulgence deprives others.[316] "The abuse and misuse of food, even for personal gratification," Cunningham argues, "is an affront to the poor of the world."[317] The desire for food and drink is corrupted when the pleasures of eating subordinate the value of others.

In summary, gluttony is the distorted desire for pleasure, a frantic "looking forward" disposition to experience a kind of euphoria in eating and drinking. Gluttony devalues God through its distracting quality, by which one seeks bodily satisfaction instead of true pleasure. Things are devalued through the corrosive quality of gluttony, by which an excessive appetite in fact abases food. Self is devalued through the depressing quality of gluttony by its immunity to meaningful pleasure, and by its enslaving quality, by which one is unable to fill one's emptiness with food. Lastly, we see how others are devalued through the isolating quality of gluttony whereby the pleasure of food is privileged over companionship, through the antagonizing quality of gluttony by which one hogs food available to others at the dinner table, and by the dehumanizing quality, evident when the fixation on eating transcends interest in others.

The disposition to gluttony is potentially inhibited by gratitude which, as joyful virtue celebrates the euphoria of fellowship with God and the wonder of his gifts. In view of the seriousness of the new world to come, gratitude celebrates the playfulness of this less serious world.[318]

Lust (*Luxuria*): The Distorted Desire for Relationship

God created Adam to be in intimate fellowship with him, but that fellowship was not immediately available. YHWH's periodic visits to the garden demonstrated that he did not intend to be with Adam every second of the day in uninterrupted face time. Adam had a need for companionship, in other words, that God did not intend to fulfill initially. Even though he enjoyed fellowship with God, there was still a sense in which he was alone and that was "not good" (Gen 2:18). "Not good" does not mean "bad" but "not the best." His fellowship with God was initially partial. History, at least in part, is about the Holy Spirit finding a bride for the Son of God and about the Son of God purchasing this bride with his blood (Acts 20:28) and sanctifying her (Eph 5:25–27). This marital union between Christ and the church, however, is not consummated until the eschaton (Rev 19:9).

316. Cunningham, *Seven Deadly Sins*, 16.
317. Cunningham, *Seven Deadly Sins*, 17.
318. This point will be expanded on in chapter 4.

A picture of this relationship (Eph 5:32), marriage is therefore an interim gift. When God first created humanity, there was no marriage and when God restores humanity in the eschaton, there will once again be no marriage. In the interim, marriage offers a foretaste of the eternal companionship God promises. Sexual arousal, for instance, is part of God's design, as the Song of Songs overwhelmingly demonstrates, and sexual intimacy is intended both to bond people together and to usher new life into the world. As such, sexual intimacy is an interpersonal gift which joins not only partners but generations of parents and children.[319] The importance of sexual intimacy cannot be devalued, DeYoung rightly states, since both love and life are at stake.[320] Even within marriage and other comparable intimate relationships, fulfillment of intimate desires is incomplete. Life on this side of glory is always attended, among married and unmarried, by a tinge of sexual frustration and discontentment, by a sense of loneliness, if not nostalgia.[321] The companionship one enjoys with God on this earth, though not the consummated intimacy of the new earth, is still rich and meaningful.

Before God introduced in Genesis 2 what we might term "erotic sexuality," he disclosed in Genesis 1 "social sexuality."[322] In other words, before there was man and woman becoming one flesh, there were male and female image-bearers. Male and female sexuality exist, therefore, apart from sexual intimacy, and this has two important implications. First of all, to be unable to engage in erotic sexuality, because of birth defect, injury, sickness, etc. does not make one less of a sexual person, and those in this predicament will still relate to others either as women or as men. Erotic sexuality, secondly, is only a small part of our identity. If sexuality is only part of identity and erotic sexuality is only part of sexuality, erotic sexuality is only a small sliver of one's total identity. For this reason, it seems dehumanizing to define people by their erotic sexuality, either as heterosexual, bi-sexual, or homosexual. Both sexual pleasure and non-erotic social bonds are gifts and both offer satisfaction and meaning, for which gratitude is appropriate.[323] Such gratitude is sabotaged by lust, the distorted desire for relationship.

Unlike love which weaves the fabric of a narrative out of the threads of commitment and faithfulness, lust produces only isolated patches and cares neither for the past nor the future. Whereas the joy of love is situated

319. DeYoung, *Glittering Vices*, 164.

320. DeYoung, *Glittering Vices*, 162.

321. Sexual frustration is a phenomenon among both married and single.

322. Marva Dawn distinguishes between "genital sexuality" and "social sexuality" (Dawn, *Sexual Character*, 9).

323. Singlehood in this conception is a noble vocation because it provides the possibility to serve God with undivided loyalty (1 Cor 7).

in a story, lust is episodic. The desire for relationship is distorted either by divorcing sexual pleasure from relationship or by pursuing the fulfillment of illicit sexual pleasure.[324] Further, sexual intimacy is a picture and foretaste of full fellowship with God. To pursue the lesser apart from the greater is both illogical and unsatisfying.

It is surprising for contemporaries to discover that lust historically was often presented as the least concerning of the vices. Christian theorists often treated it as an animal instinct unlike those vices like envy, which engage the mind.[325] Today people often feel burdened by the grip of lust, experience shame, and want to be liberated.[326] We fear lust perhaps more than other sins because we recognize that sexual desires are so strong and beautiful that we succumb easily and are often gripped before we realize it. What distinguishes lust from creational sexual desire, however, is that the former controls us whereas the latter is controlled by us.[327] The porn user enjoys the fleeting pleasure of a sham sexual moment, but high sexual satisfaction is experienced by those in faithful, monogamous marriages for whom "sexual pleasure is the fruit of love."[328]

Lust, first of all, has the capacity to devalue God. Deprivation of spiritual joys, for Augustine, generates addiction to carnal pleasures, the truth of which convicted him when through his experience of finding rest in God his restless lustful desires were finally moderated.[329] Further, sexual pleasure is so mysteriously wonderful it is transcendental. "I wonder," Willimon speculates, "if in our culture there is so much sexual passion and so little desire for God because sex has become the last means of self-transcendence."[330]

---

324. DeYoung, *Glittering Vices*, 166; Cunningham, *Seven Deadly Sins*, 22.

325. Cunningham, *Seven Deadly Sins*, 25.

326. Donald Capps sees lust as the sin peculiar to young adults who developmentally are confronted by the poles of intimacy versus isolation. As the motivator for committed relationships, the desire for intimacy is of course healthy. Hesitancy or even inability to share true intimacy generates isolation from others. Such isolation can include self-subjection by accepting what is available and thereby denying one's freedom to choose and self-abdication by choosing solitude after self-gratification and thereby surrendering our ability to give (Capps, *Deadly Sins*, 54).

327. Cunningham, *Seven Deadly Sins*, 27.

328. DeYoung, *Glittering Vices*, 169.

329. "Lust diminishes as love grows till the latter grows to such a height that it can grow no higher here" (Augustine, *Enchir.* CXXI).

330. "Willimon, *Sinning Like a Christian*, 145. "We thus confuse a temporary, momentary experience with a long-term solution, a short-lived experience of mystery with an experience of the true and living God, and that's the sin" (Willimon, *Sinning Like a Christian*, 145).

Second, lust can devalue oneself, and when sex is divorced from its purposes, human copulation is hard to distinguish from its animal counterpart. "If one is successful in becoming immune to the goods involved in sex," De Young writes, "one has also been successful in becoming less fully human."[331] Further, the pursuit of illicit sexual experiences does not represent a strong sexual appetite, but a weak one, a desire too easily satisfied with superficial and fraudulent substitutes. "Lust," Willimon claims, "is that sin that requires not a brain."[332] Love's promise of fidelity, as C. S. Lewis pointed out, is neither automatic nor guaranteed; lust is easier.[333] The happiness of an enduring marriage, for example, is attributable not to good lovers, but to good people.

Third, lust can devalue things. What lovers crave is a wholeness that transcends the intimacy of sex. There is no sin in appreciating the sexual beauty of another man or woman, even when noticed through the "involuntary turn of the head"; desiring adultery with him or her is sin.[334] The person who abstains from sexual fulfillment on grounds that it is evil or dirty "is not a Christian, but a Gnostic."[335] The starting point for a Christian view of sexuality must not be its distortions but its goodness and virtue. Understanding the goodness of sexual pleasure prevents us from both degrading it to superficial fun and elevating it to spiritual ecstasy. Far from satisfying, lust kills pleasure. With its "reductive impulses" lust limits sexual pleasure to self-gratification or to mutual pleasure divorced from any other purpose.[336] Sensual pleasure, however, is no substitute for love-giving.[337] The routine misuse of something good results in an inability to recognize and enjoy its goodness.[338] Simultaneously boring and addictive, pornography always promises more, but never delivers.[339]

One ought to question why contemporary society is so sexualized that sexual images, metaphors, and innuendo are inescapable. Dorothy Sayers

---

331. DeYoung, *Glittering Vices*, 165.

332. Willimon, *Sinning Like a Christian*, 138.

333. Lewis, *Four Loves*, 169.

334. Kreeft, *Back to Virtue*, 167.

335. Cunningham, *Seven Deadly Sins*, 27. Celibacy in the Catholic tradition is valued because sexuality is worthy to be sacrificed for the higher good of service.

336. DeYoung, *Glittering Vices*, 163.

337. DeYoung, *Glittering Vices*, 166.

338. DeYoung, *Glittering Vices*, 168.

339. Cunningham, *Seven Deadly Sins*, 30. Lust parallels gluttony in terms of the quest for self-satisfaction, and habitual self-indulgence only increases the demand. Screwtape again was accurate: "An ever increasing craving for a diminishing pleasure is the formula" (Lewis, *Screwtape Letters*, 42).

has a possible explanation: "When philosophies are bankrupt and life appears without hope—men and women may turn to lust in sheer boredom and discontent, trying to find in it some stimulus which is not provided by the drab discomfort of their mental and physical surroundings."[340] Miroslav Volf puts it strikingly, "Partners randomly 'hook up,' each hungry to sexually satisfy some inchoate craving that has no definite object and can never find rest. They crave chocolate, they grab a chocolate bar; they crave sex, they just grab the most willing partner."[341]

Lastly, lust also has capacity to devalue others. Lust is distinguished from love "when the object of lust is just that—an object and not a person."[342] Lust is far from an innocuous desire with no potential to hurt. Aquinas addressed the supposed innocuous nature of lust by arguing that it opposed the love of neighbor by opposing the good of the child to be born.[343] Aside from his argument, which many do not find compelling, lust has the potential to injure human relationships and human existence. Men who fulfill lust through pornography have distorted views of women and in some cases have difficulty relating to them.[344] Those who suffer most in overly sexualized cultures, C. S. Lewis claimed, are women: "Where promiscuity prevails, they will therefore always be more often the victims than the culprits. . . . In the ruthless war of promiscuity women are at a double disadvantage. They play for higher stakes and are also more likely to lose."[345]

Porn dehumanizes men and women and makes social sexuality impossible. "Lust isolates us from human society," Capps writes, "through its cruel and exploitative approach to individuals and its irresponsible attitude toward social obligations."[346] Further, lust easily evolves from mere internal desires to external behavior injurious to others (e.g., sex slavery, sexual abuse, rape, etc.).[347] Lust therefore is not only self-absorbing, self-serving, self-indulgent, but degrading and dehumanizing to the other. Whereas love

---

340. Sayers, *Creed or Chaos*, 121.

341. Volf, *Free of Charge*, 15. Sometimes people turn to lust out of sheer boredom and "the drab discomfort of their mental and physical surroundings" (Sayers, *Creed or Chaos*, 121).

342. Cunningham, *Seven Deadly Sins*, 28.

343. "Now fornication is contrary to the good of the child to be born" (Aquinas, *Sum* 2–2.154.2.ad4).

344. "Pornography reduces a person to a piece of meat" (Kreeft, *Back to Virtue*, 179).

345. Lewis, *God in the Dock*, 359–60.

346. Capps, *Deadly Sins*, 56.

347. Cunningham, *Seven Deadly Sins*, 28. "Cruelty usually accompanies even the seemingly more benign forms of lust" (Capps, *Deadly Sins*, 54).

is exclusive and discriminates, lust is inclusive and non-discriminating, promiscuously seeking fulfillment with whomever.

As indicated above, Marva Dawn sagely distinguishes between social and genital sexuality.[348] When genital sexuality is elevated to a defining characteristic (e.g., terms like homosexual and heterosexual) and when sexual expression is regarded as a fundamental human right, humanity is dehumanized. Conceiving of relationships between men and women only along "genital" lines seemingly precludes the possibility of non-sexual love, affirmation, and friendship between men and women. The writer of the letter to Timothy instructed him to regard women in familial categories, as sisters and mothers, "with absolute purity" (1 Tim 5:2). This notion is promising for a reconstruction of relations between men and women that acknowledges sexual differentness without assuming relationships of genital or erotic sexuality.

By contrast, lust is the distorted desire for relationship, a frantic "looking forward" disposition to enjoy others only in terms of erotic sexuality. Lust devalues God, first of all, through its distracting quality by which one seeks mere sexual pleasure instead of wholesome intimacy that God intended. Things are devalued through the corrosive quality of lust, by which sexual pleasure itself is reduced to self-indulgence. The self is devalued through the depressing character of lust, by which the shame of sham sexual pleasure leaves one empty, and by its enslaving quality, by which one is driven by an insatiable craving for a diminishing pleasure. Others are devalued through the isolating quality of lust with its exploitive approach to others, but its antagonizing quality with its unwanted sexual advances and by its dehumanizing quality in which others are reduced to mere objects.

The tendency to lust, I will argue, is potentially inhibited by gratitude which, as a personal virtue, celebrates fellowship with God and sexual others socially and sometimes erotically. It receives the gifts of others and enjoys interaction with members of the opposite sex for their sexuality without reducing them to sexual objects.

CONCLUSION

God fills human life with gifts of acceptance, equality, justice, rest, provision, pleasure, and relationship. Gratitude for these gifts is sabotaged by the seven deadly sins, socially destructive and idolatrous habits of sinful desire. The desire emerges out of an often unconscious need (desire) for communion with the Creator which amplified by willful estrangement from him

---

348. Dawn, *Sexual Character*, 9.

seeks what he promises and provides elsewhere. Because nothing outside of God is intended to satisfy, these pursuits are insatiable and idolatrous. Because such devotion arises out of estrangement from God and is directed to entities other than God, the result is a devaluation not simply of God, but of his creation in terms of self, others, and things.

CHAPTER 3

PHILOSOPHICAL REDUCTIONS OF GRATITUDE

THE PREVIOUS CHAPTER PRESENTED the seven deadly sins as saboteurs of gratitude, as habits of distorted desire which, ignoring or devaluing gifts in the past or present, relentlessly pursue illicit fulfillment and satisfaction in the future. This book argues that a potential antidote to distorted desires is gratitude, understood as a responsive virtue in which one, seeing oneself as the recipient of a gift, freely and joyfully salutes the giver for the gift received in order to perpetuate a personal and peaceable relationship. In such an understanding, gratitude is regarded as a virtue in which gifts are in some way lovingly reciprocated.

In order to obtain clarity about gratitude, this chapter invites into the conversation, utilizing the method of mutual critical correlation, the voices of philosophy and psychology in order to correlate with insights of the Christian tradition in the following chapter. The value of this chapter lies, therefore, in exposing presuppositions that might cloud a proper understanding of gratitude. In chapter 4 the insights of this chapter will be correlated with theological claims first in terms of the metanarrative of Scripture and then in terms of some prominent theologians in order to yield informed theological reflection.

To establish whether gratitude is a virtue specifically, it is advantageous to engage contrary claims, and so this chapter will probe the morality of gratitude in terms of prominent reductions or denunciations. The two most notorious detractors of gratitude are philosophersnamely, the ancient philosopher Aristotle and the post-modern philosopher Jacques Derrida.

Both adopted dim views on gratitude and the first part of this chapter will be structured around their demurrals. For Aristotle, gifts require returns, the implication of which is that gifts are intrusive burdens which subject their recipients to unwelcome relationships in which they owe the giver. For Derrida, on the other hand, gifts do not require returns, the implication of which is that returns for gifts, of which gratitude is an instance, are not simply unnecessary, but immoral. To return something for a gift poisons the gift and in fact nullifies it. In order to obtain clarity about gratitude, especially as something virtuous and helpful, the negative appraisals of Aristotle and Derrida must be engaged.

Following Aristotle and Derrida, the profile of gratitude proffered by positive psychology will be interrogated, with special attention given to Robert Emmons, the leading positive psychological researcher of gratitude. Unlike Aristotle and Derrida, Emmons values gratitude for, among other things, its psychological, physiological, social, and prosocial value. The positive psychological profile of gratitude, however, will be judged incomplete precisely because of the non-theological limitations of its inquiry. In the conclusion of the chapter, a step will be taken towards a renewed profile of gratitude that is mindful of the insights generated in this chapter. In so doing, this inquiry will engage especially, though not exclusively, the seminal work of Terence McConnell, for whom gratitude is a kind of vista through which one can entertain a variety of ethical questions and obtain ethical clarity.[1]

GIFTS REQUIRE RETURNS: GRATITUDE AS INFERIORITY

In chapter 1, I argued that in the narrative of obligatory reciprocity, dominant in the Greco-Roman world and in some non-Western hierarchical and tribal cultures, gratitude was a societal hinge connecting people together in what Margaret Visser termed a "web of obligation."[2] Because it threatened one's independence, this web with its obligations of reciprocity was not always warmly welcomed. When gift-giving is perceived as a threat to one's independence, i.e., the reception of something one did not have (and perhaps needed), then gratitude itself becomes undesirable.

---

1. McConnell wrote *Gratitude* "to show that an elucidation of the concept of gratitude requires making a commitment on many other basic issues in ethical theory" (McConnell, *Gratitude*, 7).

2. Visser, *Gift of Thanks*, 193.

Aristotle

This notion of gratitude as unwanted indebtedness finds an early precedent in Aristotle who regarded gratitude as requital for gifts received. In Aristotle's ethics of independence, gratitude is absent from his list of virtues because, in his logic, the reception of gifts "imposes dependence."[3] The cultural ideal of independence, however, is not far removed from us by time or space. In the late 1980s, Shula Sommers, a social psychologist, investigated emotional life in American, German, and Israeli societies, and observed that Americans rated gratitude low in desirability and that American men in particular often experienced gratitude as unpleasant, if not humiliating, precisely because for many gratitude assumes an admission of vulnerability and dependency.[4] The following section will present a fresh reading of Aristotle in which his historic devaluation of gratitude is both probed and evaluated.[5]

Egotistical Εὐδαιμονία

The starting point for Aristotle's ethics is not law or a categorical imperative, but inclinations to certain ends through the experience of attraction. The ultimate end sought, the goal desired above all others, is the supreme good that Aristotle identifies as happiness. Described further by Aristotle as "living well and doing well," happiness is "an activity of the soul in accordance with virtue"[6] and the perfect end because it is self-sufficient and not pursued for any reason other than itself.[7] "The εὐδαιμον (or happy man)," Barnes writes, "is someone who makes a success of life and actions, who realizes his aims and ambitions as a man, who fulfills himself."[8] Constitutive

---

3. Leithart, *Gratitude*, 37. See also, Visser, *Gift of Thanks*, 216.

4. Sommers, "Adults Evaluating Their Emotions," 313–36. In the study over 30 percent of American men preferred to conceal feelings of gratitude, though not a single woman indicated difficulty in expressing gratitude.

5. In this section, I will use "man" in a gender specific way to conform to Aristotle's (discriminatory) usage.

6. Aristotle, *Eth. nic.* 1098a15–20. According to Barnes, "activity" (ἐνέργεια) involves exercising one's powers, "soul" (ψυχή) represents being animate, and "virtue" (ἀρετή) refers to character. Even the expression ηθική ἀρετή is best understood as "excellence of character" and not "moral virtue." As such, the aim of Aristotle's ethics is not to make people morally good, but expert or successful people (See Barnes, "Introduction," xxv, xvii, xxxiii). Virtue is "a human being's capacity to act well, think well, or produce a good work" (Vanier, *Happiness*, 19).

7. Aristotle, *Eth. nic.* 1097a30–b16.

8. Barnes, "Introduction," xxxii; cf. Aristotle, *Eth. nic.* 1097b7–13.

of true happiness and distinctive to man is rational activity, the culmination of which is the theoretical life of contemplation (θεωρία), which is about enjoying, appreciating, and reflecting on the knowledge one has already acquired.⁹

Contemplation is the highest end—the most perfect, pleasurable, and pure—and the life of the divine. God is defined in Aristotle's Metaphysics as νόησις νοήσεως ("thinking of/on thinking") whose only worthy object of thought is himself.¹⁰ "The activity of the gods, which is supremely happy," Aristotle alleges, "must be a form of contemplation; and therefore among human activities that which is most akin to the gods' will be the happiest."¹¹ Pure contemplation, therefore, is self-sufficient and needs no others.¹² In this connection, Aristotle ponders whether,

> if a person be self-sufficing in every respect he will have a friend, or whether on the contrary a friend is sought for in need, and the good man will be most self-sufficing. If the life that is combined with goodness is happy, what need would there be of a friend? For it does not belong to the self-sufficing man to need either useful friends or friends to amuse him and society, for he is sufficient society for himself. This is most manifest in the case of God; for it is clear that as he needs nothing more he will not need a friend, and that supposing he has no need of one he will not have one. Consequently the happiest human being also will very little need a friend, except in so far as to be self-sufficing is impossible.¹³

---

9. Aristotle, *Eth. nic.* 1177a14ff. The Greek text I consulted is Bywater, *Aristotle's Ethica Nicomachea*.

10. "Therefore Mind thinks itself, if it is that which is best; and its thinking is a thinking of thinking" (Aristotle, *Metaph.* 1074b3; cf. *Eth. nic.* 1179a24–29). "God is the sovereign though that thinks on itself, for in God 'the intelligence and the intelligible are the same.' And Aristotle adds that God always has the immense joy of contemplation—the joy we possess only for a few fleeting moments" (Vanier, *Happiness*, 102).

11. Aristotle, *Eth. nic.* 1178b20–25. "The man who pursues knowledge in its purest form and in the most disinterested way, says Aristotle, will pursue the knowledge found in metaphysics; but he will do this because it is knowledge of the ends that inform all other forms of knowledge" (Flannery, "Friend of God," 10).

12. "That quality that we call self-sufficiency will belong in the highest degree to the contemplative activity. The wise man, no less than the just one and all the rest, requires the necessaries of life; but, given adequate supply of these, the just man also needs people with and towards whom he can perform just actions, and similarly with the temperate man, the brave man and each of the others; but the wise man can practice contemplation by himself, and the wise he is, the more he can do it" (Aristotle, *Eth. nic.* 1177a27–b1).

13. Aristotle, *Eth. eud.* 1244b2–10; cf. *Eth. nic.* 1169b26–27, 1158a23–24.

The complexity of Aristotle's thought on this point is apparent. When he affirms that "man" is a social being, he seems to indicate that this, though not ideal, is necessary.[14] Aristotle's εὐδαιμονία has been termed an egotistical εὐδαιμονία because it aims at an end which is self-sufficient and self-fulfilling. The εὔδαιμον, as will become apparent, is someone who does not receive things from others and therefore does not need to be grateful.

Friendship of Commercial Relationship

If the contemplative life should be privileged over the practical life because θεωρία is self-sufficient, then this occasions the question: what value then does φιλία (close friendship) have for intellectual activity? Here we discover that Aristotle's conception of friendship is largely mercantile and economic.

What does Aristotle say about friendship? As is true of all other virtues, friendship is a state or disposition (ἕξις) rather than a feeling (πάθος).[15] Virtue is being rightly disposed to feelings, in an intermediate relation to them (avoiding excess and deficiency) and actualizing them for the good of others.[16] As such, friendship (φιλία) is a state proceeding from a rational choice (προαίρεσις) that has a particular target—namely, τὸν φίλον (the lovable)—and friends are loveable because they are either good, pleasant, or useful.[17] Aristotle is insistent that true friendship involves wishing good things for the sake of the other, a mutual goodwill (εὔνους) that is reciprocal and mutually acknowledged.[18] Here we encounter a paradox of sorts. Is friendship based on giving or receiving? Aristotle recognizes that loving someone because of usefulness or pleasure is undesirable because it makes a person's offerings more valuable than the person.[19] A friendship according to pleasure or usefulness, however, is legitimate if the desire is mutual and reciprocal. Two individuals, for example, can enjoy a friendship of back-scratching. You can enjoy friendship with another for his or her commodity (e.g., back-scratching) so long as he or she also enjoys friendship with you for the same commodity. Though it has commercial overtones, Aristotle insists that this is not the exploitation of others, but an instance of one wishing the other well for one's own sake.[20] Perfect friendship, for Aristotle, is based

14. "For man is a social being" (Aristotle, *Eth. nic.* 1097b10–11).
15. Aristotle, *Eth. nic.* 1157b29–33; cf. 1105b29, 1106b17–25
16. Aristotle, *Eth. nic.* 1105b27.
17. Aristotle, *Eth. nic.* 1156a5–20; cf. 1155b18–19
18. Aristotle, *Eth. nic.* 1155b30–35; cf. 1156a9–10, 1166b30–1167a21
19. Aristotle, *Eth. nic.* 1156a15–20.
20. Aristotle, *Eth. nic.* 1155b30–33.

on goodness in which case "each party receives from the other benefits that are in all respects the same or similar."[21] In fact, Aristotle argues that one must be discerning in the selection of friends, and exclude those unlikely to reciprocate benefits. It is "easy to give and spend money," Aristotle argues, "but to feel or act towards the right person to the right extent at the right time for the right reason in the right way that is not easy."[22]

True friendship assumes an equal and reciprocal exchange, so much so that inequality precludes true friendship.[23] Here it becomes apparent that Aristotle's conception of human relations is decidedly hierarchical. In fact, those who are deprived of certain goods—Aristotle includes those who are ugly (not beautiful), of low birth (not noble), disabled (not healthy), enslaved (not free), with no or bad children—are incapable not just of perfecting virtues such as friendship, but of achieving εὐδαιμονία itself.[24]

Though true friendship is impossible between unequals, an inferior friendship can exist between them, among which Aristotle includes relationships between father and son, and husband and wife. These parties do not receive the same benefits from each other and the friendship is unequal in part because the one (e.g., the child) cannot repay the other (e.g., the parent) and thus remains a debtor for life.[25]

---

21. Aristotle, *Eth. nic.* 1156b30–36.

22. Aristotle, *Eth. nic.* 1109a25–30. Seneca similarly argues, "we ought to be careful to confer benefits by preference upon those who will be likely to respond with gratitude" (Seneca, *Ben.* 1.10.4–5).

23. "This becomes evident if a wide gap develops between the parties in respect of virtue or vice, or of affluence or anything else; because they no longer remain friends, and do not even expect to do so" (Aristotle, *Eth. nic.* 1158b33–36; cf. 1159a5–8).

24. Aristotle, *Eth. nic.* 1099a31–b6. "We must suppose therefore that the same necessarily holds good of the moral virtues: all must partake of them, but not in the same way, but in such measure as is proper to each in relation to his own function. Hence it is manifest that all the persons mentioned have a moral virtue of their own, and that the temperance of a woman and that of a man are not the same, nor their courage and justice, as Socrates thought, but the one is the courage of command, and the other that of subordination, and the case is similar with the other virtues. And this is also clear when we examine the matter more in detail, for it is misleading to give a general definition of virtue, as some do, who say that virtue is being in good condition as regards the soul or acting uprightly or the like; those who enumerate the virtues of different persons separately, as Gorgias does, are much more correct than those who define virtue in that way. Hence we must hold that all of these persons have their appropriate virtues, as the poet said of woman: "Silence gives grace to woman"—though that is not the case likewise with a man. Also the child is not completely developed, so that manifestly his virtue also is not personal to himself, but relative to the fully developed being, that is, the person in authority over him. And similarly the slave's virtue also is in relation to the master" (Aristotle, *Pol.* 1260a).

25. "Hence it would seem that a son may not disown his father, although a father

In all these friendships between persons of different standing, the affection must be proportionate: i.e., the better person must be loved more than he loves, so must the more useful, and each of the others similarly. For when affection is proportionate to merit the result is a kind of equality, which of course is considered to be characteristic of friendship.[26]

The individual who is entitled to more love is the more loveable one (i.e., the one who has more in terms of wealth, power, age, virtue, or the right sex) and not the one who needs more.[27]

True friendship is a commercial relationship that either enjoys or strives for equality and reciprocity in exchange of commodities.[28] Gratitude in this context is repayment. It is in these very terms that Aristotle explains the significance of a public shrine in the city of Athens to the Charites (the graces), three young beautiful naked goddesses believed to be the dispensers of *charis*, the source of all generosity (whose original province was fertility). Aristotle explains that this shrine to the Graces was constructed "to encourage the repayment of benefits (ἀνταπόδοσις); this is the distinguishing mark of gratitude (ἴδιον χάριτος), because it is right both to repay a service to a benefactor and at another time to take the initiative in benefaction."[29]

Aristotle's conception of friendship has several important dimensions relevant to gratitude. First, concern for the other is ultimately concern for oneself. An individual wishes her friend well, but for one's own sake.[30]

---

may disown his son. For a debtor ought to pay his debts, but nothing that a son can do is a due return for what he has received, so that he is permanently in his father's debt" (Aristotle, *Eth. nic.* 1163b17–23; cf. 1159a5–12). The only way for man to be a friend of God is for man to become a god and cease to be man (See Flannery, "Friend of God," 12).

26. Aristotle, *Eth. nic.* 1158b24–29.

27. "One might introduce here the relation between a handsome person and an ugly one. This is the reason why lovers sometimes make themselves look ridiculous by demanding to be loved as much as they love; if they were equally loveable, this would presumably be a reasonable demand, but when they have no such qualification it is ridiculous" (Aristotle, *Eth. nic.* 1159b15–20).

28. After warning against imposing a modern and Western contrast between gifts and commodities to non-Western cultures (Barclay, *Paul and the Gift*, 22), Barclay acknowledges the Seneca and Philo made exactly this kind of comparison (Barclay, *Paul and the Gift*, 47, 75). Barclay's warning is valid when we impose a distinction between reciprocated and unreciprocated gifts, the latter of which was virtually unknown in the ancient world.

29. Aristotle, *Eth. nic.* 1133a.

30. Wolterstorff indicates that this was common among ancient eudaimonists—namely, "the position that one may seek to promote the well-being of anyone whatsoever as an end in itself provided that doing so promises to enhance one's own overall wellbeing" (Wolterstorff, *Justice in Love*, 5).

Secondly, friendship has a commercial, economic dimension in which one strives for an equal exchange of commodities such that the value of friendship lies in reciprocity of goods. Aristotle sees friendship largely in terms of capacities and commodities and not in terms of love. He is unable to envision a fellowship in which what is shared is not impressive things, wonderful activities, or beautiful thoughts, but weaknesses and needs.

Magnanimous Rationality

Aristotle's ideas on gratitude are generated by his magnanimous rationality, the term I have chosen to describe his virtue epistemology. In terms of magnanimous rationality, the best friendship is a friendship according to virtue. This is a friendship in which the partners "wish good for other qua good, and they are good in themselves."[31] It is a friendship in which you want the other to become more fully who he or she really is. Unlike friendships according to pleasure and usefulness, friendship according to virtue involves loving others for no other reason than who they really are.

But who are we as humans, and how are we perfected? We are distinguished from plants and animals by our rationality, Aristotle contends, and it is the activity of reason that perfects human function.[32] For this reason, Aristotle gave no value to children with mental disabilities because reason seemed absent in them.[33] Rational activity produces intellectual virtues and moral virtues, and there is mutual benefit when friends consult each other about practical and intellectual matters. Friendship is profitable even for

---

31. Aristotle, *Eth. nic.* 1156b7–9; cf. 1156a9–10.

32. Aristotle, *Eth. nic.* 1097b–1098a. He also refers to "brutish" who are "rare among human beings," but "commonest among the non-Greek races, but some cases also occur that are due to disease or arrested development" (Aristotle, *Eth. nic.* 1145a30–35). The "natural slave" is also incapable of reason (see Aristotle, *Pol.* 1280a33).

33. "As to exposing or rearing the children born, let there be a law that no deformed child shall be reared; but on the ground of number of children, if the regular customs hinder any of those born being exposed, there must be a limit fixed to the procreation of offspring, and if any people have a child as a result of intercourse in contravention of these regulations, abortion must be practiced on it before it has developed sensation and life; for the line between lawful and unlawful abortion will be marked by the fact of having sensation and being alive. And since the beginning of the fit age for a man and for a woman, at which they are to begin their union, has been defined, let it also be decided for how long a time it is suitable for them to serve the state in the matter of producing children. For the offspring of too elderly parents, as those of too young ones, are born imperfect both in body and mind, and the children of those that have arrived at old age are weaklings" (Aristotle, *Pol.* 1335b).

contemplation.³⁴ Friends can help one another engage continuously in virtuous activity and perceive actions more clearly.³⁵ They can help, in other words, in the imperfect areas of virtuous activity—namely, its incompletion and its partial perceptibility.³⁶ Friends are needed for one to climb the summit of intellectual virtue, but once one arrives their necessity expires. This needs nuancing because Aristotle seems to argue that at the summit of philosophy each person is essentially νοῦς and each enjoys the same activity, the self-contemplation of the shared divine essence. Patrick Miller comments, "Philia is a way to find oneself with friends; with their help, what one finds is that there is only one self."³⁷

Aristotelian love for others, once deconstructed, is a love of oneself. This is explicit in Aristotle's construal of parental love: "Parents, then, love their children as themselves (for one's offspring is a sort of other self in virtue of a separate existence)."³⁸ Such love embraces the child not because of his or her differences, but in spite of them.³⁹ Though Aristotle attempts to distinguish his notion of self-love from narcissism, it remains the case that what is loveable in a friend is nothing unique but a generic and shared contemplation, a kind of rational mysticism. By all accounts Aristotle was unable to account for the love of a person in her differentness. Ultimately, by privileging reason over love, Aristotle has no room for alterity, no space for differentness, and no gratitude for others.

Among his moral virtues Aristotle includes liberality (situated intermediately between stinginess and prodigality) and magnificence (μεγαλοπρέπεια), which is like liberality, but involves large scale civic donations for public welfare, not least for the civic services performed in Greek cities.⁴⁰ Aristotle subsumes liberality and magnificence under the crowning virtue of his ethical system—namely, magnanimity or greatsouledness (μεγαλοψυχία).⁴¹ The magnanimous man sees himself as worthy of great

34. Aristotle, *Eth. nic.* 1177a28–b1; cf. 1178a2–8.

35. Aristotle, *Eth. nic.* 1170a5–7, 1169b33–35.

36. Patrick Lee Miller has a nice discussion of this in Miller, "Finding Oneself with Friends," 333.

37. Miller, "Finding Oneself with Friends," 344–45.

38. Aristotle, *Eth. nic.* 1161b27–29. Offspring here has sense of offshoot from a plant.

39. Miller, "Finding Oneself with Friends," 348.

40. Aristotle, *Eth. nic.* 1122a20–1123a. Prodigality, however, is better than stinginess and the one who confers benefits does not readily receive them (Aristotle, *Eth. nic.* 1122a10–15). All magnificent men are liberal, but not all liberal men are magnificent (Aristotle, *Eth. nic.* 1122a25–30).

41. Aristotle, *Eth. nic.* 1123b. "So magnanimity seems to be a sort of crown of the

things because he is worthy and is concerned with his honor because it is deserved.⁴²

The magnanimous man is the most autonomous, the most independent, and one who has no need of others. To be a free man, Aristotle avers, one cannot be dependent on any other man.⁴³ The magnanimous man "is disposed to confer benefits, but is ashamed to accept them, because the one is the act of a superior and the other that of an inferior."⁴⁴ He remembers favors he has done, but forgets those he received. Furthermore, he repays a service with interest to make his donor his debtor: "He cannot bear to live in dependence upon somebody else," Aristotle writes, "because such conduct is servile."⁴⁵ He indulges in "conspicuous consumption"⁴⁶ because "he is the sort of person to prefer possessions that are beautiful but unprofitable to those that are unprofitable and useful, because this is more consistent with self-sufficiency."⁴⁷ Finally, he "never, or only reluctantly, makes a request, whereas he is eager to help others."⁴⁸

The magnanimous man does not deny justice to slaves and weak people, but he does not concern himself with them either. Liberality, friendship, and love are bridled by a pursuit for heroic autonomy. Aristotle seems oblivious to the potential for a weak person to help a strong one.⁴⁹ Reception of gifts implies humility, inferiority, dependence, and a lack of autonomy, and therefore the virtuous man avoids being a beneficiary as much as possible.⁵⁰

---

virtues, because it enhances them and is never found apart from them" (Aristotle, *Eth. nic.* 1124a1–5).

42. Aristotle, *Eth. nic.* 1123b20–25. Aristotle's views are inextricable from the "honor and shame" culture in which he was embedded. Honor and shame are external phenomena whereas guilt, though punishable, is a private feeling and not necessarily discernible to others (Visser, *Gift of Thanks*, 259).

43. "But the man who follows the same pursuit because of other people would often appear to be acting in a menial and servile manner" (Aristotle, *Pol.* 1337b19–21).

44. Aristotle, *Eth. nic.* 1124b9–15. In contrast, Seneca recommended benefactors to forget their gifts immediately and beneficiaries to remember them always (Seneca, *Ben.* 2.10.4).

45. Aristotle, *Eth. nic.* 1124b30–32.

46. MacIntyre, *Short History of Ethics*, 79.

47. Aristotle, *Eth. nic.* 1125a10–15. MacIntryre comments, "Incidentally, he walks slowly, has a deep voice and a deliberate mode of utterance. He thinks nothing great. He only gives offense intentionally. He is very nearly an English gentleman" (MacIntryre, *Short History of Ethics*, 79).

48. Aristotle, *Eth. nic.* 1124b17–18.

49. Vanier, *Happiness*, 189.

50. Augustine understood this well. Commenting on the heroism of the Romans, which applies aptly to Aristotle, "Some, indeed, suppose that the virtues are true and honorable even when they have reference only to themselves and are sought for no

The weak should be grateful whereas the strong should prevent themselves from being drawn into gratitude.⁵¹

Appraisal

From this cursory survey of Aristotle's views the following conclusions can be made. First, in a εὐδαιμονία that, devoid of a relationship with a personal God, is self-sufficient and self-fulfilling, needing no friends and no gifts, there is no room for gratitude and no recognition of the innate dignity of creation, not least humans. Second, since friendship has a commercial dimension in which one strives for an equal and reciprocal exchange of commodities, gratitude amounts to repayment, is motivated by indebtedness, and dismisses gifts of weakness or disability. Thirdly, since friendship in contemplation involves a kind of shared rational mysticism in which what is loveable is nothing different from oneself, there can be no gratitude for differentness. Fourthly, because the man with the crowning virtue of magnanimity recalls what he gives, not what he receives (because reception of gifts implies indebtedness, weakness, and inferiority), gratitude is undesirable.

GIFTS MUST NOT REQUIRE RETURNS: GRATITUDE AS POISON

Hardly any scholar has generated more discussion on gift-giving than Marcel Mauss (1872–1950), the nephew of Émile Durkheim, who wrote *The Gift*, an extraordinarily influential book and a seminal volume for anthropologists. Without doing any fieldwork himself, Mauss studied the works of anthropologists (especially Boas, Thurwald, and Malinowski) who had written about gift practices in Polynesia, Melanesia, and among the Indians of the Pacific Northwest.⁵² Distinct from bartering and especially monetary economies, gift economies operated without contracts or laws, Mauss observed, but invariably revolved around three motions, all of which were obligatory—namely: giving, receiving, and reciprocating.⁵³ The sequence of giving and receiving was perfectly understandable to Mauss; what puzzled

---

other end. Then, however, they are puffed up and proud, and so are to be adjudged vices rather than virtue (Augustine, *City of God*, 19.25).

51. MacIntryre calls Aristotle's construal of magnanimity an "appalling picture of the crown of the virtuous life" (MacIntryre, *Short History of Ethics*, 79).

52. Visser, *Gift of Thanks*, 84. See Mauss, *Gift*.

53. Visser, *Gift of Thanks*, 85.

him was why those in le système des dons *échangés* (the system of gifts exchanged) who had received gifts returned gifts.

One of Mauss's most significant discoveries, though his source was allegedly a single informant, was the Maori concept of *hau*namely, that the spirit of the gift (and the personality of the donor) remains embodied in the gift even after it is given.[54] After eating part of a bird found in a forest, for instance, Maori priests would have a ceremony in which they returned the *hau*, the spirit of the bird, to the forest in order to generate a new harvest of birds. There is, therefore, a cycle in which the forest produces birds, people eat and enjoy them, and then they are returned to the forest.[55] In terms of purely human exchanges, the giver retains a kind of power over the recipient because the *hau* wishes to return to its homeland.[56] To give a gift was to impose an obligation, and to give widely was to exert wide power. The gift, Mauss writes, "links magically, religiously, morally, juridically, the giver and the receiver. Coming from one person, made or appropriated by him, being from him, it gives him power over the other who accepts it."[57] Keeping a gift was therefore dangerous.[58] *Hau* demands *utu* or reciprocity, the absence of which would incite revenge and initiate war against the gift's unreciprocating recipient.[59]

The point of gift-giving, Mauss contended, was not economic, but social.[60] He indicated that the distinction between persons and property, though assumed in Western societies, is alien to primitive societies.[61] The gift was, for Mauss, a primitive way of achieving peace and "the primitive analogue of social contract."[62] Sahlins argues that Mauss's views were not so

---

54. Leithart, *Gratitude*, 169. The informant was the Maori sage, Tamatri Ranapiri, whose text was translated and made available by Elsdon Best (1909). For more, see Sahlins, "Spirit of the Gift," 71.

55. Sahlins, "Spirit of the Gift," 97 n. 10.

56. Sahlins, "Spirit of the Gift" 73.

57. Mauss, "Gift," 29–30.

58. Komter, "Gift Exchange," 198. The gift "links those who partake and is always liable to turn against one of them if he would fail to honor the law. The kinship of meaning linking gift-present to gift-poison is therefore easy to explain and natural" (Mauss, "Gift," 30).

59. Visser, *Gift of Thanks*, 86. Mauss's assessments have been challenged by those who claim that *hau* (a) is the yield of the gift, not its spirit and (b) enters only at the second donation which is the *hau* of the first (See Leithart, *Gratitude*, 170; Komter, "Gift Exchange," 198). Even so, scholars are generally agreed that reciprocity was obligatory, intended to "reproduce social relations" (Barclay, *Paul and the Gift*, 18).

60. Barclay, *Paul and the Gift*, 13.

61. Barclay, *Paul and the Gift*, 13.

62. Sahlins, "Spirit of the Gift," 84.

different from Hobbes's in that both were premised on the threat of war.[63] In a significant passage, Mauss writes,

> Societies have progressed in so far as they themselves, their subgroups, and lastly, the individuals in them, have succeeded in stabilizing relationships, giving, receiving, and finally, giving in return. To trade, the first condition was to be able to lay aside the spear. From then onwards they succeeded in exchanging goods and persons, no longer only between clans, but between tribes and nations, and, above all, between individuals. Only then did people learn how to create mutual interests, giving mutual satisfaction, and, in the end, to defend them without having to resort to arms. Thus the clan, the tribe, and peoples have learnt how to oppose and to give to one another without sacrificing themselves to one another. This is what tomorrow, in our so-called civilized world, classes and nations and individuals also, must learn.[64]

Mauss concluded that the notion of a "free gift" is mythical. In his own words, gifts "were apparently free and disinterested, but nevertheless constrained and self-interested."[65] Subsequent scholarship has continued to accept, in gift-giving, a polarity between altruistic sacrifice and self-interested gain.[66] Bourdieu, in fact, argued that generosity is simply a cloak for domination.[67]

Jacques Derrida

Mauss's research sparked enormous debate about gift-giving, but the debate ultimately revolves around responses to the gift—namely, gratitude.[68] Engaging Mauss's *The Gift*, Jacques Derrida made the startling claim that Mauss's book was about "everything but the gift" because the circle of reciprocity, about which Mauss had so much to say, essentially annulled the gift.[69] For Derrida, Mauss wanted to present gifts as something other than

---

63. Sahlins, "Spirit of the Gift," 88.
64. Mauss, *Gift*, 105–06.
65. Mauss, *Gift*, 4. Mauss was contesting the scholarship of Malinowski who placed gifts along a spectrum ranging from "free" to "coerced."
66. It should be noted that Mauss acknowledged that self-sacrifice and self-interest were both present in gift-giving, but he did not present them as alternatives or polarities.
67. Bourdieu, "Selections," 219.
68. Leithart, *Gratitude*, 195.
69. "Marcel Mauss's *The Gift* speaks of everything but the gift: It deals with economy,

commercial exchanges: they require an interval of time, for instance, to elicit counter-gifts.[70] "The gift gives," Derrida says of Mauss's position, "demands, and takes time."[71] Derrida recognizes that Mauss was intent on distinguishing "cold economic reason" from the "poetic phenomena" of gift cultures because he wanted to conceive of "the economic rationality of credit on the basis of the gift and not the reverse."[72] In this way, and in contrast to "capitalist mercantilism," everything originates with the gift, and the gift "would be the true producer of value."[73] In a passage Derrida cites, Mauss writes,

> We will rediscover motives for living and acting that are still prevalent in many societies and classes: the joy of public giving; the delight in generous expenditure on the arts; the pleasure in hospitality and in private and public festival. Social security, the solicitude of the mutuality, of the cooperative, of the professional group, of all those legal entities upon which the English law bestows the name of "Friendly Societies"all are of greater value than the mere personal security that the lord guaranteed to his tenant, better than the mean life afforded by the daily wage set by management, and even better than capitalist savingwhich is only based on a changing form of credit.[74]

Derrida discerned in Mauss a discourse "oriented by an ethics and a politics that tend to valorize the generosity of the giving-being. They oppose a liberal socialism to the inhuman coldness of economism, of those two economisms that would be capitalist mercantilism and Marxist communism."[75] But Derrida argues that Mauss did not reflect sufficiently on what a gift is. He writes,

> If there is gift, the given of the gift (that which one gives, that which is given, the gift as given thing or as act of donation) must not come back to the giving (let us not already say to the subject, to the donor). It must not circulate, it must not be exchanged, it must not be exhausted, as a gift, by the process of exchange, by the movement of circulation of the circle in the form of return

---

exchange, contract (*do ut des*), it speaks of raising the stakes, sacrifice, gift *and* counter-giftin short, everything that in the thing itself impels the gift *and* the annulment of the gift" (Derrida, *Given Time*, 24).

70. Derrida, *Given Time*, 40.
71. Derrida, *Given Time*, 41.
72. Derrida, *Given Time*, 44.
73. Derrida, *Given Time*, 44.
74. Mauss, *Gift*, 68–69. A different translation is cited in Derrida, *Given Time*, 65.
75. Derrida, *Given Time*, 44.

to the point of departure. If the figure of the circle is essential to economics, the gift must remain aneconomic.[76]

For Derrida, it is impossible for a gift ever to approach its definition. "A gift is possible, there could be a gift," Derrida writes, "only at the instant an effraction in the circle will have taken place, at the instant all circulation will have been interrupted and on the condition of this instant."[77] "In this sense," he continues, "one would never have the time of a gift."[78] In order for a gift to be given, "some 'one' has to give some 'thing' to someone other."[79]

These conditions of the gift's possibility, however, "designate simultaneously the conditions of the impossibility of the gift."[80] "For there to be a gift," Derrida claims, "there must be no reciprocity, return, exchange, countergift, or debt."[81] That is obvious, he argues, when someone immediately returns the very gift one has received. The goodness in giving might just as well be "poisonous" because gifts indebt and that harms people.[82] "For there to be a gift, it is necessary [*il faut*] that the donee not give back, amortize, reimburse, acquit himself, enter into a contract, that he never have [sic] contracted a debt."[83] This for Derrida is a duty the donee has: he ought not to owe, not to give back. To do so, he must not see the gift as a gift, and if he does he has annulled the gift: "The simple recognition suffices to annul the gift" because it returns "a symbolic equivalent."[84] Furthermore, the donor must not see his gift as a gift because that too is a "symbolic recognition" whereby he gives back to himself "symbolically the value of what he thinks he has given or what he is preparing to give."[85] Thus Derrida claims that if a gift "presents itself, it no longer presents itself."[86] All of this has ethical import for Derrida and ought to make us vigilant, not least about gratitude: "the 'generous' or 'grateful' consciousness is only the phenomenon of a calculation and the ruse of an economy."[87]

---

76. Derrida, *Given Time*, 7.
77. Derrida, *Given Time*, 9.
78. Derrida, *Given Time*, 9.
79. Derrida, *Given Time*, 11.
80. Derrida, *Given Time*, 12.
81. Derrida, *Given Time*, 12.
82. Derrida, *Given Time*, 12.
83. Derrida, *Given Time*, 13.
84. Derrida, *Given Time*, 13.
85. Derrida, *Given Time*, 14.
86. Derrida, *Given Time*, 15.
87. Derrida, *Given Time*, 16.

Furthermore, in order for a gift to be given, not only must the donor and donee not perceive that a gift is given, they must forget it instantly and this is "an absolute forgetting—a forgetting that also absolves, that unbinds absolutely and infinitely more, therefore, than excuse, forgiveness, or acquittal."[88] If the gift appears as gift "as such, what it is, in its phenomenon, its sense and essence, it would be engaged in a symbolic, sacrificial, or economic structure that annuls the gift in the ritual circle of the debt."[89] Further, "the simple intention to give," Derrida writes, "insofar as it carries the intentional meaning of the gift, suffices to make a return payment to oneself . . . in a sort of auto-recognition, self-approval, and narcissistic gratitude."[90]

In *The Gift of Death*, Derrida questions the historicity of responsibility. He argues that responsibility originates in religion in which there is a realm of demonic prior to the subject, to which the subject the must give an account. Responsibility arises from one's relationship to an other of "infinite alterity."[91] Christians in particular are responsible to what corresponds to the demonic mystery—namely, the *mysterium tremendum* before whom one trembles. Analogously, one trembles before "figures of death as figures of the gift, or in fact as gifts of death [*de la mort donnée*]."[92] Derrida further explores how one gives death to oneself while assuming responsibility for it and whether sacrificing oneself means accepting the gift of death. "For what is given in this trembling," Derrida writes of Christianity, "in the actual trembling of terror, is nothing other than death itself, a new significance for death, a new apprehension of death, a new way in which to give oneself death or to put oneself to death."[93] Further, with a concern for individual autonomy, he writes,

> Everyone must assume his [sic] own death, that is to say the one thing in the world that no one else can either give or take: therein resides freedom and responsibility. . . . Even if one gives

---

88. Derrida, *Given Time*, 16. Seneca argues that, to prevent her from expecting a material return, the benefactor should immediately forget the gift (though the beneficiary should always remember it!) (Seneca, *Ben.* 2.10.4; cf. 7.22–25). Visser also suggests that "one must give and forget—or better, give without pausing to calculate. . . . The memory associated with gratitude is a virtue," Visser writes later, "not of the giver, but of the one who has received" (Visser, *Gift of Thanks*, 293–95). Aristotle had argued precisely the opposite—namely, that the magnanimous man should recall favors he has done rather those he received (Aristotle, *Eth. nic.* 4.3.1–38).

89. Derrida, *Given Time*, 23.
90. Derrida, *Given Time*, 23.
91. Derrida, *Gift of Death*, 3.
92. Derrida, *Gift of Death*, 7.
93. Derrida, *Gift of Death*, 31.

me death to the extent that it means killing me, that death will still have been mine and as long as it is irreducibly mine I will not have received it from anyone else. Thus dying can never be taken, borrowed, transferred, delivered, promised, or transmitted. And just as it can't be given to me, so it can't be taken away from me."[94]

No one can die in the place of another, in other words, because no one can live in another's place: death accepts no substitutes. Sacrifice implies exchange and yet death is a gift for which there can be no recompense. In reflecting on Kierkegaard's treatment of the story of Abraham sacrificing Isaac, Derrida argues that Abraham acted "without calculating, without investing, beyond any perspective of recouping the loss; hence, it seems, beyond recompense or retribution, beyond economy, without any hope of remuneration."[95] It seems wrong and yet, for Derrida, this is how it is in daily life, except "God" is everyone else.[96] Allegiance to the one requires the sacrifice of the other such that responsibility is ultimately undermined by otherness. To be responsible to another, in other words, requires one to sacrifice responsibility to all others. "As soon as I enter into a relation with the other," Derrida writes, "with the gaze, look, request, love, command, or call of the other, I know that I respond only by sacrificing ethics, that is, by sacrificing whatever obliges me to also respond, in the same way, in the same instant, to all others."[97]

Though Abraham's gift is the pure gift, the gift of death, God by returning his son reinscribes "sacrifice within an economy by means of what thenceforth comes to resemble a reward."[98] Derrida concludes his book by arguing that Christianity has distorted the gift by promising rewards. Though he had praised the poor in spirit, Jesus promises a reward to those who give (Matt 6) and so doing reinscribes a new economy of sacrifice, which Derrida describes as follows: "you will get a better salary if you give up your earthly salary."[99] As such, Christianity

---

94. Derrida, *Gift of Death*, 44.
95. Derrida, *Gift of Death*, 95.
96. "Everything points to the fact that one is unable to be responsible at the same time before the other and before others, before the others of the other. If God is completely other, the figure or name of the wholly other, then every other (one) is every (bit) other. *Tout autre est toute autre*" (Derrida, *Gift of Death*, 77).
97. Derrida, *Gift of Death*, 68.
98. Derrida, *Gift of Death*, 96.
99. Derrida, *Gift of Death*, 101.

begins by denouncing an offering that appears to calculating still; one that would renounce earthly, finite, accountable, exterior, visible wages . . . one that would exceed an economy of retribution and exchange . . . only to capitalize on it by gaining a profit or surplus value that was infinite, heavenly, incalculable, interior and secret. This would be a sort of secret calculation that would continue to wager on the gaze of God who sees the invisible and sees in my heart what I decline to have seen by my fellow humans.[100]

While first insisting that one should give without the expectation of reward, Christianity backtracks to say that there is a reward.

Jean Luc Marion's Response to Derrida

The French philosopher Jean Luc Marion agrees with Derrida's assessment of Mauss. "The Essay on the Gift," Marion writes, "never treats the gift, only exchange and its system."[101] Moreover, he writes, "To repay or return (a greeting, an invitation, a favor, money) already enters into an economy: the gift is followed by the countergift, the payment of a debt, reimbursement for what has been borrowed."[102] Further, he agrees with Derrida that the recipient should not repay a gift, and that such a refusal should not be construed as ingratitude because "ingratitude comes up only within an already constituted economy of exchange and reciprocity."[103]

Marion believes that a pure gift does exist and can be located through a phenomenal reduction of givenness. Unlike Husserl who was still bound to the metaphysical paradigm of the object, Marion argues that some things cannot be treated merely as objects. A painting, for instance, must be apprehended as a thing, but its beauty transcends this and cannot be reduced to a description.[104] The key reality, and this is ultimate phenomenology, is its effect, what it gives.[105] "While the gift according to exchange is stymied in the natural attitude," Marion argues, "the gift in terms of givenness arises in the realm of reduction."[106] Such givenness requires the bracketing not only of

100. Derrida, *Gift of Death*, 109.
101. Marion, *Being Given*, 75.
102. Marion, *Being Given*, 76. "If there is givenness, it implies the suspension of exchange" (Marion, *Being Given*, 76).
103. Marion, *Being Given*, 76.
104. Marion, *Being Given*, 43.
105. Marion, *Being Given*, 51.
106. Marion, *Being Given*, 114.

the recipient, but also of the giver because the very consciousness of giving generates a return in one's consciousness which establishes "an economic exchange in self-immanence."[107] Then, lastly, "the economic interpretation of givenness as a system of exchange not only freezes giver and givee as parties to commerce, but also submits the exchanged gift to the gaze that they direct toward it, and this exchanging gaze fixes only an object of exchange."[108] The permanent sight of the gift as such requires the bracketing of the gift.

In his phenomenological reduction, therefore, Marion brackets the giver, the gift itself, and the recipient, claiming that none of them is essential to the gift. First, he brackets the recipient in order to consider the gift only from the perspective of giver. A gift which is "pure loss" cannot be returned because the recipient is unknown and thus it functions outside an economic horizon.[109] An example of this for Marion is a contribution to the United Way where the donor does not know the recipient. "For the giver, during the time of the gift (the collection campaign)," Marion writes, "it's not about expecting a return or an exchange; it's about a gift given with abandon."[110] Further, a gift given to an enemy who refuses it remains a gift: "The enemy alone, who is the figure for the givee in the realm of the reduction, the de-negating givee, receives the gift without repaying it—but by the same token, admits it as such, a gift according to givenness, without any commerce."[111] The same applies to gifts to an ingrate who, by refusing to be grateful, "manifests, a contrario and in all its purity, the gift reduced to givenness, since he proves that this gift is perfectly accomplished without the givee's consent."[112] Marion further provides an example of a recipient who is neither absent, nor hostile, from Jesus's instruction to his disciples about clothing the naked and visiting the imprisoned (Matt 25).[113] In giving to the least of his brothers, Jesus says, they gave to him, whom they did not see, but who received their gifts.

Secondly, Marion brackets the giver in order to consider the gift from the perspective of the recipient. In an instance of an inheritance from a dead benefactor or an anonymous gift and therefore the inability to respond to

---

107. Marion, *Being Given*, 76, 77.

108. Marion, *Being Given*, 77.

109. Marion, *Being Given*, 79. "The gift, to be given, must be lost and remain lost without return. In this way alone does it break with exchange, where one gives only to have it repaid" (Marion, *Being Given*, 86).

110. Marion, *Being Given*, 88.

111. Marion, *Being Given*, 89. Think of Jesus's call to love one's enemies.

112. Marion, *Being Given*, 91.

113. Marion, *Being Given*, 92.

the giver, "the economy of exchange is thus suspended perfectly."[114] Marion, thirdly, brackets the gift itself as something which, without donor or recipient, gives itself. The reduced gift may consist of making a promise or forging a friendship, something "accomplished solely on the occasion of its own happening."[115] Similarly, the conferring of power or the giving of one's word involves the transference of no objects. "In the realm of the reduction," Marion writes, "the gift is accomplished all the better when it is not reified in an object."[116] The gift gets its given character from givenness. "To recognize the gift," Marion concludes, "implies a strict and particular phenomenological gaze: that which, faced with the fact, sees it as a gift.... The gift is given intrinsically to give itself."[117]

Appraisal

For both Derrida and Marion gifts are compromised by reciprocation. Such a conception of gift-giving, however, is completely foreign to both traditional and global practices which, as Visser demonstrates, have nearly always assumed reciprocity and the creation or strengthening of mutual ties and social cohesion. The insistence that gift-giving must be free of reciprocation necessarily results in a radical depersonalization of gifts and an endorsement of a world in which people must for moral reasons be unhinged from each other. For Derrida, only a spontaneous gift to a random person approaches true giftedness.[118] For someone to give a bag of money, for example, to anyone on the street "would appear quixotic rather than straightforwardly generous."[119] "Derrida's concern for purity of intention," Hart writes, "partakes of a certain Enlightenment mythology; there seems also to be an unspoken solicitude for the recipient of the gift, that other subject whose indivisible interior freedom would somehow be compromised by the imposition of any exterior obligation or debt."[120]

Furthermore, the inability to conceive of gift-giving outside of commerce (especially true of Derrida) is unwarranted. The reciprocation of

---

114. Marion, *Being Given*, 96.
115. Marion, *Being Given*, 103.
116. Marion, *Being Given*, 106.
117. Marion, *Being Given*, 112–13.
118. Even here Derrida would object because the giver has rewarded himself with the knowledge that he is the giver. "A true gift would be from no-one, to no-one and of nothing" (Milbank, "Can a Gift," 130).
119. Milbank, "Can a Gift," 124.
120. Hart, *Beauty of Infinite*, 263.

gratitude, historically, was distinguished from repayment by a delay in time (i.e., thus not immediate) and by a distinction in value (i.e., thus not commensurate).[121] The distinction is illustrated by consideration of other kinds of gifts. If one speaks, and thus offers a verbal gift, is it inappropriate to expect a response? Does a response poison the verbal gift with repayment? Are conversations contaminated with commerce?[122] The gifts of romantic love are freely given, though with expectations that are mutually shared.[123] "A gift differs from other forms of exchange," Hart writes, "not because it 'generously' demands nothing in return, but solely by the style of return it elicits; and so it is only by obligation (albeit a particular fashion of obligation) that the gift is recognizable as a gift that has been given and received."[124] The grateful reception of a gift by a beloved, far from poisoning it, honors the gift and is precisely the response the romantic gift pursues. In terms of romantic love, "giving here is most free where it is yet most bound, most mutual and most reciprocally demanded."[125]

Further, why is it necessary to insist that returns are necessarily obligated? "There is no reason," Hart argues, "why it is more correct to say that the gift forces a return than to say that the gift allows or even liberates a response, and so is the occasion of communion."[126] As such, the notion of romantic love, in Derrida's and Marion's conceptions, is problematic if not impossible because unrequited love is not romantic love. A conception of gift-giving in only commercial categories is, as Barclay concludes, neither "natural" nor "necessary."[127] Not only do most gifts receive something back, there is something right about returns. Derrida allows for the possibility of a pure gift outside of commercial relationships, but cannot find it. Through

---

121. Especially Seneca (to a lesser degree Aquinas) makes distinctions of this sort. Similarly, Bourdieu indicates that counter-gifts that do not insult are "deferred and different" (Bourdieu, "Selections," 198). Similarly, for Milbank a "purified gift exchange" is one in which there is a "delayed" and "non-identical" repetition of the gift (Milbank, "Can a Gift," 131).

122. Milbank, "Can a Gift," 123.

123. "Human erotic attachments are only sustained by the incessant exchange of gifts, which are always tokens of further, future gifts, such that desire is never fulfilled as possession, for a constitutive lack of desire will always prove its own thwarting. If desire does know moments of fulfillment, then this is in the coincidence of giving and giving back" (Milbank, "Can a Gift," 124).

124. Hart, *Beauty of Infinite*, 260–61.

125. Milbank, "Can a Gift," 124.

126. Hart, *Beauty of Infinite*, 263.

127. Barclay, *Paul and the Gift*, 63.

his method of phenomenological reduction, Marion is able to locate the gift in the mode of pure givenness, but not without sacrificing gratitude.[128]

POSITIVE PSYCHOLOGY: GRATITUDE AS ADVANTAGEOUS

Among non-theological "texts" that resource theological reflection on gratitude, not all are critical, however. Unlike Aristotle and Derrida who have little space for gratitude, positive psychologists recommend gratitude as something that contributes to human wellbeing. In what follows the insights generated by positive psychology will be summarized and appraised in order to enhance theological reflection on gratitude.

Positive Psychology

A school of thought founded largely by American psychologist Martin Seligman, positive psychology researches, scientifically, the ingredients in humanity that enable flourishing and studies, specifically, positive emotion (e.g., confidence, trust, hope), positive traits (e.g., strengths, virtues, and skills), and positive institutions (e.g., democracy, family).

Positive psychologists have registered some striking observations about the constitution of happiness.[129] Fifty percent of happiness, psychologists surmise, is determined by what is called one's set point, the genetic baseline one inherits. On the basis of one's genetic programming, some are far more predisposed to happiness than others, just as some are far more likely to experience depression. Research suggests that only ten percent of human happiness relates to life circumstances and whether one is wealthy or poor, healthy or unhealthy, educated or uneducated, married or unmarried.[130] Achieving happiness through winning the lottery or undergoing an extreme makeover is, it turns out, largely mythical. People generally return to prior happiness levels after a year of experiencing such reversals in life circumstances. Though today we are better educated and live in larger houses with multiple appliances and numerous conveniences, we score lower on happiness levels (7.2 out of 10) than those in the 1940s (7.5 out of 10), a third of whom lived in homes without running water, half of whom did

---

128. See also Leithart, *Gratitude*, 210.

129. The information that follows is derived from Lyubomirsky, *Happiness*, 39–68. Emmons discusses this in Emmons, *Thanks*, 21–25.

130. Lyubomirsky, *Happiness*, 21.

not have central heating, and only a quarter of whom graduated from high school.[131]

What accounts for the inverse relationship between prosperity and happiness? Positive psychologists talk about hedonic adaptation, becoming so accustomed to certain pleasures and privileges that their initial appeal fades.[132] Hedonic adaptation is observable in marriages: within only two years of their weddings, married couples are statistically likely to return to their prior happiness levels.[133] Much of hedonic adaptation can be accounted for by rising aspirations (e.g., those who purchase a big home soon want one that is bigger) and social comparisons (e.g., you want what those in your social network have).[134]

What especially interests positive psychologists is the remaining forty percent in the happiness equation, attributable not to a set point or circumstances, but to decisions we make about how we live. What patterns of behavior are objectively discernible in happy people? Here it became apparent to researchers that happy people are generally those who nurture social relationships with family and friends, forgive offenders, readily offer help to others, express gratitude for what they have, etc. Among early positive psychologists who researched gratitude, Michael McCullough and Robert Emmons discovered that those who practiced gratitude in their daily routines experienced a surge of joy, happiness, and contentment, and were less likely to suffer depression.[135]

The Positive Psychological Profile of Gratitude

Positive psychologists research gratitude under the rubric of emotion (as opposed to, say, virtue), in part because one can experience and express gratitude without being a grateful person.[136] For gratitude to be embodied

- 131. Lyubomirsky, *Happiness*, 42.
- 132. Lyubomirsky, *Happiness*, 50.
- 133. Lyubomirsky, *Happiness*, 49.
- 134. Lyubomirsky, *Happiness*, 50.
- 135. Seligman, *Authentic Happiness*, 75.

136. Emmons, "Introduction," 8. As an emotion, gratitude defies the categories. Most emotions involve agitation, and unlike other emotions it is difficult to prompt grateful feelings in a lab. Further, gratitude emerges out of relationships, requires reflection, lacks facial expressions, can exist without feeling, and is supposed to endure, though emotions are typically short-lived. Gratitude must be taught to children before they feel it. As an emotion, gratitude reacts, recognizes, and reflects, and so motivated, generates a decision. As such gratitude exists in the heart and is displayed through giving back (Visser, *Gift of Thanks*, 325–41).

the following sequence occurs: (a) There is an elicitor—something external to oneself, i.e., a gift or gesture, (b) the perception of which generates a feeling and (c) then provokes a measurable, physiological reaction (e.g., welling in the throat) (d) which alters our thinking (e.g., motivating us to respond) and (e) results in the expression of our feeling.[137] The same sequence, interestingly, occurs in anger where (a) there is an elicitor, often an offence, (b) the perception of offence, (c) the physiological reaction of elevated heart rate and a surge of stress hormones, (d) the wish to see the injustice redressed, and (e) the expression of anger through facial reaction or physical action.[138]

The emotion of gratitude, further, is recognized to have an action tendency—namely, to reciprocate the gift(s) and so contribute to the wellbeing of the benefactor, but one which is distinct from action tendencies typically associated with indebtedness.[139] Those who are grateful are driven, Fredrickson claims, not by mindless reciprocity, but by creative interest in the wellbeing of others, especially their benefactors.[140] In this way gratitude differs significantly from anger since one cannot be grateful to oneself, Emmons argues, though one can be angry with oneself.[141] As such, gratitude develops a person's skill in showing love and kindness.[142]

Gratitude, for Emmons, is a personal recognition, "the perception of a positive personal outcome, not necessarily deserved or earned, that is due to the actions of another person."[143] More specifically, gratitude for Emmons involves the recognition (a) that one has been the recipient of someone's kindness, (b) that a benefactor has intentionally given something to you, often at some expense on her part and (c) that the gift has value in eyes of a recipient.[144] Gratitude is therefore forged in our hearts through acknowl-

---

137. Emmons, *Thanks*, 59. Though most emotions (e.g., anger, happiness, disgust) have accompanying universally recognizable facial expressions, gratitude does not (Emmons, *Thanks*, 60).

138. Emmons, *Thanks*, 59.

139. Emmons, "Introduction," 9.

140. Fredrickson, "Gratitude," 150–51.

141. "It would be bizarre to say that a person felt grateful to herself. Even if you bought yourself a lavish dinner . . . it would be peculiar if I were to give thanks to myself. Thanks are directed outward to the giver of gifts" (Emmons, *Thanks*, 4). Emmons, however, leaves room for another kind of gratitude, what he terms capital G gratitude—namely, the gratitude we feel for contributions we make, including the giving of thanksgiving (Emmons, *Thanks*, 120). It is difficult to interpret this as something other than self-gratitude.

142. Fredrickson, "Gratitude," 152.

143. Emmons, "Introduction," 5.

144. Emmons, *Thanks*, 5.

edging the goodness of the gift, the goodness of the giver, and the gratuitousness of the gift.[145]

What especially distinguishes the positive psychological appraisal of gratitude are the benefits attributed to it. In one of their first studies, McCullough and Emmons assembled three groups of people for research purposes. The first group had to identify, at the conclusion of a week, five things for which they were grateful. The second similarly had to identify five "hassles." The third was a control group asked simply to list five things that affected them in the previous week. McCullough and Emmons discovered that not only was the "grateful" group a full 25 percent happier than the others, its participants reported fewer health complaints, and exercised more.[146] Moreover, McCullough and Emmons discovered that when the notion of gift was broadened to include everyday pleasures, people, kind gestures, etc., nearly half of the gifts identified by participants fell into the categories of interpersonal or spiritual gifts. Furthermore, they discovered that these things were viewed more positively when perceived as gifts.[147]

A correlation exists, therefore, between levels of being grateful and levels of personal satisfaction.[148] Not only do people have pleasant associations with gratitude, preliminary research suggests that being grateful can actually generate mood improvement.[149] When people are asked to identify feelings associated with gratitude they speak of contentment, joy, peace, etc.[150] In fact, in terms of the determinants of happiness listed above, gratitude has the capacity to "counteract the effects of hedonic adaptation."[151] "Adaptation to satisfaction," Emmons writes, "can be counteracted by constantly being aware of how fortunate one's condition is."[152]

Philip Watkins accounts for this function of gratitude. The first mechanism, he suggests, is the recognition that what you have is not just any commodity, but a gift someone has intentionally given you, the enjoyment of which is partially restrained until our appreciation can be expressed.[153] The

---

145. Emmons, *Thanks*, 38.

146. Emmons, *Thanks*, 30. Similar studies conducted with young children generated similar results (Emmons, *Thanks*, 52).

147. Emmons, *Thanks*, 37.

148. Watkins, "Gratitude and Subjective Well-being," 169.

149. Watkins, "Gratitude and Subjective Well-being," 173.

150. Emmons, *Thanks*, 25.

151. Emmons, *Thanks*, 35.

152. Emmons, *Thanks*, 42.

153 Gratitude is therefore indicative of a healthy psychology because it is generated especially when the beneficiary, in an empathic moment, imagines the sacrifice the benefactor made to provide the gift (McCullough and Tsang, "Parent of the Virtues?," 125).

second mechanism is the manner in which gratitude, by taking inventory of how good life is, counteracts the law of habituation by which people adapt to ongoing circumstances and become accustomed to levels of satisfaction such that increases in salary, for example, ultimately do not produce increases in happiness. The third mechanism is gratitude's capacity to prevent one from making comparisons to those who have more. Gratitude, as such, is "inversely related to dispositional envy."[154] If one is grateful for his or her house, he or she is less likely to be envious of his or her neighbor's house. From this line of reasoning, it seems sensible to hypothesize that grateful people will not have an inordinate desire for things they do not have and will enjoy more capacity to delay gratification.[155] The converse also holds true: those focused on what they lack will be unable to enjoy what they have.[156] Positive emotions like gratitude have the capacity to replace harmful negative emotions, thereby restoring psychological balance.[157] According to the well-established psychological principle of emotional incompatibility, it is impossible for stress and relaxation to co-exist.[158]

Studies also demonstrate that the more grateful one is, the less depressed she is and, conversely, the more depressed, the less grateful.[159] Grateful and depressed individuals therefore have inverse relationships to a positive memory bias.[160] At some level this is unremarkable, but studies also demonstrate that gratitude enhances the "encoding" (i.e., formation) of experiences in which we have a positive outlook.[161] This in turn enables grateful people to recall gifts more readily and to elicit a positive recall bias. "To the extent that gratitude helps an individual direct their attention to blessings they have and away from things they lack," Emmons writes, "this should decrease the likelihood of depression."[162] Finally, gratitude weakens depression by directing attention away from oneself and thereby inhibiting the gloom that self-focus can generate.[163]

---

154. Watkins, "Gratitude and Subjective Well-being," 177.
155. Watkins, "Gratitude and Subjective Well-being," 177.
156. Emmons, *Thanks*, 42.
157. Emmons, *Thanks*, 74.
158. Emmons, *Thanks*, 74.
159. Emmons, *Thanks*, 38.
160. Watkins, "Gratitude and Subjective Well-being," 171.
161. Emmons, *Thanks*, 39.
162. Emmons, *Thanks*, 40. Studies show that those with significant prefrontal dysfunction, including individuals with Parkinson's disease, have greater difficult recalling gratitude memories and no change in mood when they do (Emmons, *Thanks*, 80).
163. Emmons, *Thanks*, 41.

Gratitude is a way of coping with disaster, a kind of resiliency. When people narrate their life stories, they often identify "redemption sequences" for which they are grateful.[164] The distinction between feeling grateful and being grateful is important here. The feeling is a natural response, and no one feels grateful in the moment of tragedy. Being grateful is "a chosen posture toward life."[165] Humans are extraordinarily resilient and respond to loss reasonably well. In one study, it was discovered that only three months after losing a child through Sudden Infant Death Syndrome (SIDS), most parents had more positive than negative emotions.[166] Following the war in which he spent time in Auschwitz, Elie Wiesel went around saying to people, "Thank you just for living, for being human . . . and to this day, the words that come most frequently from my lips are 'thank you.'"[167] Emmons speculates, having studied gratitude for years, that deeply held gratitude often requires "some degree of contrast or deprivation."[168] In one study, students were asked to recall 9/11 and report on how often they had felt in terms of a variety (twenty in fact) of emotions. The second most experienced emotion was gratitude.[169]

Gratitude is also being acknowledged for its prosocial nature. The emotion of gratitude, first of all, functions as a moral barometer in the sense beneficiaries feel most grateful when a gift was rendered intentionally, incurred cost to the benefactor, and was valuable to the recipient.[170] Secondly, the emotion of gratitude functions as a moral reinforcer in the sense that benefactors who are thanked for their gifts are more likely to work harder on behalf of others than those who are not thanked.[171] Thirdly, gratitude functions as a moral or prosocial motivator when recipients of gifts are inclined to enhance the welfare of the benefactor.[172] Just as grudges maintain a hostile orientation in relationships, so gratitude facilitates positive and healthy relationships.[173]

Gratitude not only generates positive feelings towards others, it forges social bonds and relationships by fueling reciprocal altruism and motivates

164. Emmons, *Thanks*, 178.
165. Emmons, *Thanks*, 180.
166. Emmons, *Thanks*, 164.
167. Wiesel quoted in Emmons, *Thanks*, 183.
168. Emmons, *Thanks*, 165.
169. Emmons, *Thanks*, 171.
170. McCullough and Tsang, "Parent of the Virtues?," 126.
171. McCullough and Tsang, "Parent of the Virtues?," 129. Relatedly, servers who write "thank you" on a restaurant bill are more likely to receive greater tips than those who do not (McCullough and Tsang, "Parent of the Virtues?," 129).
172. McCullough and Tsang, "Parent of the Virtues?," 128
173. McCullough and Tsang, "Parent of the Virtues?," 124.

faithfulness in existing relationships, especially those in which commensurate reciprocity is impossible (e.g., a child's loyalty to parents).[174] Consumerism, on the other hand, is destructive to relationships because it fuels ingratitude. Consumer psychologists indicate that much of advertising creates a wedge between parents and children by depicting parents as outdated and out of touch. "Gratitude can serve as a firewall of protection," Emmons writes, "against some of the effects of these insidious advertising messages."[175] Psychologist John Gottman discovered that marriages were far more likely to survive with high "positivity ratios" (i.e., positivity in emotion and speech-acts outpacing related negativity), the implications of which enabled him, when observing couples in his marriage lab, to predict with 90 percent accuracy whether the marriage would last.[176] For Gottman, one of the chief ways to create a positivity ratio is through the practice of gratitude.[177]

Moreover, the practice of gratitude contributes to one's physical health. Some surmise that as much as 75 percent of our longevity is predicated on psychological/behavioral variables.[178] Those who are prone to anger, for instance, are three times more likely to have a heart attack than those who are not.[179] In emotional responses such as anger or frustration, our heart rhythms become irregular and jagged, our blood pressure rises, and our blood vessels constrict. In emotional responses such as love and appreciation, however, the heart produces smooth rhythms indicating "cardiovascular efficiency" and generating "enhanced immunity."[180] In fact, positive emotions have the capacity to repair damage done by negative emotions by "restoring physiological and emotional balance."[181] Studies repeatedly demonstrate, for instance, that exercises in positive emotion generate positive and measurable changes, including increased immunoglobulin (a vital antibody) and decreased cortisol (a stress hormone).[182] In one study lasting a number of weeks, participants who were required to identify five things

---

174. Frederickson, "Gratitude," 151. See also Emmons, *Thanks*, 45.

175. Emmons, *Thanks*, 43. Similar studies involving women in relationships looking at pornographic images of attractive men did not generate the same results, i.e., there was no change in terms of their views of husbands or boyfriends.

176. Emmons, *Thanks*, 46.

177. Emmons, *Thanks*, 46.

178. Emmons, *Thanks*, 66.

179. Emmons, *Thanks*, 64. "Negative emotions create a chain reaction in the body—blood vessels constrict, blood pressure rises, and the immune system is weakened" (Emmons, *Thanks*, 71).

180. Emmons, *Thanks*, 72–73.

181. Emmons, *Thanks*, 74.

182. Emmons, *Thanks*, 73.

for which they were grateful reported fewer physical complaints and more frequent physical exercise than those required to identify five hassles or stressors.[183] Other studies suggest that gratitude also has the capacity to reduce pain ratings among those whose suffering is chronic.[184]

How do positive psychologists account for ingratitude? Some point to what is termed "a negativity bias," a predisposition to be pessimistic that generally translates into diminished gratitude.[185] Gratitude can also be resisted in scenarios where the recipient believes the gift violated boundaries (e.g., to manipulate a decision) or feels psychological conflict (e.g., anger and indebtedness to a parent) or fears that gratitude implies approval of what the donor does (e.g., a gift from a drug dealer).[186] Other obstacles to gratitude include comparison thinking, which incites envy and resentment, and the perception of victimhood.[187] Similarly, narcissism impedes gratitude because "if one is entitled to everything, then one is thankful for nothing."[188] Though narcissists can be grateful, studies reveal they are less grateful than others, are more grateful for things than for people, and have lower "gratitude density," i.e., are grateful to fewer people on average.[189] One study demonstrated that when people displayed high scores on Narcissistic Personality Inventory on account of feelings of pride, for example, and competency, they were less likely to be grateful.[190]

Appraisal

The positive psychological account of gratitude is fruitful for theological reflection. First, its depiction of how gratitude emerges warrants a construal of gratitude that includes vision or perception. In the progress of Western civilization, as chapter 1 documented, gratitude became increasingly seen as an emotion, a recognition endorsed by positive psychology. If an emotion is, as Roberts defines it, "a concern based construal," then gratitude is

---

183. Frederickson, "Gratitude," 156.
184. Emmons, *Thanks*, 76.
185. Emmons, *Thanks*, 127.
186. Emmons, *Thanks*, 131–36.
187. Emmons, *Thanks*, 136–37. Emmons reports on studies concluding that the psychological industry, by "manufacturing victims" incites resentment and retaliatory impulses rather than gratitude. Emmons indicates that the positive psychology movement is a corrective to this mentality.
188. Emmons, *Thanks*, 150.
189. Emmons, *Thanks*, 152.
190. McCullough and Tsang, "Parent of the Virtues?," 131.

an emotion which construes a situation in a particular way—namely, that one is the recipient of a gift.[191] Secondly, gratitude is understood by positive psychologists as an "action-tendency." This corresponds to what Roberts calls "an emotion-disposition," an inclination to act in accord with how one construes the world.[192] If one conceives of virtue as a character trait disposing one to proper emotions and conduct, perhaps gratitude can be understood a virtue that evolves from a way of seeing the world that subsequently disposes one to proper grateful emotions.

Thirdly, the moral value of gratitude for positive psychologists is often located in its benefits more than in its justice or appropriateness. To a degree, Emmons and others are guilty of the naturalistic fallacy in which what "ought" to be is derived from what "is." That gratitude generates all sorts of psychological, physiological, and social benefits and impedes several unhealthy behaviors does not prove its moral necessity. On the other hand, the wealth of data accumulated by Emmons and others is strongly suggestive of gratitude's moral necessity. A full portrait of gratitude, I contend, is not possible without an affirmation of an ontology of communion in which people are situated not only in relationships with each other and the world, but with God himself. It seems that Emmons, in his psychological portrait of gratitude, approaches this ontology very closely in the sense that gratitude is for him a counter-cultural force because it challenges "the illusion of self-sufficiency" and enables people not only to see themselves "as part of a larger, intricate network of sustaining relationships" but to affirm "dependency on others."[193] "Until this dependence is acknowledged," Emmons concludes, "gratitude remains a potentiality at best."[194] To add the prepositional phrase "on God" to the noun "dependence" is nearly to complete the picture.

If one's construal of gratitude excludes God, gratitude is necessarily shortchanged and one is unable to recognize that the value of self, things, and others—all gifts—is derived especially from their creation by God. This book will argue that any conception of gratitude that excludes a notion of God as creator and redeemer is ultimately inhospitable to gratitude. One's perspective on life, especially for Christian believers, is shaped by the recognition of God's sovereignty, his creation, and his purposes. From a strictly positive psychological perspective, it seems unlikely that one could or should be grateful in a life defined by suffering, a life in which tragedy yields no apparent benefits.

191. Roberts, *Spiritual Emotions*, 11, 132–33.
192. Roberts, *Spiritual Emotions*, 13.
193. Emmons, *Thanks*, 54.
194. Emmons, *Thanks*, 54.

CONCLUSION: A PRELIMINARY PROFILE OF GRATITUDE

Having interacted with the demurrals of Aristotle and Derrida, and the positive psychological depiction, a preliminary profile of gratitude will now be offered. It is apparent from the discussion above that philosophical systems which morally devalue gratitude are inclined to regard it as reciprocation approximating repayment in a commercial sense. For Aristotle, gifts require returns, and thereby subject their recipients to unwelcome relationships in which they must repay the giver. For Derrida, on the other hand, gifts do not require returns because all returns are forms of repayment that annul the gift. Since gratitude is a return for a gift it is poisonous. In what follows, I will argue contra Aristotle and Derrida that the reciprocation inherent in gratitude is distinct from repayment in a commercial context. In so doing, I will engage especially Terence McConnell and Robert Roberts, both of whom have written extensively on gratitude from largely philosophical perspectives.

To obtain a commodity or service from a vendor in the realm of commerce, one must pay the price set by the vendor. Outside of purchase, there are no alternatives to obtaining a vendor's product. One is therefore constrained to pay the price, and such payment is ordinarily immediate and unaccompanied by delight. Gratitude, however, is freely and gladly extended by beneficiaries and not because of expectations set forth by a benefactor who has no legal or moral duty to give and has not made demands for a return.[195] "Before I give you a gift," Volf argues, "I can't tell you what I want in return and when; if I did, I wouldn't be giving a gift, but proposing a deal."[196]

The extent to which gratitude is fitting depends in part on the extent to which the benefit received is a gift. McConnell rightly argues that the duty to give on the part of the donor does not always preclude the appropriateness of a grateful response, surmising that gratitude is still owed a lifeguard who saves a drowning person when he or she is hired to save those who are drowning.[197] Though this is the lifeguard's general obligation, he or she has succeeded in fulfilling it in a personal way that involves special effort (perhaps even risk) on his or her part that constitute his or her action as a gift. By itself, special effort on the part of the benefactor, however, is not necessary for gratitude to be a fitting response. If, as McConnell suggests, you oblige the request of a colleague struggling with severe depression to stay by the

---

195. McConnell, *Gratitude*, 5. See also, Roberts, "Blessings of Gratitude," 61.
196. Volf, *Free of Charge*, 40.
197. McConnell, *Gratitude*, 16.

phone at night when your typical evening activity involves reading beside the phone, you are still owed gratitude.[198] For McConnell, gratitude is only owed if a gift is given gratuitously and not exclusively out of self-interest. A person who saves you in order to kill you in a more painful way is not owed gratitude, but a person who saves you in order to be a hero is, McConnell surmises, because the latter gift is gratuitous, even though it includes self-interest.[199]

It is difficult to imagine how Roberts would evaluate these scenarios since he argues that gratitude is only owed to those from whom we want to receive a benefit because to be grateful is to be willingly indebted and happily "bound" (i.e., gratified) to someone so as to reciprocate by a return of some sort.[200] "To have the virtue of gratitude is to be disposed," Roberts argues, "not just to be grateful, but to be grateful in the right way, to the right people, for the right things."[201] Such a view of gratitude, however, seems parsimonious. It seems that gratitude can and should be given to parties from whom we do not want to receive a benefit. Perhaps what makes the scenario objectionable is Roberts's previous assertion that gratitude involves being "bound" to those to whom one reciprocates with gratitude. The language of "binding" is too suggestive of commerce.

For gratitude to be appropriate, must the gift have been desired? Should one not be grateful to one's grandmother, for example, who lovingly gives cookies one does not want? Roberts argues that gratitude is not possible in scenarios where the gift is "repugnant," but does insist that one can be grateful for the "thought" rather than the gift, if given with good intentions.[202] But if it is the "thought" that counts—assuming the thought is a kind one—how can an unwanted gift be "repugnant"? McConnell insists that gratitude is owed so long as the gift is received, regardless of one's feelings about the gift or toward the benefactor.[203] If the gift is such a significant benefit, e.g., tuition for an unwanted college education, and one receives it,

---

198. McConnell, *Gratitude*, 18.

199. McConnell, *Gratitude*, 23.

200. Roberts, "Blessings of Gratitude," 63. Gratitude is inappropriate when the recipient has no desire to be "indebted" to the giver (Roberts, "Virtues and Rules," 335).

201. Roberts, "Blessings of Gratitude," 61. Similarly, Visser, "Expressing gratitude that is not meant and returning a favour entirely out of duty may be polite, but they do not constitute gratitude" (Visser, *Gift of Thanks*, 329). McConnell similarly argues that if a person shows gratitude begrudgingly for no fault of his own, for instance, it seems that a negative moral assessment is still required (McConnell, *Gratitude*, 91).

202. Roberts, "Virtues and Rules," 335.

203. McConnell, *Gratitude*, 39.

even if unwillingly, McConnell argues, one should be grateful.[204] Such delimitations of gratitude, however, seem incongruent with the general Christian ethic of loving one's enemies, esteeming others better than oneself, and living peaceably with all people. In other words, one should be disposed to gratitude for unwanted gifts because one should be disposed to viewing unwanted donors charitably.

Given the variables discussed above, McConnell presents the following account of gratitude:

> A person discharges a debt of gratitude to another when she acknowledges and appreciates what the other has done, is prepared to provide the benefactor willingly with a commensurate benefit if the proper occasion for doing so arises, and does so because she (or a loved one) has been benefited by the other.[205]

With this definition McConnell has distinguished "debt of gratitude" from commercial repayment, but insufficiently so. Though he has accented the gratuitous feature of gratitude, the language he uses is still indicative of a commercial relationship. The language of "discharges a debt," for instance, implies a burden, and the language of "commensurate benefit" resembles repayment. In fact, there is little in his account of gratitude that would exclude a commercial transaction.

Robert Roberts defines gratitude similarly, but distinctively: "To experience gratitude is gladly to construe some person as giver of some benefice (gift) to oneself, and thus gladly to construe oneself as recipient of some benefice from a benefactor, and thus as a kind of debtor."[206] The advantage that Roberts's definition has, and its distinctive accent, is the willingness and delight of the beneficiary to be in relationship with the benefactor. This sharply distinguishes the reciprocity in gratitude from the reciprocity of repayment since repayment implies no such relationship. Both McConnell and Roberts underscore the voluntary, intentional, joyful, and social dimensions of gratitude, though for Roberts the reciprocal motion of the recipient is more personal or relational.

---

204. McConnell, *Gratitude*, 34–35. McConnell also grants that in a scenario in which you do not receive the benefit someone attempted to give (e.g., find you a job), the very attempt to provide a benefit can be grounds for gratitude (McConnell, *Gratitude*, 42).

205. McConnell, *Gratitude*, 56. Relatedly, McConnell identifies four moral failures with respect to gratitude: One can (a) fail to appreciate the toll it took for someone to provide a benefit or (b) fail to return to a benefactor, where appropriate, a commensurate benefit or (c) return a benefit to a benefactor grudgingly or (d) return a benefit to a benefactor for the wrong reason (McConnell, *Gratitude*, 55–56).

206. Roberts, "Virtues and Rules," 334.

Roberts's definition, however, does not account for why a recipient would happily construe someone as giver of a gift and oneself as recipient. Using the language of "discharging a debt" and providing, ideally, a "commensurate benefit," McConnell does, though unsatisfactorily. I would argue that the objective of gratitude is *peaceable* and *fitting*. Put differently, gratitude seeks a relationship of harmony (i.e., peaceable) with the giver that is just (i.e., fitting). McConnell's term "commensurate" approaches the notion of "fitting" or "just" but approximates "proportional." In terms of gratitude, however, justice does not require proportionality, or even make it an ideal to be attained. To insist on proportionality as the ideal return is to approach the category of repayment.

Given the discussion above, gratitude has several salient features, all of which are italicized in what follows. Gratitude, first of all, implies a prior action (i.e., the giving of a gift) and thus is preeminently *responsive*. Attempts to re-define gratitude in non-responsive ways as mere appreciation, for instance, involve more than a benign category mistake. Such redefinitions can easily be conscripted in support of an atheistic worldview. Along these lines, Robert C. Solomon recently expressed interest in the question, to whom should an atheist feel cosmic gratitude?[207] Even among those who define gratitude as an emotion, many insist it must have an object (i.e., someone or something to thank). Being grateful to the "universe" or to "destiny" are "limp" solutions, Solomon suggests, and instances of "manufacturing an evasive impersonal agent" to whom one can be thankful.[208] Solomon suggests, in order to answer his question, that gratitude should not simply be conceived in terms of interpersonal relationships, but as a "philosophical emotion."[209] This is comparable, Solomon conjectures, to being grateful to a stranger one will never see again. How should we conceive of this philosophical emotion? Solomon describes it as "being aware of one's whole life" and in so doing recognizing "how much of life is out of one's hands, how many advantages one owes to other people."[210] If gratitude is mere awareness, however, it no longer presupposes a gift from another. If it no longer presupposes a gift from another, it may be appreciation, but it is not gratitude.

The same critique applies to Oliver Sacks's wonderful memoir, *Gratitude*, written on the eve of his death. Sacks expresses his *joie de vivre*, his affirmation of life. "I am grateful," he writes, "that I have experienced many

---

207. Solomon, "Foreword," vii.
208. Solomon, "Foreword," ix.
209. Solomon, "Foreword," ix.
210. Solomon, "Foreword," ix–x.

things."[211] As death became imminent, he wrote, "I cannot pretend I am without fear. But my predominant feeling is one of gratitude. I have loved and have been loved; I have given much and I have been given much in return; I have read and travelled and thought and written. I have had an intercourse with the world, the special intercourse of writers and readers."[212] What Sacks is referring to here might be termed an appreciative awareness of life, and in particular its goodness, but, because it does not acknowledge a gift or respond to a giver, falls short of gratitude.

The response of gratitude, furthermore, is given freely. Unlike commercial transactions in which repayment is strictly owed, recipients freely chose to reciprocate. Donors should not demand gratitude and recipients should not show gratitude merely because it is fitting. These are exactly the dimensions involved in love, and precisely those variables that pose a dilemma. Robert Bellah et al. explain,

> The sharing and commitment in a love relationship can seem, for some, to swallow up the individual, making her (more often than him) lose sight of her own interests, opinions, and desires. Paradoxically, since love is supposed to be a spontaneous choice by free individuals, someone who has 'lost' herself cannot really love, or cannot contribute to a real love relationship.[213]

The free response of gratitude is also joyful. For Cicero and Seneca, gratitude was exclusively an action, and therefore not a feeling.[214] Yet gratitude is, as positive psychology has underscored, an emotion and particularly a positive emotion. The grateful person sees oneself as the recipient of a gift and that perception is a joyful one. As Roberts argued (see above), the grateful person is happily connected to the donor.

Also unlike any business transaction, gratitude salutes the giver in order to perpetuate a personal relationship. To reciprocate a benefit with no interest in a relationship with the benefactor is to complete a commercial transaction. It is analogous to tipping in which a return gift for service ends both the business transaction and the relationship to the server.[215] Even gratitude to a lifeguard who saves out of duty is personally motivated, though a meaningful relationship might prove impossible. This is perhaps most apparent by considering ingratitude (and not simply non-gratitude).[216]

---

211. Sacks, *Gratitude*, 7.
212. Sacks, *Gratitude*, 20.
213. Bellah et al., *Habits of the Heart*, 93.
214. Visser, *Gift of Thanks*, 326.
215. Visser, *Gift of Thanks*, 249.
216. By non-gratitude I mean the omission of thanks in negligence; by ingratitude I mean a deliberate refusal to give thanks.

To reject a gift is to reject a person, and to ignore a dinner invitation is a hostile response.[217] Gratitude, in other words, should be given randomly, haphazardly or with disinterest (*pace* Derrida). Gratitude requires one to look beyond gift to giver, and the recipient freely consents to a relationship with the donor (accepting is thus generous).[218]

Finally, the responsive salute of gratitude is peaceable, fittingly directed to a particular giver. The absence of gratitude, in other words, suggests that something is morally amiss. Gratitude seeks harmony, equity, and equilibrium in a seemingly "unequal" relationship with the consequence that both parties are givers and receivers. In North American culture, gratitude functions much like greeting or apologizing, instances of what linguists call "conversational routines."[219] It is part of an exchange and plays "a compensatory role" such that refusals to say "thanks" can create imbalance and provoke hostility.[220] There is a sense in which a gift indebts a recipient and distorts moral equilibrium. Equilibrium is restored by gratitude, however, not through payment, but through a "token" gesture, the value of which does not compensate for the gift.[221]

I will argue that gratitude as agapic, a variant of love, and as such escapes many of its critiques, particularly those advanced by Derrida and Marion.[222] To speak of a "debt" of gratitude, for example, complies with the apostle Paul's exhortation in Romans to "owe" no one anything but love. Furthermore, the reciprocation of love, far from poisoning the original gesture of love, is precisely the response such a gesture endeavors to elicit.

It is precisely this claim that Aldo de Martelaere disputes in his warnings about the dangers of gratitude. Reflecting on Marcel Mauss's theory that gifts are reciprocal, de Martelaere disputes the universality of Mauss's claim that gifts imply obligations to give, to receive, and to return.[223] Though he sees good reasons to construe love as a gift, he denies the threefold obligation to love, to accept love, and to return love. In reverse order, the obligation to return someone's love, for de Martelaere, seems absurd on the surface and would likely lead people to feign love. To accept love seems reasonable to de

217. Visser, *Gift of Thanks*, 109.
218. Visser, *Gift of Thanks*, 452.
219. Visser, *Gift of Thanks*, 11.
220. Visser, *Gift of Thanks*, 63.
221. The language of "token" for gratitude is helpfully introduced in Roberts, *Spiritual Emotion*, 136.
222. Visser acknowledges this point in claiming that gratitude, to function well, "cannot stand on its own, but needs to grow from other virtues, principally love and justice, that must come first" (Visser, *Gift of Thanks*, 417).
223. de Martelaere, "Personal Obligations," 209–25.

Martelaere but only if one loves the lover in return. Without return love, the acceptance of love is at best insincere (i.e., communicating a false impression) and at worst immoral (i.e., taking advantage of someone). Lastly, de Martelaere addresses the question whether there is an obligation to love in the first place. Whereas returning love and accepting love concern someone else (for whom the possibility of manipulation or deception exists), the act of love concerns oneself. Here de Martelaere argues in a complex manner that the obligation to love necessarily presupposes the existence of love.[224] Apart from general obligations one has to everyone (e.g., not to kill) there are special obligations one might have to those with whom one is in a personal relationship, but "the reason why one has those obligations is love."[225]

The above discussion leads de Martelaere to consider whether there are gifts for which Mauss's three obligations do apply. He answers affirmatively, pointing to gratitude which obliges people "to be grateful and to act out of gratitude (analogous to the obligations to accept and to return)."[226] In these instances, the beneficiary is obligated because of something done by someone else. From this assessment, de Martelaere sharply distinguishes gratitude from love and cautions his reader "to be careful in giving a place to gratitude in personal relations."[227] Though he concedes that they are not "utterly incompatible," a tension exists between love and gratitude "which implies that gratitude must never get too firm a foothold in a personal relation. Too much gratitude, I think, ruins love and hence destroys the personal relation."[228] Though he fails to explain precisely why gratitude has the capacity to "ruin" and "destroy," the implication is that the language of obligations, appropriate for gratitude, assumes an economic relationship or market transaction outside of which love ought to operate.

Rather than think of love and gratitude as distinct, however, one should see gratitude as a subset of love. This becomes viable especially when one considers the phenomenon of gifts of romantic love. For de Martelaere,

224. de Martelaere defines love as an emotion (which seemingly overtakes a passive subject and over which she seemingly has no choice) (de Martelaere, "Personal Obligations," 210). Defining love as emotion, however, makes it extraordinarily difficult to speak of love as a duty. "What is done in a personal relation *falls outside* the scope of economics, morality, and law" since, unlike market transactions, what one does out of love in a personal relationship, for de Martelaere, is unconditional, non-obligatory, and unenforceable (de Martelaere, "Personal Obligations," 214–15). It seems far better to define love as a duty which, in the context of personal relations, is ordinarily invested with emotion.

225. de Martelaere, "Personal Obligations," 217.
226. de Martelaere, "Personal Obligations," 224.
227. de Martelaere, "Personal Obligations," 224.
228. de Martelaere, "Personal Obligations," 224–25.

love per se is not a gift that demands reciprocation, though a gift per se does. If one conceives of a gift of love or love as a gift, however, then one can grant that it ought to be reciprocated. The mutuality of love seemingly transcends the reciprocity of commercial transactions.

Putting all these ingredients together, I define gratitude as a responsive virtue in which one, seeing oneself as the recipient of a gift, freely and joyfully salutes the giver in order to perpetuate a personal and peaceable relationship. Gratitude so conceived is a potential solvent for distorted and destructive desires.

CHAPTER 4

A THEOLOGICAL PROFILE OF GRATITUDE

To claim that Christians historically have had a positive appraisal of gratitude is unsurprising. According to Brian Gerrish, "true religion," for the celebrated church father Augustine, "was gratitude for our justification."[1] Such regard for gratitude seemingly comports with the mindset of the apostle Paul who, according to Paul Schubert, "mentions the subject of thanksgiving more frequently per page than any other Hellenistic author, pagan or Christian."[2] On the other hand, there are grounds for bridling enthusiasm about a Christian appraisal of gratitude. Claus Westermann concluded that the concept of thanksgiving is absent in the Old Testament.[3]

Moreover, the value of interpersonal gratitude is relativized by several biblical scholars and theologians. New Testament scholar David Pao, for instance, argues that gratitude, though morally important, is limited in scope, "reserved for God and not human beings."[4] Arguing similarly that, biblically speaking, "recipients owe thanks and grateful service not to the giver but to God."[5] Peter Leithart contends that "Christians introduced a corrosive ingratitude."[6] Though circumscribed by an infinite circle (i.e., God rewards those who give), gift-giving in Scripture, for Leithart, is linear

1. Gerrish, *Grace and Gratitude*, ix.
2. Schubert, *Form and Function*, 41.
3. Westermann, *Praise of God in the Psalms*, 25.
4. Pao, *Thanksgiving*, 20.
5. Leithart, *Gratitude*, 7.
6. Leithart, *Gratitude*, 6.

(i.e., without the expectation of human returns). Gratitude, he claims, is nowhere presented in Scripture as reciprocation, response, or return for human gifts, but only "as right use of the gift."[7] An extreme version of this approach, in which one hears echoes of Derrida's position, is the economy of grace recommended by Kathryn Tanner who insists that God's giving is unilateral and unconditional:

> Indeed, the meaning of giving is proved, almost refined, by efforts to exclude from it all aspects of loan and sale. *No reciprocity or exchange is at all necessary for it.* A gift is offered freely and not as any kind of tit-for-tat, certainly not a return for services rendered. It comes with no strings attached of an obligatory kind, as loans do; you are free to respond as you like and only if you feel like it. A gift is offered for nothing, without compensation, apart from any consideration of a return being made for it. Giving is *completely disinterested*, without self-concern, solely for the well-being or pleasure of others.[8]

Tanner further clarifies that in an economy of grace one need not worry so much about motives or the extent to which giving is disinterested. Giving, in the economy of grace, is not simply unconditioned by payments or returns, it is at a structural level unconditional, without any conditions.[9] God's giving is unilateral, and returns to him are unnecessary: "God's purpose in giving is to benefit creatures, and therefore the proper return for God's giving is not so much directed back to God as directed to those creatures.... A proper return displays what the gifts of God are good for."[10]

This practical theological inquiry endeavors to rethink gratitude theologically in order to renew its practice. Attention is given to both theological and non-theological texts or voices, though both are approached with a hermeneutic of suspicion in the recognition that human fallenness has potential to misconstrue and misinterpret reality. In the previous chapter, hospitality was extended to divergent voices in philosophy and psychology to bring clarity to the nature of gratitude, what it means, and whether it is virtuous. There it became apparent that, within the history of philosophy at least, gratitude is not without its detractors. Convinced that the reception

---

7. Leithart, *Gratitude*, 71. See Leithart, *Gratitude*, 7. "In Paul, the proper reception of gifts includes the giving of thanks to God, but he accents making good use of the gift" (Leithart, *Gratitude*, 6). This point itself is indisputable; the question that concerns me is whether gratitude is reciprocation or return.

8. Tanner, *Economy of Grace*, 57 (emphasis added).

9. Tanner, *Economy of Grace*, 62.

10. Tanner, *Economy of Grace*, 68–69.

of gifts implied weakness and inferiority, Aristotle did not celebrate gratitude while Derrida, convinced that any return for a gift amounts to repayment and as such nullifies the gift, essentially condemned gratitude. Both Aristotle and Derrida view gratitude in terms of reciprocal repayment. For Aristotle, the reciprocal repayment of gratitude is dishonorable; for Derrida, it is immoral.

The previous chapter also demonstrated how contemporary positive psychologists are far more affirmative of gratitude, and their research invites theological reflection on gratitude as an emotion, for instance. Ultimately, a merely psychological account of gratitude, by excising God from the picture, is inhospitable to gratitude. Engaging the deconstructions of gratitude by Aristotle and Derrida and the reduction of gratitude by positive psychology, this chapter will present a constructive proposal of gratitude through theological reflection nested in the metanarrative of Scripture. Among others, the following questions will be addressed: What does the Bible say about gratitude? What is peculiar about Christian gratitude? What function does gratitude have in the Christian life? To answer these questions, this chapter will investigate how gratitude is depicted in Scripture. Furthermore, this chapter will develop the views of prominent theologians, beginning with Thomas Aquinas, an attractive conversation partner given his Aristotelianism and the critique of Aristotle in the previous chapter. From Aquinas, this chapter moves to John Calvin, the magisterial sixteenth-century reformer who framed the Christian life in terms of gratitude. This chapter also considers the theology of Karl Barth, arguably the most prolific of twentieth-century theologians, who as an admirer of Calvin's theology demurred somewhat from his theology of gratitude. Finally, this chapter concludes with theological reflection on gratitude in terms of the material assembled thus far in order to present a seven-fold theological profile of gratitude. This book argues that gratitude is a responsive virtue in which one, seeing oneself as the recipient of a gift, freely and joyfully salutes the giver in order to perpetuate a personal and peaceable relationship.

GRATITUDE IN THE NARRATIVE OF SCRIPTURE

Consideration of gratitude in terms of the narrative of Scripture will proceed along the lines of what N.T. Wright regards as the five acts of the biblical story: Creation, Fall, Israel, Jesus, and the Church (the first scene of includes much of the New Testament).[11]

---

11. Wright, *New Testament*, 141.

Creation

The creation account of Genesis 1 indicates that humanity is created in the image of God. Significantly, God speaks in the plural in indicating this intent: "Let us make humankind in our image, according to our likeness" (Gen 1:26). The prototype for the image humanity bears, therefore, is the Triune God. In order to understand something of human identity and ontology one must be familiar with the dynamics of the Trinity.

The doctrine of the Trinity has been significantly revived in recent years. Early Trinitarian debates revolved around a metaphysics of substance and subsequent theological reflection followed suit. In recent years, however, a theological shift has occurred in which "*relationship* has replaced *substance* as the central term."[12] This has generated what has been termed an "ontology of communion" in which the three Persons of the Trinity cannot be separated ontologically, but form part of "one ontological dynamic," or what John Zizioulas calls "being as communion."[13] Moreover, the theological focus today is less on intra-Trinitarian relationships and more on how the Trinity relates to the world, less on the so-called ontological or immanent Trinity (God *in se*) and more on the so-called economic Trinity (God *ad extra*).[14]

How do the Persons of the Trinity relate to each other? The term *perichoresis*, first used by Gregory of Nazianzus (d. 390), captures a theological concept regarding the Trinity denoting "the conjunction of unity and distinction, stability and dynamism, symmetry and asymmetry."[15] If we suppose that the Trinity is involved in the world today as a "mutually involved personal dynamic," Gunton argues, "it would appear to follow that in eternity Father, Son and Spirit share a dynamic mutual reciprocity,

---

12. Pembroke, *Renewing Pastoral Practice*, 8. This is the fruit of especially the Trinitarian reflection of the Cappadocian theologians, e.g., Basil the Great (d. 379), Gregory of Nyssa (d. 394), and Gregory of Nazianzus (d. 390).

13. Gunton, *One, Three, and Many*, 214. "The Father gives the Son, whose being and will is inseparable from his. He and the Father are one, while he is also sent to do the will of the Father on earth. After his glorification, the Son will ask the Father to send the Spirit who will perform towards the church and the world similar and yet distinct functions, again without a suggestion that anything is *individual action*. God appears to be conceived neither as a collectivity nor as an individual, but as a communion, a unity of persons in relation" (*One, Three, and Many*, 215). See also Zizioulas, *Being as Communion*.

14. Webb, "Christian Giving," 341. Karl Rahner famously argued that the economic Trinity is the immanent Trinity (Rahner, *Trinity*, 22).

15. Harrison, "Perichoresis," 63.

interpenetration and interanimation."[16] The doctrine of perichoresis, in other words, "implies that the three persons of the Trinity exist only in reciprocal eternal relatedness."[17]

The symmetry of this indwelling, first of all, is captured by ways in which the persons of the Trinity give lavishly to each other. "The Father gives all that he is to the Son," Verna Harrison writes. "In return, the Son gives all that he is to the Father, and the Holy Spirit, too, is united to the others in mutual self giving. This relationship among the persons is an eternal rest in each other but also an eternal movement of love, though without change or process."[18] In addition to symmetry in terms of their mutual dwelling, there is also asymmetry in terms of the priority of the Father as the origin of the Son and Spirit. Moreover, Gunton claims, there is "a dynamic personal order of giving and receiving" which, because giving prioritizes receiving, is "asymmetrical rather than merely reciprocal."[19]

If humanity is created in the image of God, it follows "that human beings should in some way be perichoretic beings."[20] Analogy is not identity, however, and human perichoresis must be distinct from divine perichoresis. Gunton helpfully distinguishes between God who *is* spirit and humans who *have* spirit.[21] As the Spirit opens the person of the Trinity to each other, we are open to God, others, and the world, though our openness is not unqualified. Human beings are "able to relate, to love, hate, cherish, exploit, to enter into relations that enslave them and to be redeemed for relations that do not by the love of God."[22] Yet like the Trinity, humanity has no being apart from

16. Gunton, *One, Three, and Many*, 163. Prior to the creation of the world, "the Trinitarian God is already full of fellowship, joy, and glory, and requires no sacrifice of worldly love—no commerce of totality—to make his glory replete; the world adds nothing to the triune God" (Hart, *Beauty of Infinite*, 255).

17. Gunton, *One, Three, and Many*, 164. Many of the biblical texts behind the notion of perichoresis are found in the Gospel of John, including John 1:18; 10:37–38; 14:9–11, 20; 17:20–23.

18. Harrison, "Perichoresis," 64. "The life of God is a life of self-giving and other-receiving love. As a consequence, the identify of each Trinitarian person cannot be defined apart from the other persons" (Volf, *Exclusion and Embrace*, 128).

19. Gunton, *One, Three, and Many*, 225.

20. Gunton, *One, Three, and Many*, 168. "We are what we are in perichoretic reciprocity" (Gunton, *One, Three, and Many*, 170). Gunton in fact argues that we live in a perichoretic universe, as opposed to a mechanistic universe. We are related to each other, in other words, and we are related to everything else (Gunton, *One, Three, and Many*, 173). The universe, after all, is not held together by something, but by someone, the one "through whom, in the unity of the Father and the Spirit, all things have their being" (Gunton, *One, Three, and Many*, 179).

21. Gunton, *One, Three, and Many*, 188.

22. Gunton, *One, Three, and Many*, 188.

being-in-relation. "The merely *individual* state," Gunton writes, "is a denial of human fullness."[23] Further, "the heart of human being and action is a relationality whose dynamic is that of gift and reception."[24] Yet the gift and response is non-reciprocal, for Gunton, since for both divine and human giving the term "sacrifice" is used.[25]

The Trinity, however, is not simply the model for human ontology. The triune God accounts for life and defines human identity and purpose. "God's being is in giving," according to Stephen Webb, and "giving is who God is."[26] "Our personhood," Webb further claims, "is the result of God's giving, just as God is God because God gives."[27] We have no existence apart from God's gift of life. "God encompasses the whole trajectory of the gift" and as such "is thoroughly involved in the origin, use, and return of God's gifts."[28] God is the *giver*, and he gives selectively and deliberately, freely and extravagantly as the source of all we are and have. He is also the *given*, especially in his Son Jesus Christ, through whom we understand and enjoy his other gifts. He is thirdly the *giving*, inclusive of our ability to return gifts to God, so that when we give we participate in the ongoing life of the Trinity. Here Webb envisions especially the Holy Spirit who not only bonds together Father and Son, but who overflows into the world (Rom 5:5).[29]

In response to God's giving up his Son and the Son laying down his life, we are to present ourselves by the giving power of his Spirit as "living sacrifices" (Rom 12:1).[30] The notion of sacrifice is bound up with the notion of gift and it is only because of the Fall that the sacrifice of Christ, for example, requires the spilling of blood.[31] Similarly, the objective of life is to "give" in praising God, though prior to the unveiling of the new earth, this giving will be practiced in terms of toil and carrying one's cross.[32] "The

---

23. Gunton, *One, Three, and Many*, 216.

24. Gunton, *One, Three, and Many*, 225.

25. Gunton, *One, Three, and Many*, 225. The word "sacrifice" fittingly describes all three forms of giving The Father "gives up" the Son and the Son "lays down" his life and Spirit-enabled believers present their bodies to God as a "living sacrifice" (See Gunton, *One, Three, and Many*, 225). "The very nature of the triune God is reflected on the cross of Christ" (Volf, *Exclusion and Embrace*, 127).

26. Webb, "Christian Giving," 342.

27. Webb, "Christian Giving," 342.

28. Webb, "Christian Giving," 343.

29. Webb, "Christian Giving," 345.

30. Gunton, *One, Three, and Many*, 225.

31. Gunton, *One, Three, and Many*, 225n19.

32. Gunton, *One, Three, and Many*, 226.

logic of sociality," Gunton writes, is "gift and reception," a reality that demonstrates that " the other is central for our being."[33]

For Gunton, "the true end of all human action" is to render to God "due response for his goodness."[34] This also has tremendous implications for our cultural activity in relation to the non-personal world.[35] All action should therefore be a sacrifice of praise and this means "that action toward the world is action directed to allowing that world truly to be itself before God."[36] Everything is related to God, and everything—truth, beauty, and goodness—can and should be offered to him. "It is for such reasons," Gunton writes, "that the practice of both art and the proper dominion of the natural order are Trinitarian imperatives, for both are ways of fulfilling the command of the creator to those created male and female in his image."[37] Humanity is conscripted for service by God, and redeemed humanity returns to the ends for which it was created. "The created world," Gunton claims, "becomes truly itselfmoves towards its completionwhen through Christ and the Spirit, it is presented perfect before the throne of the Father."[38]

All of life is a response to the Triune God's excessive gifts and yet the human response is not external to the Trinity. "We participate in the Trinitarian exchange," Milbank writes, "such that the divine gift only begins to be a gift to us at all (since in this case there is no neutral 'desert') after it has been received—which is to say returned with the return of gratitude and charitable giving-in-turn—by us."[39] As Todd Billings explains, "one gives the love one receives from God to one's neighbor even as one is receiving it from God. It is impossible to receive God's gift while refusing to give to one's neighbor."[40] This is what Milbank terms "active reception."[41] "As we

---

33. Gunton, *One, Three, and Many*, 227. "What we receive from and give to others is constitutive: not self-fulfillment but relation to the other as the other is the key to human being, universally (Gunton, *One, Three, and Many*, 227).

34. Gunton, *One, Three, and Many*, 227.

35. Whereas people in relation to each other or to God are marked by sociality, people and creation are marked by relationality because only "personal beings are social beings" (Gunton, *One, Three, and Many*, 229).

36. Gunton, *One, Three, and Many*, 227.

37. Gunton, *One, Three, and Many*, 228.

38. Gunton, *One, Three, and Many*, 231. "The sacrifice of praise which is the due human response to both creation and redemption takes the form of that culture that enables both personal and non-personal worlds to realize their being" (Gunton, *One, Three, and Many*, 231).

39. Milbank, "Can a Gift," 136.

40. Billings, "Milbank's Theology," 89. The term Coakley uses for Milbank is "participatory response" (Coakley, "Gift, Gender," 228n12).

41. Milbank, "Gregory of Nyssa," 95.

are drawn into the life of the Triune God," Stephen Fowl writes, "we find that the world is transformed in ways that tend to collapse any straightforward notions of gift, giver, and recipient."[42] God is preeminently a giver and his intra-Trinitarian love overflows into the world, enters lives, and invites human participation in his being.[43] Webb argues that

> true gifts create return gifts, but it does not follow that giving therefore is always controlled by a logic of equivalence, of measuring this for that. For the return response to be solicited, the gift itself must be excessive, wonderful, unexpected. My governing insight, then, is the following: *divine excess begets reciprocity*. Without excess, reciprocity becomes calculation, bartering, exchange; without reciprocity, excess becomes irrelevant, anarchic, and wasteful.[44]

Human participation in the life of the Trinity is located specifically in Christ, through whom there is access to the Father. This is apparent in, for example, 2 Corinthians 8 and 9 where Paul refers to Christ as God's "indescribable gift" (2 Cor 9:15) and speaks of Christ's "generous act" (2 Cor 8:9). The gift of Christ, for Paul, is "the definitive act of divine beneficence, *given without regard to worth*."[45] As recipients and beneficiaries of this definitive gift, believers participate in it freely and fully, sharing in the grace of Christ.[46] Believers, in other words, are called not simply to imitate God's display of grace but to embody it through participation in Christ.[47] Further, there is a sense in which for Paul "grace begets grace" so that "the reception of God's grace in Christ results in gracious acts."[48]

The implications of this for a theology of gratitude are immense. The first is that humanity, in terms of an ontology of communion, is inextricably situated in relationships of giving and receiving, first with the Triune God and then with other people. Secondly, the Trinity is both the model

---

42. Fowl, "Wealth, Property, and Theft," 459.

43. "The baptized are brought into relation with God and with each other in the same act, by virtue of sharing in communion with the one Father, mediated by the Son and realized in the Spirit. Those who are in Christ are in the church: brought into relation to God through him and into community simultaneously" (Gunton, *One, Three, and Many*, 218). "The divine desire that constitutes created beings ventures 'beyond' the Trinitarian dance only because that desire always possesses the generosity that gives differenced, the beauty that declares itself" (Hart, *Beauty of Infinite*, 256).

44. Webb, *Gifting God*, 90.

45. Barclay, *Paul and the Gift*, 350.

46. Gorman, *Becoming the Gospel*, 252.

47. Gorman, *Becoming the Gospel*, 252.

48. Dunn, *Theology of Paul*, 323.

for our giving and receiving and its matrix. Gifts within the Trinity are given, received, and returned in love without a hint of commerce. In terms of gratitude, this means that gifts should be "returned" in non-commercial ways even if the motive for giving is not a return. Thirdly, the definitive gift God gives is Christ, and those who receive the gift participate in it. The responsive return of gratitude to Christ for his self-gift and to God for the gift of Christ is never merely passive but involves participation in the gift, through the Spirit.

The Fall

Given the discussion above, one must recognize that relationality with God and others is not constructive, but is constructed, i.e., ontological. This means that already in the prelapsarian Garden of Eden, there is giving and receiving and that the fitting way for humanity to respond to the goodness of the Creator is through the response of praise that amounts to a kind of gratitude. Gratitude, therefore, has a primal quality. "The creation that is good (Gen 1)," Millar writes, "praises the Creator whose power and glory are reflected in the creation" for which praise language "may be viewed as the one speech that is truly primal and universal."[49] Unlike other responsive virtues, such as forgiveness, gratitude does not require the fall into sin. Moreover, it is not hard to imagine the appropriateness of gratitude in the beginning since the Genesis narrative indicates that Adam was placed into a generous and bountiful world of untarnished beauty.[50] His first words could have been "Thank you!" When the apostle Paul chronicles the sin of rebellious people in Romans 1, he references those "who though they knew God . . . did not honor him as God or give thanks to him" (Rom 1:21). There is a strong exegetical argument, Morna Hooker argues, for seeing Adam and Eve as within Paul's purview there and therefore for seeing ingratitude as the original sin.[51] Behind Paul's account, James D. G. Dunn similarly

---

49. Millar, "Enthroned on the Praises," 14. The praise of gratitude is elicited throughout the Old Testament not just among human individuals and communities, but in the entire cosmos (e.g., Ps 29; 148). The praise of the cosmos "de-divines" the natural world (Millar, "Enthroned on the Praises," 14).

50. I set aside peculiarly evangelical debates about whether the early chapters of Genesis are best construed as history or myth. In both scenarios, Adam is a paradigmatic figure in Scripture and the events of his life are regarded in subsequent revelation as crucial for theological reflection.

51. Morna Hooker argues that Paul has Adam and Eve in view as he chronicles the rebellion of wicked people in Romans 1 (Hooker, "Adams in Romans 1"). It is also possible that Paul envisions Adam in Rom 3:3 where sin results in one's deprivation of God's glory. "In every sin there is material ingratitude to God" (Aquinas, *Sum* 2–2.107.2ad1).

claims, "we should probably see the figure of Adam, the archetypal human who deliberately refused to give God his due, by refusing to obey God's one command."[52] Solomon Schimmel captures the sentiment perfectly: When God asked Adam if he had eaten from the forbidden tree, Adam responded with "hutzpah and ingratitude," blaming Eve.[53]

Because relations of giving and receiving are constructed and not constructive, there is a real sense in which ingratitude is the original sin. Adam did not respond to the gift with the return of gratitude and thereby offended the Creator and denied something about his ontology by virtue of creation. Just as gifts are lovingly returned within the Trinity, so humanity ought lovingly to return thanks to the Creator.

Israel

Given the claims above regarding human ontology and the logic of returning gifts, one would expect gratitude to be a dominant motif in the Old Testament. It is therefore surprising to note Claus Westermann's claim that since the εὐχαριστεῖν word-group is completely absent in canonical portions of the Septuagint the concept of thanksgiving is absent in the Old Testament.[54] David Pao rightly rejects this interpretation on the grounds that Israel responded to God's gifts with praise (תודה) that can hardly be distinguished from thanksgiving.[55]

---

52. Dunn, *Theology of Paul*, 91.

53. Schimmel, "Gratitude in Judaism," 45. Schimmel also indicates that the Talmud faults Adam for ingratitude, but provides no citation.

54. "The fact that there is no word for 'to thank' in Hebrew has never been properly evaluated. The ignoring of this fact can be explained only in that we live so unquestionably in the rhythm between poles of thanks and request, of 'please!' and 'thank you!', and the thought does not occur to anyone that these concepts are not common to all mankind, and have not been present as a matter of course, do not belong to the presuppositions of human intercourse nor to those of the contrast of God and man" (Westermann, *Praise of God in the Psalms*, 25). Westermann argued that תודה had the sense either of "praise" or "confess."

55. Pao, *Thanksgiving*, 23–25. In fact תודה often appears in the Old Testament as a parallel or in close proximity to ברך (typically translated "to bless") and הלל (typically translated "to praise"). The text of Psalm 100, for example, reads, "Enter his gates with thanksgiving (תודה), and his courts with praise (הלל). Give thanks (ידה, "to praise") to him, bless (ברך) his name." Furthermore, ברך and הלל are both translated by εὐλογέω in the Septuagint, a word closely connected in the New Testament to εὐχαριστέω, the former used for the bread and the latter for the cup in the Matthean and Markan accounts of the institution of the Lord's Supper, though εὐχαριστέω is used of both bread and cup in Luke (22:17–19) and Paul (1 Cor 11:24) (Pao, *Thanksgiving*, 30).

How did Israel understand and practice gratitude? In what follows, features of Psalm 116 will be presented as a window through which to answer this question. Psalm 116 is particularly useful for this purpose because it weaves together several important threads in terms of Israel's expression of gratitude: as a *song* of thanksgiving, like Psalms 66 and 107, it refers to the *sacrifice* of thanksgiving.[56] Situated in a wider collection of Psalms called the Hallel (Pss 113–118),[57] Psalm 116 is a hymn of thanksgiving penned by an individual saved from peril, possibly sickness.[58] At the heart of the Psalm, the Psalmist poses the question, "What shall I return (שוב) to the Lord for all his bounty to me?" (Ps 116:12). The verb שוב is also used in verse 7 ("Return [שוב], O my soul, to your rest, for the Lord has dealt bountifully with you"), leading Goldingay to allege that what is required of the grateful worshipper is both an internal (Ps 116:7) and an external (Ps 116:12) turn or return.[59] Dahood argues that מָה in verse 7, when used adverbially as an interrogative, expresses a seeming impossibility, i.e., how is such a return for all God's favors possible?[60] The Psalmist answers his own question in verses 13 and 14: "I will lift up the cup of salvation and call on the name of the Lord, I will pay (שלם) my vows to the Lord in the presence of all his people." In similar words a few verses later, he says, "I will offer (זבח) to you a thanksgiving sacrifice (תודה זבח) and call on the name of the Lord. I will pay (שלם) my vows to the Lord in the presence of all his people" (Ps 116:17–18).

What precisely is the תודה זבח? In Leviticus 3 instructions are given regarding the peace (or well-being) offering (זבח שלמים) which is then associated in chapter 7 with three sacrifices in particular—thanksgiving (תודה), votive (נדר), and voluntary or freewill (נדבה)—which may represent three subgroups or three different stages.[61] The peace offerings are distinguished in part by the celebratory contexts in which they are offered, whether in communal festivals or personally (e.g., Num 10:10).[62] The תודה offering was

---

56. The motif of gratitude is also prominent in certain psalms of lament (e.g., Ps 22; 27; 40; 51; 54; 56; 61; 69).

57. These Hallel Psalms were sung in connection with the Passover celebration: Psalms 113, 114 before the meal and Psalms 115–118 after (Dahood, *Psalms*, 3:130).

58. Dahood, *Psalms*, 3:145; Allen, *Psalms 101–150*, 115.

59. Goldingay, *Psalms*, 3:344–45. "God valued a tangible response to his blessings more than a mere verbal profession of gratitude which might or might not be sincere" (Harrison, *Leviticus*, 79).

60. Dahood, *Psalms*, 3:148. Similarly, Allen, "So indebted does he feel that he despairs of responding adequately to divine blessing. But the unpayable nature of the debt does not absolve him from making what contribution he can" (Allen, *Psalms 101–150*, 115).

61. Boda, "Words and Meanings," 289.

62. Miller, *Religion of Ancient Israel*, 113.

the most common peace offering such that the terms "peace offering" and "peace offering for thanksgiving" are nearly synonymous (e.g., 1 Chr 29:31; Jer 17:26).[63] Whereas the votive offering was connected the fulfilment of a vow and the voluntary offering to an act of obedience to the Lord where no vow was made, the thanksgiving offering acknowledged God's mercy for deliverance (e.g., Ps 107:22), recovery from sickness (e.g., Ps 116:17), or escape from enemies (e.g., Ps 56:12).[64] "The chief function" of the sacrifices of thanksgiving, Courtman alleges, "is a public memorial to honour God for what he has done."[65]

A sharp distinction between thanksgiving (תודה) and votive (נדר), however, is unwarranted. Miller argues that the votive offering itself was closely connected to gratitude, even approximating a kind of payment.

> The payment of a vow suggests a gift to the deity in return for the deity's help. The very character of the vow assumes that the deity desires the gift and responds in the light of the vow, as well as suggesting that without the offer of the sacrificial gift the deity might not respond. The vow indicates that as gift, the vow and sacrifice had an instrumental character, in some manner effecting, from the perspective of the offerer, divine assistance and returning a gift to the Lord in both thanksgiving and obligation.[66]

One discerns in the זבח שלמים, therefore, a parallel with the tithe and first-fruit offerings, both return gifts for the Lord's generosity. "Here again," Miller writes, "thanksgiving and obligation join as motivating forces for the offering, and the gift further symbolizes the recognition of the one who is the Lord of the land and provider of life."[67] There is such joy in these return

---

63. Milgrom, *Leviticus 1–16*, 413. There are also passages in which תודה denotes a verbal expression, in some cases in contrast to material praise, e.g., Ps 69:31; cf. Ps 42:5; Isa 51:3. Further there are passages in which תודה is used in both verbal and material modes, e.g., Jonah 2:10 (verbal praise accompanying material sacrifice); Ps 26:6–7 (worshipper encircles altar with voice of thanksgiving); Ezra 10:11. Boda argues that what unites the material and verbal expressions may be "the close bond between תודה and vows made in times of distress" (e.g., Lev 3; Ps 26:7; 42:5; 95:2; 100:1, 4; 147:7) (Boda, "Words and Meanings," 296). He further argues on this basis that one should "avoid imposing false dichotomies (confession versus praise; verbal versus material) onto the texts" (Boda, "Words and Meanings," 297). David Pao argues that what God demanded was "a heart of thanksgiving" and not "outward ritual," (Pao, *Thanksgiving*, 53), though in contradiction with his subsequent claim that thanksgiving for Israel was "a public act when the mighty deeds of God are published" (Pao, *Thanksgiving*, 73).

64. See Harrison, *Leviticus*, 79; cf. Miller, *Religion of Ancient Israel*, 113.

65. Courtman, "Sacrifice in the Psalms," 53.

66. Miller, *Religion of Ancient Israel*, 129.

67. Miller, *Religion of Ancient Israel*, 129.

gifts, however, that the notion of obligation "is replaced by an overwhelming sense of gratitude."[68]

This is precisely the dynamic observable in Psalm 116 where the psalmist offers to "pay" (שׁלם) a vow in return for God's deliverance. The verb שׁלם has a wide semantic range that includes the notions of paying, repaying, rewarding, completing, finishing, etc.[69] The payment of a vow conveyed, at least in some instances, a state of shalom: "The payment of a vow (Ps 50:14) completes an agreement so that both parties are in a state of shālôm. Closely linked with this concept is the eschatological motif in some uses of the term. Recompense for sin, either national or personal, must be given. Once that obligation has been restored, wholeness is restored (Isa 60:20; Joel 2:25)."[70] In fact, there is speculation among scholars that the peace offering is so denominated because it "brings about 'agreement' or 'reconciliation.'"[71] In the grateful "payment" of a vow we have an instance of asymmetrical reciprocity that restores a kind of "equilibrium," a return that is not commensurate with the gift, but a token of its value.[72]

It is also important to note, in this connection, that the Old Testament is devoid of the reciprocal relations (i.e., *do ut des*) that characterized the Greco-Roman world. One searches the Old Testament in vain, Leithart argues, for instructions regarding repayment so prominent in Cicero and Seneca.[73] Though human generosity is everywhere recommended, it is not to be motivated by interpersonal or horizontal repayment common in the ancient world. The traditional motivation for hospitality in ancient cultures—namely, to form friendships (ξενία) for political purposes, for

68. Courtman, "Sacrifice in the Psalms," 53.
69. Holladay, *Hebrew Lexicon*, 373.
70. Carr, "שׁלם," *Theological Wordbook*, 931.
71. Jenson, "Levitical Sacrificial System," 31.

72. Though it cannot be conflated with patron-client reciprocity of the Greco-Roman world, there are also instances, in the Old Testament, of mutually obligatory asymmetrical reciprocity in inter-personal relationships that Crook defines as "covenantal exchanges" (Crook, "Reciprocity," 87). For helping the spies, Rahab makes a *quid pro quo* request, "Now then, since I have dealt kindly with you, swear to me by the Lord that you in turn will deal kindly with my family" (Josh 2:12) and she is rewarded by Joshua with protection from the imminent destruction of Canaan (Josh 6:25). Boaz rewards Ruth's loyalty and piety (Ruth 3:10–11) (Leithart, *Gratitude*, 62). Mutual, inter-personal love in a marriage would perhaps be an instance of such reciprocity. The lover and beloved, in the Song of Songs, converse with each other, love each other and desire each other in reciprocal ways. He says to her (Song 2:2), "As a lily among brambles, so is my love among maidens" and she immediately reciprocates (Song 2:3), "As an apple tree among the trees of the wood, so is my beloved among young men." Within this love there is non-identical reciprocation.

73. Leithart, *Gratitude*, 62.

instance, is nearly absent and located instead in compassion.[74] The Torah legislated care for the poor, the widow, and the orphan (e.g., Exod 22:25–27; Deut 15:8–11; 24:10–15, 19–22), creating in the ancient world a distinctive ethic of "almsgiving."[75] Giving to the poor was "both (unusually) a matter of legislation and integral to a religious piety that pervaded all spheres of life."[76] "The Jewish ideology is undergirded," Barclay argues, "not by the ethos of a 'pure,' unreciprocated gift, but by an emphasis on the certainty of reciprocation from God."[77] Leithart observes that whereas human beneficence in the Greco-Roman orbit ran *parallel* to the divine-human exchange, it was *integrated* into the divine-human exchange in the Old Testament. Instead of multiple circles of exchange, in other words, the Hebrew Bible imagined one "socio-religious circle" initiated and completed by the Creator's generosity.[78] The reward from the Lord encouraged the donor and the recipient, who was liberated from felt obligation to reciprocate.

The thanksgiving offering, finally, was a communal meal in which food was shared with the Lord, the priest, and others.[79] Each of the different types of bread (see Lev 7:12) would be shared with the priest (Lev 7:14), though never sacrificed on the altar.[80] The donations to the priests were

---

74. Leithart, *Gratitude*, 60. See also Barclay, *Paul and the Gift*, 30.

75. Barclay, *Paul and the Gift*, 41. For example, "You shall not harden your heart, nor close your hand from your poor brother; but you shall open your hand to him, and shall generously lend him sufficient for his need" (Deut 15:8–9). Though completely absent in Philo, this theology is acknowledged by Josephus in these comments on generosity to the poor: "When thou hast been assistant to his necessities, think it thy gain if thou obtainest their gratitude to thee; and withal that reward which will come to thee from God, for thy humanity towards him" (Josephus, *Ant*. 4.8.25).

76. Barclay, *Paul and the Gift*, 43.

77. Barclay, *Paul and the Gift*, 44. The promised reward of the Lord's blessing (Deut 14:29; 15:4–5,10; 24:19, etc.) delivered Israel from the book-keeping mentality of Cicero, or even Seneca, who feared distributing gifts too widely for fear recipients might be unable to repay. "A third party is involved in every transaction, the generous God who guarantees that the circle of reciprocity will be closed by promising to reward those who share and practice his generosity" (Leithart, *Gratitude*, 61). The "most important return" came "not from the human recipient but from *God*" (Barclay, *Paul and the Gift*, 43).

78. Leithart, *Gratitude*, 61.

79. "The Israelites were as aware as anyone that God did not physically eat food, but eating is a rich symbolic resource for theological reflection" (Jenson, "Levitical Sacrificial System," 31).

80. These offerings resembled the Nazarite offerings and offerings for priestly consecrands (cf. Exod 29:25–28; Num 6:19–20). "In the thank offering, then, even daily bread could be offered on the altar, where nothing with leaven was otherwise allowed" (Lindsay, "*Todah* and Eucharist," 88).

given "as a gift to the Lord" (Lev 7:14).⁸¹ Unlike the עולה (traditionally called the "whole burnt offering"), only *part* of the תודה was offered in smoke and the remainder was enjoyed, along with the bread, by the priests and friends or family of the grateful one (Ps 30:4; cf. Amos 4:5).⁸² This dimension to the thank offering, Lindsay argues, has "an eschatological dimension. This becomes obvious in Isaiah 25:1–10 where a song of thanksgiving transforms the eschatological feast into a thank offering of the entire spiritual community of God."⁸³ This is one of several ways in which the תודה זבח anticipates the Eucharist.⁸⁴ Relatedly, one must also recall that four cups were raised throughout the Passover celebration and that Psalms 115–18 were recited in connection with the fourth cup. In the raising of "the cup of salvation" in Psalm 116:13 there is a "a ritual reference" to this fourth cup and an antecedent to the cup of wine in the Eucharist.⁸⁵

There are several features to Israel's thanksgiving that are noteworthy. The first is that gratitude was deeply embedded with Israelite culture and worship. God had prescribed sacrifices for gratitude which indicates that he wanted and expected grateful worship. This should not exclude the reality that gratitude was often spontaneously generated and could be expressed verbally and not just by means of a material sacrifice. The second is that gratitude was understood as a response to God's gifts, even a kind of asymmetrical "payment" that restored a kind of equilibrium (i.e., shalom). The third is that generosity was not to be motivated by interpersonal returns, but anticipated a reward from the Lord that liberated one to give charitably. The fourth is that the תודה sacrifice, as a ritual of gratitude, anticipates the Eucharist in multiple ways.

81. "Gift" is a translation of תרומה, which, according to Milgrom, has the sense of "contribution" or "dedication."

82. Unique among the sacrifices, the offerer would eat part of the thanksgiving sacrifice, both of the animal and the bread (Lev 3:15) and, unlike the other peace offerings, the meat had to be eaten in one day. Wenham sorts through a variety of explanations, favoring the notion that if the meat was left it might spoil and so be inappropriate for worship (e.g., Lev 1:3, 10) (Wenham, *Leviticus*, 124). Though the sacrifice was not offered because of sin, the priest would dash "the blood of the offering," an "expiatory function" for a "nonexpiatory sacrifice" (Milgrom, *Leviticus 1–16*, 417). See Harrison, *Leviticus*, 80. The paradox is resolved, for Milgrim, in the recognition that the crime of taking the animal's life is absolved if the worshipper offers its blood (see Lev 17:3–4, 11) (Milgrom, *Leviticus 1–16*, 417). Milgrom also argues that, according Rabbinic sources, all sacrifices would be annulled in the world to come but the sacrifices of thanksgiving (Milgrom, *Leviticus 1–16*, 413–15).

83. Lindsay, "*Todah and Eucharist*," 89.

84. Interestingly, the Septuagint often translates תודה as "sacrifice of thanksgiving" (θυσίαν αἰνέσεως) which in Hebrews 13:15 is a possible allusion to Eucharist.

85. Mays, *Psalms*, 371.

Jesus

To understand gratitude in the New Testament, one must be familiar with Greco-Roman conceptions of reciprocity. Those who received benefaction were obligated to gratitude. In Seneca's formulation, "The person who intends to be grateful, immediately while receiving, should turn his or her thought to repaying."[86] Further, gratitude was often expressed in terms of ascribing honor, "because honor," Aristotle says, "is the reward for virtue and beneficence."[87]

Religion in the Greco-Roman world was decidedly reciprocal, encapsulated by the Latin slogan *do ut des* ("I give that you may give"). By offering sacrificial gifts, one could purchase favors from the gods and thus put them into debt.[88] Through rituals of prayer and sacrifice, properly performed in devotion, gods were incited to respond favorably and when they did, more prayer was elicited.[89] It was of course possible, however, for gods to be oblivious to requests or ignore them. Apart from the Epicureans who alleged that the gods were indifferent to human life, the Greek philosophers saw religious life as a circle in which gifts are returned to those who give.[90] Reciprocity in these scenarios was more relational than commercial and therefore carefully distinguished from mere bribery.[91]

Leithart indicates that the reciprocal exchange of gifts in heroic Greece was often tied to achievement such that victorious warriors were rewarded by chiefs and rulers with goods and relationships, though they were expected to be generous in turn.[92] In political Greece, especially wealthy citizens attempted to curry favor with the polis/ruler through civic euergetism or liturgies of civic donations by which endeavor to enhance the civic realm through funding expanses taxation could not cover—namely, military equipment, for example, banquets, the construction and renovation of public buildings and temples, etc.[93] These contributions were regarded as gifts, for which the "grateful" return was public honor through inscriptions,

---

86. Seneca, *Ben.* 2.25.3

87. Aristotle, *Eth. nic.* 1163b4–5. Similarly, "The greater the favor, the more earnestly we must express ourselves, resorting to such compliments as: . . . 'I shall never be able to repay you my gratitude, but, at any rate, I shall not cease from declaring everywhere that I am unable to repay it'" (Seneca, *Ben.* 2.24.2).

88. Leithart, *Gratitude*, 21.

89. Leithart, *Gratitude*, 21.

90. Leithart, *Gratitude*, 24.

91. Leithart, *Gratitude*, 21, 25.

92. Leithart, *Gratitude*, 27.

93. Leithart, *Gratitude*, 30–31.

statues, etc.⁹⁴ Civic euergetism, Barclay argues, paved the way for "the imperial cult," and the public honors one gave to a benevolent emperor.⁹⁵

A significant development in Roman culture was the emergence of patronage by which patrons with access to the Senate could offer clients financial help and political influence, for instance, in exchange for public honor and political support. This network of patronage extended to the Mediterranean world as Roman power expanded and sometimes included complete cities.⁹⁶ "Romans were explicit and completely unapologetic about the fact," Barclay writes, "that gifts create ties of obligation."⁹⁷ Moreover, the patron-client bond was an immense source of security for both parties. For this reason, ingratitude is elevated as a vice because it robbed people of the provision (for client) or loyalty (for patron) needed in difficult circumstances.⁹⁸

That gifts were expected to be reciprocated in Greek social relations is obvious from the way in which χάρις denoted initially both "a favor given and a favor returned" and the way εὐχαριστία ("thanks") is nearly synonymous with χαριστήριον ("favor").⁹⁹ Specifically, χάρις can refer, as does the Latin *gratia*, to: (a) the delight in the object of one's favor (e.g., Luke 1:30; 2:52; Acts 7:46; 1 Pet 2:19-20); (b) the favor in the giver (e.g., Gal 1:6,15; Rom 3:24), the act of giving (e.g., Rom 5:15-21; Gal 2:21; 2 Cor 6:1), or the gift itself (2 Cor 4:5; 9:1, 8); (c) gratitude, the return of favor (e.g., 1 Cor

---

94. Leithart, *Gratitude*, 30–31. In attempt to extricate itself from such mutual obligations and the bribery they implied, Athens experimented with democracy, the "victory of community over hero," and implemented a system in which public officials were paid from a public treasury (Leithart, *Gratitude*, 33). The circle of gifts remains in political Greece, though those who are bound together are no longer rulers and heroes, but rulers and people.

95. Barclay, *Paul and the Gift*, 35. In some cases, such benefaction would address an economic crisis, though Theognis underscored the futility of helping the poor since they are unable to repay (Barclay, *Paul and the Gift*, 34). For Aristotle, giving to a beggar did not fall under "magnificent" giving. (Aristotle, *Eth. nic.* 1122a26-28). "Since the destitute could give nothing worthwhile back to the donor . . . the motivation for giving to the poorest members of society is comparatively weak" (Barclay, *Paul and the Gift*, 43).

96. Barclay, *Paul and the Gift*, 37.

97. Barclay, *Paul and the Gift*, 39. Unlike the modern world where giving to the poor is often motivated simply by virtue, "the proper expression of gift" in the ancient world, "is reciprocal exchange" (Barclay, *Paul and the Gift*, 51).

98. "There is nothing that so effectually disrupts and destroys the harmony of the human race as this vice" (Seneca, *Ben.* 4.18.1).

99. Barclay, *Paul and the Gift*, 26. Not until the first century did εὐχαριστία arrive, initially referring especially to outward expressions of gratitude (Pao, *Thanksgiving*, 81n68).

10:30; 2 Cor 9:11–12; 15).[100] In some cases, divine χάρις, in the sense of gift, is connected to human εὐχαριστία to indicate reciprocity.[101] Furthermore, the language of "debt" (ὀφείλημα) was frequently used to communicate the obligation of reciprocity[102] and the word μισθός connoted "reward" in the context of gift but "wage" in the realm of commodities.[103]

It is very apparent from his ministry that Jesus subverted the conventional notions of reciprocity among both Jews and Hellenists. In this sense, Leithart claims, Jesus is portrayed in the Gospels as an ingrate because he endorsed "hating" one's parents, railed against the reciprocal mindset of the Pharisees, encouraged generosity without regard for the prevailing honor system, instructed his disciples to renounce "calculating hospitality," and regarded Jews who gave as Gentiles as hypocrites.[104] Unlike Cicero who advocated the restraint of excessive generosity and Seneca who had encouraged selective giving to the just who would feel moral compulsion to give back, Jesus urged his disciples to distinguish themselves from Gentile benefactors who lord it over their subjects by creating debts of gratitude.[105]

We see further evidence of Jesus subverting Hellenistic notions of reciprocity in his parable of the undeserving servant in Luke 17. In the Hellenistic religious world χάρις denoted both one's offering to a god and the god's response. Here is where Marshall Sahlins's categories are helpful. Sahlins distinguished between different kinds of reciprocity in "primitive" communities (i.e., essentially tribal and "lacking a political state"[106]): *generalized* reciprocity, i.e., disproportionate open-ended giving and receiving between those in an affective relationship (e.g., hospitality among friends);

---

100. Barclay, *Paul and the Gift*, 576–77. Visser argues that eventually *charis* came to refer, as did the Latin *gratia*, to (a) the delight in the object of one's favor; (b) the favor in the giver, the act of giving or the gift itself (c) gratitude, the return of favor (Visser, *Gift of Thanks*, 464). Thus both the Roman *gratia* and the Greek *charis* include notions of favor and delight, and from the Greek, via the Romans, we have inherited the language of grace and gracefulness to connote beauty (Visser, *Gift of Thanks*, 205). Christian *charis* includes Jewish notion of divine blessing and mercy, the delight of Greek charis, and the gratitude for favors of Roman *gratia* (Visser, *Gift of Thanks*, 205).

101. Barclay, *Paul and the Gift*, 578.

102. Barclay, *Paul and the Gift*, 27.

103. Barclay, *Paul and the Gift*, 32. Reciprocity is often presented in the Greco-Roman world in terms of friendship (ξενία) and for this reason it was sometimes virtuous, especially when an enemy offered a gift, to abstain from a gift exchange Barclay indicates that there's no ancient Greek word for "bribe" (Barclay, *Paul and the Gift*, 30).

104. Leithart, *Gratitude*, 68, 70. Jesus faulted the Pharisees for wanting the best seats in the synagogue, arguing that one should seek the low seat in expectation that God would reward the humble with a high seat. See Luke 6:30–35; 14.

105. Leithart, *Gratitude*, 70. See Luke 22:25.

106. Sahlins, *Stone Age Economics*, 188.

balanced reciprocity, i.e., giving and receiving with an eyes to equivalence and proportionality among those in distant and impersonal relationships (e.g., commercial, contractual arrangements); and *negative* reciprocity, i.e., wanting or obtaining disproportionate benefits from another in mercenary exploitation (e.g., bartering, stealing, and raiding).[107] The god's response in Hellenistic offerings is not payment in a mercantile sense, but one in which the god recalls the gift and is inclined to give in the future. The giving of thanks for Hellenistic worshippers was not a pleasant feeling, therefore, but a recognition of one's indebtedness to the gods in relationships in which χάρις is reciprocated.[108]

In verse 9, Jesus asks his disciples whether they would "thank" a slave for doing what was commanded. The χάριν ἔχειν combination in verse 9 typically means "to give thanks," though Knowles suggests that here it might have the "balanced" reciprocal sense of "to owe thanks," typically expressed by χάρις ὀφείλειν.[109] The likelihood that this is the sense in this parable is enhanced by recognition that both χάρις and ὀφείλειν are used elsewhere in Luke's text in the sense of religious indebtedness.[110] Luke's non-Jewish audience would have expected the slave in the parable to receive χάρις from the master (representing God) in exchange for his χάρις. That is the import of Jesus's statement in verse 9, which Knowles renders, "he should favor the slave, shouldn't he?"[111] In a Judeo-Christian economy, however, God's χάρις is not subject to conventional reciprocal relationships of Hellenistic religion but transcends them.

The golden rule in Luke 6:31, however, seems at first glance to be an exception to this observation. In a golden rule mindset, a giver expects to receive back what he has given, and a lover expects to receive love back.[112]

---

107. Sahlins, *Stone Age Economics*, 198–201. Zeba Crook similarly distinguishes between familial reciprocity, symmetrical reciprocity, and asymmetrical reciprocity (Crook, "Reciprocity," 81–82).

108. Seneca depicts the intense bond forged by benefaction: "If you wish to make a return for a favor, you must be willing to go into exile, or to pour forth your blood, or to undergo poverty, or . . . even to let your very innocence be stained and exposed to shameful slanders" (Seneca, *Ep.* 81.27). Cf. Seneca's description of gratitude as "an utterly happy condition of the soul" (Seneca, *Ep.* 81.21).

109. Knowles, "Reciprocity," 258.

110. Knowles indicates that χάρις is used by Jesus to connote religious merit in Luke 6:32–33 and by Stephen of David finding "favor" with God in Acts 7:45–6. In Luke 11:4, ὀφείλειν is used in terms of religious debt; cf. Luke 13:4 and the parables in Luke 7:41–8 and 16:1–9 (Knowles, "Reciprocity," 260).

111. Knowles, "Reciprocity," 260.

112. "Its criterion of action is one's desire for the beneficent responses from others" (Kirk, "Love Your Enemies," 685).

This is especially striking in the context where Jesus denounces loving "those who love you" (Luke 6:32) and commands the love of enemies with no expectation of return (Luke 6:35). Whereas the golden rule complies with a conventional sense of justice as equity, the love of enemies transcends it. Put differently, while the golden rule embraces the "logic of equivalence," loving one's enemies embraces the "logic of superabundance."[113] Bilateral justice, for Ricoeur, is now transformed "by the spirit of unilateral mercy that animates the love command."[114]

While conventional reciprocity is subverted, Alan Kirk argues, it is not rejected wholesale. Luke 6:29, first, envisions scenarios of negative reciprocity characteristic in exchanges with enemies.[115] Instead of retaliation, the explicit mode of negative reciprocity, Jesus urges benefaction. In verse 30, secondly, Jesus subverts conventional Greek wisdom about the virtuous discrimination in the selection of beneficiaries.[116] Even in general or affective reciprocity one discerningly and deliberately chose friends who could give back.[117] "The operative moral axiom in Greek reciprocity ethics," Kirk writes, "was that one helps friends and harms enemies, and that it is justthe justice of the *talio*"to do so." By urging the love of enemies, Kirk argues, Jesus does not abandon reciprocity entirely, but recommends that general reciprocity replace negative reciprocity and that one treat an enemy as one would a friend.[118] In fact, verses 32–34 are expressions of general reciprocity and the "lending" of verse 35 is indicative of "open-ended lending among friends, widely practiced among all social strata in Greece and Rome."[119]

Lastly, the generosity of the Most High in verse 35, indicative of noble and wealthy magnanimity, is not disinterested. "Benefactors seek by these means," Kirk argues, "to awaken gratitude, create social bonds, and thereby a devoted clientele."[120] Though this is the response intended, the generosity is not contingent on it, and as such it is a model for believers in verses 27–30.

---

113. Ricoeur, "Golden Rule," 392–93.

114. Kirk, "Love Your Enemies," 670.

115. Kirk, "Love Your Enemies," 681.

116. Kirk, "Love Your Enemies," 682.

117. It is "easy to give and spend money," Aristotle argues, "but to feel or act towards the right person to the right extent at the right time for the right reason in the right waythat is not easy" (Aristotle, *Eth. nic.* 1109a26–28). See also Seneca, "we ought to be careful to confer benefits by preference upon those who will be likely to respond with gratitude" (Seneca, *Ben.* 1.10.4–5).

118. Kirk, "Love Your Enemies," 682.

119. Kirk, "Love Your Enemies," 682. The generosity commended by Aristotle and Seneca always envisions friends as objects.

120. Kirk, "Love Your Enemies," 683.

Such generosity is distinguished from conventional Greco-Roman reciprocity by not discriminating against the ungrateful as a less worthy recipient.[121] This in turn shows how the reciprocity of the golden rule is not completely forsaken in the command to love enemies. "Without the reciprocity motif," Kirk writes, "the command to love enemies remains orphaned from a social context; it is just an emotive slogan, not the inaugural note of a comprehensive social vision."[122]

Neither Kirk nor Leithart see in these verses an argument for altruism. For Leithart, to give with the expectation of reward is mistaken, unless the reward sought is the one promised by the Father who sees in secret.[123] The reward of the Father is, of course, significant and Jesus has no inhibitions, as Leithart rightly indicates, about embedding commercial language into the theological notion of reward (e.g., "lay up treasures in heaven," Matt 6:20).[124] The expectation of a reciprocal reward is of course misplaced, but this does not mean that the desire for such reward is impious. Not only is such a return implied in the golden rule stated by Jesus and so treasured by Christians, as Kirk helpfully demonstrates, it belongs to the nature of healthy relationships, not least romantic relationships. Reciprocal love should not be rejected, but must be transcended. Greco-Roman reciprocity in particular must be transcended by refusing to limit one's love only to those who can repay or to view those unable to repay as less worthy recipients of beneficence. Return love is wonderful, though one's offer of love should not be motivated by expectation of the return one rightfully desires.

The parable of the unworthy servant considered above is immediately followed in Luke's Gospel by Jesus's encounter with the ten lepers on his way to Jerusalem. In response to their pleas for mercy, Jesus instructs them to show themselves to the priests to verify cleansing. As they go, they are cleansed. Not having travelled far, one of the lepers, identified as

---

121. Kirk, "Love Your Enemies," 684.

122. Kirk, "Love Your Enemies," 686. "The rule connects the programmatic love command to the social relia of human relations, thereby preventing 'love your enemies' from degenerating into empty sentimentality" (Kirk, "Love Your Enemies," 686).

123. Leithart, *Gratitude*, 69. Jesus says both "Love your enemies, and do good, and lend, expecting nothing in return" (Luke 6:35) and "Your Father who sees in secret will repay (ἀποδίδωμι) you" (Matt 6:4). For Derrida, this implicates Jesus for endorsing commercial conceptions of gift-giving (see Derrida, *Gift of Death*).

124. Leithart, *Gratitude*, 69. In my view, this must be balanced by instances where Jesus demonstrates that the economy of grace does not conform to the economy of commerce. The worker who shows up at the eleventh hour, for example, receives the same wage as those who have worked all day (Matt 20:1–16). Leithart would of course agree, arguing that the Father's "repayment" of rewards, though promised to those who fulfill certain obligations, is still undeserved.

a Samaritan, sees that he is cleansed, praises God, and falls at Jesus's feet "giving him thanks" (εὐχαριστῶν) (Luke 17:16). Jesus responds by posing three uninterrupted questions: "Were not ten made clean? But the other nine, where are they? Was none of them found to return and give praise to God except this foreigner?" (Luke 17:17–18). At first glance, the questions are nearly troubling. The other lepers did precisely what Jesus commanded—going to the priest, and the Samaritan disobeyed! The sequence in the Samaritan leper's response counters Leithart's claim that Christian gratitude is the "right use of the gift" rather than "return."[125] Gratitude is the fitting response to a gift, marked in this account, among other things, by a physical "return." The fact that Jesus expected gratitude for his gift of healing is arguably an exception to Leithart's claim that "givers look to the Father not to the recipients for repayment"[126] Interestingly, the thankful Samaritan leper receives the verification from Jesus that the priests would seemingly give: "Your faith has made you well" (Luke 17:19).

Prior to his death, at the observance of Passover, Jesus instituted a commemorative meal called the Lord's Supper which arguably became the church's central ritual. At this meal, Jesus offered two prayers of thanks.

> Jesus offered thanks over the bread and wine before passing it among his disciples, of whom one had betrayed him, one would deny him, and all would desert him. Still he offered thanks, saying grace by offering up both words and his very life. Jesus graced the dreadful evening of his betrayal with gratitude.[127]

So central are the thanksgiving prayers in his ritual that the Lord's supper, in many quarters, is called the Eucharist.[128] The prominence of gratitude recalls the תודה such that the "sacrifice of praise" (θυσία αἰνέσεως, the translation of תודה in Leviticus in the Septuagint) in Hebrews 13:15 is a possible reference to the Eucharist.[129] As a ritual, it is foreshadowed by

---

125. Leithart, *Gratitude*, 7. "Human givers give, but recipients owe thanks and grateful service not to the giver but to God" (Leithart, *Gratitude*, 7). "In Paul, the proper reception of gifts includes the giving of thanks to God, but he accents making good use of the gift" (Leithart, *Gratitude*, 6).

126. Leithart, *Gratitude*, 71.

127. Williams, *Saying Grace*, 33–34.

128. Leithart, *Gratitude*, 71.

129. On seeing תודה as the background of the Eucharist, see Lindsay, "*Todah* and Eucharist." Jacob Milgrom argues that the rabbis taught תודה was never offered for forgiveness (see Milgrom, *Leviticus 1–16*), leading Leithart to suggest that this makes it "the perfect model for the sacrifice that persists after the final sacrifice has been offered" (Leithart, *Gratitude*, 249n101).

the peace offering in which food was shared by God and his people (Lev 7:11–38) to communicate fellowship and the restoration of shalom.[130]

The Church

Beyond Jesus, how do New Testament conceptions of reciprocity compare with prevailing Greco-Roman views? New Testament writers seemingly encourage euergetism among believers in expectation of civic gratitude (Rom 13:3–4; 1 Pet 2:14–15), as Leithart admits,[131] and the praise that God's gift of grace elicits in some ways parallels, for Paul, the honor clients would ascribe patrons.[132] Notions of Greco-Roman reciprocity also lie in the backdrop to the summons to follow Jesus in Hebrews 13. DeSilva argues, for instance, that when readers are exhorted (Heb 13:13) "to show this measure of gratitude to Jesus, going out to him 'outside the camp, bearing his reproach,'"[133] it comports with Seneca's counsel: "If you wish to make a return for a favor, you must be willing to go into exile, or to pour forth your blood, or to undergo poverty, or . . . even to let your very innocence be stained and exposed to shameful slanders."[134]

Yet Paul's theology of grace diverges from traditional Greco-Roman notions of reciprocity in numerous ways.[135] The superabundance feature of God's grace abandons, Dunn claims, "the benefaction ideology of the Greco-Roman world."[136] Words such as overflow, abound, surpassing, and abundant leave no room "for any thought that the human recipient of divine grace can somehow repay it."[137] Though the possibility exists of balanced

---

130. Longman, *Immanuel*, 90.

131. Leithart, *Gratitude*, 58; cf. Winter, "Public Honoring of Christian Benefactors."

132. In Ephesians, the redemption of believers leads to "the praise of God's glory" (Eph 1:14). See DeSilva, *Perseverance in Gratitude*, 475n78.

133. DeSilva, *Perseverance in Gratitude*, 476.

134. Seneca, *Ep.* 81.27.

135. In Barclay's estimation, scholars often privilege one facet over others or worse, single out facet of grace to the exclusion of others. Specifically, he argues that reciprocity need not be contrasted with grace. We must careful, Barclay argues, not to restrict oneself to one definition, far less reduce grace to one essential meaning. Grace is Paul's theology, for Barclay, is polyvalent and multi-faceted, characterized by (a) superabundance—the more lavish, the more perfect; (b) singularity—benevolence is the giver's sole mode of operation; (c) priority—the gift precedes the recipient's initiative; (d) incongruity—the gift should be give selectively and thoughtfully though perhaps incongruent with worth of the recipient; (e) efficacy—the gifts performs its intention; and (f) non-circularity—the gift is unreciprocated (Barclay, *Paul and the Gift*, 70–75).

136. Dunn, *Theology of Paul*, 323.

137. Dunn, *Theology of Paul*, 323. Paul asks rhetorically, "Or who has given a gift to

reciprocity with other people, there is no possibility of balanced reciprocity with God. God cannot be indebted to us. Even when we mishandle his gifts, "God gives us more—the gift of freedom from the guilt and power of sin" (see Rom 3:23–25).[138] God cannot be indebted to people, but are people indebted to him? The God who covers all debts, Leithart claims, does not impose "burdens of gratitude" on recipients.[139] Yet the superabundance and excessiveness of God's grace is not disinterested, but solicitous.

There is, first of all, a sense in which God's gifts are intended for us and they oblige a response.[140] Though what we have is given by God, and though he has everything and needs nothing from us, he obliges us to respond with faith, for example, and receives delight in our grateful service as living sacrifices (Rom 12:1).[141] "The one to whom *charis* has been given," Dunn says, "should return *charis* indeed, but always in the sense of 'thanks,' never in the

---

him to receive a gift in return?" (Rom 11:35). To oblige God to reciprocate, we would have to be able to give him something first. "If all things come from God, then nobody can give anything to God in a way that obliges God to give in return" (Volf, *Free of Charge*, 33). Similarly, Paul asks, "What do you have that you did not receive?" (1 Cor 4:7). The implied answer is: absolutely nothing (Volf, *Free of Charge*, 34). We "give" gratitude to God and yet nothing is "given" (Volf, *Free of Charge*, 47). "We give ourselves for God's *use* to benefit creation, not to benefit God" (Volf, *Free of Charge*, 48).

138. Volf, *Free of Charge*, 37.

139. Leithart, *Gratitude*, 74.

140. Throughout the New Testament one finds commands to be thankful. First, there scenarios where Paul gives thanks and assumes his readers will join him (e.g., 2 Cor 2:14; Col 1:3). There also instances in which he commends (without commanding) gratitude (e.g., Eph 5:4, 20; Phil 4:6; Col 2:7; 3:16, 17; 4:2; 1 Thess 3:9; 1 Tim 2:1; 4:3–4; among letters not attributed to Paul, Heb 12:28; 13:15). In some instances, Paul outright commands gratitude, as in 1 Thess 5:18: "Give thanks in all circumstances; for this is the will of God in Christ Jesus for you." "All circumstances" parallels "at all times and for everything" (Eph 5:20). On the other hand, the Macedonian churches who gave as expression of love (2 Cor 8:8), Paul says, "voluntarily gave according to their means, and even beyond their means" (2 Cor 8:3). Similarly, he writes, "So I thought it necessary to urge the brothers to go on ahead to you, and arrange in advance for this bountiful gift that you have promised, so that it may be ready as a voluntary gift and not as an extortion" (2 Cor 9:5). Further, he writes, "Each of you must give as you have made up your mind, not reluctantly or under compulsion, for God loves a cheerful giver" (2 Cor 9:7).

141. In many ancient cultures, the gods would only give in response to human action. Jesus himself confirms this in his Sermon on the Mount (Matt 6:7–8) when he teaches that prayer should not be offered in the manner of pagans who "think that by using many words they will make themselves heard." Further Jesus says, "Do not be like them; your Father knows what you need before you ask him." Normally, sacrifices were dead, and were offered to the gods to nourish them, but Paul indicates that God requires a living sacrifice, so that we are "ready to do God's work in God's world" (Volf, *Free of Charge*, 48).

sense of 'favour' returned."¹⁴² In several passages, in fact, New Testament writers employ a word play in which εὐχαριστία corresponds to χάρις, as in 1 Corinthians 1:4: "I give thanks (εὐχαριστία) to my God always for you because of the grace (χάρις) of God that has been given you in Christ Jesus."

But how precisely does one return χάρις? The sequence of grace evoking gratitude is exemplified in the collection Gentile churches took for the needy church in Jerusalem. The sequence began with the "generous act of our Lord Jesus Christ, that though he was rich, yet for your sakes he became poor, so that by his poverty you might become rich." Christ's self-gift to believers in their poverty flows onward from them with their material possessions to help the materially impoverished.¹⁴³ He is the "indescribable gift" believers receive, and they are called "as beneficiaries of this greatest gift, to participate in it more fully and responsibly—yet freely, cheerfully, and without worry—by sharing in the grace of Christ."¹⁴⁴ The Corinthians, in other words, were not simply to imitate God's grace in Christ, but to participate in it and extend it forwards.¹⁴⁵ The Corinthian experience of grace induced them to gratitude which they expressed by sending gifts to Jerusalem.¹⁴⁶ Christian believers have new selves (Rom 6:1–11; Eph 4:22–24) in which Christ lives and acts: "we give because we *are* givers, because Christ living in us is a giver."¹⁴⁷ Paul's exhortation to the Corinthians to give charitably to this cause concludes with an exclamation, "Thanks be to God for his indescribable gift" (2 Cor 9:15).

Gifts obligate a response, and since the gifts of God are sovereignly given, gratitude is enjoined "in all circumstances; for this is the will of God in Christ Jesus for you" (1 Thess 5:18).¹⁴⁸ To understand how gratitude might be fitting in all circumstances we are helped by the insights of the Christian philosopher Robert Roberts who defines emotion as "concern-based construal."¹⁴⁹ What generates emotion, in other words, is not simply

---

142. Dunn, *Theology of Paul*, 323.

143. Gorman, *Becoming the Gospel*, 253.

144. Gorman, *Becoming the Gospel*, 252.

145. Gorman, *Becoming the Gospel*, 252.

146. "The gratuitous God of Christianity does not summon gratitude as either dependence or exchange; instead, the divine giver begets further giving, the obligation to continue the gift, not to substitute giving with the attitude of thanksgiving" (Webb, *Gifting God*, 146–47).

147. Volf, *Free of Charge*, 66. Volf compares this to the feeling of liberty a musician has following a musical score, or to sense of freedom a sailor on a sailboat has, going where the wind directs (Volf, *Free of Charge*, 67).

148. "All circumstances" parallels "at all times and for everything" (Eph 5:20).

149. Roberts, *Spiritual Emotions*, 11.

a concern but how one construes the concern. Anger, for example is generated by an elicitor, i.e., something happens external to oneself, and it's the perception of what happens which in turn produces the feeling (that subsequently provokes a reaction). In Roberts's language there is a concern, and how one construes the concern generates the emotion. How one responds to a scratch on one's car, for instance, depends on the value one places on an unscratched car.

How one can give thanks in all circumstances, therefore, depends on how one sees the world or perceives life or construe events.[150] The sight of tragedy, for example, suggests a chaotic world, an unhinged a world, a world out of control, careening towards self-destruction. The Christian worldview, however, teaches that God is sovereign and that Christ has secured a certain future.[151] Shaped by Christian teaching and the biblical narrative, therefore, gratitude remains a possibility even in the face of tragedy.

The language of Ephesians 5:20 is still stronger: "giving thanks to God the Father at all times and for everything in the name of our Lord Jesus Christ." The seemingly categorical injunction to gratitude, however, is textually qualified in two ways.[152] Gratitude must be consistent with the devoted Fatherhood of God and grounded in "the name of our Lord Jesus Christ." Sin and Satan, for example, are enemies Christ came to defeat and adversaries Christians must battle; they are not gifts of the loving Father for which gratitude is enjoined.

There is, secondly, a sense in which gratitude forms part of the motivation to develop a closer walk with God.[153] The writer to Hebrews exhorts

---

150. Think of how the disciples, for instance, responded to persecution. Once out of prison, the disciples were ordered by the Sanhedrin not to speak in the name of Jesus, and yet the responded with joy (Acts 5:41). There was an elicitor, a concern—persecution. There was emotion—joy. The emotion, however, does not match the concern: where one expects anger or frustration, one finds joy. Between the concern and the emotion is perception, interpretation, seeing. They interpreted the persecution as suffering disgrace for Jesus and it generated joy.

151. Roberts, *Spiritual Emotions*, 133.

152. Stott, *God's New Society*, 207.

153. This claim is disputed by American Pastor John Piper who claims that it reeks of a "debtor's ethic" and reintroduces Christian believers under the guise of gratitude to a kind of repayment plan which amounts to "works-righteousness" or earning one's salvation through good works. In language reminiscent of Derrida, Piper claims that in a debtor's ethic what is "offered as free grace is nullified by distorted gratitude" (Piper, *Future Grace*, 32). Piper defines gratitude as "a spontaneous response of joy to receiving something over and above what we paid for" (Piper, *Future Grace*, 32). Forgetfulness of this definition, Piper argues, "is the birthplace of the 'debtor's ethic.'" Furthermore, John Piper claims that "the Bible rarely, if ever, explicitly makes gratitude the impulse of moral behavior, or ingratitude, the explanation of immorality" (Piper, *Future Grace*,

his readers, "Therefore, since we are receiving a kingdom that cannot be shaken, let us give thanks, by which we offer to God an acceptable worship with reverence and awe" (12:28). The expression ἔχειν χάριν can be legitimately translated either as "have grace" or "have thanks" since χάρις can denote both gift and return. Whatever word one chooses to translate χάρις, however, seems irrelevant since it is indisputable that the writer is talking about the reciprocal response of believers to eternal benefaction (see also 6:17; 9:15) and its motivating function for service.[154] There is legitimate debate about whether ἔχειν χάριν denotes balanced reciprocity rather than gratitude *per se*, though DeSilva argues that "since ἔχειν χάριν results in honoring God and pleasing God, and results from receiving a great gift from God, 'gratitude' is the aspect that fits."[155] For DeSilva, in fact, this is the "basic summons of the whole letter" in which gratitude and ingratitude are "the two courses of action open to believers."[156] Further, DeSilva argues that the "stability and security" God provides as Patron "requires a proportionate commitment to living gratefully," expressed through worship and the sundry obligations of the believing community in chapter 13.[157]

Relatedly, gratitude is presented in the New Testament in terms cultivating a closer relationship with God. New Testament writers acknowledge, in connection with gratitude, human weakness and dependency and thus the need for God's ongoing power and provision (e.g., Rom 14:6; 1 Cor 10:30; 1 Tim 4:4; Phil 4:6). Unlike Aristotle, they believe that God's gifts enhance our dignity because we have no existence independent of God. "God's gifts establish," Volf writes. "They come with the message 'You are loved, and therefore you exist.'"[158]

There may be a sense, thirdly, in which gratitude consecrates God's gifts. Paul indicates that God intended humanity to be grateful for food, for example, "which God created to be received with thanksgiving by those who believe and know the truth" (1 Tim 4:3). Further, such food is "sanctified by God's word and by prayer" (1 Tim 4:5). Envisioning the requirement of Old Testament priests to touch only holy things (e.g., holy food, implements,

---

34). In terms of the New Testament, Piper does engage Hebrews 12:28–29 which says, "let us show gratitude, by which we may offer to God an acceptable service." He argues that "let us have grace," however, is the "literal rendering" which might in fact be the "accurate" reading (Piper, *Future Grace*, 44).

154. DeSilva, *Perseverance in Gratitude*, 473.

155. DeSilva, *Perseverance in Gratitude*, 473n71.

156. DeSilva, *Perseverance in Gratitude*, 473. DeSilva also refers in this connection to 6:4–10 and 10:26–31.

157. DeSilva, *Perseverance in Gratitude*, 476.

158. Volf, *Free of Charge*, 47.

incense etc.) to prevent their priesthood from being defiled, Leithart hypothesizes in this connection that gratitude had a "performative function" in which gifts are consecrated as holy fit for use by holy ones (*hagioi*).[159] There is no New Testament rite of consecration other than thanksgiving, for which reason Leithart calls it "the liturgy of Christian living" and "the continuous sanctification of the world."[160]

Finally, gratitude in the New Testament has an ethical function insofar as it is presented as the alternative to obscenity or coarse joking (Eph 5:18–20).[161] In fact, Paul's exhortations to be grateful often occur within instructions on how to live as God's holy and redeemed community (Col 3:15; Eph 5:3–4; 1 Thess 5:18). This should not be entirely surprising because in the Old Testament thanksgiving was connected to compassion for the poor, the orphans, and the widows.

One significant question about gratitude remains. What does the New Testament teach about inter-personal gratitude? As mentioned above, Leithart and Pao argue that, for Paul, gratitude is offered exclusively to God and nearly exclusively for benefits given to others.[162] I am not convinced by these claims. They are seemingly undermined, first, by Romans 16:4 where Paul speaks of Prisca and Aquila "to whom not only I give thanks, but also all the churches of the Gentiles" (for "risking their necks to save him.").[163] Similarly, Paul instructs Philemon to welcome Onesimus and to charge anything he owes to Paul's account (Phil 1:18). Further, he writes (Phil 1:19–20), "I, Paul, am writing this with my own hand: I will repay it. *I say nothing about your owing me even your own self.* Yes, brother, let me have this benefit from you in the Lord." Paul mediates gifts of salvation from the Divine Patron and, as such, lays claim to a kind of "repayment."

The complex "giving and receiving" (Phil 4:15) relationship that Paul has with the Philippians, secondly, also reveals inter-personal gratitude. Paul thanks God, the Philippians' Patron, and not the Philippians, for their

---

159. Leithart, *Gratitude*, 72.

160. Leithart, *Gratitude*, 72.

161. Pao, *Thanksgiving*, 20. Further, in Ephesians 5, the one who give thanks is contrasted with the idolater (Eph 5:5); cf. 1 Tim 4:5.

162. David Pao argues that gratitude is "reserved for God and not human beings" (Pao, *Thanksgiving*, 20). Elsewhere he narrows and qualifies his bold claim in stating that εὐχαριστία, in particular, is "almost always used by Paul in reference to God." He does concede that other ways of acknowledging debt can be construed as gratitude and cites Phil 4 as an example (presumably Phil 4:18, BDJ) (Pao, *Thanksgiving*, 22n37).

163. Pao cites Rom 16:4 as a possible exception but the inclusion of "all the churches of the Gentiles" in giving thanks demonstrates, for Pao, that Paul's concern is for the work of God (Pao, *Thanksgiving*, 20n27). On the other hand, Paul gives them thanks because they "risked their necks" for his life.

gift (Phil 1:3).[164] Moreover, he promises them no repayment, but assures them that "my God shall supply all your needs" (Phil 4:18), thereby modifying the traditional rules of reciprocity by highlighting the divine reward and removing the sense of debt a beneficiary would have.[165] Those who supply the needs of others will find their own needs supplied because God is the great benefactor and he balances things out.[166] Though Paul did not seek the gift from the Philippians, he delighted in it and "seeks profit that accumulates to your account" (4:17). What is often overlooked, however, is that Paul clearly interpreted the Philippians' gift as a return gift for his initial gift of service, even using the language of "payment" (ἀπέχω, 4:18)![167] "It would be a mistake," Moisés Silva writes, "to infer that such language suggests coldness or aloofness. On the contrary, we may well imagine a warm Pauline smile as he dictated these words."[168] No one should give with the expectation of returns (Leithart's cyclical category), but returns are both natural and wonderful. One does not have to envision the parameters of Greco-Roman reciprocity to recognize that "Paul views gifts are simply part of a circulation of goods between Christian friends that takes place as they make common offerings to God."[169]

Lastly, Paul can sound Aristotelian by insisting that one must owe (ὀφείλω) nothing to another but love (Rom 13:8). This does not mean that one should not receive gifts, as it did for Aristotle. Leithart claims that gifts should always be received in terms of the divine patron so that gratitude is owed, not to human benefactors, but to him.[170] Paul, however, does not say that we do not owe each other anything, but that we owe each other only love. Gifts, including the gift of thanks, are expressions of love, and thus make fitting returns.

164. Leithart, *Gratitude*, 73; cf. 1 Cor 1:4; Eph 1:16; 1 Thess 1:2; 2 Thess 1:3; 2:13; 2 Tim 1:3.

165. "Here, Paul does not return the favor in kind, but assures them instead that it is 'his' God who will repay them" (Bockmuehl, *Epistle to Philippians*, 266; see also Barclay, *Paul and the Gift*, 180).

166. Leithart, *Gratitude*, 74. We are liberated to give generously because God provides compensation.

167. "The money of course has been given to God not directly but by being invested in the cause of the gospel" (Bockmuehl, *Epistle to Philippians*, 266). The notion of giving gifts or gratitude to restore "equilibrium" is also apparent in 2 Cor 8:13–14, "I do not mean that there should be relief for others and pressure on you, but it is a question of a fair balance between your present abundance and their need, so that their abundance may be for your need, in order that there may be a fair balance."

168. Silva, *Philippians*, 206.

169. Fowl, "Wealth, Property, and Theft," 458.

170. Leithart, *Gratitude*, 74

In conclusion, both Old and New Testaments recommend a reciprocity in gift-giving that cannot be equated with traditional Greco-Roman reciprocity. This counters the claims not simply of Derrida, but of Leithart and Pao who make Derrida-like statements. Jesus certainly encouraged giving without the expectation of returns (apart from the returns of the Father), but one must not for this reason disparage returns or redefine gratitude, as Leithart does, as "right use" of gift rather than "return" for gift. Returns for gifts are what one would expect in an ontology of communion, especially in relationships of mutual love.

The question remains, how have theologians in history conceived of gratitude? The next section will begin to the answer this question by exploring the contributions of three notable theologians—namely, Thomas Aquinas, John Calvin, and Karl Barth.

THEOLOGIANS OF GRATITUDE

Theology should never be "done" in abstraction from the theological contributions of others, as if it were an autonomous pursuit, and so the next section will explore the views of three significant theologians who have all devoted considerable space in their theologies for gratitude, beginning with Thomas Aquinas.

Thomas Aquinas

Thomas Aquinas is particularly relevant for this inquiry, not simply because of his prodigious writing and theological reputation, but because of his Aristotelian approach. Given the negative appraisal Aristotle's views received in the previous chapter, how does Aquinas fare?

Godward Beatitudo

Though Aquinas approximates Aristotle regarding the place of reason in identifying upright moral character, the importance of character formation, and the identification of happiness as the practical goal of the study of ethics, he parts company with the philosopher on account of differing metaphysical commitments generally and the precise identity of happiness as the ultimate end. Whereas for Aristotle the goal of life is a flourishing rationality, for Aquinas it is a life of intimate union with God.[171] Humanity

---

171. "Therefore God alone constitutes man's [sic] happiness" (Aquinas, *Sum*

was created in the image of God and therefore flourishes most when God is most resembled. Aquinas situates his understanding of happiness in terms of creation in God's image, which includes intellect, will, and ability to act on one's own power.[172] Humanity is teleological, created with a particular function and purpose, to know and love God. Aquinas sees the highest good as happiness, but with God. Since humans are unique among animals as created in God's image, having intellect and will, perfect human happiness involves knowing God through our intellect and loving God through our wills.[173] Unlike Aristotle, Aquinas argues that happiness is unattainable in this life because, unlike Aristotle, Aquinas identifies perfect happiness with the full contemplation of God himself, the vision of God's nature.[174] Because humanity's creation involves divine endowment with goods and its destiny includes divine presence and favor, gratitude is protological and eschatological.[175] Humanity moves from giftedness to giftedness and thus from gratitude to gratitude.

1-2.2.8); "Final and perfect happiness can consist in nothing else than the vision of the Divine Essence" (Aquinas, *Sum* 1-2.3.8). "Thomas argues that will's desire for happiness can be satisfied by God alone as the Final End of all its desiring" (O'Reilly, "Significance of Worship," 455).

172. Aquinas, *Sum* 1.93.

173. For Aquinas, the cognitive and volitional dimensions to a unitary human anthropology exclude the possibilities of "pure reason" and "pure will" (O'Reilly, "Significance of Worship," 454). There is debate about the place of the disabled in Aquinas's view. Identifying will and movement as part of the image of God seems to exclude some disabled. There are also passages in which God's grace takes priority over reason. For, e.g., "The spiritual regeneration effected by Baptism is somewhat like carnal birth, in this respect, that as the child while in the mother's womb receives nourishment not independently, but through the nourishment of the mother, so also children before the use of reason, being as it were in the womb of their mother the Church, receive salvation not by their own act, but by the act of the Church (Aquinas, *Sum* 3.68.9.ad1). Furthermore, Aquinas rejects the argument that the severely mentally impaired should not be baptized any more than non-human animals (*Sum* 3.68.12.ad2). In fact, God gives the gift of wisdom to infants and mentally impaired "naturally foolish" in baptism (*Sum* 2-2.45.5.ad3). For more see, Berkman, "Persons with Profound Intellectual Disabilities," 83-96; cf. Reinders, *Receiving the Gift*, 88-90.

174. Aquinas, *Sum* 1-2.5-6

175. "Now the cause of our debt is found primarily and chiefly in God, in that He is he first principle of all our goods" (Aquinas, *Sum* 1-2.106.1). "For He brought things into being in order that His goodness might be communicated to creatures, and be represented by them; and because His goodness could not be adequately represented by one creature alone, He produced many and diverse creatures, that what was wanting to one in the representation of the divine goodness might be supplied by another. For goodness, which in God is simple and uniform, in creatures is manifold and divided and hence the whole universe together participates the divine goodness more perfectly, and represents it better than any single creature whatever (Aquinas, *Sum*

Though Aquinas is Aristotelian in his ethics he embraces the rubric of the four cardinal virtues of prudence (or wisdom), courage (or fortitude), justice, and temperance first mentioned in Plato's *Republic*.[176] His consideration of the cardinal virtues is preceded by a discussion of the three theological virtues of faith, hope, and love because it is in the context of the Christian life that the cardinal virtues are perfected.[177] For Aquinas, these four virtues "lead us to the door of heaven while the theological virtues bring us behind the door."[178]

Friendship of Intentional Relationship

Where does Aquinas situate gratitude specifically? Whereas other virtues direct a person in relation to himself, justice directs a person in relation to others, and therefore Aquinas considers gratitude under the rubric of justice.[179] It is not a *principal* virtue of justice, however, but an *annexed* virtue

---

1.47.1). Eschatological happiness (*beatitudo*) is also a gift of God's grace (Aquinas, *Sum* 1–2.5–6).

176. Aristotle includes prudence as one five intellectual virtues, and fortitude, temperance, and justice as three of eleven moral virtues. Early church fathers often referred to the four virtues from Platonic sources though they are explicitly mentioned in the Book of Wisdom 8:7: "And if a man love justice: her labours have great virtues: for she teacheth temperance, and prudence, and justice, and fortitude, which are such things as men can have nothing more profitable in life" (Douay-Rheims Bible). It was Ambrose who coined the term *virtutes cardinals* (See Bejczy, *Cardinal Virtues*, 12). Aquinas emerges out of a context in which there were competing theological systems. Peter Abelard and followers were progressive, philosophical, appreciative of Aristotle and saw the cardinal virtues as common ground between ancient and Christian morality whereas Peter Lombard and followers) were conservative, theological, oriented by Augustine, and contended that the cardinal virtues had no value in their ancient conception (See Bejczy, *Cardinal Virtues*, 70).

177. This was common already in the eleventh century, though absent in earlier formative theologians such as Ambrose, Jerome, and Augustine (Bejczy, *Cardinal Virtues*, 44). "The cardinal virtues . . . are discussed after the theological virtues because they are understood to be retained and perfected within the Christian life" (Pope, "Virtue Ethics in Thomas Aquinas," 4). As nature is perfected by grace, so is the will by love, and the cardinal virtues by the theological virtues.

178. Bejczy, *Cardinal Virtues*, 184.

179. "A man's [sic] work is said to be just when it is related to some other by way of some kind of equality, for instance the payment of the wage due for a service rendered" (Aquinas, *Sum* 2–2.57.1). As such, gratitude is a virtue linked to justice because it involves rendering to someone her due. Similarly, in religion believers give to God what is his due. Since there is no equality between creature and God, and we can never return anything equal to benefits received from God. "It is not possible to pay God as much as we owe Him" and there is a kind of "equality in consideration of man's [sic] ability

because it is an imperfection of justice in one of two ways—by "falling short of the aspect of equality" or "by falling short of the aspect of due."[180] Gratitude falls short of the aspect of equality in the sense that what is returned in gratitude does not always equal the value of the gift. In terms of "the aspect of due" Aquinas distinguishes, as did Aristotle, between *legal* debt as "that which one is bound to render by reason of a legal obligation" and *moral* debt as "that which to which one is bound in respect of the rectitude of virtue."[181] Aquinas argues that "the repayment that belongs to the virtue of thankfulness or gratitude answers to the moral debt and is paid spontaneously."[182]

What is significant is that for both Aquinas and Aristotle gratitude repays a debt. Even if the giving is not legal (i.e., contractual), Aristotle argues, "the giver expects to recover the equivalent or more"[183] and the recipient "ought to repay as much benefit as he enjoyed, or even more, because this will be a finer gesture[184] Similarly, Aquinas argues that "gratitude should incline to do something greater" because the objective is not simply to fulfill a contract or conclude a relationship, but to perpetuate it.[185] Yet since his reflection on gift-giving was based chiefly on Seneca, Aquinas's views are also different from Aristotle's. Unlike Aristotle who was unable sufficiently to distinguish gift-exchange from commercial transactions, Seneca argued that repayment of benefits in gratitude differs from commercial repayment in timing and quantity. If you are eager to repay a gift to a friend you are unwilling to be in his debt and thus are ungrateful.[186] Similarly Aquinas

---

and God's acceptance" (Aquinas, *Sum* 81.5.ad3). Like gratitude, therefore, religion is an imperfect justice and thus an annexed virtue.

180. Aquinas, *Sum* 2-2.80.1.

181. Aquinas, *Sum* 2-2.80.1; 2-2.106.4.ad1; cf. Aristotle, *Eth. nic.* 1162b20-25. Aristotle's distinction between legal and moral debt is not nearly as pronounced as Aquinas's. For Aquinas, repayment of a legal debt is necessary; repayment of a moral debt is virtuous. Aristotle describes moral debt in ways similar to legal debt: "The giver expects to receive an equivalent or greater return, as though it had not been a free gift, but a loan ... it ought to be in a friendship as it is in a business partnership" (Aristotle, *Eth. nic.* 1163a20-25).

182. Aquinas, *Sum* 2-2.106.1.ad2; cf. 2-2.106.5.

183. Aristotle, *Eth. nic.* 1162b30-35 (the context is utilitarian friendship). "Friendship is preserved by repayment of favours" (Aquinas, *Sum* 2-2.106.1.ad3).

184. Aristotle, *Eth. nic.* 1163a20-21. Earlier, he says, "Now it is a fine thing to confer a benefit without any thought of return, but the profitable thing is to receive benefits. So one ought, if one can, to repay a kindness at its full value; for one should not make a man one's friend—against his will" (Aristotle, *Eth. nic.* 1162b35-1163a5).

185. Aquinas, *Sum* 2-2.106.6. Similarly, Seneca argues that beneficiaries should not return the exact amount, but more if possible, in part to remain connected to others (Seneca, *Ben.* 2.18.5).

186. Seneca, *Ben.* 4.40.5; 6.35.3; 41.2; cf. Aquinas, *Sum* 2-2.106.5.ad1.

argues that if you endeavor to repay immediately "it would not seem to be virtuous, but a constrained repayment."[187]

There remains, however, one significant difference between Aquinas's and Aristotle's conceptions of gratitude. Unlike commercial reciprocity, where payments correspond to the value of the commodity regardless of intentions, gratitude for Aquinas responds with favor to the will.[188] Seneca had insisted that donors should not operate with a bookkeeping sense of reciprocity nor think about their gifts unless reminded by someone endeavoring to repay them.[189] The value of gratitude, for Seneca, does not consist simply in the thing given, but in the spirit in which it is given.[190] Aquinas similarly sees gratitude not simply as the return of things, but as a reciprocity of feelings. Feelings are irrelevant for Aristotle, though he does argue that "the one who is benefitted financially or morally should give honour in return, making such payment as is in his power."[191] Aquinas's view is similar, though he situates gratitude in the heart: "A poor man is certainly not ungrateful if he does what he can. For since kindness depends on the heart rather than the on the deed, so too gratitude depends chiefly on the heart."[192]

Following Seneca, Aquinas identifies the three features of gratitude as recognition, expression of thanks, and repayment, at a suitable time, place, and way.[193] In fact, Aquinas argues (again in line with Seneca) that the joyful reception of a gift is already a repayment of sorts.[194] A corollary of this is that ingratitude is always a sin "because the mere will suffices for the repayment of the debt of gratitude."[195] This, in fact, is what distinguishes legal

---

187. Aquinas, *Sum* 2-2.106.4

188. "Thanksgiving is less thankful when compelled" (Aquinas, *Sum* 2-2.106.1.ad2).

189. Seneca, *Ben.* 1.2.3.

190. Seneca, *Ben.* 1.6.1; 1.2.4.

191. Aristotle, *Eth. nic.* 1163b10–15.

192. Aquinas, *Sum* 2-2.106.3.ad5. Similarly, "repayment of a favor depends chiefly on the affection of the heart" (Aquinas, *Sum* 2-2.106.3.ad6). "There is no need for a man to desire neediness or distress in his benefactor before repaying his kindness" (Aquinas, *Sum* 2-2.106.3.ad5).

193. Aquinas, *Sum* 2-2.107.2. Seneca indicates how the "three graces" were allegorized by those who alleged that they are cheerful, as are those who give and receive gifts; young, because memory of gifts should not grow old; maidens, because benefits are pure and undefiled; and naked, because gift-giving should be transparent because benefits "desire to be seen." Seneca himself described the *charites* as (a) those who confer benefits, (b) those who return them, and (c) those who accept and return simultaneously (See Seneca, *Ben.*1.3.2–1.3.10).

194. Aquinas, *Sum* 2-2.106.3ad5.

195. Aquinas, *Sum* 2-2.107.1.ad2. "The will to pay back would be sufficient for gratitude" (Aquinas, *Sum* 2-2.106.6.ad1).

debt from moral debt. Whereas a legal debt is repaid according to the gift, moral debt is repaid "with regard to the choice or disposition of the giver."[196] Here Aquinas expressly distances himself from Aristotle who had claimed that a son cannot make repayment to a father. In line with Seneca, Aquinas alleges "that if we consider the will of the giver and of the repayer, then it is possible for a son to pay back something greater to his father."[197]

Sacrificial Charity

"The debt of gratitude," Aquinas wrote, "flows from charity."[198] Charity is "the form of the virtues" which sustains all other virtues and directs them (including justice) to its end.[199] Of the theological virtues, it alone persists into eternity. Charity is a grace-inspired friendship of person of God which includes benevolence, mutuality, and communication in a shared good.[200] "Whereas Aristotle's civic ideal is that of the magnanimous man," John Milbank claims, "Aquinas's ecclesial ideal is that of 'the person of charity.'"[201] The charitable person does not accumulate resources in order to dispense them with *largesse*, as does the magnanimous man, but lives in a mode of giving. Motivated by "heartfelt sympathy for another's distress," the charitable person gives to the poor without expectation of reciprocity.[202] His/her love of the poor is the love of friendship, and involves not simply the

---

196. Aquinas, *Sum* 2-2.106.5.

197. Aquinas, *Sum* 2-2.106.6.ad1; cf. Aristotle, *Eth. nic.* 1163b20-25. Seneca believed that donors should be strategic about gift-giving in singling out recipients who are able to reciprocate with gifts of their own (Seneca, *Ben.* 1.10.5; 2.11.4-5). At the same time, gratitude should be expressed by donees. The way to elicit gratitude from a an ungrateful donee, Seneca advises, is to shower him with more gifts until eventually you "squeeze gratitude even from a heart that is hard and forgetful. . . . Besiege him with your benefits" (Seneca, *Ben.* 1.3.1). Seneca recommends giving without the expectation of return and yet "the donor who gives without the expectation of return will maximize his return" (Seneca, *Ben.* 5.1.4). He who gives gifts widely and generously ensures that he is surrounded by subordinates he could call upon when support was needed (see Blanton, "Benefactor's Account-book," 407).

198. Aquinas, *Sum* 2-2.106.6.ad2. The full statement is, "The debt of gratitude flows from charity, which he more it is paid the more it is due, according to Rom 13:8, *Owe no man anything, but to love one another.* Wherefore it is not unreasonable if the obligation of gratitude has no limit."

199. Aquinas, *Sum* 2-2.23.8. It is "what makes virtue virtuous" (Milbank, *Theology and Social* Theory, 360).

200. Aquinas, *Sum* 2-2.23.1.

201. Milbank, *Theology and Social Theory*, 359.

202. Aquinas, *Sum* 2-2.30.1; 31.3.ad1

donation of goods, but a giving of oneself.[203] Everyone is a neighbor, created in image of God, capable of eternal fellowship with God, and thus no one is beyond the reach of charity.[204] The person of charity is not first and foremost a benefactor, but a recipient of charity from God such that "charity begins and ends in gratitude."[205]

What does Aquinas make of the magnanimous man? Does magnanimity not conflict with humility? Humility makes us think little of ourselves in terms of our deficiencies, Aquinas argues, but magnanimity makes us think high of ourselves in terms of God's gifts.[206] What about Aristotle's claim that the magnanimous man should recall gifts given and not gifts received? Aquinas interprets Aristotle in this way: "This points to the fact that he takes no pleasure in accepting favors from others unless he repay them with yet greater favor; this belongs to the perfection of gratitude, in the act of which he wishes to excel, even as in the acts of other virtues."[207] Aquinas argues, in fact, that an act of magnanimity can be considered great not only when "it consists of the best use of the greatest thing" but also "proportionately, even if it consist in the use of some small or ordinary thing."[208] Furthermore, he argues that those who are unable to perform the *act* of magnanimity might still possess the *habit* of magnanimity whereby one is "disposed to practice that act if it were competent to him according to his state."[209] Aquinas claims that the virtue is mainly an inward choice which may not always be accompanied by "outward fortune" such that "even a poor man may be magnificent."[210]

Appraisal

Aquinas is particularly interesting because of his Aristotelian outlook, though a comparison with Aristotle yields significant differences. Whereas chapter 3 observed that gratitude languishes in Aristotelian ethics because it: (a) recommends a εὐδαιμονία that, devoid of a relationship with a personal God, celebrates at the summit of virtue heroic achievement, self-fulfillment,

---

203. Aquinas, *Sum* 1–2.114.4.ad3.

204. Aquinas, *Sum* 1.93.4; 2–2.25.1, 6; 78.1

205. Milbank, *Theology and Social Theory*, 360.

206. "There is in man [sic] something great which he possesses through the gift of God" (Aquinas, *Sum* 2–2.129.3.ad4).

207. Aquinas, *Sum* 2–2.129.3.ad5.

208. Aquinas, *Sum* 2–2.129.1.

209. Aquinas, *Sum* 2–2.129.3.ad2.

210. Aquinas, *Sum* 2–2.134.3.ad4.

egotism, autonomy, independence, and inequality; (b) reduces friendship to commerce; (c) privileges rationality over charity; and (d) marginalizes poverty, weakness, and disability, this chapter concludes that gratitude flourishes in Thomistic ethics because it: (a) prizes the endowment of divine gifts at creation, not least the *imago Dei*; (b) anticipates the giftedness of divine presence in the eschaton; (c) construes friendship in terms of intentionality; (d) envisages "debts" in friendship and "repayment" of gifts in non-commercial ways; (e) privileges love over rationality; and (f) sees value in poverty, weakness, and disability.

On the other hand, Thomistic gratitude is not without its problems. Though there is a sense in which his sense of repayment is non-commercial, there is also a sense in which it stands in the shadow of commerce. First, Aquinas retains the language of "repayment" and "debt" which, though acceptable, is not optimal because of the commercial implications. On the other hand, he distinguishes the "repayment" of gratitude from mere commerce, not only by distinguishing moral from legal debt as did Aristotle, but by eschewing immediate repayment, in line with Seneca. Second, his Senecan restrictions regarding time, place, and manner, while distinguishing gratitude from commercial repayment, potentially conflict with the apostle Paul's exhortation to give thanks in all circumstances. Thirdly, Aquinas's insistence that the grateful person should attempt to repay the donor in greater measure has potential to recast gratitude as a burden.

John Calvin

It could be argued that Thomas Aquinas, because of certain affinities with John Calvin in terms of the doctrine of predestination, was a proto-Protestant. On the other hand, their views are also remarkably different, especially on the doctrine of justification. What place does gratitude have in Calvin's theology? Brian Gerrish claims that Calvin's entire theology had a "eucharistic shape."[211] It could be argued that, especially in the final edition of his *Institutes* (1559), the father's liberality and his children's responsive gratitude is "the most fundamental theme."[212] Calvin's theology is pastoral, not a *summa theologiae*, but a *pietatis summa*, not a contemplation of God's essence, but something responsive. "It consists," Nicholas Wolterstorff explains, "in the appropriate *response* to his works. Knowledge of God consists

---

211. Gerrish, *Grace and Gratitude*, ix. As such, Gerrish writes, Calvin "belonged self-consciously within the tradition of St. Augustine, for whom true religion was gratitude for our justification" (Gerrish, *Grace and Gratitude*, ix).

212. Gerrish, *Grace and Gratitude*, 20.

in acknowledgment of God. And acknowledgement of God occurs in life as a whole, comprising such things as trust, reverence, gratitude, service."[213] Calvin yearned for people to understand "that they owe everything to God, that they are cherished by his fatherly care, that he is the author of their every good, so that they should ask for nothing apart from him."[214] In fact, Calvin's favorite image for God is "the fountain of all good" (*fons omnium bonorum*). Though the source for this image is likely Plato, Calvin emphasizes the reciprocal responsibility creatures have to their generous Creator.[215] Such natural imagery (i.e., fountain) gives way in the *Institutes* to predominantly familial imagery, leading Warfield to dub Calvin "the theologian of divine fatherhood."[216] God created the world and then tends it with pure goodness and loving care, but humans are "the privileged recipients of the father's special care."[217]

Calvin's assessment of the world is quite complex. There is, first of all, a sense in which the world invites contempt. Since the fall, Calvin averred, humanity was plagued with a love affair with the present world, creating a "blockishness" that cannot see beyond this world and therefore endeavors to locate happiness on earth.[218] "The heart also," he writes, "occupied with avarice, ambition, and lust, is so weighed down that it cannot rise up any higher."[219] For this reason, God sends us the discipline of the cross, diseases, and peril, to wean us from the present life and arouse desire for the life to come.[220] Calvin goes so far as to suggest that there is no middle ground between an inordinate love of the world and a contempt for it.[221]

Though seemingly Stoic, Calvin's theology must be distinguished from Seneca's Stoic theology in multiple ways: (a) Seneca's god is strict, refusing to spoil a good person; (b) deep access to the Father's love was possible for

213. Wolterstorff, *Until Justice and Peace Embrace*, 13.

214. Calvin, *Instit.* 1.2.1. The subtitle of Calvin's 1536 edition of the *Institutes* described it as a *summa pietas*.

215. Gerrish, *Grace and Gratitude*, 39.

216. Gerrish, *Grace and Gratitude*, 27. The language of God as fountain of all good is found in Luther and Zwingli, and likely derives from Plato.

217. Gerrish, *Grace and Gratitude*, 30. See Calvin, *Instit.* 1.4.3; 1.14.2.

218. Calvin, *Instit.* 3.9.1.

219. Calvin, *Instit.* 3.9.1.

220. Calvin, *Instit.* 3.9.1.

221. Calvin, *Instit.* 3.9.2. The theological error in Calvin's depreciation of the world becomes apparent especially when he chides those "gripped by great fear of death, rather than a desire for it" so that we can be delivered from "the rotting tabernacle of our body" (Calvin, *Instit.* 3.9.5). His demurral from those who, though they have reasons to do so, celebrate birthdays "with sorrow and tears" and "funeral rites with solemn joy" (Calvin, *Instit.* 3.9.4).

Calvin only through Christ; (c) the fatherhood of God, for Calvin, did not exclude motherhood and (d) Stoicism, Calvin judged, was "an iron philosophy" in which sadness and tears at the plight of the world were unwelcome.[222] Yet Calvin insisted, like Seneca, that the fitting response among sons and daughters to a generous parent is gratitude, though Calvin distinguished between humanity before and after the Fall. Gerrish writes,

> The heart of the matter can then be summed up if we say that the existence of humanity in God's design is defined by thankfulness, the correlate of God's goodness, and the existence of humanity in sin is defined by thanklessness, the antithesis of God's goodness.[223]

Humans in fact are special mirrors of God's glory, distinct from mute creation, by the ability to "reflect God's glory in a conscious response of thankfulness."[224] When Calvin reflects on the world as created by God, he moderates his views about contempt for it: we should not display any "hatred of it or ingratitude against God."[225] Moreover, if we discern in this life "no divine benefit, we are already guilty of grave ingratitude toward God himself."[226] Not only do some earthly things reveal his glory and goodness, God gives us benefits whereby we "taste the sweetness" of divine generosity to whet our appetite for its future fullness and so be "freed from too much desire" of this life.[227] Further, Calvin distances himself from those—one thinks of Augustine's views on sex—who argue that that one must abstain from everything unnecessary which, if true, would require satisfaction with a diet of "plain bread and water."[228]

Ultimately, Calvin settles on the principle that "the use of God's gifts is not wrongly directed when it is referred to that end to which the Author himself created and destined them for us, since he created them for our good, not for our ruin."[229] Refusal to see God's goodness and abstinence

---

222. Gerrish, *Grace and Gratitude*, 39; Calvin, *Instit.* 3.8.9.

223. Gerrish, *Grace and Gratitude*, 41.

224. Gerrish, *Grace and Gratitude*, 43.

225. Calvin, *Instit.* 3.9.3.

226. Calvin, *Instit.* 3.9.3

227. Calvin, *Instit.* 3.9.3.

228. Calvin, *Instit.* 3.10.1.

229. Calvin, *Instit.* 3.10.2. Apart from necessity, food is for delight, for example, and clothing for comeliness and decency. "Grasses, trees, and fruits, apart from their various uses, there is beauty of appearance and pleasantness of odor. . . . Did God not "render many things attractive to us, apart from their necessary use?" (Calvin, *Instit.* 3.10.1).

from his gifts "robs a man of all his senses and degrades him to a block."[230] Calvin questions, "Where is your thanksgiving if you so gorge yourself with banqueting or wine that you either become stupid or are rendered useless for the duties of piety and of your calling?"[231] God's generosity includes gifts in the arts and sciences, gifts of reason, philosophy, and civic virtue.[232] Because such gifts are distributed unequally, it is clear for Calvin that they are "peculiar gifts of grace" and therefore should incite gratitude.[233] To deny that this is so is to be guilty of "ingratitude into which not even the pagan poets fell."[234] Further, we must be grateful for God's gifts which reach us through other people. Calvin's *Geneva Catechism* poses the question (237), "But should we not be grateful to other people when they perform some service to us?" Calvin's answer is:

> Of course we should, precisely because God honors them by channeling through their hands the good things that flow to us from the inexhaustible fountain of his generosity. In this way he puts us in their debt, and he wants us to acknowledge it. Anyone, therefore, who does not show gratitude to other people betrays ingratitude to God as well.[235]

Whereas Augustine rooted human sin in pride, Calvin argued that infidelity preceded pride and with pride came ingratitude.[236] "Calvin's disgust at human ingratitude, not disgust with humanity," writes Gerrish, "lies behind his rhetoric of sin and depravity."[237] At the fall, when true human knowledge of God was lost, it was no longer possible for people to render the grateful piety (*grata pietas*) due to the almighty Father and creator.[238]

When he deals with redemption, Calvin makes clear that access to the fountain, and also to the Father, is possible only through Christ.[239] In some places, Calvin describes Christ as the fountain.[240] Faith, for Calvin, is recognizing God's fatherhood and being convinced that he is a kind

---

230. Calvin, *Instit.* 3.10.3.
231. Calvin, *Instit.* 3.10.3.
232. See Plantinga, "Concern of the Church," 193–97.
233. Calvin, *Instit.* 2.2.14.
234. Calvin, *Instit.* 2.2.15. See Gerrish, *Grace and Gratitude*, 44–45.
235. Calvin, *Catechism of the Geneva Church*.
236. Calvin, *Instit.* 2.1.4; cf. *Instit.* 1.4.1–2.
237. Gerrish, *Grace and Gratitude*, 47.
238. Calvin, *Instit.* (1536).
239. See Calvin, *Comm.* Heb 7:25.
240. See Calvin, *Comm.* John 6:11.

father.[241] Without faith, such recognition is impossible.[242] Not surprisingly, Calvin often regards the gospel as the good news of adoption, signified by baptism. Without adoption, we would have no confidence to call God "father."[243] Moreover, the remission of sins summons nothing but love and gratitude.[244] "By faith, then, we obtain forgiveness," Calvin writes, "by love we give thanks and bear witness to the kindness of the Lord."[245] We must do good works, and we are promised rewards for them, but these rewards are not merited—something Calvin thought was proved by the parable of the laborers in the vineyard, where those who worked different hours were paid the same.[246]

The emergence in the modern world of an "unreciprocated" gift, Barclay argues, is "distinctively Protestant in origin," architected especially by Martin Luther.[247] To pit Catholic reciprocity against Reformed gratuitousness, however, is tenuous since Calvin argued that in response to the free gift of salvation, believers should return to God a grateful life of obedience. In fact, though he affirmed that the covenant is unilateral in some sense, Calvin "makes extensive use of the language of a mutual, bilateral covenant, particularly when he wants to emphasize human responsibility."[248] Mak-

241. Calvin, *Instit.* 3.2.2.

242. Calvin, *Instit.* 2.6.4.

243. Calvin, *Instit.* 3.20.36.

244. The Lord's Supper was also significant for his theology of gratitude. For Calvin, the Lord's Supper had two uses: to confirm faith in God's promise and to awaken gratitude, the latter receiving a separate chapter in the final edition of the *Institutes* (4.18) (Gerrish, *Grace and Gratitude*, 126). The Lord's Supper is a holy banquet (*sacrosanctum epulum*) and a genuine feast (*convivium*) which moves communicants to gratitude and love. Gerrish presents several propositions to capture Calvin's doctrine of the Lord's Supper. First, the Lord's Supper is a gift. In this way, he distinguished himself from Zwingli who emphasized our thankful recollection of the cross, which Calvin regarded as secondary. "The Supper is a gift," Gerrish writes, "it does not merely remind us of a gift" (Gerrish, *Grace and Gratitude*, 136). Second, the gift is Jesus Christ himself. In the Eucharist, we commune with the whole Christ, in his humanity and deity. Third, the gift is given with signs. Unlike the Roman Catholics for whom sign was transformed into thing signified, and the Zwinglians, who divorced sign and reality, Calvin argues that the signs are not bare signs but "present what they represent" (Gerrish, *Grace and Gratitude*, 137). Fourth, the gift is given by the Holy Spirit.

245. Calvin, *Instit.* 3.4.37.

246. Calvin, *Instit.* 3.18.3.

247. Barclay, *Paul and the Gift*, 56. In Luther's theology, God "gives freely and without strings attached, and believers are to do likewise" (Barclay, *Paul and the Gift*, 57). The unreciprocated gift "may have roots in Lutheran theology, but was universalized in Kantian ethics with its resistance to externally imposed obligation" (Barclay, *Paul and the Gift*, 185).

248. Billings, "Milbank's Theology," 92. This is an important corrective to Tanner's

ing much of the prayer in Romans 8 in which the Spirit enables one to cry out "Abba Father," Calvin insisted, for example, that the believer is far from passive.[249] On the other hand, the grateful life of the believer is merely a response and not a means to earning a future gift from God.[250] "Human praise and obedience are never instrumental in Protestant theology," Barclay claims, "never part of a repeatable pattern of gift and return."[251] The former statement seems obvious, but the latter questionable. Calvin regarded the whole of the Christian life as a return for the gift of life in creation and redemption and did not hesitate to denominate the return as a "debt."

The remission of sins, for Calvin, summons gratitude and therefore gratitude functions as an impetus for life and obedience. The influence of Calvin in this area is discernible especially in the Heidelberg Catechism, one of the most popular sixteenth-century Reformation confessions. Divided into fifty-two "Lord's Days" (hereafter, LD), the content of the catechism was designed to be taught over the course of the fifty-two Sundays of a year. The threefold structure of catechism, set forth in the first LD (1:2) moves from the depth of sin to the manner of deliverance and concludes with "how I am to be thankful to God for such deliverance." Moreover, the catechism teaches that knowledge of God's creation and providence enables us to be patient in adversity and "thankful in prosperity" (LD 10:28). The persistently "ungrateful and impenitent" cannot be saved (LD 32). Christ's redemption enjoins believers to offer themselves as a "living sacrifice of thankfulness" (LD 11:32; cf. LD 16:43), "to bring forth fruits of thankfulness" (LD 24:64), and with their whole lives to show themselves "thankful to God for his benefits" (LD 32:86). The Ten Commandments and the Lord's prayer, ethics and spirituality, are explained under the rubric of "gratitude," the third and longest section of the catechism (LDs 32–52). Furthermore, prayer is necessary because it is the most important part of "the thankfulness which God requires of us" and God will give his grace and Holy Spirit "only to those who constantly and with heartfelt longing ask him for these gifts and thank him for them" (LD 45:116).

Calvin's theology of gratitude is predicated on his theology of God's excessive generosity. Because God's generosity is so lavish, ingratitude is inexcusable. There are wonderful statements in Calvin's theology about the diversity of God's gifts located in the arts and sciences, but also in other

---

insistence that all divine giving is by nature unconditional and unilateral.

249. "He means that the prompting of the Spirit empowers us so to compose prayers as by no means to hinder or hold back our own effort, since in this matter God's will is to test how effectually faith moves our hearts" (Calvin, *Instit.* 3.20.5).

250. Barclay, *Paul and the Gift*, 56.

251. Barclay, *Paul and the Gift*, 56.

people, to whom we should return thanks as well. His was an ontology of communion in which humanity is inextricably connected to God, others, and the world. Moreover, the Senecan restrictions apparent in Aquinas are absent in Calvin.

Two features of Calvin's theology of gratitude are, nevertheless, concerning. The first is a statement to which Gerrish draws attention which offers a small window into Calvin's mentality: "The thought repeatedly returns to my mind," Calvin writes, "that there is danger of my being unjust to God's mercy when I labor with such great concern to assert it, as if it were doubtful or obscure. But since our ill will is such that it never yields to God that which is his, unless it is powerfully compelled, I am obliged to dwell on this a little longer."[252] One sometimes gets the sense from Calvin that gratitude is hard work. Something must be returned to God, and so we give gratitude, but it is laborious and never really suffices.[253] Not unrelatedly, the joy in Calvin's gratitude is muted. If it is muted in Calvin, however, it is prominent in Karl Barth, to whom we turn next.

Karl Barth

As an heir to Calvin's theology, Barth too was a theologian of gratitude and, even more than Calvin, Barth affirmed an ontology of communion. His *Church Dogmatics* are laced with wonderful affirmations and expositions of gratitude, some of which are cited below. God's grace comes first, for Barth, and it calls for gratitude: "Χάρις calls for εὐχαριστία. But εὐχαριστία is itself the substance of the creature's participation in the divine χάρις."[254] But so constituted, gratitude describes the essence of redeemed humanity: "Gratitude is to be understood not only as a quality and an activity but as the very being and essence of this creature. It is not merely grateful. It is itself gratitude. It can see itself only as gratitude because in fact it can only exist as this, as pure gratitude towards God."[255] In this respect, gratitude is simply acknowledgement.

252. Calvin, *Instit.* 3.14.6.
253. Webb expresses similar concerns in Webb, *Gifting God*, 98.
254. Barth, *CD* 2/1:670. This expression makes one think of 1 Corinthians 1:4: "I give thanks (εὐχαριστία) to my God always for you because of the grace (χάρις) of God that has been given you in Christ Jesus." Elsewhere, Barth writes, "And if God requires and made possible that He should be served by the creature this service itself means that creature is taken up in to the sphere of divine Lordship. We have always to remember that God's glory really consists in His self-giving, and that this has its centre and meaning in God's Son, Jesus Christ" (Barth, *CD* 2/1:670).
255. Barth, *CD* 2/1:669. "This creature is itself a new creature, not taken out of

> As the work of gratitude, it cannot try to be requital and therefore be a reply in equal terms to what has been said to man by God. Where man [sic] repays like with like, there is no question of thanksgiving but only a transaction: we are at the market which is ruled by the mutual adjustment of supply and demand, value and price. The giving of thanks for anything can only be acknowledgment, and the one who acknowledges places himself and his action consciously and expressly under the giver and his gift. Even the richest gift given in return as a mark of thanks will then—if it does not spring from the wrong intention of discharging the thanks—be designed only to emphasize the acknowledgment of the giver and the gift and the subordination of the recipient to the giver in accordance with the very nature of thanks.[256]

Yet gratitude is more than mere acknowledgment; it is joyful acknowledgment. "Joy is the simplest form of gratitude," Barth writes. "When we are joyful, time stands still for a moment or moments because it has fulfilled its mean as the space of our life-movement and, engaged in this movement, we have attained in one respect at least the goal of our striving."[257] The fact that joy and gratitude are commanded simply means for Barth that "we should hold ourselves in readiness for joy."[258]

> We live in expectation, but are moments in which life manifests itself as 'God's gift of grace,' in which something of fulfillment shines out in the midst of the movement experienced and executed by him, in which gratitude that he may live break through all his running and striving and fighting and struggling. In respect for life, he is necessarily confident that there will be such moments. He is prepared and ready for the arrival of such moments and therefore for joy. He is ready, then, not merely to hurry on with his own work, but to pause in gratitude for what life is really is as the gift of God before and after and over all his own works.[259]

---

darkness by its own powers and efforts but by the light which has fallen upon it from God, and of which it has become witness and been made the reflection. This creature is free for God's glory, not because it was able or willed to be so on its own account, but because it has been made free for it by the God's glory itself. This creature is grateful. It knows God, and itself becomes a new creature, by being thankful. To believe in Jesus Christ means to become thankful" (Barth, CD 2/1:669).

256. Barth, CD 2/1:217.
257. Barth, CD 3/4:376.
258. Barth, CD 3/4:377.
259. Barth, CD 3/4:378. "In so far and for so long as we know true joy, we desire

Moreover, it is significant that Barth situates the grateful person in relation to God. "True gratitude enquires—and it does not enquire in a soliloquy, but it enquires after him to whom it wants to show gratitude.... But it enquires after Him, and enquiring after Him, it acts."[260] The grateful person, however, is also united to others.

> Joy is a social matter. There may be cases where a man [sic] can be really merry in isolation. But these are exceptional and dangerous. To be sure, life is a gift to each individually. But it is made to each in his [sic] relationship with his [sic] fellows. And as man [sic] cannot live it alone, he [sic] cannot basically claim as his [sic] own the manifestation of its character as a divine gift of grace, nor can he [sic] be basically grateful for its fulfillments in any kind of solitude and egotism.[261]

Statements of this order, according to Stephen Webb, are "majestically focused" and Barth provides a "theocentric celebration of God's central and abiding excess" and yet "cannot provide the foundation for a Christian theory of mutual generosity, a language that encompasses God's involvement in acts of giving that are also our own."[262]

In Webb's treatment of Barth's theology of gratitude, however, he largely ignores Barth's early lectures on ethics in which he pays substantial attentional to gratitude and there mitigates, I suspect, some of Webb's concerns. In 1928 Barth delivered stirring lectures on ethics in which he depicted theological ethics as "presenting the claiming of man [sic] by the Word of God" specifically as the Word of divine creation, divine reconciliation, and divine redemption.[263] Whereas the Word of divine creation means life, is revealed as calling, demands order, and gives faith, the Word of divine reconciliation means law, is revealed as authority, demands humility, and gives love, the Word of divine redemption means promise, is revealed as conscience, demands gratitude, and gives hope.[264]

---

only the duration of this fulfillment, of life in the form of a gift, and therefore of the joyful moment. This is achieved, of course, only in the case of what is called in Holy Scripture eternal joy and felicity in perfect fellowship with God. But this is one instance has an exemplary significance. The desire for duration, even if realized only in a single case, is an essential characteristic of all joy as such. Why? Quite simply because joy is gratitude for an effected fulfillment" (Barth, *CD* 3/4:377).

260. Barth, *CD* 2/1:218
261. Barth, *CD* 3/4:380.
262. Webb, *Gifting God*, 105.
263. Barth, *Ethics*, 45, 52.
264. See Barth, *Ethics*, 52. In this section Barth demonstrates how the "commands" issuing from the Word of God in these three senses align with what the Protestant

To those he has reconciled, God promises his presence and summons "to wait for this future of his and to hasten toward it."[265] Furthermore, in fellowship with God the redeemer, his command strikes us and claims us, supplying us with his Spirit, the source of our conscience, and we "have to listen to it."[266] This claim of his Word, which we must obey, "wins me not only for the commanded orderliness and humility, but also for the God to whom I owe my existence, my salvation, and my final relationship to him."[267]

Gladly Embracing God's Pure Gift

For Barth, God and humanity are united through redemption, so that we belong to him and are partakers of his divine nature, though not in a way that obliterates the Creator/creature distinction. This unity, after all, is not something people attain, but what Barth dubs "the pure gift of God."[268] "As we live by the fact that it is promised to us, we are pointed to God's *gift*," Barth writes, "and what is required of us, the measure by which our conduct is measured from this third standpoint, is *gratitude*.[269] Barth interprets gratitude to mean "specifically that I am gladly, i.e., voluntarily and cheerfully, ready for what God wills of me in acknowledgment of what is given to me by God and as my necessary response to God's gift."[270] Implied in the adverb "gladly" is that God "unequivocally wants me myself," that he wants obedience to be our choice.[271] God's intentions for us are not fulfilled by us as mere creatures, or mere sinners saved by grace, but only by "the eschatological reality of our divine sonship."[272] This is true because in this eschatological context, the Word of God regarding our sonship enters our own word so that God's claim "you are" is echoed with our affirmation "I am."[273] We cannot be summoned except by ourselves: "Gratitude cannot be

---

Reformed called the Three Uses of the Law—namely, the civil use of the law (for creation), the pedagogic use of the law (for reconciliation), and the normative use of the law (for redemption). Note to self: interesting how new life is to be future-oriented, though characterized by gratitude.

265. Barth, *Ethics*, 461.
266. Barth, *Ethics*, 475.
267. Barth, *Ethics*, 497.
268. Barth, *Ethics*, 499; cf. Derrida's remarks about the impossibility of "pure" gifts.
269. Barth, *Ethics*, 499.
270. Barth, *Ethics*, 499–500.
271. Barth, *Ethics*, 500.
272. Barth, *Ethics*, 500.
273. Barth, *Ethics*, 501.

commanded," Barth writes, "I must really command it of myself."[274] We are thus liberated in this eschatological phase in a way that is not true of creation or reconciliation. Yet we must be clear that we have not experienced redemption itself and thus are still sick and frail, imprisoned and confined in some sense. We sigh, but "there is a release and relaxation even in this sighing, even in the despair which often does overpower the comfort."[275]

Playing before God: Art and Humor

Barth proceeds to reflect on the end for which believers are liberated. It is for goodness, for what is pleasing to God and yet we are also "released from the seriousness of life and can and should simply play before God."[276] He defends this proposition with three arguments. First, we are still God's "little" children, not like adult children who relate to their father on his level.[277] Second, we have not yet entered the final consummation, and therefore "cannot allot final seriousness to what we do here and now."[278] Third, because God's command is something one gladly embraces, the strangeness and the hostility of his command has evaporated and what one does therefore amounts to play.[279]

This notion of play leads Barth to consider art and humor, which "have in common that, strictly and exactly, only the children of God are capable of them."[280] Both art and humor, though practiced "gladly, voluntarily, and cheerfully," are "sustained by an ultimate and very profound pain."[281] The children of God suffer with a groaning creation, with suffering that cannot be overlooked, but joyfully accept it in terms of future redemption. Only those who anticipate the resurrection truly understand death. Art does not belong to creation or salvation, but eschatological redemption, and is created only by the truth of the promise of a new heavens and a new earth. "In

274. Barth, *Ethics*, 501.
275. Barth, *Ethics*, 502.
276. Barth, *Ethics*, 504.
277. Gratitude "cannot take place except in joyfulness. A gratitude that consists in an involuntary, mutinous and therefore forced and unjoyful action is not thanksgiving. A tribute to tyranny, however, is paid, not thanks. A sacrifice offered in dread and constraint is not, in the biblical sense at least, a real sacrifice. Sacrifice and thanks are only what is offered gladly. . . . It is not the undertaking of a slave, but of a child (Barth, *CD* 2/1:219).
278. Barth, *Ethics*, 505.
279. Barth, *Ethics*, 506.
280. Barth, *Ethics*, 506.
281. Barth, *Ethics*, 506–7.

principle all artistic creation is *futuristic*."[282] It plays with reality and presents it, created and reconciled, as redeemed—new and changed. Human words are transcended in poetry; the human voice in song; the voices of creation in instrumental music; the reality of life and society, sin and forgiveness in novels and plays; forms and nature in painting and sculpture, all "creating anew in a better way."[283] In fact, "to be unaesthetic is to be immoral and disobedient . . . fundamentally to reject the signs that point beyond the present."[284]

To have humor, for Barth, is to persevere in the recognition that we "cannot change the future into the present and the present into the future."[285] Like art, humor does not take the present seriously because the future is more serious. Humor does not dismiss the present, but wrestles with it gladly, voluntarily, and joyfully, with "liberated laughter."[286] Close your eyes to the riddles of existence and you will lack humor; true humor presupposes rather than excludes knowledge of suffering. Its favorite target is oneself, seeing both a question mark and exclamation point behind its "very important and serious heavenly existence."[287] "When we have first laughed at ourselves," Barth argues, "we can laugh at others, and we can stand cheerfully the final test of being laughed at by them."[288]

In conclusion, Barth replicates Calvin's theology of God's excessive generosity, though the gratitude he recommends is free not simply from the shadow of commerce in Aquinas but from the somber sense of obligation one finds in Calvin. Barth himself acknowledges this: "A serious problem one might have with Calvin is that he seems not to have been able to laugh, or to do so only bitterly."[289] Furthermore, in his ethics Barth provides something for which Webb finds him deficient—namely, he demonstrates how gratitude is reciprocal and how grateful people participate in God's generosity, particularly through art and humor.

---

282. Barth, *Ethics*, 508.
283. Barth, *Ethics*, 509.
284. Barth, *Ethics*, 510.
285. Barth, *Ethics*, 511.
286. Barth, *Ethics*, 511.
287. Barth, *Ethics*, 511.
288. Barth, *Ethics*, 511.
289. Barth, *Ethics*, 512.

CONCLUSION: A THEOLOGICALLY REFLECTIVE PROFILE OF GRATITUDE

The concluding section of this chapter will offer a profile of gratitude, mindful of the preliminary profile presented in chapter 3 and the material accumulated in this chapter. Gratitude, first of all, is a *responsive virtue* because it presupposes a gift. Even prior to the Fall, there was the gift of creation, an instance of divine generosity. After the Fall, there is the gift of Christ, a second instance of divine generosity. Accepting the world and life as given realities, gratitude is primal. "If we are in fact creatures who are contingent and dependent," Mitchell writes, "then at least one disposition we ought to possess is gratitude."[290] Both life and salvation are gifts, and humanity is dependent on Another for both. "To live in sync with who we truly are," Volf writes, "means to recognize that we are dependent on God for our very breath and are graced with many good things; it means to be grateful to the giver and attentive to the purpose for which the gifts are given."[291] The grateful person therefore responds especially to the gifts God gives in creation and salvation, but he or she also responds to the gifts of others (which are ultimately still God's gifts). Gratitude, therefore, represents a turn or return to the giver. This is represented by the Samaritan leper who physically turned to thank Jesus. It is also a sense obtained from Psalm 116 where the Psalmist asks about what can be returned to the Lord for his gifts.

Like the returns of romantic love, gratitude is the normal and natural response to a gift, without which something would be morally amiss. Yet the return of gratitude is also given *freely*, just as each person within the Trinity freely gives and returns gifts to the other. In Old and New Testaments, gratitude is both commanded and voluntary, illustrated in the תודה sacrifice, which was regulated by God and yet often offered spontaneously. This is what one should expect in believers in whom Christ the giver lives. This note of freedom is minor in John Calvin and more so in Thomas Aquinas, but prominent in Karl Barth for whom gratitude was the voluntary embrace of what God wants of people namely, that he wants them for himself. Gratitude, in this sense for Barth, cannot be commanded, but must be commanded of oneself.

The return of gratitude is also *joyful*. In hierarchical cultures, gratitude was often expressed without emotion. In Scripture, however, joy is an inseparable feature of gratitude. In both Old and New Testaments, commands to be grateful are conjoined to commands to be joyful. Just as the תודה sacrifice

---

290. Mitchell, *Politics of Gratitude*, 17.
291. Volf, *Free of Charge*, 36.

in the Old Testament was a meal in which the worshipper celebrated God's gifts of deliverance in particular, so the Eucharist in the New Testament is a festive meal celebrating Christ's redemption. Furthermore, for Aquinas the joyful reception of a gift is already a repayment of sorts and for Barth joy is the simplest form of gratitude. In fact, for Barth, this present world with its sorrows and pains can be joyfully accepted with gratitude because a future world is promised.

In the response of gratitude, one *sees oneself as the recipient of a gift*. In a Christian worldview, one ought always to see oneself as the recipient of gifts—namely, the gifts of life and redemption through Christ. This is why the injunction in Scripture, "Be thankful in all circumstances" is not just wishful thinking. Believers operate with a perspective in which they see the world differently. One ought not to be grateful for death, for instance, but gratitude is possible for one facing death because one sees life beyond the grave and all other blessings secured by Christ's redemption.

Gratitude further *salutes the giver in order to perpetuate a personal relationship*. Whether through words or gestures, gratitude expresses honor and respect to a giver. The gratitude of Old Testament believers included a dimension of praise in which God was honored, often publicly, for his benevolence. Similarly, in the New Testament, the expression of gratitude is coupled with praise and given to God who is deserving of honor and praise. The gratitude of the Samaritan leper includes a vocal and public expression of praise to God. Moreover, Christians affirm that life is teleological and purposeful, moving towards the end for which God created everything. For John Calvin, "the existence of humanity in God's design is defined by thankfulness."[292] Given the paradigmatic character of Adam's sin in Scripture, it could be argued that all sin is the repetition of Adam's sin. As such, all sin is ingratitude—refusing to thank God for what he has given and wanting, ungratefully, what he has not. Within the medieval church, this notion was so accepted that a Latin slogan was coined to verbalize it—namely, *ingratitudo peccatum maximum* (ingratitude is the greatest sin of all).[293]

Unlike any business transaction, gratitude is directed to a particular giver in order to perpetuate a relationship. Put differently, gratitude is not ordinarily expressed impersonally, much less anonymously. Gratitude requires one to look beyond the gift to giver, and the recipient freely consents to a relationship with the donor.[294] The Israelites practiced gratitude verbally and materially, often with expressed intent (as is apparent in the Psalms)

---

292. Gerrish, *Grace and Gratitude*, 41.
293. Visser, *Gift of Thanks*, 363.
294. Visser, *Gift of Thanks*, 452.

to deepen a relationship with YHWH. In the New Testament, gratitude is expressed with the admission of weakness and powerlessness, and the need for God's ongoing and loving provision. Furthermore, gratitude for God's generosity is presented in Hebrews (in particular) as a motive for Christian obedience and service. Though Aquinas can be critiqued for recommending that one should endeavor to return to donors something greater than what was received, his objective in so doing was to perpetuate a relationship, rather than conclude it. Both Calvin and Barth interpreted gratitude in terms of a father-child relationship as the appropriate way for children to respond to their father's generosity. Moreover, for Barth, the childlike dimension of gratitude liberates people to play before the Father.

Lastly, gratitude endeavors to maintain a *peaceable relationship*. Supposing an ontology of communion with God, others, and the world, gratitude is constructed, not constructive. Much like the Trinity, humanity is situated in giving-and-receiving relationships in which reciprocating gifts with returns of some sort are both natural and necessary. God situated humanity in community, in relations with him and others. By prizing self-sufficiency and self-fulfillment, Aristotle resisted this ontology and therefore misconstrued gratitude. By rejecting God's existence, Robert Solomon is unable to accept this ontology and therefore misconstrues gratitude for an experience of awareness or a feeling of appreciation. In the Old Testament, God is often thanked and praised for who he is and for what he has done, such that gratitude is never an isolated or abstract activity. In the New Testament, gratitude is nearly exclusively directed to God, though there are instances in which Paul, in particular, expresses thanks to others. When the Samaritan leper reflected on his healing, he returned to thank Jesus, and Jesus commended him for his gratitude and chided the ungrateful conduct of the nine lepers. The notion of self-gratitude, therefore, is a category mistake.

Among the persons of the Trinity, however, the one reciprocates gifts with return gifts, and similarly within humanity. If a gift does not elicit gratitude, something is morally amiss. For this reason, Aquinas subsumed gratitude under justice. Gratitude, for John Calvin, is the most fitting response to God a believer could possibly have. Jacques Derrida argued that gratitude poisoned a gift by repaying something gratuitous. Similarly, Peter Leithart contends that gratitude is not reciprocity or a return, but the right use of a gift, and that people owe gratitude only to God and not to others. While it is true that the New Testament takes a dim view of Greco-Roman reciprocity and encourages giving without the expectation of returns, it is nevertheless the case that such returns, when received, are welcome and wonderful.

It is in this sense that gratitude even marks a kind of "payment" for God's gifts. In the Old Testament, for example, one "pays" a vow in return for God's deliverance. This "payment" restores shalom or peace and a kind of moral equilibrium, though the "payment" is an asymmetrical return for the gift, a mere token of the gifts value. Even among inter-personal giving and receiving there is a sense of equilibrium that is achieved when gifts are reciprocated. The apostle Paul, for example, understood the gift of the Philippians as "payment." To receive is, in some sense, to be indebted, and to return thanks is, in some sense, to make payment. What one gives in gratitude, however, is a token of the value of the gift.

CHAPTER 5

GRATITUDE RITUALIZED AND PRACTICED

NORTH AMERICA IS HOME to widespread greed peacefully co-existing with equally widespread gratitude. Though few are inclined to admit greed, many are public about their gratitude. How can a culture that so prominently values gratitude (enjoying what one has) so vigorously succumb to greed (pursuing what one does not have)? The relevance of this question extends for pastors beyond greed to all sinful desires which so easily enslave people, the dynamics of which were explored in chapter 2 through a consideration of the seven deadly sins. Defined as distorted, forward-looking desires for superficial fulfillment which devalue God, self, others, and the world, the seven deadly sins were interpreted as saboteurs of gratitude which reject or deny an ontology of being-in-communion.

Utilizing the method of mutual critical correlation and attending to interpretations from the realms of philosophy and psychology, this book has probed gratitude theologically in order to generate a renewed understanding. Chapter 3 identified how gratitude was devalued by Aristotle for implying dependence, and by Derrida for contaminating gifts through a kind of repayment, and reduced by positive psychology (in excising God from the purview) to a merely horizontal dimension of human flourishing. Chapter 4 argued on biblical-theological grounds for positioning (rehabilitating) gratitude as a virtue in terms of agapic, asymmetrical reciprocity. On analogy with intra-Trinitarian, perichoretic giving and receiving that approximates the response of lovers to each other and eschews commercial repayment, gratitude is defined as a responsive virtue in which one, seeing oneself as the recipient of a gift, freely and joyfully salutes the giver in order to perpetuate a personal and peaceable relationship.

This final chapter pursues the objective of this practical theological inquiry—namely, to recommend, from this the renewed understanding, practices of gratitude that can potentially rehabilitate distorted human desires. In a technological framework in which practical theology is misconstrued as applied theology, practices tend to be regarded pragmatically in terms of what someone does and the effects of such activity rather than its content.[1] When practical theology is properly understood as a theological discipline, practices are acknowledged as theory-laden, invested with particular theological meaning and content.[2] In this perspective, practices are never merely individual but situated in "communities with specific histories and traditions which give meaning, value, and direction to the particular forms of practice."[3] This social dimension is captured by Dorothy Bass who defines practice as "a dense cluster of ideas and activities that are related to a specific social goal and shared by a social group over time."[4]

Christian practices are a particular variant—namely, "things Christian people do together over time to address fundamental human needs in response to and in light of God's active presence for the life of the world."[5] Further, Christian practices embed both normative and formative elements:

> Christian practices are set in a world created and sustained by a just and merciful God, who is now in the midst of reconciling this world through Christ.... When they participate in such practices, Christian people are taking part in God's work of creation and new creation and thereby growing into a deeper knowledge of God and of creation.[6]

Though considerable attention has been paid to practices within the realm of practical theology in recent years, the association between practical

---

1. Swinton and Mowat, *Practical Theology*, 18.
2. Swinton and Mowat, *Practical Theology*, 20.
3. Swinton and Mowat, *Practical Theology*, 21. See also Alasdair MacIntryre's definition: "Any coherent and complex form of socially established cooperative human activity through which goods internal to that form of activity are realized in the course of trying to achieve those standards of excellence which are appropriate to, and partially definitive of, that form of activity, with the result that human powers to achieve excellence, and human conceptions of the ends and goods involved, are systematically extended" (MacIntryre, *After Virtue*, 187).
4. Bass, "Introduction," 2–3.
5. Dykstra and Bass, "Theological Understanding," 18.
6. Dykstra and Bass, "Theological Understanding," 21.

theology and virtue is much more fixed.[7] This chapter will attend to the practice of gratitude as a *virtue*.

Sometimes regarded as dispositions to act in certain ways or simply as skills/character traits, virtues are best understood when both notions are included. Such a comprehensive account is recommended by Gilbert Meilaender who defines virtues as "traits of character which not only suit us for life but shape our vision of life, helping to determine not only who we are but what world we see."[8] Much like practices, virtues are inescapably public and social, not simply because human behavior affects others, but because they dispose one to see others in certain ways and relate to them accordingly.[9]

If practices are ways of incarnating certain ideals, then virtues are ways of seeing situations and inclining one to certain ideals. "An ethic of virtue," Meilaender writes, "is dominated by the eye, by metaphors of sight and vision. To know what traits of character qualify as virtues we must *see* our world and human nature rightly. To see rightly, in turn, requires that we have virtues. Virtue enhances *vision*; vice darkens and finally *blinds*."[10] A key component of such vision are the emotions, defined by Robert Roberts as "concerned-based construals" and a "way of seeing."[11] Robert indicates

---

7. Already decades ago, Donald Browning surmised it was the task of practical theology to unite theological ethics and the social sciences to formulate a normative vision of life and that pastoral care and counselling should be grounded in ethics (Browning, *Religious Ethics*, 18). More recently, Phil Zylla has argued that "the moral life of virtue is at the heart of the enterprise of pastoral theology" (Zylla, *Consent to Being*, 111). In some of the recent volumes attentive to practice, however, there is a curious neglect of virtue. Consider, e.g., Volf and Bass, *Practicing Theology*; Bass and Dykstra, *For Life Abundant*.

8. Meilaender, *Theory and Practice of Virtue*, 11. See also Joseph Kotva's definition: "Virtues are those states of character or character traits acquired over time that contribute to the human good. The virtues involve both the intellect and will, both the rational and affective parts of the self. They also are the tendencies, disposition and capabilities necessary to the human good, to the best kind of human life" (Kotva, *Christian Case*, 38).

9. "The exercise of the moral virtues inescapably brings the person into relationship with others. . . . For theological ethics, there exists a general, but real, sense in which every virtue remains ordered to the kind of social communication which befits the unity of believers in Christ" (Cessario, *Moral Virtues*, 20).

10. Meilaender, *Theory and Practice of Virtue*, 11. Meilaender argues further that the "ear" is also important for virtue in terms of being "ready to hear the divine word which—seeing us whole—condemns even the best of our virtues, and again—seeing us whole in Christ—says, even with reference to much that does not get into the self-conscious life stories we narrate, "well done" (Meilaender, *Theory and Practice of Virtue*, 17).

11. Roberts, *Spiritual Emotions*, 11.

that, in the New Testament at least, some virtues are known by the names of emotions (e.g., gratitude, peace, joy, etc.) while others are not (e.g., patience, courage, self-control, etc.).[12] "As Christian construals," Roberts writes, "spiritual emotions are a subject's perceptions of the situation of his or her life in terms of the Christian teachings about what the world is like, who we are, and what God has done for us."[13] How does this relate to virtue? Virtue (Robert uses "Christian character") for Roberts is "the set of dispositions to experience the Christian emotions" and "is not just proper passion, but also the well-engrained habit of seeing the world in Christian terms."[14]

In what follows, this chapter will attempt to unite the notions of virtue and practice under the rubric of pastoral theology and recommend the practice of gratitude as a virtue to inhibit idolatries of desire. This endeavor will begin by identifying the inadequacy of Protestant law-ethics and the advantages of traditional virtue ethics in terms of redressing ingratitude. Secondly, a slightly renewed virtue ethics will be recommended in which the necessity of transformation and community are acknowledged. The remaining part of the chapter will present the Eucharist as a normative meal with capacity to form the people of God into a grateful people. This chapter will then conclude with some suggestive recommendations of practices of gratitude.[15]

DEFICIENCIES OF LAW-ETHICS IN RELATION TO INGRATITUDE

In chapter 1, the suggestion was made that something is deficient in Reformed ethics in relation to sins of desire. The section that follows will argue that this deficiency lies in the preference for law-ethics over virtue ethics. What accounts for this preference? To answer the question requires a brief sojourn back into history to trace the evolving theological assessments of virtue that led to the Protestant demurral. Both Peter Abelard (1074–c.1142) and Peter Lombard (c.1100–1160), two significant medieval theologians, distinguished between the cardinal virtues (justice, courage, prudence, and temperance) and the theological virtues (faith, hope, and love), but they reflected on them in alternative ways. In contrast to Abelard, an admirer of

---

12. Roberts, *Spiritual Emotions*, 9.
13. Roberts, *Spiritual Emotions*, 31.
14. Roberts, *Spiritual Emotions*, 31.
15. In so doing, I am participating in a wider project pioneered by Stanley Hauerwas and recently reinvigorated in new ways by James K. A. Smith, both of whose books will be referenced in what follows.

Aristotle, who saw virtues as habits through which one could act morally and merit beatitude, Lombard believed, as an Augustinian, that virtue was resourced only by God's grace.[16] Whereas Abelard and his followers saw the cardinal virtues, at least, as common ground between ancient and Christian morality, Lombard contended that the cardinal virtues had no value in their ancient conception.[17] Aquinas held that the cardinal virtues (justice, prudence, courage, and temperance) were available, to some degree, to all human beings, whereas the theological virtues (faith, love, and hope) were the unique province of Christians. More significantly, Aquinas argued that if supernatural beatitude were the goal of humanity, "only the power of the Holy Spirit can create capacities proportionate" to attaining that goal.[18] What was necessary for salvation, therefore, were infused (by the Spirit) virtues and not just acquired (by human potential) virtues.[19] In this way, the righteousness with which one attained beatitude was Spirit-infused human righteousness.

Where did the Protestant Reformers stand in relation to this? Martin Luther, first of all, had little fondness for Aristotle in whom he detected nothing of the grace of God. In his *Disputation against Scholastic Theology* (1517). Luther writes, "We do not become righteous by doing righteous deeds but, having been made righteous, we do righteous deeds" (thesis 40).[20] Consequently, "virtually the entire Ethics of Aristotle is the worst enemy of grace" (thesis 41) and "the whole of Aristotle is to theology as darkness is to light" (thesis 50).[21] Luther, however, also strongly objected to Aquinas's view about infused virtues, against which he set forth his prized doctrine of justification by faith alone.[22] Luther insisted instead that if there were any righteousness that leads us to God, it is not an infused righteousness (in which God props up human righteousness), but the alien, imputed righteousness of Christ. John Calvin sided with Luther in his view that believers are justified by an alien and imputed righteousness and so rejected Aquinas's view of justification involving cooperative and infused grace as synergistic. Calvin recoiled at the notion that sinners could contribute to

---

16. Porter, "Virtue Ethics," 78.

17. Bejczy, *Cardinal Virtues*, 70.

18. Cessario, *Moral Virtues*, 106.

19. By human potential, one can restrain oneself from eating to attain a measure of health, but in fasting, the Spirit molds one for God's presence (Cessario, *Moral Virtues*, 106).

20. Luther, *Disputation against Scholastic Theology*, 16.

21. Luther, *Disputation against Scholastic Theology*, 16. "Indeed, no one can become a theologian unless he becomes one without Aristotle" (Thesis 44).

22. Vos, "Christelijke Deugden," 31–32.

their standing before God and "avoid living in complete dependence on God's grace."[23] Further, the Protestant reformers were convinced that all desire has been corrupted, so that apart from the grace of God the sinner has no hope for renewal.[24]

Instead of formulating an ethics around virtue, therefore, the Reformers presented ethics primarily in terms of the law of God, particularly the Ten Commandments.[25] This approach, however, betrays significant liabilities in relation to sinful desires. What, after all, is a moral life? What are its characteristics? What criteria does one use to assess whether a life is moral? Consider the morality of the following scenarios: An upright person is diagnosed with a terminal illness, but now lives without joy. A man successfully resists sexual temptation but is frustrated. A woman obeys all the traffic rules but is an impatient driver. A man refuses to take revenge but is seething in bitterness. A woman stays within her budget but purchases frivolous things and goes on extravagant vacations. Traditional Protestant law-ethics, which conceives of morality primarily in terms of the Ten Commandments, is deficient in addressing these sorts of scenarios. In what follows, the nature of these deficiencies will be explained with special reference to gratitude.

Law-ethics, first of all, cannot generate what we sense are significant dimensions to being human such as joy, laughter, celebration, and gratitude.

23. Hauerwas, "Christian Ethics," 42. See also Meilaender, *Theory and Practice of Virtue*, 36.

24. All of this must be balanced with the recognition that the Protestant reformers did not completely abolish the tradition of virtue ethics. For John Calvin, for instance, the emphasis is never on virtuous self-improvement, but on participation in Christ. Only through communion with Christ can the virtues truly blossom (Vos, "Christelijke Deugden in de Gemeente," 32). Calvin admits that wonderful virtues can be located in the world, but none of these make a person righteous. In order to have value, the virtues must be linked to Christ. Calvin endorses the church fathers who conceived of the Christian life in terms of cardinal virtues and their derivatives (Calvin, *Instit.* 3.6.1). He chose for practical reasons to write about the Christian life in terms of the ten commandments, but not without references to the virtues, which for Calvin, are traits like piety, justice, sobriety, generosity, and perseverance (Vos, "Christelijke Deugden," 32) and especially humility, which he regarded as the mark of our regeneration (Nolan, *Reformed Virtue After Barth*, 17). For Calvin, the Christian life cannot be reduced to a back-and-forth movement between sin and absolution without any progress. Through the work of the Spirit of Christ one can be renewed, not least in one's character and attitudes (Vos, "Christelijke Deugden," 32–33).

25. All of the Protestant catechisms, for example, and countless Protestant books present ethics in terms of the Ten Commandments. Consider *inter alia*: Douma, *Ten Commandments*; *Responsible Conduct*; Frame, *Doctrine of the Christian Life*; Horton, *Law of Freedom*; Murray, *Principles of Conduct*; Smedes, *Mere Morality*. By way of contrast, the Catholic Catechism also has sections on virtue and the fruit of the Spirit, and Catholic ethicists, for centuries, have conceived of the Christian life not simply in terms of law and conscience, but in terms of virtue and character.

Law-ethics will effectively address sins of desire such as greed and lust, for instance, but is powerless to generate gratitude. Not without its own shortcomings in this area, traditional virtue ethics revolves around human desires for the good with a view to attaining happiness and satisfaction. Aristotle observed that humans are inclined to the good.[26] For Aristotle, in fact, there is a hierarchy of goods and a gradation of desires: we want health in order to study, in order to find a job, in order to have an income and so forth.[27] The deep desire beneath all our superficial desires is what we desire for its own sake and not for the sake of anything else—namely happiness.[28] For us happiness is subjective, associated with the feeling of pleasure, but for Aristotle it was the subjective satisfaction of objectively living morally and productively.[29] Thomas Aquinas similarly saw our highest good as happiness, but with God. Since humans are unique among animals as created in God's image, having intellect and will, perfect human happiness involves knowing God through our intellect and loving God through our wills.[30] Unlike law-ethics whose objective is prescribing and forbidding conduct, traditional virtue ethics presents a way of life whose objective is happiness, variously defined. As such, traditional virtue ethics seems more congenial to gratitude.

Secondly, traditional Protestant law-ethics recommends nothing to uproot the source of sin, whether ingratitude or radical self-centeredness. By simply prescribing and forbidding behaviors, law-ethics often introduces a recurring cycle in which a person feels powerless: The law condemns the sin, the sinner repents, Jesus forgives, and then the cycle repeats.[31] Though

26. Vanier, *Happiness*, 6.

27. Vanier, *Happiness*, 4.

28. Vanier, *Happiness*, 14. Aristotle, *Eth. nic.* 1097b14–16. Happiness (εὐδαιμονία) is the highest good (i.e., good by itself and not as a means to some further good such as wealth, honor, health, pleasure).

29. Charry, *God and the Art of Happiness*, 3; cf. Aristotle, *Eth. nic.* 1098a7–17; Russell, "Virtue Ethics," 11. Ultimate happiness, the highest good, for Aristotle, is located in contemplation (θεωρία)enjoying, appreciating, and reflecting on the knowledge one has already acquired (Aristotle, *Eth. nic.* 1095a10). "The activity of God which surpasses all others in blessedness," Aristotle alleges, "must be contemplative; and of human activities, therefore, that which is most akin to this must be most of the nature of happiness" (Aristotle, *Eth. nic.* 1178b25–27). "The man who pursues knowledge in its purest form and in the most disinterested way, says Aristotle, will pursue the knowledge found in metaphysics; but he will do this because it is knowledge of the ends that inform all other forms of knowledge" (Di Blasie et al., *Virtue's End*, 10).

30. Unlike Aristotle, Aquinas argues that happiness is unattainable in this life because, unlike Aristotle, Aquinas identifies perfect happiness with the full contemplation of God himself, the vision of God's nature.

31. "Moreover, simply to obey a moral rule cannot effect the radical transformation

law-ethics has potential to restrain the heart, it is unable, Hauerwas says, "to train our desires and direct our attention; to make us into moral people."[32] Law-ethics can inform a greedy person that greed is wrong, that the sin of greed should be acknowledged, and that there is forgiveness for greedy people. Virtue ethics, on the other hand, recommends the development of a second nature in which greed, for instance, can potentially be reduced.[33] For Aristotle, happiness emerges from the deepest part within us and that which distinguishes us from animals—namely, λόγος or reason, the principle that enables us to contemplate, understand, order, name, control, and therefore also realize our full potential of becoming autonomous.[34] Virtue therefore requires φρόνησις or practical wisdom, a distinctive human ability to think rationally about how to live and so change the way things are.[35] In so doing, we determine what is essential to virtue—namely, the "mean," the optimum middle between two extremes, deficiency and excess.[36] As such, virtue is not simply about fulfilling desire or curbing it, but about pursuing the fulfillment of "deliberated desires."[37]

Relatedly, by locating moral norms for life external to a person (i.e., in commands), the currency of traditional Protestant law-ethics diminishes in what Charles Taylor calls "a culture of authenticity," which he defines as:

---

in a human person which the Christian life seeks to accomplish in us" (Cessario, *Moral Virtues*, 16).

32. Hauerwas, *Peaceable Kingdom*, 11. "Moral norms may serve societies to enhance life in ways that promote civility, order, and lawfulness, but they cannot instill virtue" (Zylla, *Virtue as Consent*, 108).

33. Kamtekar, "Ancient Virtue Ethics," 36. See also Aristotle, *Eth. nic.* 1103a30–b25. Habit (ἕξις) for Aristotle is the acquisition of a kind of 'second nature' (Aristotle, *Eth. nic.* 1152a31), a disposition that empowers one to act in a certain way. "The aim of Aristotle's ethics," Vanier writes, "is to help human beings choose the activity from which they will derive the greatest pleasure of joy, and thus become as happy as possible by divorcing themselves from activities that give them more superficial and temporary pleasure, but prevent them from progressing towards the finest activities and pleasures" (Vanier, *Happiness*, 43–44).

34. Vanier, *Happiness*, 18.

35. As such, it is distinguished from scientific knowledge (of unchanging things) or the study of nature (where things change by nature, not decision) (See Kamtekar, "Ancient Virtue Ethics," 36–37).

36. The classic example is courage: if you fear danger too much (excess) you are a coward and if you fear danger too little (deficiency) you are reckless.

37. Kamtekar, "Ancient Virtue Ethics," 35; Aristotle, *Eth. nic.* 1113a2–12. For Aristotle virtue, good reason in concert with one's desire, must be distinguished from mere continence, good reason opposed by one's desire. Virtues are good character traits or attitudes (such as courage, friendship, trust, and wisdom) which influence one's conduct and reactions and determine, consciously or unconsciously, the choices one made.

the understanding of life which emerges with the Romantic expressivism of the late-eighteenth century, that each one of us has his/her own way of realizing our humanity, and that this is important to find and live out one's own, as against surrendering to conformity with a model imposed on us from the outside, by society, or the previous generation, or religious or political authority.[38]

But what if the authentic self is greedy or envious? What must be done in scenarios when the freedom of one clashes with the freedom of another? In terms of virtue ethics, by habituating, in the pursuit of happiness, strengths (virtues) of character, practiced repeatedly, an internal "second nature" is generated that can translate "head knowledge" into "heart knowledge" and make extraordinary challenges rather simple and the virtuous life inescapable.[39] In this conception, one is guided by a virtuous character to do what is right in a scenario which for others might represent a moral quandary. Marva Dawn illustrates this with the following story about her and her husband.[40] They were on their way to the doctor's office and stopped at a red light. When the light turned green, the car in front did not move. Marva grew impatient and told her husband he could safely go

---

38. Taylor, *Secular Age*, 275. "It is only in the era after the Second World War, that this ethic of authenticity begins to shape the outlook of society in general. Expressions like 'do your own thing' become current; a beer commercial of the early 70s enjoined us to 'be yourselves in the world of today.' . . . Therapies multiply which promise to help you find yourself, realize yourself, release your true self, and so on" (Taylor, *Secular Age*, 475). This is true of ethical systems that associate authentic morality with freedom and autonomy—namely, existentialism and situationalism, and what Alasdair MacIntyre and others have called emotivism (See MacIntyre, *After Virtue*; cf. Hauerwas, *Peaceable Kingdom*, 7). This penchant for autonomy and freedom also plagues the morality of social relations. Anything is permissible that does not infringe on the freedom of others, as if goodness were the sum of individual desires and choices. Such a position leads to self-deception because it is impossible for anyone to live in a way that does not impinge on the liberty of others. This self-deception in turn generates manipulation as we attempt to locate "moral" ways to satisfy self-interest. The family bond between parents and children, for instance, is not conducive (perhaps "opposed") to self-interest and generates resentment and bargaining (Hauerwas, *Peaceable Kingdom*, 10).

39. In the ancient world, virtues spoke to your identity, who you were, as a free man or a courageous woman or a merciful person (Vos, "Christelijke deugden," 27). They were good character traits or attitudes such as courage, friendship, trust, and wisdom, that influenced one's conduct and reactions and determined, consciously or unconsciously, the choices one made. Especially because of the influence of Aristotle, classical virtue ethics typically located virtue in the so-called "golden mean," the optimum middle between two extremes, deficiency and excess (Aristotle, *Eth. nic.* 1152a31). See also Dunnington, *Addiction and Virtue*, 52).

40. Dawn, *Sexual Character*, 33–34.

around in the open lane next to them. Her husband turned to her and said, "I'm waiting to make sure the woman in front of us is all right." It was her husband's nature to be observant of other people's needs. Many things had contributed to that nature: his parent's influence, his childhood experiences, etc. Given the prevailing culture of authenticity in which one endeavors "to follow one's heart" rather than conform to an external standard, virtue ethics has capital. Individuals would need to be compelled, however, that their "heart" needs tweaking.

Traditional Protestant law-ethics is deficient, thirdly, because it is unsure in some scenarios whether a commandment is being transgressed and, if so, which commandment. Protestant ethicists have struggled, for example, with whether Rahab sinned in lying to the Canaanites about the Israelites she hid.[41] For our purposes, what commandment does ingratitude transgress? One could argue that ingratitude violates the tenth commandment, and it does, but it seems improper to reduce ingratitude to covetousness. Lust (seventh commandment), for instance, should be distinguished from covetousness (tenth commandment), and yet lust can be a manifestation of ingratitude.

Fourthly, traditional Protestant law-ethics tends to address the morality of conduct only when there are moral quandaries and, as such, proves extraordinarily helpful in morally complex situations, e.g., when is it permissible to remove life-support. Suppose a scenario, however, in which a woman, already owning six luxury purses, chooses to purchase a seventh. She is not violating any commandment and yet her purchase suggests something is morally amiss (i.e., possibly ingratitude). Virtue ethics, on the other hand, is concerned with "one's whole life" rather than just moments when something moral is in question.[42] If law-ethics is about what is done, virtue ethics is about how one lives.[43] In virtue ethics, what matters is to be a certain kind of person—namely a person of virtue.[44] While commands play a part in shaping who we are, the focus is not on rules, but on the people we

---

41. Absolute Absolutists (as opposed to Graded Absolutists) such as John Murray find fault with Rahab (See his *Principles of Conduct*).

42. Russell, "Introduction," 1.

43. In a Protestant worldview character is often addressed outside of ethics in terms of vocation, discipleship, spiritual formation spirituality, spiritual disciplines. Virtue ethics envisions a "more expansive field of human action" that includes all these (Nolan, *Reformed Virtue After Barth*, 22).

44. In comparison to law-ethics which asks, "what is the right thing to do," virtue ethics asks, "what is the best way to live, what sort of people should we be?" "What is significant about us morally, Hauerwas writes, "is not what we do or do not do, but how we do what we do" (Hauerwas, *Community of Character*, 113). "The only way to a good society is through good individuals" (Kreeft, *Back to Virtue*, 16).

want to be. This is not to diminish what we do, but to subordinate it to who we are, to see it as the fruit of good character. If the metaphor for law-ethics is a timeless dialogue that occurs mid-air, the metaphor for virtue ethics is a situational journey that takes place on the ground.[45]

This dimension of virtue ethics seems especially congenial to pastoral theology. Rather than address specific questions, pastoral theology is on a "quest" to articulate and address challenges with hope.[46] This quest, Phil Zylla argues, has the following four characteristics: it is, first, a pursuit of something better (i.e., a new world); secondly, it pushes towards the boundaries courageously and challenges the status quo; thirdly, it is imaginative and empathic, willing to enter into the sufferings of another in order to articulate a "resonant word"[47]; and, fourthly, it deepens and illumines experiences to make explicit what is implicit.[48] There is space within virtue ethics for pastoral theology to launch this quest.

Lastly, traditional Protestant law-ethics feeds pride by giving one a sense of satisfaction through one's compliance with the commandments and thus nurtures sin at the heart of one's moral life. Suppose again the wealthy woman purchasing her seventh luxury purse. She is purchasing something for which she has the money and is neither stealing from the vendor nor spending beyond her means. Blindness to her ingratitude, and compliance with the sixth commandment. can nurture an illegitimate sense of satisfaction.

REDRESSING INGRATITUDE

Chapter 2 summarized Merleau-Ponty's view that all habits, sinful or otherwise, are deeply embodied and that, for habits to change, the body must be sedimented with new deposits of meaning, i.e., the solidification of new habits. Misdirected desires, therefore, must be reformed and redirected, in part at least, through practices. The practices of gratitude, specifically, have potential to deposit new meaning in order to solidify new habits that rewrite the old habits of sinful desire. If the body is the locus for the sedimentation of harmful deposits of meaning, however, how can that same body effect liberation? Whereas Derrida finds such liberation in "the gift of death," I

---

45. "For Christians, the moral life is to be seen as a journey through life sustained by fidelity to the cross of Christ, which brings a fulfillment no law can ever embody (Hauerwas, "Theological Ethics," 70).

46. Zylla, *Virtue as Consent*, 89.

47. Zylla, *Virtue as Consent*, 95.

48. Zylla, *Virtue as Consent*, 89–96.

locate it in the grace of God. To effect change, liberation from the outside is necessary. "To worship God rather than the idols of our own making," Miroslav Volf writes, "we must allow God to break apart the idols we create, through the Spirit's relentless and intimate work within our lives."[49]

The Holy Spirit: Agent of Transformation

It is tempting to present the Christian life as the true fulfillment of human desire, as if our desires were simply underdeveloped, as Aristotle argued. This book has argued that because thoughts, desires, and attitudes have been corrupted by sin, they must be thoroughly reshaped and reformed into the form of Christ. To become a believer, biblically speaking, is not to add religion to one's identity, but to become a thoroughly new person ("new creation," 2 Cor 5:17).[50] In the New Testament, Jesus recommends transformation as a kind of via media between external and internal ethical models because it generates a lifestyle that both transcends mere alignment with rules and conforms to oneself, though this self is a new and redeemed self.[51] Rules are still kept, not as an imposition from the outside, but from a transformed character inside, which the Holy Spirit produces (Gal 5:16–26; Eph 5:18). One still follows one's heart, but now only after a disciplined and transformed lifestyle.[52]

At the heart of Jesus's program is the summons to deny oneself, take up one's cross, and follow him. As such, Christianity represents a new way of being human characterized by a new kind of virtue. Whereas Aristotle's

---

49. Volf, *Free of Charge*, 23.

50. Believing the gospel message, therefore, must be transformative. "If no one was transformed," Leithart writes, "then the message that announced the transformation could not possibly be true" (Leithart, *Against Christianity*, 99).

51. Wright, *After You Believe*, 7.

52. This is illustrated for N. T. Wright in the story in the Gospels of the rich young ruler (Matt 19:16–30; Mark 10:17–22; Luke 18:18–30) who poses the question, what must I do to inherit eternal life? For a Jew, Wright explains, this is analogous to asking, what kind of person must I be to enjoy the age to come? This, in turn, is not so different from the question, how do I experience fulfillment, meaning, and happiness in life? The young man viewed his life as one of compliance with the ten commandments, but feels incomplete. Jesus's answer—namely, sell your possessions, give proceeds to the poor, and follow me—does not set the moral bar higher by adding commandments, but summons a character transformation (Wright, *After You Believe*, 15–16). "The New Testament," Cessario argues, "presents virtue as the interior principle of the moral life which directs the individual's relationship with God and neighbor. As such, Christian virtue remains a stable reality, something which firmly establishes in the believer the capacity to accomplish those deeds that are worthy of the Kingdom of God" (Cessario, *Moral Virtues*, 1).

virtues make a person a hero, a moral giant who should be applauded, the virtues prized by Christ are just the opposite. The virtues recommended by Jesus in the Sermon on the Mount are meekness, for example, and poverty in spirit. Throughout his entire ministry, Jesus resocializes human habits, desires, and affections to be godly.[53] This, in fact, is what Jesus does throughout the Gospels, and therefore readers ought to be open to having their affections and habits changed and conformed to God's coming kingdom.[54] The practices that can deposit new meanings to solidify new behaviors, therefore, are impressed upon us by Jesus and attainable through the transformation of the Holy Spirit. "An account of the virtues," Jonathan Wilson argues, "is a description of how Christ is being formed in us by the Holy Spirit."[55] There remains, however, another ingredient requisite for the virtuous life—namely, the church.

The Church: Locus of Transformation

What was lost after the Reformation was the role of "the church as the indispensable context in which order might be given to the Christian life."[56] Under the assumption that everyone knows what it means to be a Christian, the sacrament of penance (acknowledging sin, receiving forgiveness, pursuing restoration) was discarded by Protestants.[57] The Protestant view of morality that prevailed was that decisions could (and should) be justified from the vantage point of *anyone*. With the role of church receding to the background, Hauerwas argues, Protestants increasingly resorted to philosophy for resources.[58] For Hauerwas, this was an ill-fated move

---

53. I really like the term "resocialization" which is used by Leithart (Leithart, *Against Christianity*, 16) and recently by Pennington who defines it as "an intentional re-forming of our habits, desires, affections (a proper ordering of loves), a re-making of disciples to be like their Father God ("to be holy as I am holy") to be god-like/godly" (Pennington, "Sermon on the Mount," 3).

54. Pennington, "Sermon on the Mount," 4.

55. Wilson, *Gospel Virtues*, 45.

56. Hauerwas, "Christian Ethics," 43.

57. "If the church is the locus and vehicle of the sacred, then we are brought closer to God by the very fact of belonging and participating in its sacramental life.... Once the sacred is rejected, then this kind of mediation is also. Each person stands alone in relation to God: his or her fate—salvation or damnation—is separately decided" (Taylor, *Sources of Self*, 216).

58. Ethics, however, is not an autonomous discipline, free of religious and/or traditional presuppositions, as Kant held. Haunted by fear of relativism and the notion that moral convictions are arbitrary, Kant wanted to ground morality, not in religion or tradition from the Enlightenment liberated people, but in reason itself (Hauerwas,

which birthed meta-ethical (or mid-air or unqualified ethical) approaches that attempt to locate an (often unchanging and absolute) objective basis for moral concepts and human conduct (assuming that the question "what ought we to do" must be answered before, "what ought we to be?").[59] Such approaches require individuals, Hauerwas argues, to "assume a stance external to our commitments and cares, which are the lifeblood of any morality" and thereby ignore the fact that ethical actions obtain intelligibility from their function in a community's history.[60] In contrast to this assumption, Hauerwas contends that all ethical reflection is "relative to a particular time and place."[61] Christian ethics must be grounded (not simply mid-air), concrete (not simply abstract), and character oriented (not simply conduct oriented). Phil Zylla casts a compelling vision of virtue along these lines:

> The language of symbol, myth, dialogue, and story will be given priority to the prescribed teaching of religious moralism. Perspective will be drawn from "life below" rather than from the extractions of moralism. Love for God will ground a pastoral theology of virtue as a truly religious and ethical construct rather than as a function of prescribed morality. Attention to experience (primary and secondary) will ground ideas about authentic virtue in concreteness, not in moral abstraction. Critical reflection on the ambiguities, depth, and mystery of the moral life will replace the blind faith of obsessive moralism. Attention to character, to "being" over "doing" will confront the tendency of religious piety to act in the right ways, but without a pure heart. The demand for social justice will be intrinsic to the vision of virtue in pastoral theology rather than the religious piety that pretends to care for the other but is actually preoccupied with religion.[62]

The only missing ingredient here is community. The ethical power of a community is apparent in the following two examples. "After the long uncertainty and bloody confusion that attended the breakdown of the Roman empire," Lewis Mumford writes, "there was an alternative community waiting in the wings.[63] In the rise of the monastery, the desire for order and

---

"Christian Ethics," 45). Kant therefore formulated as the basic principle of ethics the categorical imperative: "Act only according to that maxim by which you can at the same time will that it should become a universal law" (Kant, *Foundations*, 39).

59. Hauerwas, *Peaceable Kingdom*, 22.
60. Hauerwas, *Peaceable Kingdom*, 18.
61. Hauerwas, *Peaceable Kingdom*, 1.
62. Zylla, *Consent to Being*, 112.
63. Mumford, "Monastery and the Clock," 121.

power was realized apart from "the military domination of weaker men."⁶⁴ As communities, monasteries functioned as an ethical force to reorient society by reshaping desires.

During oppressive communist rule, secondly, the dissident playwright Vaclav Havel who became president of the Czech Republic, pondered the future. Mary Jo Leddy explains,

> So Havel and other dissidents began to ask, "How can we live the truth in a culture based on a fundamental lie, especially since the lie is in our heads? How can we begin to live into the truth? We desire so much more than just things. We want something to hope in, a reason to believe."
>
> So in his country, as in other iron-curtain countries, people began to set up what he called "parallel cultures." They had underground study groups. They studied Plato. They had drama. They had music groups. They wrote novels and poetry, and published them underground. He called this a "parallel culture." It was not a counter-culture because, he said, it was impossible for us to live totally outside the system. You cannot live outside a culture. But you can create within it zones and spaces, where you can become who you really are. It is in such places that one can speak the truth, where one can gather with others who share that truth. This went on for years, not without difficulties, but for years. Over time, the truth became stronger and stronger, and at a certain point people began to walk in the streets and to say to the system, "We don't believe you anymore." And the system fell. It fell, not because of the power of Western nuclear equipment, but because the people said within the system, "We don't believe you anymore." It was a vision that had been nourished within those parallel cultures.⁶⁵

The church can be such a parallel culture to effect change. What is original about Christians, after all, is not their beliefs, but their existence as a community which, unlike any other, challenges proud pretensions and provides skills for the humility necessary for becoming not just good, but holy.⁶⁶ The place of the church reminds us that Christianity's new way of

---

64. Mumford, "Monastery and the Clock," 121.
65. Leddy, "People of God," 311. See also Havel, *Living in Truth*.
66. Hauerwas, "Theological Ethics," 73. "Christianity is not a continuation of the Greek understanding of the virtues, but rather the inauguration of a new tradition that sets the virtues within an entirely different telos in community" (Hauerwas and Pinches, *Christians Among Virtues*, 63).

being human is "a new way of being human *together*."[67] Churches, Hauerwas claims, must be communities of character in which certain practices encourage virtue in its members who, in turn, strengthen the community by embodying these virtues. Through sermons, we hear the narrative that teaches us who Jesus is and what his people are like and we are shaped by expositions of idolatry and encouraged by the cross and resurrection and the defeat of evil. Though preaching should aspire "to renew the church through conviction, its primary goal is to constitute the church through conversion."[68] In the community's fellowship we experience the embodiment of these virtues and in the community's discipline we are rebuked, warned, instructed, and loved when we choose values other than those of Christ's kingdom. In the community's strength, we are bolstered with courage to continue holding to the teachings of Scripture. But there remains one particular dimension to the church that is especially important for its ethical implications—namely, the practice of the Eucharist. The next section proposes the Eucharist as the community paradigm for transformation.

EUCHARIST: PARADIGM FOR TRANSFORMATION

James K. A. Smith regards humans as inescapably desiring beings and therefore life as inescapably liturgical.[69] By "liturgy," Smith is thinking of the sequence of embodied practices that habituate a particular vision, narrative, and imagination that shapes desires and love (and, consequently, action).[70] Not only churches, but professional sporting events and shopping malls have liturgies.

The notion that liturgical practices shape desires and conduct is gaining immense traction. Stanley Hauerwas and Samuel Wells, for instance, depict Christian ethics as "informed prayer" and by presenting "the discipline of Christian ethics through the lens of Christian worship, most particularly the Eucharist."[71] Hauerwas and Wells want to dispel, in particular, the assumed dichotomies that envision ethics as objective, public, action-oriented, and normative, and worship as subjective, private, word-oriented, and aesthetic. They define worship as "an ordered series of activities that Christians carry out regularly together in obedience to Jesus's command,

---

67. Leithart, *Against Christianity*, 16.
68. Hauerwas and Wells, "Gift of the Church," 18.
69. Smith, *Desiring the Kingdom*, 40.
70. Smith, *Desiring the Kingdom*, 55–63.
71. Hauerwas and Wells, "Christian Ethics as Informed Prayer," 3.

as a way of becoming more like him, and as a witness to God's world."[72] Further,

> The liturgy offers ethics a series of ordered practices that shape the character and assumptions of Christians, and suggest habits and models that inform every aspect of corporate life—meeting people, acknowledging fault and failure, celebrating, thanking, reading, speaking with authority, reflecting on wisdom, naming truth, registering need, bringing about reconciliation, sharing food, renewing purpose.[73]

In what follows, we will pursue ways in which the Eucharist, in particular, functions as ethical paradigm to reorder sins of desire. Given the importance of the Eucharist as a ritual Jesus intended to repeat, gratitude is arguably a central motif in the ministry of Jesus. In the Reformed churches, the Lord's Supper, in spite of John Calvin's arguments to the contrary, is rarely celebrated weekly. Moreover, its meaning is frequently reduced to a mere invitation to remember (i.e., think about) Jesus's death. Furthermore, theological treatments of the Lord's supper in Reformed theology rarely explicate the function of the ritual for the church and world.[74]

The following section will offer a corrective to this deficiency by presenting the Eucharist as an ethical paradigm. As a ritual, the Eucharist embodies important features to gratitude. First, the Eucharist celebrates the ontology of communion because there is giving and receiving with God, inter-personal giving and receiving, and even giving and receiving with the created world. By denying the dualisms of spiritual/material, the Eucharist can help rewrite the trajectory of the historical narratives identified in chapter 1 in which gratitude was increasingly minimized. Secondly, the Eucharist features each of the dimensions to gratitude as simultaneously social, inclusive, gratuitous, peaceable, personal, joyful, and purposeful. So understood and practiced, the Eucharist has potential to resocialize ungrateful people in reciprocal love and so mitigate the sabotaging influence of the seven deadly sins.[75]

72. Hauerwas and Wells, "Christian Ethics," 7.

73. Hauerwas and Wells, "Christian Ethics," 7.

74. Typical treatments of the Lord's Supper in Reformed theology rehearse the alternative views held at the time of the Reformation regarding the presence or absence of Christ in the bread and wine, comment on the meaning of the elements of bread and wine, and make some remarks about the frequency with the Lord's Supper should be celebrated and who should be admitted (See, for example, Letham, *Lord's Supper*).

75. To my knowledge, no case has yet been made in print for seeing the Eucharist as a solvent for the seven deadly sins. Articles pointing in this direction include Newman, "Diagnosing Vice and Prescribing Virtue"; Webb, "Sin of Gluttony."

The Eucharist as a Social Ritual that Celebrates Acceptance

When he instituted the Eucharist, Jesus did not eat of the bread or drink of the wine without first giving thanks to the Father he loved and served.[76] After taking the bread, Jesus blessed it (Matt 26:26; Mark 14:22) and/or gave thanks (Luke 22:19; see also 1 Cor 11:24) and after taking the cup, he gave thanks (Matt 26:27; Mark 14:23; Luke 22:17; see also 1 Cor 11:25).[77] This pattern follows the sequence in John 6 where Jesus gave thanks between taking the loaves and distributing them (John 6:11) and anticipates the sequence in Luke 23 where Jesus blesses the bread between taking it and breaking it (Luke 23:30). In other words, Jesus did not see the meal in terms of isolated or abstract entitlement, but as a loving gift from his Father. In thanking the Father, Jesus lovingly reciprocated for the gift.

Eucharistic celebrations also reciprocate love to Christ for the gift of life and acknowledge absolute dependence on his gift. Far from a reward for good behavior, the Eucharist is "the food we need," Williams writes, "to prevent ourselves from starving as a result of our own self-enclosure and self-absorption, our pride and our forgetfulness."[78] Just as the eyes of Adam and Eve were opened when they "took" and "ate," so the eyes of the two individuals on the road to Emmaus were opened as Jesus dined with them (Luke 24:31). Both the meal of human autonomy and rebellion and the meal of faith and reconciliation lead to open eyes, but at the Eucharist eyes are opened by the Spirit to the risen Christ.

---

76. The word εὐχαριστίας is present in all four Gospel accounts. Though some conjecture that it represents later Christian editing, its link with the Jewish Passover feast makes Jesus's giving thanks "contextually plausible in a first-century Jewish Passover context" (Pitre, *Jesus and the Last Supper*, 429). The Passover "was not regarded as just any kind of sacrifice, but as a sacrifice of thanksgiving for deliverance" (Pitre, *Jesus and the Last Supper*, 427).

77. The argument that εὐλογέω, as a close parallel to εὐχαριστέω, is a prayer to the Father (e.g., Ps 103) and not a consecration of the bread or wine per se is strong. Some in fact have argued that Luke uses εὐχαριστέω where Mark uses εὐλογέω on the grounds that εὐλογέω is a semitism and Luke is writing for a Gentile audience (and thus εὐχαριστέω a graecism; similarly, 1 Cor 11:24). See, e.g., Bubbers, *Scriptural Theology*, 127–28; cf. Witherington, *Gospel of Mark*, 374. Note too that when Jesus blesses food in Mark 6:41 he looks heavenward, which is suggestive of a prayer to the Father. Bubbers argues that εὐλογέω in Mark 14:22 has "a broader meaning" than the "obvious meaning of the term which is to offer praise or thanksgiving to God" which includes "action by God" (Bubbers, *Scriptural Theology*, 126). France argues the parallel between εὐλογέω and εὐχαριστέω in Mark 14:22 suggests that εὐλογέω is the traditional prayer, i.e., "Blessed are you, Lord our God, king of the world" (France, *Gospel of Mark*, 568; cf. Marshall, *Supper*, 41).

78. Williams, *Being Christian*, 53.

The Eucharistic formularies used in Anglican and Reformed churches remind worshippers that the Lord's Supper was instituted "on the night when Jesus was betrayed." The human capacity to betray is universal, and the Eucharist reminds believers of the need for repentance. "To frequent the Eucharist full of my own self-righteousness and worthiness," Moloney writes, "is to leave no space for the presence of a Eucharistic Lord who seeks me out in my brokenness. He challenges me to go on taking the risky and difficult task of the Christian life, in imitation of him."[79] The Eucharist is enjoyed not as a destination, but as step in a journey, as a meal on the go.

Reciprocating love for Christ's gift at the Eucharist also includes the expression of mutual acceptance at the Eucharistic table. Believers eat with Jesus and with one another, passing bread and wine to each other and refusing to see themselves as isolated individuals. "In the Eucharist," Williams writes, "we are absorbed into a larger body. The small individual self is decentered and put in the context of a much wider community of participation with others in the divine life."[80] Believers retain their individual identities, but as members of the body of Christ (1 Cor 12:12–27). The Eucharistic participant does not simply take in Christ but is taken into Christ's body (John 6:56; cf. 1 Cor 10:16–17).[81] "Instead of simply consuming the body of Christ," Cavanaugh writes, "we are consumed by it."[82]

The de-centered individual is the individual in whom pride evaporates and space is wedged open for others. Just as he had said to Zacchaeus earlier, "for I must stay at your house" (Luke 19:5), the risen Jesus asks the disciples in the upper room for whom he had given his life, "Have you anything here to eat?" (Luke 24:41). "And so the flow of giving and receiving, of welcome and acceptance," Williams writes, "moves backward and forwards without a break."[83]

At the Eucharist, Jesus can potentially resocialize believers to conceive of life as a life of mutual acceptance, a life of receiving and giving, of being guests and being hosts, of receiving and offering hospitality. Believers are guests at the Eucharistic table, and they are free to invite other guests too. By means of the Eucharist, Jesus can open hearts for him and for others.

---

79. Moloney, *Body Broken*, 200.
80. Cavanaugh, *Being Consumed*, 55.
81. Cavanaugh, *Being Consumed*, 54.
82. Cavanaugh, *Being Consumed*, 54.
83. Williams, *Being Christian*, 43.

From Pride to Gratitude for Acceptance

The Eucharist displays how disordered desires for acceptance in pride can potentially be rehabituated by gratitude. Just as Jesus thanked the Father for gifts of love, so must believers. Jesus presented himself as one who accepts believers with an affirming and mirroring love, who sacrificed himself for them in his death, and now nourishes them with his life. "Not to be able to be grateful," Cunningham writes, "is an apt description of one who is proud."[84]

By being grateful, believers relinquish their place at the center of attention and center themselves in God, which is the way, Capps suggests, "to correct exaggerated self-centeredness.[85] "As soon as I say 'God exists,' my existence no longer can remain in the center, because the essence of the knowledge of God reveals my own existence as deriving its total being from his."[86] Mary Jo Leddy narrates the story of catholic writer Dorothy Day who, at a moment in her life when religion did not captivate her, gave birth to a daughter, having resigned herself, because of a previous abortion, to the impossibility of children. Overwhelmed with gratitude, she asked, "To whom should I give thanks for so much joy?" At the heart of faith, Day found gratitude.[87]

Gratitude generates humility which both leads believers to concede that they are far from self-sufficient and frees them to ask for help from others.[88] Believers can be further resocialized to see others around them who are similarly the objects of his sacrificial, nourishing, accepting love—the last, the least, the lost, the little and the languishing.

The Eucharist as an Inclusive Ritual that Celebrates Equality

At the Eucharist, there are no boundaries—no division between rich and poor, haves and have-nots. "The very distinction between what is mine and what is yours," Cavanaugh writes, "breaks down in the body of Christ."[89] Yet in Corinth there was a factious spirit and rampant division for which Paul upbraids the congregation with an appeal to the Eucharist. Addressing the divided congregation, Paul says, "Examine yourselves!" (1 Cor 11:28).

---

84. Cunningham, *Seven Deadly Sins*, 77.
85. Capps, *Deadly Sins*, 52.
86. Nouwen, *Show Me*, 37.
87. Leddy, *Radical Gratitude*, 49.
88. Cunningham, *Seven Deadly Sins*, 77.
89. Cavanaugh, *Being Consumed*, 56.

To celebrate the Eucharist while perpetuating divisions (1 Cor 11:20) is to eat and drink in "an unworthy manner," for which people "will be answerable for the body and blood of the Lord" (1 Cor 11:27).

Table fellowship throughout Scripture is a means by which bonds of friendship are formed. Jacob and Laban's peace covenant was symbolically ratified with a meal (Gen 31:54). In ways suggestive for the Eucharist, Jesus feasted with sinners and tax collectors. "All the downtrodden," Cavanaugh writes, "are Christ's brothers and sisters."[90] Within the Greco-Roman world, where meals were "carefully regulated," it would have been "embarrassing" to narrate stories of how the visionary leader "shared his table with the broken and unworthy."[91] Francis Moloney argues that this supplies evidence that the Eucharist "was not invented by the early church" but was "one of the authentic practices of Jesus's public life."[92] Referring to mentally disabled persons as gifts for others, Reinders writes,

> In the eyes of the world what we have received does not count for much. For the world, the brokenness of God is as absurd as the brokenness of profoundly disabled human beings is scandalous. The world sees no cause whatsoever to be grateful for the presence of disabled people. Having enjoyed the communion of the Lord's Supper, Christians may begin to think and see differently.[93]

Further, racial, ethnic, political, and even (to a degree) theological divisions contradict the meaning of Eucharist.

When Peter first arrived in Antioch, he freely dined with Gentiles without consideration for traditional Jewish taboos. When the delegation from Jerusalem arrived, however, Peter suddenly felt pressure to accommodate the sensitivities of the Judaizers and withdrew from table fellowship with the Gentiles. This exclusive behavior invited a stern rebuke from the apostle Paul who, when he visited Antioch, confronted Peter publicly and alleged that Peter's action constituted a denial of justification by faith (Gal 2:11–21). Justification by faith explains how Jews and Gentiles relate in the church. When Peter retreated from table fellowship with the Gentiles, he was, regardless of what he intended, objectively denying the Gentiles a place in the church community, treating them as unbelievers, and denying justification

---

90. Cavanaugh, *Being Consumed*, 55. The identity of "brothers and sisters" in Matthew 25 as only Christians is unlikely given the reference to "all the nations" (Matt 25:32).

91. Moloney, *Body Broken*, 189.

92. Moloney, *Body Broken*, 190.

93. Reinders, "Being Grateful," 439.

by faith. The boundaries of table fellowship, in other words, mark out those who are justified—namely, those who believe in Jesus.[94] The Lord's supper is not about whom we want to eat with, about our guest list, but about God's. The lesson here is that we are to treat as friends those whom God regards as friends. Here we sometimes learn, as James K. A. Smith says, "to love people we really don't like that much."[95] We are obliged to see those next to us with new eyes, to see others as God's guests, as company desired by God.[96]

We see this remarkable dimension of the Eucharist in a story narrated by Vincent Donovan, a Roman Catholic priest sent to evangelize the Masai people of Tanzania in the 1960s. Donovan indicates that he simplified the Mass by eliminating all rituals that traditionally preceded and followed it. The ritual itself was transformative. "Masai men," Donovan writes, "had never eaten in the presence of Masai women. In their minds, the status and condition of women were such that the very presence of women at the time of eating was enough to pollute any food that was present."[97] But if they accepted it, Donovan writes, "they were accepting the truth that in the Eucharist . . . 'there is neither slave nor free, neither Jew nor Greek, neither male nor female.'"[98]

The Eucharist, therefore, has potential to resocialize us to see the true equality that exists among all those who believe in Jesus, regardless of race, wealth, status, politics, ethnicity, nationality, etc. In the soil of this community, envy languishes. There is no rank at the Eucharist and therefore our impulses to compare and see each other as rivals and competitors dissipates. At the Eucharist Jesus resocializes us to be grateful that God includes us, and others, in his love.

From Envy to Gratitude for Equality

Jesus teaches us to view people in non-comparative and non-competitive ways. At the table where we share food, we are encouraged to share common goods as a way of divesting a competitive mentality.[99] To embrace the gift of Christ liberates one to be thankful for gifts in others without the need to

---

94. Leithart has a stimulating discussion of this in Leithart, *Blessed are the Hungry*, 141–46.
95. Smith, *Desiring the Kingdom*, 202.
96. Williams, *Being Christian*, 51–52.
97. Donovan, *Christianity Rediscovered*, 121.
98. Donovan, *Christianity Rediscovered*, 121.
99. DeYoung, *Glittering Vices*, 55.

diminish one's own value or worth.[100] Those who see the world in terms of competition and rivalry "become blinded by their own concerns and desire for power (or fear of death); they are unable to see and appreciate the beauty of others."[101]

Many have observed the parallels between resentment and gratitude. In both instances, the recipient reciprocates the "gift" of another, though in resentment the gift is an offense. The differences are also striking. Unlike resentment which pushes one away from another or initiates relationships of hostile reciprocity, "gratitude tends to bind us together in relationships of friendly and affectionate reciprocity."[102] Whereas a resentful person is quick to observe offences and blame others, a grateful person is eager to see goodness in others and inclined to reciprocate with similar kindness.

The envious person is unhappy with him/herself and feels small and worthless around others who are regarded as better. Relationships for such individuals are easily degraded by envy. "If *Invidia* were a grateful rather than an envious person," Roberts writes, "she would not focus on the ways she falls short of Grace's excellences, but on the abilities and endowments that she herself possesses."[103] If she were a talented musician, she would not look at others comparatively, much less think competitively, about others who perform better than she. "She will be freer to value her musical excellence for its own sake," Roberts avers, and "she will be inclined to thank somebody for it."[104]

Here it becomes plain again how gratitude manifests love. "Love is not envious," Paul writes (1 Cor 13:4). "It is not irritable or resentful" (1 Cor 13:5). "It bears all things, believes all things, hopes all things, endures all things" (1 Cor 13:7). Gratitude has the potential to dispel resentment since "the corresponding dispositions will tend to exclude one another"[105] Roberts conjectures, "I should think that the virtue tends to exclude the vice."[106]

Sometimes we might sense we are powerless, a recognition that can generate lasting resentment. "Resentment," according to Nouwen, "is thus a sign of our having become victims of the darkness of this world and of having lost faith in the One who is the light."[107] The opposite of resent-

---

100. DeYoung, *Glittering Vices*, 54.
101. Vanier, *Community and Growth*, 19.
102. Roberts, "Blessings of Gratitude," 68.
103. Roberts, "Blessings of Gratitude," 75.
104. Roberts, "Blessings of Gratitude," 75.
105. Roberts, "Blessings of Gratitude," 69.
106. Roberts, "Blessings of Gratitude," 69.
107. Nouwen, *Peacework*, 116.

ment, gratitude involves "finding the living Christ in our life together" and showing "each other in a concrete way that something new is happening."[108] Nouwen's perspective was radically altered by working among impoverished people in Peru and discovering, to his surprise, joy in the midst of sadness and care in the midst of oppression. One cannot be a real peacemaker if motivated simply by guilt or the sense that one is needed by others. "When I could be with them to exchange gifts and live gratefully," he writes, "it could become a relationship without limits."[109]

A community of peaceworkers must recognize and affirm the great human gifts. "The greatest service we can offer each other," Nouwen writes, "is mutual support in our conversion from resentment to gratitude."[110] The reverse is also true. If there is mutual support to begin with, resentment is less likely to evolve.[111]

The Eucharist as a Peaceable Ritual that Celebrates Justice

On Maundy Thursday, at the last Supper, Jesus breaks bread and says, "do this in remembrance of me."[112] He indicates that what was going to happen to him, i.e., the tearing of his flesh and shedding of his blood, is going to be the definitive sign of God's welcome.[113] The invitation God extends to us to share a meal indicates, much like the peace offering in the Old Testament, that we have peace with him, now explicitly through Jesus (cf. "sacrifice of praise," Heb 13:15). We reciprocate his love gift by giving thanks, "by which we offer to God an acceptable worship with reverence and awe" (Heb 12:28).

When the risen Jesus appeared to his disciples to dine with them, he did so only after greeting them with the words, "Peace be with you" (Luke 24:36). In light of the peace one has with God, peace should be pursued

---

108. Nouwen, *Peacework*, 116.

109. Nouwen, *Peacework*, 117.

110. Nouwen, *Peacework*, 118.

111. "Everyone is called to manifest a particle of the glory of God—in communion with others. When they do not work together, groups create apartheid. Walls are built up between them, rivalry and competition set in. This leads to jealousy which, in turn, leads to hatred and warfare" (Vanier, *Community and Growth*, 19).

112. Scholars are generally agreed that the Last Supper occurred on the evening following the slaughter of the lambs in the Temple, and therefore on Thursday evening (see esp. Mark 14:12; Luke 22:7). The conjecture that the date is different in John's Gospel loses some strength if "before the feast of the Passover" (John 13:1) is understood as "before 15 Nisan" rather than "before 14 Nisan." In such an instance eating the Passover (John 18:28) refers to consuming the Passover peace offerings which were eaten on 15–21 Nisan. For these and other arguments, see Pitre, *Jesus and the Last Supper*, 251–73.

113. Williams, *Being Christian*, 47.

with others. Those sensitive to the dynamic of the Eucharist "know, in their bones, by an increasingly second nature, that we are forgiven and so we forgive."[114] The Eucharist is a meal of reconciliation, not alienation, a meal of cooperation, not competition. "In the Eucharist, then," Volf writes, "we celebrate the giving of the self to the other and the receiving of the other into the self that the triune God has undertaken in the passion of Christ and that we are called and empowered to live such giving and receiving out in a conflict-ridden world."[115]

Donovan describes a peace ritual through gift-giving for the Masai people (reflective in many ways of the peace rituals Visser identifies among tribal people) in which one person would accept from other the offer of a tuft of grass (i.e., vital food for cattle). On some occasions, "if someone, or some group, in the village had refused to accept the grass as the sign of the peace of Christ, there would be no Eucharist at this time."[116] The Eucharist, as such, promoted peace.

Justice is more than equality. Whereas equality can be acknowledged, justice is something that can be implemented. Because God has created all with equality, no one should be alienated or disadvantaged. No one should hoard, and no one should go hungry. The Eucharist is the revelation of God's final act and purpose to bring the end of the world closer. It is "the beginning of the end of the world."[117] At the table, the church becomes what it is supposed to be—namely, "a community of strangers who have become guests together and are listening together to the invitation of God."[118] At Eucharist, the world and people can be viewed properly, filled with the Holy Spirit and equipped. It lasts only seconds but happens again and again. The Lord's Supper is a meal on the run.[119] The full kingdom meal has not yet arrived, and the Eucharist is anticipatory.

It would be a colossal error, however, to insist that every celebration of the Eucharist now is peaceable. For some, not least disabled people, it can be "a ritual of exclusion and degradation."[120] Nancy Eiesland comments,

> I have been part of several congregations whose practice of receiving Eucharist includes filing to the front of the sanctuary and kneeling at the communion rail. Often, because I am either

---

114. Wright, *After You Believe*, 279.
115. Volf, *Exclusion and Embrace*, 130.
116. Donovan, *Christianity Rediscovered*, 127.
117. Williams, *Being Christian*, 57.
118. Williams, *Being Christian*, 58.
119. Smith, *Desiring the Kingdom*,
120. Eiesland, "Encountering the Disabled God," 10.

in a wheelchair or using crutches, an usher alerts me that I need not go forward for the Eucharist. Instead, I am offered the sacrament at my seat after everyone has been served. The congregation is trying to accommodate my presence in the service.... But, in effect, they are transforming the Eucharist from a corporate experience to a solitary one for me, from a sacralization of Christ's broken body to a stigmatization of my disabled body.[121]

The peace of the Eucharist does not always shine; sometimes it only flickers, and the church must admit its shortcomings. It is striking that at the Last Supper, as Gethsemane began to cast its shadow, Jesus gave thanks.[122] He did not disconnect the looming darkness with God the Giver, recognizing that God continues to give in dark places.[123] When he was reviled, Jesus did not revile in return but entrusted himself to the all-seeing, all-knowing Judge (1 Pet 2:23). Too frequently in this world, the Eucharist is celebrated in the context of oppression. In so doing, the church gives thanks in dark places. In the face of injustice, there is a place for subdued anger in the recognition that God is the Judge who judges justly. The notion of a final judgment reduced Miroslav Volf's angry impulses to take vengeance into his own hands as he witnessed ethnic genocide.[124]

The Eucharist, however, conveys the message that justice will prevail and that in the end God will vindicate the oppressed and punish perpetrators of injustice.[125] The marriage feast of the Lamb, previewed at the Eucharist, is announced with shouts of joy: "Salvation and glory and power to our God, for his judgments are true and just; he has judged the great whole who corrupted the earth with her fornication, and he has avenged on her the blood of his servants" (Rev 19:2). When Jesus appears on the white horse, followed by the armies of heaven, he has protruding from his mouth "a sharp sword with which to strike down the nations, and he will rule them with a rod of iron; he will tread the wine press of the fury of the wrath of God the Almighty" (Rev 19:15).

---

121. Eiesland, "Encountering the Disabled God," 10.

122. Williams, *Being Christian*, 48.

123. Williams, *Being Christian*, 48.

124. "It takes the quiet of a suburban home for the birth of the thesis that human nonviolence corresponds to God's refusal to judge. In a scorched land, soaked in the blood of the innocent, it will invariably die. And as one watches it die, one will do well to reflect about many other pleasant captivities of the liberal mind" (Volf, *Exclusion and Embrace*, 304).

125. The Eucharist "commemorates God's victory over every cosmic and historical force of evil by a lion—no, of all things!—by a lamb who was slain and by the blood of the martyrs who follow this lamb" (Schlabach, "Peace and War," 367).

From Anger to Gratitude for Justice

The death and resurrection of Jesus are the guarantees that he will rid it of injustice. Gratitude is an expression of trust that the world is God's, and that his promises will be fulfilled. "A posture of grace in the midst of trouble," Christine Pohl writes, "does not mean that we are feeling grateful for the inconvenience . . . but it does say that we trust God in all of the circumstances of our lives."[126] In recognition that the all-seeing Creator and Judge will right wrongs and judge justly, unhealthy anger can be purged. We must look for joy even in the shadow of the cross. In the words of Barth,

> He judges the world . . . once for all in Jesus Christ, and thus gives the cosmos its hope and our life its promise. But the cosmos still stands, and our life still proceeds, under the shadow of the cross on this judgment has been accomplished for the salvation of the world and our own. We must be surprised and angry that we live in this shadow. . . . We must also realize that all the provisional light which we believe we can recognize and enjoy as such really breaks forth from this shadow, that all the little fulfillments in which we may rejoice are only reflections of the great fulfillment which has taken place in the darkness into which God Himself entered for us in His Son, and that every recognition and experience of these fulfillments is only an advance towards the comprehensive and conclusive revelation of this great fulfillment. But this means in practice that the real test of our joy of life as commanded and therefore a true and good joy is that we do not evade the shadow of the cross of Jesus Christ and are not unwilling to be genuinely joyful even as bear sorrows laid upon us.[127]

Death is an intrusion into the created realm, a disturber of shalom. "The wages of sin" or just desserts, death was for the apostle Paul no less an invasive enemy to be vanquished. The hymn text Bach melodized, *Komm süßer Tod* (Come, Sweet Death) is understandable for someone on the brink of death, but is otherwise unsound theology. Wolterstorff's poignant *Lament for a Son* grapples with the loss of a son: "I can do nothing else than endure in the face of this deepest and most painful of mysteries. I believe in God the Father Almighty, maker of heaven and earth and resurrector of Jesus Christ."[128] In other words, "faith endures; but my address to God is

---

126. Pohl, *Living into Community*, 29.
127. Barth, *CD* 3/4:383.
128. Wolterstorff, *Lament for a Son*, 67–68.

uncomfortably, perplexingly, altered."[129] Gratitude can survive the pain of loss, though it is muted, sung in a lower a key. "All these things I recognize," Wolterstorff writes, "I remember delighting in them—trees, art, house, music, pink, morning sky, work well done, flowers, books. I still delight in them. I'm still grateful. But the zest is gone."[130]

In some difficult scenarios, we can still be grateful for the presence of God and of his people. As such, gratitude can be an "uncomfortable reminder that we need other people and that our lives are dependent on their gifts and generosity."[131] When you are suffering, you discover that some people are gifted with words. "For such, one is profoundly grateful."[132] In grief we learn from others. "I have been daily grateful," Wolterstorff writes, "for the friend who remarked that grief isolates."[133] For Christine Pohl, gratitude prevents death from defining us and can sometimes be a "spiritual bludgeon used to smash the heart of grief out of people."[134]

Paul enjoins gratitude in all circumstances and for all things. While the comprehensiveness of this injunction excludes evil, as was indicated in the previous chapter, there is a sense in which gratitude can be appropriate even in the face of evil. God works *against* evil and suffering, but in his wisdom, he also works *through* evil and suffering.[135] In this connection, one wonders whether gratitude for disability is ever appropriate. On the surface, disabilities seem to imply the brokenness of the world, the diminishment of life, and the negation of abilities others enjoy. Yet within the corpus of Vanier's and Nouwen's writings, for instance, the word "gift" is often used in connection with disabilities and those with disabilities.[136] Others locate biblical warrant for this nomenclature in Jesus's statement in John 9 that a certain man was born blind "so that God's works might be revealed in him" (John 9:3) which is interpreted to mean that blindness itself is the revelation

---

129. Wolterstorff, *Lament for a Son*, 70.
130. Wolterstorff, *Lament for a Son*, 51.
131. Pohl, *Living into Community*, 28.
132. Wolterstorff, *Lament for a Son*, 34.
133. Wolterstorff, *Lament for a Son*, 56.
134. Pohl, *Living into Community*, 26.
135. Volf, *Free of Charge*, 30.
136. Referring to, among others, those with disabilities, Vanier writes: "These people should not be sucked into the structure of the community; that would deflect them from their gift, which is to love and serve or, even more, to call out for love and awaken compassion and service in the hearts of others" (Vanier, *Growth and Community*, 262). Nouwen repeatedly refers to the gifts of Adam, an individual with severe disabilities with whom Nouwen worked (Nouwen, *Adam*, esp. 58–59). Nowhere could I find an instance where disabilities themselves were called gifts.

of "God's works," for which gratitude is appropriate.[137] A more plausible interpretation, however, understands the works of God to be revealed not as the blindness with which the man is born, but the gift of sight he receives. The works of God, elsewhere in the narrative of John's Gospel, are restorative works Jesus performs (e.g., John 5:36) in order for people to believe that he is sent by the Father (e.g., John 10:38; cf. 9:34).[138]

The kingdom Jesus introduces is a kingdom in which ability (e.g., sight, as in John 9) is often restored to those with disability (e.g., blindness). If we suppose that blindness is a gift, for instance, are we not required to interpret the conferral of sight as the removal of a gift? Yet the Samaritan leper, at least, regarded his cleansing as a gift for which Jesus should be thanked, and Jesus commended him for his gratitude (Luke 17:18).

Gratitude for disability, therefore, seems unimaginable. To insist that one who cannot see or walk or remember should be thankful seems extremely offensive. Further, it contradicts the wisdom of the psalmists for whom the diminishment of life often generated lament, not gratitude. Such a perspective, however, might be ableist, the product of a tired normate hermeneutic.[139] After all, for many in the New Testament blindness was a scourge not primarily because one could not see but because one was not accepted.

To obtain wisdom in this area, the situation must be complexified.[140] Disabilities themselves vary. Not all those with disability suffer and for some disability in one area (e.g., Asperger's) means heightened ability in another. The causes of disability vary: some experience disability from birth and others only in adulthood. For some disability is genetic and for others the

---

137. Hans Reinders, in fact, widens the referent to include "disabled lives" (Reinders, "Being Thankful," 432). Later he unpacks this: "The work of God that is revealed in the disabled person, then, is that she does not reject me for the limited person that I am" (Reinders, "Being Thankful, 438).

138. "The chaos and misery of this present world is, it seems, the raw material out of which the loving, wise and just God is making his new creation" (Wright, *John for Everyone*, 134). Out of the ultimate chaos and darkness of his crucifixion, Jesus establishes "a new world of light and healing" (Wright, *John for Everyone*, 134).

139. I am touched by accounts of those who envision themselves in the eschaton with disability. Disability is so constitutive of their identity that future reconstitution without disability implies an unwelcome loss of identity. This exposes a measure of ableism within my theological understanding and necessarily challenges my normate vision of the eschaton. From Nancy Eiesland I've learned to see Jesus, in his resurrected and glorified body, as a scarred God. "The foundation of Christian theology is the resurrection of Jesus Christ. Yet seldom is the resurrected Christ recognized as a deity whose hands, feet, and side bear the marks of profound impairment" (Eiesland, "Encountering the Disabled God," 14).

140. See Zylla, *Roots of Sorrow*, 56.

consequence of human recklessness or even evil. Persons with disabilities vary in terms of their psychological constitutions, personal histories, and cultural contexts. Here are just a sample of reasons why it would be imprudent and insensitive, not least for a person with no outstanding disabilities, to wax categorical about whether disability is a gift for which one should be grateful.

Yet disability that causes suffering, depending on the person, time, and situation, might be recognized as a gift. Christians learn from the psalms of lament that to express one's frustration and pain to God is not faithlessness. "Lament occurs in the context of the gap," Phil Zylla writes, "between the hope for God's intervention and the distress of being left by God alone in one's suffering."[141] Psalms of lament involve, in John Swinton's categories, not a "crisis of faith" but "a crisis of understanding."[142] Yet these Psalms, Swinton elaborates, "are not designed simply to *express* human pain and suffering. They are also designed to *form* human pain and suffering in quite specific ways."[143] They are, in Jürgen Moltmann's terms, protests in hope.

Is it possible for a lament for disability, voiced in authentic piety, to give way to gratitude, expressed with no less piety? It seems that *some* disabilities at *some* moments for *some* people, initially formed by lament, can become gifts. This was case for Miroslav Volf whose struggle with infertility prompted him and his wife to adopt two boys. Years later, as he was enjoying his two sons, he found himself in a position he once thought unimaginable—namely, being thankful for the infertility that plagued him and his wife for years. "Since it gave me what I now can't imagine living without," Volf writes, "poison was transmuted into a gift, God's strange gift."[144]

The Eucharist as a Gratuitous Ritual that Celebrates Rest

By means of the Eucharist, Jesus conveys a message of rest and so liberates us both from insatiable quests to change ourselves and the world and from the corresponding feelings of powerlessness and fatigue. The Eucharist is not an invitation first and foremost to accomplish something, to effect revolution, or to earn status; it is an invitation to see and taste what Christ has done. The work is done by Christ on the cross and the Eucharist proclaims his death. Referring to his broken body, Jesus says, "This is my body that is for you" (1 Cor 11:24). Henri Nouwen writes:

141. Zylla, *Roots of Sorrow*, 79–80.
142. Swinton, *Raging with Compassion*, 111.
143. Swinton, *Raging with Compassion*, 108.
144. Volf, *Free of Charge*, 32.

> We take from the earth what sustains us and lift it up to him who makes it his own. Small, insignificant human gifts become God's greatest gift, the gift of himself to all of us. We give God part of ourselves; he gives us all of himself. We ask God to understand our hunger and thirst; he gives us more than we even asked for. We express a reasonable desire; he responds to a greater desire than we were aware of, a desire to dwell forever in his house and share in his table. . . . Everything about the Eucharist proclaims: all is given . . . just be grateful![145]

Jesus responds to our great desire "to dwell" with him and commune with him. At the Eucharist, Jesus binds time for believers to do nothing but be together, eat and drink. If it were not a community meal, it could take place whenever. The Eucharist, therefore, gives the church the "regular rhythm of celebration."[146] Each celebration looks back and looks forward, back to cross and resurrection and forward to final banquet.[147] Further, the Eucharist also binds space for celebration. You cannot be anywhere, but must come somewhere. In the Eucharist, the church is visible at that time and in that place.[148]

At the Eucharist, prayers are offered to the Holy Spirit to transform, not so much the gifts of bread, but the people who eat.[149] The Spirit who made Jesus alive enlivens people at the Eucharist to see world as the realm of God's redemption and to see themselves as profoundly liberated. When they celebrated the Passover, the disciples reclined.[150] Only slaves would stand for meals and, though they did not fully understand it, the disciples were about to be set free from the power of sin. Anticipated by the Passover which celebrated liberation from Egyptian bondage, the Eucharist is a freedom party in which we celebrate release from all our burdens, not least the debilitating sense that we must be agents of change.

---

145. Nouwen, *Peacework*, 119.
146. Hauerwas and Wells, "Gifts of the Church," 19.
147. Hauerwas and Wells, "Gifts of the Church," 20.
148. Hauerwas and Wells, "Gifts of the Church," 20.
149. Williams, *Being Christian*, 56.
150. Wright, *Holy Communion for Amateurs*, 13. Though standing to eat was the ancient Passover custom, the rabbis recommended the Gentile posture of reclining because of the associations standing had with slavery.

From Sloth to Gratitude for Rest

The burdens of the world can sometimes overwhelm to such a degree that one sees no purpose in doing anything and abdicates his or her responsibilities. When a pastor works in a church community that routinely disappoints or critiques excessively, for instance, his or her energy is quickly depleted, hope diminishes, and the temptation of sloth arises. One does not look at everything—certainly not suffering—and say, "This is what God wants."

> It's about the capacity to see into depth of situation or person and recognize that somewhere there is God the giver, and so there is the possibility of more and more giving on the part of God which will bring something new and transforming. And somehow, as I struggle to change myself, the person I am with, the situation I am experiencing, I find that what I am looking for, what I am opening myself to, is that buried reality: God the Giver, who is never exhausted.[151]

In gratitude, one sees a world in which Christ provides rest for the weary and heavy-laden. Life is perceived as grace-filled. In gratitude, one recognizes that God has not simply commissioned work, but has provided resources and abilities in Christ. The gift celebrated in gratitude is the "easy" yoke of Christ. Further, one enjoys the cadence of rest God embeds in creation and in life, in the daily rhythm of day and night and in the weekly rhythm of a day for worship (i.e., the Lord's Day).

Gratitude reminds us that, in God's economy of gifts, everything is free because it cost Christ everything. Nothing for us is earned and nothing is deserved. Gifts are received "without payment" (Matt 10:8), and out of the overflow of joy in one's heart, one spontaneously runs to Jesus, as did the Samaritan leper, to say, "Thank you." The Eucharist enables one to see the grace and goodness of Christ, even in the face of distress, and to say with the Psalmist: "I will both lie down and sleep in peace for you alone, O Lord, make me lie down in safety" (Ps 4:8). Believers can take hold of Christ in the recognition that he has first taken hold of them (Phil 3:12).

The Eucharist as a Purposeful Ritual that Celebrates Provision

At the Eucharist, Jesus resocializes believers to see the Father as the owner of all. What he has received he has been given, and therefore he regards the bread and wine as gifts. When he takes the bread, he pauses to say, "Thank

---

151. Williams, *Being Christian*, 59.

you, Father," and when he takes the cup, he repeats his gratitude. He does not see the bread and cup as something he earned, as something to which he is entitled, in order to use as he pleases. He regards them as gifts for which his grateful prayer is loving reciprocation. Frequent neglect to pray before a meal represents the extent to which ingratitude characterizes life.[152]

Jesus resocializes people to see themselves selves as empty and needy, and to see his body and blood as ultimate provisions. The table is approached with open hands that are filled. On one occasion, Willimon was struck by people

> streaming toward the altar, and there they hold out empty hands like little children, like the famished folk they really are, empty, needing a gift in the worst sort of way.... What's normal, and natural, is the clenched fist, the hands grabbing and holding tight to what they can get. What's strange, from the world's point of view, is the openhanded, needy, empty request for grace.[153]

At the Eucharist, Jesus offers his body and blood for our consumption in order to satisfy. "I am the bread of life," he says. "Whoever comes to me will never be hungry, and whoever believes in me will never be thirsty" (John 6:35). Here is power to dispel our greed. "The insatiability of human desire," Cavanaugh writes, "is absorbed by the abundance of God's grace in the consumption of Jesus's body and blood" (John 6:27,54).[154]

Hunger is a sign of dependence. "If there is a physical body," Paul writes, "there is also a spiritual body" (1 Cor 15:44), implying that, for hunger, there is eschatological satisfaction. Such satisfaction is previewed in the gift of the Eucharist, for which gratitude is the appropriate response. "One of the ways the Eucharist overflows into the rest of our life," Rowan Williams writes, "is precisely in giving us the energy and vision for thanksgiving in all things, for making the connection between the God the Giver and everything we experience."[155]

Further Jesus resocializes people at the Eucharist to see the world not as something to be exploited out of self-interest, but as God's good matter to be stewarded and developed. In ritualizing the most common of human activities to depict his kingdom (i.e., eating and drinking), Jesus was not separating holy activity from profane, but demonstrating that his kingdom involves this material world. The use of ordinary bread and ordinary wine conveys that all of creation is to be used in the kingdom of God. The

---

152. Macquarrie, *Guide to the Sacraments*, 102.
153. Willimon, *Sinning Like a Christian*, 36.
154. Cavanaugh, *Being Consumed*, 54.
155. Williams, *Being Christian*, 59.

Eucharist is the special sacramental meal through which everything can, in some sense, be seen as sacramental.[156] God the Giver is present in everything. Regardless of where one is, some connection to God is possible, and therefore the whole material world must be taken seriously.[157] Reverence for bread and wine is the beginning of reverence for the material world.

At the Eucharist, Jesus takes the bread and blesses it, rendering a judgment, much like at creation when God said, "This is good." Vincent Donovan indicates that at the Mass he would preside over with the Masai people, there would sometimes be musicians and dancers. "There were some dances they were ashamed to bring into the Eucharist" Donovan writes. "By that very fact, a judgment had been made on them. Such dances should no longer be part of their lives at all. Eucharist served as a judgment for them."[158]

Jesus, therefore, resocializes people to see the purpose of his provision and the vocation of stewardship this implies. In the depths of every moment and every material thing, God must be seen as the Giver.[159] In some Eucharistic traditions, the consecrated bread cannot be thrown away. If the world is sacramental, the problems of overconsumption and waste must be taken seriously. This also has implications for how science and technology should be viewed. At the Eucharist, Jesus was not only demonstrating the sacramental side to material creation, he was endorsing science and technology. He did not serve wheat and grapes, but bread and wine, and therefore endorsed the scientific discoveries and processes of leavening and fermentation.

At the Eucharist, there ought to be no exclusion of others because of self-indulgence. Rather, there ought to be sharing with others in what has been received, in what has been given. At the Lord's table, there is no "my cup," but only "the cup of the Lord." The church in Corinth featured a factious spirit in which some remained hungry while others got drunk (1 Cor 11:21). "When you come together to eat," Paul says, "wait for one another" (1 Cor 11:33). At the Eucharist, bread is not hoarded, but distributed, and the cup is not gripped in a possessive way, but passed to the next person.

From Greed to Gratitude for Provision

Gratitude acknowledges that God is the creator and, as such, the source of all material goods. Such acknowledgement generates humility on two fronts.

---

156. Williams, *Being Christian*, 49.
157. Williams, *Being Christian*, 49.
158. Donovan, *Christianity Rediscovered*, 125.
159. Williams, *Being Christian*, 50.

First, there is ultimately no self-production. Whatever is made depends on materials and resources that God provides. Gratitude that sees God as creator readily embraces a reality in which houses cannot be constructed, for example, apart from the trees that God supplies. For Aristotle, gratitude was something inferior and dependency something to be avoided. He had no view, however, of life as a personal gift from God. Christian believers do not regard it as degrading to be cast as recipients of gifts. In fact, worship extols God as generous giver and believers embrace their status as needy recipients.[160]

Acknowledging God as creator implies, secondly, that people are creatures with lives characterized by finitude. Human needs are modest, infinitely far from infinite, and, with very little, contentment is attainable. "But if we have food and clothing," Paul writes, "we will be content with these" (1 Tim 6:8). There is justification for including under the rubric of clothing what we typically denominate "shelter." Across the globe, this is what most people have access to—food, clothing, and shelter—though in some locales in very modest amounts. Gratitude to our provider liberates us from the insatiable quest for more and more (Heb 13:5–6). Capacity for gratitude is not tied to abundance of resources.[161]

Christine Pohl reflects on spiritual greed, i.e., a craving for more spiritual growth, more dramatic experiences, greater success in ministry. It is a cultural emphasis on growth and success that undermines gratitude in and outside the church.[162] Pohl draws attention to this insight from Thomas á Kempis:

> Be thankful for the smallest blessing, and you will deserve to receive greater. Value the least gifts no less than the greatest, and simple graces as especial favors. If you remember the dignity of the Giver, no gift will seem small or mean, for nothing can valueless that is given by the most high God.[163]

Gratitude prevents one from simply enjoying the goods God has given and leads one to pause—before, in, and even after enjoyment—to thank him in prayer. As the hands learn the habit of folding in prayer first, the habit of immediately grasping will be dispelled. Every time one pauses to thank God for a good, one is reminded of how many goods one has. The world is seen with new eyes, and all of creation is perceived as something sanctified by

---

160. Roberts, "Blessings of Gratitude," 73.
161. Pohl, *Living into Community*, 27.
162. Pohl, *Living into Community*, 21.
163. á Kempis quoted in Pohl, *Living into Community*, 22.

God's word, "It is good." Everything is therefore received with thanksgiving and nothing is rejected. Gratitude consecrates material goods for service in the kingdom of Christ (1 Tim 4:4–5).

Gratitude to God as creator for his provision accepts the calling of stewardship and resists the quest to possess and exploit. Stewards in his creation are tasked with using his gifts wells, caring for his creation, and developing it in ways that honor it. Through gratitude, labor is seen as a vocation rather than a means to a paycheck. Industry is no longer viewed as a commodity itself, but as the avenue to make quality goods available for human use and enjoyment, and science as something that honors the giver. In so doing, one experiences liberation from excessive consumption of the earth's resources and from the exploitation of others for cheap labor.

The Eucharist as a Joyful Ritual that Celebrates Pleasure

At the Eucharist, Jesus invites his disciples to the pleasure of communion with him. The food he offers is not simply bread, but his life-giving body. The drink he supplies is not simply wine, but his sin-forgiving blood. At the Eucharist, in other words, Jesus offers a deep joy that transcends the pleasure of mere eating. What the bread and wine of the Eucharist supply transcends the energy to stay physically alive; the bread and wine convey the life of Christ to remain spiritually vibrant.

There is a sense in which the Eucharist today features the absence of Christ. But there is an even more profound sense in which the Eucharist features the presence of Christ, albeit a spiritual presence. When the Eucharist is celebrated today, there is a sense in which Jesus returns, and the return of Jesus is marked by joy. "So you have pain now," Jesus says, "but I will see you again, and your hearts will rejoice, and no one will take your joy from you" (John 16:22).

This is why the eschatological wedding feast depicted in Revelation 19, of which the Eucharist is a foretaste, is ultimately celebratory. This feast, which features the presence of Christ in way previously not experienced, begins with multiple shouts of praise, first from the great multitude, "Hallelujah! Salvation and glory and power to our God!" (Rev 19:1). Then the twenty-four elders and four living creatures say, "Amen. Hallelujah!" (Rev 19:4), followed by a voice from the throne, "Praise our God all you his servants" (Rev 19:5) and the voice of a great multitude, "Hallelujah! For the Lord our God the Almighty reigns" (Rev 19:6). Though this feast is not described as eternal, it clearly points to an eschatological feast.

From Gluttony to Gratitude for Pleasure

Gluttony is not interested so much in the food, much less in the company with which one eats, but in the pleasure derived from food. In gratitude, God is acknowledged not only as the giver of food and drink, but as the author of joy. He does not merely supply nourishment necessary for life on analogy of an IV bag at the hospital, but as food and drink laced with taste. To eat hastily, therefore, is ingratitude towards God as benevolent creator.

In gratitude, one does not simply acknowledge gifts, but one receives them with joy. "It is really when the Holy Spirit comes and is present, Karl Barth wrote, "that one experiences true joy. But this means that joy comes and is present as it lists, and no one knows whence it comes or whither it goes."[164] "When our lives are shaped by gratitude," Pohl writes, "we're more likely to notice the goodness and beauty in everyday things."[165] Grateful people also recognize that part of the pleasure of eating is the pleasure of companionship. When the Father is thanked, he is thanked for the friends with whom eats and drinks. Eating, therefore, must envision the good of others and should reflect sensitivity to those with whom one lives or in whose community one finds oneself.

We stand with Heideggerian awe at the wonder of the world, but the experience is not impersonal. The experience of transcendence defies our comprehension, as it did for Qoheleth, but not in a way that depresses us. God's transcendence implies our creaturehood, and in that acknowledgement we conclude that "there is nothing better for mortals than to eat and drink, and find enjoyment in their toil. This also, I saw, is from the hand of God; for apart from him, who can eat or who can have enjoyment?" (Eccl 2:24–25). The liturgy of Israel, her cultic practices, are never separated from the fact that the king of glory, who dwells with her in the temple, is creator God. For the earth and its fullness are the Lord's. Every bit of existence, including our eating and drinking, is like an ongoing hymn: "So whether you eat or drink or whatever you do," Paul says, "do everything for the glory of God" (1 Cor 10:31).

But, as Karl Barth argued, one should not take this world too seriously because the future world must be taken very seriously. Believers are liberated to play, to celebrate the little things, the small and ordinary, etc.[166] The new creation is instantiated by writing poetry and so transforming words, by making music and so transforming notes, by producing film, and

---

164. Barth, CD 3/4:379.
165. Pohl, Living into Community, 22.
166. Pohl, Living into Community, 20.

so transforming images. Through art, old worlds are "redeemed" and new worlds are created. One learns to laugh because the world God promises is so much greater than this one.

In gratitude, one acknowledges that the God who supplies food also promises pleasure. Yet God did not appoint food to fill eternal cravings. To eat excessively is ingratitude towards God as one's eternal portion and delight. Further, one ignores the calling to be stewards by misappropriating food for personal gratification and slighting those in the world who are needy. In gratitude for food and drink, God is acknowledged as the true source of joy.

The Eucharist as a Personal Ritual that Celebrates Relationship

At the Eucharist, Jesus invites believers to dine with him, not simply to be with them, but to be in them. He wants believers to ingest him, to receive him in their bodies and into their lives. "His welcome," Rowan Williams writes, "gives us the courage to open up to him."[167] The Eucharist means that Jesus wants to be with his people, to be their dependable companion, and he gives them everything needed to follow him. Much like hunger, sexual desire is protological and satisfaction eschatological (1 Cor 15:42–49). The ultimate satisfaction of the eschaton is previewed in the Eucharist.

The Eucharist, as the apostle explains, is a participation in, or communion with, the body and blood of Christ (1 Cor 10:16). Overtones of sexual intimacy are discernible when we recall that the feast the Eucharist previews is a marriage feast in which Jesus is the bridegroom and the church, his bride. At the Eucharist, Jesus does not only nourish and care for the church (Eph 5:29), he becomes one with the church, on analogy of husband and wife becoming one flesh (Eph 5:31). By ingesting the bread and the wine, one receives Christ and become members of his body, "bone of his bones, and flesh of his flesh" (Eph 5:30, KJV). In fact, the mystery of marital intimacy is disclosed in the union and communion between Christ and the church (Eph 5:32).

Jesus can resocialize believers through Eucharist to see others as brothers and sisters in a family, to see the "sexual other," not first and foremost in terms of erotic sexuality, but in terms of social sexuality. Jesus himself provides an example of social sexuality, interacting throughout his life with many women, but without a hint of erotic sexuality.

---

167. Williams, *Being Christian*, 43.

From Lust to Gratitude for Relationship

God must be thanked for friendships and relationships available in the church community. The church is an intimate community, depicted in Scripture as a family consisting of brothers and sisters. Envisioning women and men in the church interacting as family, the apostle urges Timothy to speak "to older women as mothers, to younger women as sisterswith absolute purity" (1 Tim 5:2). Gratitude to God for existing relationships has potential to dispel lust. Sexual temptation, for those who are single, is reduced when one's relationship to sexual others (e.g., father-daughter, mother-son, brother-sister) is healthy.

During a period in her life when she was very lonely, theologian Marva Dawn faced what she called "the inviting possibility of an affair." She shared her feelings with a close Christian friend who said to her, "I want to be here for you when you come back." When she asked him to clarify, he said, "If you have an affair, you'll regret it. I want to help pick up the pieces when you hate yourself." She writes, "If my Christian brother loves me like that, who needs an affair?"[168] Gratitude to God for other women and men in our lives honors them as individuals and reduces our impulses to see them as objects or to mistreat or injure them sexually.

Gratitude to God for one's spouse has similar power for those who are married. When one is grateful for one's spouse, one is grateful for shared experiences and shared stories. When God is thanked for a spouse, he is acknowledged as the one who judges those who defile the marriage bed (Heb 13:4) and that he ordained marriage to depict the relationship between Christ and church. To regard intimacy with a spouse purely in terms of sensual pleasure is ingratitude to God. When God is thanked for relationships, one recalls that he promises the greatest relational intimacy, of which marriage and especially the Eucharist is a foretaste. We recall that Jesus is the groom who will never leave, nor forsake us (Heb 13:5).

PRACTICES OF GRATITUDE

If the ritual of the Eucharist is the ethical paradigm, then Christian practices ought to be Eucharist-like. Such practices potentially resolve the paradox of Merleau-Ponty's position—namely, that to change the self the body must be changed, but since the self is the body, one is requiring the problem to be the solution. To effect change, liberation from the outside is necessary. The agent of this liberation is the Spirit, the locus is the Church, and the

---

168. Dawn, *Sexual Character*, 8.

paradigm is the Eucharist. Through Eucharist-like practices, the Spirit can deposit new meanings to solidify new behaviors.

There is documentation, on a purely psychological level, that "religious practices" can enhance human life and health.[169] One recent social-scientific study, for example, revealed that people who "engaged in more religious activities had more spiritual experiences" and that "on days they had more spiritual experiences they more strongly felt moral emotions (empathy, gratitude, and forgiveness)."[170] Further, "the positive associations between religiosity, spirituality, and moral emotions seem to be evident at both the between-person and within-in person levels of functioning."[171] But is it not possible that the self is still reinforced even when bad habits are replaced with religious ones? How can one be sure that one is being transformed?

By pursuing Christian practices of prayer, hospitality and community, for example, one can open oneself to the Spirit's transformative power to rewrite bad habits. This inquiry regards gratitude as one way the Spirit can reverse distorted desires. Not insignificantly, therefore, New Testament writers recommends gratitude to displace vice. To the Ephesians, the writer says (5:3–5),

> But fornication and impurity of any kind, or greed, must not even be mentioned among you, as is proper among saints. Entirely out of place is obscene, silly, and vulgar talk; but instead, let there be thanksgiving. Be sure of this, that no fornicator or impure person, or one who is greedy (that is, an idolater), has any inheritance in the kingdom of Christ and of God.

A few verses later, he continues in the same vein (5:18–20):

> Do not get drunk with wine, for that is debauchery; but be filled with the Spirit, as you sing psalms and hymns and spiritual songs among yourselves, singing and making melody to the Lord in your hearts, giving thanks to God the Father at all times and for everything in the name of our Lord Jesus Christ.

What is necessary to dispel bad habits, for the biblical writer, are practices of gratitude. This concluding section will identify, only in preliminary and suggestive ways, three such practices—namely, the practices of prayer,

---

169. Those who engage in religious practices tend to avoid risky behaviors, e.g., substance abuse, and have better health, e.g., lower depression. For documentation, see Smith and Snell, *Souls in Transition*; Smith and Denton, *Soul Searching*.

170. Hardy et al., "Daily Religious Involvement," 344. Religious practices included, e.g., prayer and attendance at worship services. Religious experiences included, e.g., sensations of God's presence or comfort.

171. Hardy et al., "Daily Religious Involvement," 344.

of hospitality, of community.[172] Each of these practices is Eucharist-like, underscoring communion with God and with others and involving reciprocal giving-and-receiving.

Prayer, first of all, is Eucharist-like because it acknowledges the ontology of communion with God, others, and the world. Chapter 1 identified how the hegemony of reason, especially in Descartes, disenchants the world and reduces it to a machine. When God is approached in prayer, one admits that there is more to the world than meets the eye. Behind the gifts of life, there is a gracious Giver. In prayer, one does not only acknowledge that there is God who hears, but that he is the creator of the world and of all people and that he has created humanity to live in relationship to him, the world, and others. "Prayer enacts an entire cosmology," Smith writes, "because implicit in the very act of prayer is an entire ontology construal of the God-world relationship."[173] By praying, "we are engaged in a sort of performative ontology."[174]

Prayer has the capacity to reshape pride. Instead of seeking audiences with others who might give their approval, one seeks in prayer an audience with God who blesses people with his countenance and addresses them with his voice.[175] A good mother mirrors love to her child and smiles at the child's expressions of joy and happiness. Capps points that for Erik Erikson, "the mirroring event is ritually affirmed in the sacrament of baptism, and repeated in the funeral service."[176] Much like a mother "does God greet us by name and lift us up, and we sense the joy and warmth of the glow on God's face that corresponds to our own."[177] In so doing, one begins to be healed of "narcissistic injury" and is restored to balanced self-esteem. To be grateful is to reciprocate love to a giver and to acknowledge the wonder of the gift.

Prayer can be a way one responds to illegitimate enemies created by envy or to legitimate enemies guilty of injustice. The practice of praying for an enemy can alter (recalling Merleau-Ponty's categories) one's (a) perceptual level (how one sees the object) by recasting him or her as a friend for whom one is concerned, (b) motor level (how one thinks, feels, and postures oneself toward the object) by subduing one's anger towards this person and

---

172. Other grateful practices might include the practices of art, humor, conversation, celebration, and friendship.
173. Smith, *Desiring the Kingdom*, 193.
174. Smith, *Desiring the Kingdom*, 193.
175. DeYoung, *Glittering Vices*, 75.
176. Capps, *Depleted Self*, 68.
177. Capps, *Depleted Self*, 68.

generating appreciation (c) tactile level (how one acts in relation to the object) by generating hospitality and interaction instead of avoidance.[178]

The practice of hospitality, secondly, includes "guests" and "hosts." According to Margaret Visser, hospitality in ancient cultures often ritually domesticated and disarmed guests, including enemies who were potentially hostile.[179] You gave to friends because they had potential to be your helpers and you gave to strangers because they had potential to be your enemies.[180] "When hostility is converted into hospitality," Nouwen writes, "then fearful strangers can become guests, revealing to their hosts the promise they are carrying with them. Then, in fact, the distinction between host and guest proves to be artificial and evaporates in the recognition of newfound unity."[181] In this newfound unity, there is a reciprocal exchange of gifts. "In the context of hospitality," Nouwen says, "guest and host can reveal their most precious gifts and bring new life together."[182]

In gratitude, one acknowledges not only being-in-communion, but being-for-others. Jesus provided an example of welcoming the disadvantaged and marginalized. Grateful hospitality is eager to provide access to the disabled, for example, but access must transcend merely accommodating the disabled—"not as the 'abled' serving the weaker disabled, but as people in interdependent relationships infused by the Holy Spirit, mutually giving and receiving."[183] Christians must embrace the stranger, but inclusion must move beyond something perfunctory.

Thomas Aquinas's view of magnanimity recast Aristotle's because he envisioned something Aristotle could not—namely, the magnanimity of the poor. Nouwen contended that poverty enables people to be good hosts because in poverty they have fewer defenses and therefore more room for enemies.[184] If one has nothing to lose, one has everything to give. "Who wants to sneak in our back door," Nouwen asks, "when our front door is wide open?"[185]

Through the practice of community, thirdly, one can practice asymmetrical reciprocal relationships. One way to illustrate this is to envision a

178. Bennett, *Involved Withdrawal*, 45–46.
179. Visser, *Gift of Thanks*, 28.
180. Visser, *Gift of Thanks*, 28–29.
181. Nouwen, *Show Me*, 30.
182. Nouwen, *Show Me*, 31.
183. Edgar-Smith et al., "Youth with Special Needs," 57.
184. "We can perceive the stranger as an enemy only as long as we have something to defend" (Nouwen, *Show Me the Way*, 31).
185. Nouwen, *Show Me The Way*, 32.

community in which mentally disabled children are regarded as gifts. This is precisely the question with which Hans Reinders grapples, and he does so in terms of John 9 and the invitation to see the disabled in the light of Jesus. A man is born blind "so that God's works might be revealed in him" (John 9:3).[186] There is a real sense in which a disabled person is a gift, though such a claim is often said "by the wrong people at the wrong time."[187] Unlike the Pharisees who do not know God, Jesus says, "But I do know him and I keep his word" (John 8:55). To say a disabled child reveals the works of God, therefore, requires people to "be prepared to take up their part in making these works visible."[188] But it also requires "appropriate self-knowledge" which begins with "practicing humility to lay down our pride."[189]

How does one acquire such self-knowledge? At l'Arche, a global network of homes for disabled founded by Jean Vanier, the staff consists of people who prioritize being with the disabled over doing something for them.[190] Such a community, in Vanier's words, expresses "mutual belonging and bonding."[191] Vanier elaborates, "We announce the goals the spirit that unites us. We recognize together that we are responsible for one another. We recognize also that this bonding comes from God; it is a gift from God. It is he who has chosen us and called us together in a covenant of love and mutual caring."[192] When people chose to live with disabled people rather than do something for them, they who have authentic self-knowledge embark on a journey that consists largely of "receiving."[193] Reinders elaborates,

> Yet this receiving comes from mentally disabled people who because of their need for assistance in the eyes of the world do not have much to give. This is what seeing the person in her relationship to oneself and to God entails. To learn how to receive from those who have nothing to give but what and who they are, this is the task that new assistants at l'Arche have to master. Without knowing how to receive, their days will be filled with frustrating experiences.[194]

---

186. For a brief discussion about this verse, see above.
187. Reinders, "Being Thankful," 432.
188. Reinders, "Being Thankful," 432.
189. Reinders, "Being Thankful," 433.
190. "But before 'doing for them,' we want to 'be with them'" (Vanier, *Community and Growth*, 11).
191. Vanier, *Community and Growth*, 17.
192. Vanier, *Community and Growth*, 18.
193. Reinders, "Being Thankful," 435.
194. Reinders, "Being Thankful," 435.

The disabled person becomes a mirror into which one begins to see oneself for whom one really is, as fragile and limited. "What is received," Reinders writes, "is a truth about our limits in the face of a human begin who wants to be accepted unconditionally."[195] What is learned, he goes on to say, is not from acting, but from responding, not how to love, but how to be loved, "not to strive toward your own perfection but to learn to live with your imperfections."[196] Reinders concludes, "The disabled person is genuinely a gift. But in order to see that, we first have to learn to say the words of thanksgiving to God for what we receive, which is not necessarily the same as that we would like to be given."[197] Relationships in a community in which there are disabled children must be reciprocal because disabled children have something to contribute. The church must offer access and be inclusive, but true hospitality, Zylla argues, transcends access and inclusivity to include reciprocity.[198]

CONCLUSION

The situation that prompted this practical theological inquiry is the surprising co-existence, in the Western world, of both greed and gratitude, of a vice which wants more and of a virtue that celebrates what one has. Widening the lens, one sees society as populated by people gripped by desires for something in the illusionary future. These desires are interpreted theologically as desires to return home, to access the place of human origins in the sinless Garden of Eden and, even more, the peaceful new creation of the eschaton. These healthy desires for acceptance, equality, justice, rest, provision, pleasure, and relationship, however, are sabotaged by cravings for superficial substitutes which are quickly enslaving and destructive. The sinful sabotage of human desire denies an ontology of being-in-communion in which humans are inextricably related to God, others, and the world. Sin separates what God has joined together and devalues what God dignifies, and so these distorted desires isolate people from God and each other, for example, and generate destructive behavior. These are the implications that confront pastors who are often at a loss how to respond or what to recommend.

195. Reinders, "Being Thankful," 436.
196. Reinders, "Being Thankful," 436.
197. Reinders, "Being Thankful," 438.
198. "Integrating the vision of the biblical witness," Phil Zylla writes, "requires true reciprocity" (Zylla, "Practices of Acceptance," 708).

This book hypothesized that gratitude, freshly understood, could function as a pastoral antidote to the issues generated by distorted desires. Gratitude, however, has not been universally embraced as a virtue, and this inquiry investigated, through mutual critical correlation, alternative accounts in Aristotle and Jacques Derrida, both of whom critiqued gratitude. Aristotle judged gratitude to be an inferior virtue and Derrida condemned gratitude as an immoral response. This inquiry further explored the assessment of gratitude rendered by positive psychology. Positive psychologists recommend gratitude for its psychological, physiological, and pro-social benefits. By excluding God from their considerations, however, gratitude for life is ignored and gratitude in the face of overwhelming tragedy is seemingly impossible.

Gratitude was then probed in terms of the narrative of Scripture. By virtue of their creation in God's image, human beings have an ontology of beings-in-communion in which they are inextricably situated giving and receiving relationships with God, others, and the world. In these relationships, gifts must be acknowledged and reciprocated, albeit in agapic, asymmetrical ways, and givers must be saluted to perpetuate peaceable relationships. Life and redemption are especially significant gifts because of their ontic qualities and in recognizing them, one is able to be grateful even as one encounters tragedy and loss. In union with Christ and through his grace, believers respond to these and other gifts freely and joyfully.

Through the Holy Spirit enabled acquisition of virtue, one acknowledges the ontology of being-in-communion, sees God's gifts, and is disposed to practice gratitude. In the church community, the Eucharist especially has potential to resocialize people in the way of Jesus by inculcating the features of gratitude as social, inclusive, peaceable, joyful, gratuitous, purposeful, and personal. Practicing gratitude, so comprehensively understood, has tremendous potential to inhibit the sins of desire as one increasingly recognizes that in Christ one has what one desires—namely, acceptance, equality, justice, rest, provision, pleasure, and relationship. Mindful of such a paradigm, the church as community, with pastors and parishioners, can recommend the practices of prayer, for example, hospitality, and community to foster relationships of giving and receiving with God above, with one other, and with the surrounding world in order to decenter people and so potentially reduce their vulnerability to the destructive potential of distorted desires.

BIBLIOGRAPHY

Alexander, Donald L. *Christian Spirituality: Five Views of Sanctification*. Downers Grove, IL: InterVarsity, 1988.

Allen, Leslie C. *Psalms 101–105*. Word Biblical Commentary 21. Waco, TX: Word, 1993.

Andresen, Jensine. "Introduction: Towards a Cognitive Science of Religion." In *Religion in Mind: Cognitive Perspectives on Religious Belief, Ritual, and Experience*, edited by Jensine Andresen, 1–44. Cambridge: Cambridge University Press, 2001.

Aquinas, Thomas. *Commentary on Aristotle's Nicomachean Ethics*. Translated by C. J. Litzinger. Notre Dame, IN: Dumb Ox, 1964.

———. *Summa Theologiae*. Translated by the Fathers of the English Dominican Province. 5 vols. 2nd ed. New York: Benzinger, 1947–48.

Aristotle. *Art of Rhetoric*. Translated by J. H. Freese. Loeb Classical Library 193. Cambridge: Harvard University Press, 1959.

———. *Eudemian Ethics*. Translated by H. Rackman. Loeb Classical Library 295. Cambridge: Harvard University Press, 1935.

———. *Metaphysics*. Translated by Hugh Tredennick. Loeb Classical Library 287. Cambridge, MA: Harvard University Press, 1935.

———. *The Nicomachean Ethics*. Translated by J. A. K. Thompson. Rev. ed. Harmondsworth: Penguin, 2004.

———. *Politics*. Edited and translated by H. Rackham. Loeb Classical Library 264. Cambridge: Harvard University Press, 1932.

Arnsperger, Christian. "Gift-Giving Practice and Noncontextual Habitus: How (Not) to Be Fooled by Mauss." In *Gifts and Interests*, edited by Antoon Vandevelde, 71–92. Leuven: Peeters, 2000.

Augustine. *The City of God against the Pagans*. Edited and translated by R. W. Dyson. Cambridge: Cambridge University Press, 1998.

———. *The Confessions of St. Augustine*. Translated by Rex Warner. New York: Mentor, 1963.

———. *The Enchiridion on Faith, Hope, and Love*. Translated by J. B. Shaw. South Bend, IN: Regnery, 1961.

Baker, David L. *Tight Fists or Open Hands? Wealth and Poverty in Old Testament Law*. Grand Rapids: Baker, 2009.

Ballard, Paul, and Stephen R. Holmes. *The Bible in Pastoral Practice: Readings in the Place and Function of Scripture in the Church*. Grand Rapids: Eerdmans, 2006.

Barclay, John. "Manna and the Circulation of Grace: A Study of 2 Corinthians 8:1–15." In *Word Leaps the Gap: Essays on Scripture and Theology in Honor of Richard B. Hays*, edited by J. Wagner, et al., 409–26. Grand Rapids: Eerdmans, 2008.

———. *Paul and The Gift*. Grand Rapids: Eerdmans, 2015.

Barfield, Owen. *History, Guilt, and Habit*. Middletown, CT: Wesleyan University Press, 1979.

Bargh, John A., and Erin L. Williams. "The Automaticity of Social Life." *Current Directions in Psychological Science* 15 (2006) 1–4.

Bargh, John A., and Tanya L. Chartrand. "The Unbearable Automaticity of Being." *American Psychologist* 54 (1999) 462–79.

Barnes, Jonathan. "Introduction." In *The Nicomachean Ethics*, by Aristotle, ix–xli. Translated by J. A. K. Thompson. Rev. ed. Harmondsworth: Penguin, 2004.

Barrett, William. *Irrational Man: A Study in Existential Philosophy*. New York: Anchor, 1962.

Barth, Karl. *Church Dogmatics*. 4 vols. Edinburgh: T. & T. Clark, 1936–77.

———. *The Epistle to the Romans*. Translated by Edwyn C. Hoskyns. 6th ed. Oxford: Oxford University Press.1933.

———. *Ethics*. Translated by Geoffrey W. Bromiley. New York: Seabury, 1981.

Bartholomew, Craig. "In Front of the Text: The Quest of Hermeneutics." In *The Bible in Pastoral Practice: Readings in the Place and Function of Scripture in the Church*, edited by Paul Ballard and Stephen R. Holmes, 135–52. Grand Rapids: Eerdmans, 2006.

Bass, Dorothy C. "Introduction." In *Practicing Theology: Beliefs and Practices in Christian Life*, edited by Miroslav Volf and Dorothy C. Bass, 1–9. Grand Rapids: Eerdmans, 2002.

Bass, Dorothy C., and Craig Dykstra. *For Life Abundant: Practical Theology, Theological Education, and Christian Ministry*. Grand Rapids: Eerdmans, 2008.

Bavinck, Herman. *Reformed Dogmatics*. 4 vols. Grand Rapids: Baker Academic, 2003–2008.

Beckwith, Roger T., and Martin J. Selman. *Sacrifice in the Bible*. Grand Rapids: Baker, 1995.

Bejczy, István P. *The Cardinal Virtues in the Middle Ages: A Study in Moral Thought from the Fourth to the Fourteenth Century*. Leiden: Brill, 2011.

Bellah, Robert, et al. *Habits of the Heart: Individualism and Commitment in American Life*. 3rd ed. Berkeley: University of California Press, 2008.

Belliotti, Raymond Angelo. *Dante's Deadly Sins: Moral Philosophy in Hell*. Chichester: Wiley-Blackwell, 2011.

Bennett, Kyle D. "Involved Withdrawal: A Phenomenology of Fasting." PhD diss., Fuller Theological Seminary, 2013.

Berkhof, Louis. *Systematic Theology*. 4th ed. Grand Rapids, Eerdmans, 1949.

Berkman, John. "Are Persons with Profound Intellectual Disabilities Sacramental Icons of Heavenly Life? Aquinas on Impairment." *Studies in Christian Ethics* 26 (2013) 83–96.

Berkouwer, G.C. *Sin*. Translated by Philip C. Holtrop. Grand Rapids: Eerdmans, 1971.

Billings, Todd. "John Milbank's Theology of the 'Gift' and Calvin's Theology of Grace: A Critical Comparison." *Modern Theology* 21 (2005) 87–105.

Blanton, Thomas R., IV. "The Benefactor's Account-Book: The Rhetoric of Gift Reciprocation according to Seneca and Paul." *New Testament Studies* 59 (2013) 396–414.
Bloch, Marc. "The Feudal World." In *Medieval Society: 400–1450*, edited by Norman F. Cantor and Michael S. Werthman, 33–83. 2nd ed. New York: Crowell, 1972.
Bockmuehl, Markus. *The Epistle to the Philippians*. Black's New Testament Commentary. London: A. & C. Black, 1998.
Boda, Mark. "Words and Meanings: הדי in Hebrew Research." *Westminster Theological Journal* 57 (1995) 277–97.
Boersma, Hans. "Being Reconciled: Atonement as the Ecclesio-Christological Practice of Forgiveness in John Milbank." In *Radical Orthodoxy and the Reformed Tradition: Creation, Covenant, and Participation*, edited by James K. A. Smith and James Olthuis, 183–202. Grand Rapids: Baker, 2005.
Boone, Mark. *The Conversion and Therapy of Desire: Augustine's Theology of Desire in the Cassiciacum Dialogues*. Eugene, OR: Wipf & Stock, 2016.
Bourdieu, Pierre. "Selections from *The Logic of Practice*." In *The Logic of the Gift: Toward an Ethic of Generosity*, edited by Alan D. Schrift, 190–230. New York: Routledge, 1997.
Brown, Colin. *Philosophy and the Christian Faith*. Downers Grove, IL: InterVarsity, 1969.
Browning, Don S. *A Fundamental Practical Theology: Descriptive and Strategic Proposals*. Minneapolis: Fortress, 1991.
———. *The Moral Context of Pastoral Care*. Philadelphia: Westminster, 1976.
———. "Pastoral Theology in a Pluralistic Age." In *Practical Theology: The Emerging Field in Theology, Church, World*, edited by Don Browning, 192–201. San Francisco: Harper & Row, 1983.
———. *Religious Ethics and Pastoral Care*. Philadelphia: Westminster, 1983.
Bubbers, Susan. *A Scriptural Theology of Eucharistic Blessings*. London: Bloomsbury, 2013.
Buck, Ross. "The Gratitude of Exchange and the Gratitude of Caring: A Developmental-Interactionist Perspective of Moral Emotion." In *Psychology of Gratitude*, edited by Robert A. Emmons and Michael E. McCullough, 108–22. Oxford: Oxford University Press, 2004.
Bywater, J., ed. *Aristotle's Ethica Nicomachea*. Oxford: Clarendon, 1894.
Calvin, John. *Catechism of the Church of Geneva*. In *The School of Faith: The Catechisms of the Reformed Church*, edited and translated by Thomas F. Torrance, 3–65. Eugene, OR: Wipf & Stock, 1996.
———. *The Epistles of Paul the Apostle to the Hebrews and The First and Second Epistles of St. Peter*. Translated by William B. Johnston. Calvin's Commentaries. Grand Rapids: Eerdmans, 1996.
———. *The Gospel According to St. John 1–10*. Translated by T. H. L. Parker. Calvin's Commentaries. Grand Rapids: Eerdmans, 1996.
———. *Institutes of the Christian Religion*. Edited by John T. McNeill. Translated by Ford Lewis Battles. 2 vols. Philadelphia: Westminster, 1960.
Campbell, Alastair. *The Gospel of Anger*. London: SPCK, 1986.
Cantor, Norman F., and Michael S. Werthman, eds. *Medieval Society: 400–1450*. 2nd ed. New York: Crowell, 1972.
Capps, Donald. *Deadly Sins and Saving Virtues*. Philadelphia: Fortress, 1987.

———. *The Depleted Self: Sin in a Narcissistic Age.* Philadelphia: Fortress, 1993.
———. *Pastoral Care and Hermeneutics.* Philadelphia: Westminster, 1984.
Caputo, John D. *God, the Gift, and Postmodernism.* New ed. Bloomington: Indiana University Press, 1999.
———. *On Religion: Thinking in Action.* Abingdon: Routledge, 2001.
———. *The Prayers and Tears of Jacques Derrida: Religion without Religion.* Bloomington: Indiana University Press, 1997.
Carlisle, Clare. "Creatures of Habit: The Problem and the Practice of Liberation." *Continental Philosophy Review* 38 (2006) 19–39.
Carr, G. Lloyd. "מלש." In *Theological Wordbook of the Old Testament*, edited by Robert Laird Harris, et al., 931–32. Chicago: Moody, 1980.
Catholic Church. *Catechism of the Catholic Church: Revised in Accordance with the Official Latin Text Promulgated by Pope John Paul II.* Vatican City: Libreria Editrice Vaticana, 1997.
Cavanaugh, William. *Being Consumed: Economics and Christian Desire.* Grand Rapids: Eerdmans, 2008.
Cessario, Romanus. *The Moral Virtues and Theological Ethics.* Notre Dame: University of Notre Dame Press, 1991.
Charry, Ellen. *God and the Art of Happiness.* Grand Rapids: Eerdmans, 2010.
Chesterton, G. K. *A Short History of England.* Seven Oaks: Fisher, 1994.
Coakley, Sarah. "Gift, Gender and Trinitarian Relations in Milbank and Tanner." *Scottish Journal of Theology* 61 (2008) 224–35.
Collins, Elizabeth. "Reflections on Ritual and on Theorizing about Ritual." *Journal of Ritual Studies* 12 (1998) 1–7.
Collins, Mary. "Ritual Symbols and Ritual Process: The Work of Victor W. Turner." *Worship* 50 (1976) 336–46.
Courtman, Nigel. "Sacrifice in the Psalms." In *Sacrifice in the Bible*, edited by Roger T. Beckwith and Martin J. Selman, 41–58. Grand Rapids: Baker, 1995.
Cox, James L. *A Guide to the Phenomenology of Religion: Key Figures, Formative Influences and Subsequent Debates.* London: T. & T. Clark, 2006.
Crawford, Allan. "What Explains Trends in Household Debt in Canada?" *Bank of Canada Review* (Winter 2012) 3–15.
Crook, Zeba. "Reciprocity: Covenantal Exchange as Test Case." In *Ancient Israel: The Old Testament in Its Social Context*, edited by Philip F. Esler, 78–91. Minneapolis: Fortress, 2006.
Cunningham, Lawrence. *The Seven Deadly Sins: A Visitor's Guide.* Notre Dame: Ave Maria, 2012.
Curran, Charles E., and Lisa A. Fullam, eds. *Virtue.* Readings in Moral Theology 16. New York: Paulist, 2011.
Dahood, Mitchell. *Psalms.* 3 vols. Anchor Bible 16–17a. Garden City: Doubleday, 1965–1970.
Dawn, Marva. *Sexual Character: Beyond Technique to Intimacy.* Grand Rapids: Eerdmans, 1993.
Derrida, Jacques. *The Gift of Death.* Translated by David Wills. Chicago: University of Chicago Press, 1995.
———. *Given Time, I: Counterfeit Money.* Chicago: University of Chicago Press, 1992.
Descartes, René. *Discourse on Method and Meditations on First Philosophy.* Translated by Donald A. Cress. Indianapolis: Hackett, 1999.

———. *The Passions of the Soul*. Translated and annotated by Stephen Voss. Indianapolis: Hackett, 1989.

DeSilva, David A. "Exchanging Favor for Wrath: Apostasy in Hebrews and Patron-Client Relationships." *Journal of Biblical Literature* 115 (1996) 91–116.

———. *Honor, Patronage, Kinship and Purity: Unlocking New Testament Culture*. Downers Grove, IL: InterVarsity, 2000.

———. *Perseverance in Gratitude: A Socio-Rhetorical Commentary on the Epistle to the Hebrews*. Grand Rapids: Eerdmans, 2000.

DeYoung, Rebecca Konyndyk. *Glittering Vices: A New Look at the Seven Deadly Sins and Their Remedies*. Grand Rapids: Brazos, 2009.

Di Blasi, Fulvio, et al. *Virtue's End: God in the Moral Philosophy of Aristotle and Aquinas*. South Bend, IN: St. Augustine's, 2008.

Donovan, Vincent. *Christianity Rediscovered*. London: SCM, 1982.

Douma, Jochem. *Responsible Conduct: Principles of Christian Ethics*. Translated by Nelson D. Kloosterman. Phillipsburg, NJ: P & R, 2003.

———. *The Ten Commandments: Manual for the Christian Life*. Translated by Nelson D. Kloosterman. Phillipsburg, NJ: P & R, 1994.

Dunn, James D. G. *The Theology of the Apostle Paul*. Grand Rapids: Eerdmans, 1998.

Dunnington, Kent. *Addiction and Virtue: Beyond the Models of Disease and Choice*. Downers Grove, IL: InterVarsity Academic, 2011.

Dykstra, Craig, and Dorothy C. Bass. "A Theological Understanding of Christian Practices." In *Practicing Theology: Beliefs and Practices in Christian Life*, edited by Miroslav Volf and Dorothy C. Bass, 13–32. Grand Rapids: Eerdmans, 2002.

Edgar-Smith, S., et al. "Bringing Youth with Special Needs into the Church Community: A Practical Guide." *Journal of Youth Ministry* 11 (2013) 57–72.

Eiesland, Nancy L. "Encountering the Disabled God." *The Other Side* 38 (2002) 10–15.

Eitel, Aiden. "Virtue or Art? Political Friendship Reconsidered." *Journal of Religious Ethics* 44 (2016) 260–77.

Emmons, Robert A. "The Psychology of Gratitude: An Introduction." In *Psychology of Gratitude*, edited by Robert A. Emmons and Michael E. McCullough, 145–66. Oxford: Oxford University Press, 2004.

Emmons, Robert A., and Michael E. McCullough. "Counting Blessings versus Burdens: An Experimental Investigation of Gratitude and Subjective Well-Being in Daily Life." *Journal of Personality and Social Psychology* 84 (2003) 377–89.

———, eds. *The Psychology of Gratitude*. Oxford: Oxford University Press, 2004.

Emmons, Robert A., and Teresa T. Kneezel. "Giving Thanks: Spiritual and Religious Correlates of Gratitude." *Journal of Psychology and Christianity* 24 (2005) 140–48.

Esler, Philip, ed. *Ancient Israel: The Old Testament in Its Social Context*. Minneapolis: Augsburg Fortress, 2006.

Fairlee, Henry. *The Seven Deadly Sins Today*. Notre Dame: University of Notre Dame Press, 1979.

Farley, Edward. "Interpreting Situations: An Inquiry into the Nature of Practical Theology." In *The Blackwell Reader in Pastoral and Practical Theology*, edited by James Woodward and Stephen Pattison, 118–27. Oxford: Blackwell, 2007.

———. *Theologia: The Fragmentation and Unity of Theological Education*. Philadelphia: Fortress, 1983.

Flannery, Kevin L. "Can an Aristotelian Consider Himself a Friend of God?" In *Virtue's End: God in the Moral Philosophy of Aristotle and Aquinas,* edited by Fulvio Di Blasi, et al., 1–12. South Bend, IN: St. Augustine's, 2008.

Forde, Gerald. "The Lutheran View." In *Christian Spirituality: Five Views of Sanctification,* edited by Donald L. Alexander, 13–46. Downers Grove, IL: InterVarsity, 1988.

Fowl, Stephen. "Wealth, Property, and Theft." In *The Blackwell Companion to Christian Ethics,* edited by Stanley Hauerwas and Samuel Wells, 455–67. 2004. Reprint, Chichester: Wiley-Blackwell, 2006.

Frame, John. *The Doctrine of the Christian Life.* Phillipsburg, NJ: P & R, 2008.

France. R.T. *The Gospel of Mark.* The New International Greek Testament Commentary. Grand Rapids: Eerdmans, 2002.

Fredrickson, Barbara. "Gratitude, Like Other Positive Emotions, Broadens and Builds." In *Psychology of Gratitude,* edited by Robert A. Emmons and Michael E. McCullough, 145–66. Oxford: Oxford University Press, 2004.

Gerkin, Charles V. *The Living Human Document: Re-Visioning Pastoral Counseling in a Hermeneutical Mode.* Nashville: Abingdon, 1984

———. *Widening the Horizons: Pastoral Responses to a Fragmented Society.* Philadelphia: Westminster, 1986.

Gerrish, Brian. *Grace and Gratitude: The Eucharistic Theology of John Calvin.* Eugene, OR: Wipf & Stock, 2002.

Goldingay, John. *Psalms.* 3 vols. Baker Commentary on the Old Testament Wisdom and Psalms. Grand Rapids: Baker, 2006–8.

Gorman, Michael J. *Becoming the Gospel: Paul, Participation, and Mission.* Grand Rapids: Eerdmans, 2015.

Graham, Elaine, et al. *Theological Reflection: Methods.* London: SCM, 2005.

Grethlein, Christian. *An Introduction to Practical Theology: History, Theology, and the Communication of the Gospel in the Present.* Translated by Uwe Rasch. Waco, TX: Baylor University Press, 2016.

Gunton, Colin. *The One, the Three, and the Many: God, Creation, and the Culture of Modernity.* Cambridge: Cambridge University Press, 1993.

Guthrie, Harvie. *Theology as Thanksgiving: From the Psalms to the Church's Eucharist.* New York: Seabury, 1981.

Hardy, Sam A., et al. "Daily Religious Involvement, Spirituality, and Moral Emotions." *Psychology of Religion and Spirituality* 6 (2014) 338–48.

Harpham, Edward J. "Gratitude in the History of Ideas." In *Psychology of Gratitude,* edited by Robert A. Emmons and Michael E. McCullough, 19–36. Oxford: Oxford University Press, 2004.

Harris, R. Laird, et al., eds. *Theological Wordbook of the Old Testament.* Chicago: Moody, 1980.

Harrison, R. K. *Leviticus: An Introduction and Commentary.* Tyndale Old Testament Commentaries Series 3. Downers Grove, IL: InterVarsity, 1980.

Harrison, Verna. "Perichoresis in the Greek Fathers." *St. Vladimir's Theological Quarterly* 35 (1991) 53–65.

Hart, David Bentley. *The Beauty of the Infinite: The Aesthetics of Christian Truth.* Grand Rapids: Eerdmans, 2004.

———. "A Gift Exceeding Every Debt: An Eastern Orthodox Appreciation of Anselm's Cur Deus Homo." *Pro Ecclesia* 7 (1998) 333–49.

Hauerwas, Stanley. *Approaching the End: Eschatological Reflections on Church, Politics, and Life*. Grand Rapids: Eerdmans, 2013.
———. *A Community of Character: Towards a Constructive Christian Social Ethic*. South Bend, IN: University of Notre Dame Press, 1981.
———. *The Hauerwas Reader*. Edited by John Berkman and Michael Cartwright. Durham, NC: Duke University Press, 2001.
———. "On Keeping Theological Ethics Theological." In *The Hauerwas Reader*, edited by John Berkman and Michael Cartwright, 51-74. Durham, NC: Duke University Press, 2001.
———. *The Peaceable Kingdom: A Primer in Christian Ethics*. Notre Dame: University of Notre Dame Press, 1993.
———. *Vision and Virtue: Essays in Christian Ethical Reflection*. Notre Dame: Fides, 1974.
Hauerwas, Stanley, and Charles Pinches. *Christians Among the Virtues: Theological Conversations with Ancient and Modern Ethics*. Notre Dame: University of Notre Dame Press, 1997.
Hauerwas, Stanley, and Samuel Wells, eds. *The Blackwell Companion to Christian Ethics*. 2004. Reprint, Chichester: Wiley-Blackwell, 2006.
———. "Christian Ethics as Informed Prayer." In *The Blackwell Companion to Christian Ethics*, edited by Stanley Hauerwas and Samuel Wells, 3-12. 2004. Reprint, Chichester: Wiley-Blackwell, 2006.
———. "The Gift of the Church and the Gifts God Gives It." In *The Blackwell Companion to Christian Ethics*, edited by Stanley Hauerwas and Samuel Wells, 13-27. 2004. Reprint, Chichester: Wiley-Blackwell, 2006.
Havel, Miroslav Vaclav. *Living in Truth*. Edited by Jon Vladislav. London: Faber and Faber, 1989.
Hawkes, Gerald. "The Role of Theology in Practical Theology." *Journal of Theology for South Africa* 49 (1984) 29-61.
Heidegger, Martin. *Being and Time*. Translated by Joan Stambaugh. Albany: State University of New York Press, 2010.
———. *What Is Called Thinking?* Translated by J. Glenn Gray. San Francisco: HarperCollins, 1976.
Heitink, Gerben. *Pastoraat als Hulpverlening: Inleiding in de Pastorale Theologie en Psychologie*. Kampen: Kok, 1984.
Herman, Arthur. *The Cave and the Light: Plato Versus Aristotle and the Struggle for the Soul of Western Civilization*. New York: Random House, 2013.
Hiltner, Seward. *Preface to Pastoral Theology*. New York: Abingdon, 1958.
Hobbes, Thomas. *Leviathan or the Matter, Forme and Power of a Commonwealth Eccleiasticall and Civil*. Edited by Michael Oakeshott. Oxford: Basil Blackwell, 1946.
Holladay, William L., ed. *A Concise Hebrew and Aramaic Lexicon of the Old Testament*. Grand Rapids: Eerdmans: 1988.
Hooker, Morna. "Adam in Romans 1." *New Testament Studies* 6 (1960) 297-306.
Horton, Michael S. *The Law of Perfect Freedom*. Chicago: Moody, 1993.
Hunsinger, Deborah. *Theology and Pastoral Counselling: A New Interdisciplinary Approach*. Grand Rapids: Eerdmans, 1995.
Janicaud, Dominique. *Phenomenology and the Theological Turn: The French Debate*. New York: Fordham University Press, 2000.

Jenson, "The Levitical Sacrificial System." In *Sacrifice in the Bible*, edited by Roger T. Beckwith and Martin J. Selman, 25–40. Grand Rapids: Baker, 1995.

Josephus, Flavius. *The Works of Josephus: Complete and Unabridged*. Translated by William Whiston. Peabody, MA: Hendrickson, 1987.

Joubert, Stephan. "1 Corinthians 9:24–27: An Agonistic Competition?" *Neotestamentica* 35 (2001) 57–68.

———. "Religious Reciprocity in 2 Corinthians 9:6–15: Generosity and Gratitude as Legitimate Responses to *Charis tou theou*." *Neotestamentica* 33 (1999) 79–90.

Kamtekar, Rachana. "Ancient Virtue Ethics." In *The Cambridge Companion to Virtue Ethics*, edited by Daniel C. Russell, 29–48. Cambridge: Cambridge University Press, 2013.

Kant, Immanuel. *Foundations of the Metaphysics of Morals*. New York: Liberal Arts, 1959.

———. "Fundamental Principles of the Metaphysics of Morals." In *The Enlightenment*, edited by Leonard Marsak, 90–106. New York: John Wiley & Sons, 1972.

Kapic, Kelly. *God So Loved, He Gave: Entering the Movement of Divine Generosity*. Grand Rapids: Zondervan, 2010.

Kass, Leon. *The Hungry Soul: Eating and the Perfecting of Our Nature*. New York: Free Press, 1994.

Keller, Timothy. *Counterfeit Gods: The Empty Promises of Money, Sex, and Power*. New York: Dutton, 2009.

Kennedy, James, and Pieter Vos. *Oefenen in Discipelschap: De Gemeente als Groeiplaats van het Goede Leven*. Zoetemeer, NL: Uitgeverij Boekencentrum, 2015.

Kirby, Jason. "Canada's Fatal Attraction to Debt." *Macleans*, January 7, 2014. http://www.macleans.ca/economy/business/canadas-fatal-attraction-to-debt.

Kirk, Alan. "'Love Your Enemies,' The Golden Rule, and Ancient Reciprocity (Luke 6:27–35)." *Journal of Biblical Literature* 122 (2003) 667–86.

Klein, Melanie. *Envy and Gratitude & Other Works, 1946–1983*. New York: Delta, 1975.

Klosko, George. "Four Arguments Against Political Obligations from Gratitude." *Public Affairs Quarterly* 5 (1991) 33–48.

Knowles, Michael P. "Reciprocity and 'Favour' in the Parable of the Undeserving Servant (Luke 17.7–10)." *New Testament Studies* 49 (2003) 256–60.

Kohut, Heinz. *The Kohut Seminars on Self Psychology and Psychotherapy*. Edited by Miriam Elson. New York: Norton, 1987.

———. *The Restoration of the Self*. New York: International Universities Press, 1977.

Komter, Aafke Elisabeth. "Gratitude and Gift Exchange." In *Psychology of Gratitude*, edited by Robert A. Emmons and Michael E. McCullough, 195–212. Oxford: Oxford University Press, 2004.

Kotva, Joseph J. *The Christian Case for Virtue Ethics*. Washington, DC: Georgetown University Press, 1996.

Koyzis, David. *Political Visions and Illusions: A Survey and Christian Critique of Contemporary Ideologies*. Downers Grove, IL: InterVarsity, 2003.

Krause, Neal. "Religious Involvement, Gratitude, and Change in Depressive Symptoms over Time." *International Journal for the Psychology of Religion* 19 (2009) 155–72.

Kreeft, Peter. *Back to Virtue: Traditional Moral Wisdom for Modern Moral Confusion*. San Francisco: Ignatius, 1992.

Kromminga, Carl. "Introduction." In *The Pastoral Genius of Preaching*, by Samuel Volbeda, 1–6. Grand Rapids: Zondervan, 1960.

Kuitert, H. M. *Everything Is Politics, but Politics Is Not Everything*. Translated by John Bowden. Grand Rapids: Eerdmans, 1986.

Lartey, Emmanuel. "Practical Theology as a Theological Form." In *Blackwell Reader in Pastoral and Practical Theology*, edited by James Woodward and Stephen Pattison, 128–34. Oxford: Blackwell, 2000.

Lasch, Christopher. *The Culture of Narcissism: American Life in an Age of Diminishing Expectations*. New York: Norton, 1978.

Leddy, Mary Jo. "The People of God as a Hermeneutic of the Gospel." In *Confident Witness---Changing World: Rediscovering the Gospel in North America*, edited by Craig Van Gelder, 303–16. Grand Rapids: Eerdmans, 1999.

———. *Radical Gratitude*. Maryknoll, NY: Orbis, 2002.

Lee, Philip J. *Against the Protestant Gnostics*. Revised ed. Oxford: Oxford University Press, 1981.

Leithart, Peter J. *Against Christianity*. Moscow, ID: Canon, 2003.

———. *Gratitude: An Intellectual History*. Waco, TX: Baylor University Press, 2014.

Lester, Andrew. *The Angry Christian: A Theology for Care and Counseling*. Louisville: Westminster John Knox, 2003.

Letham, Robert. *The Lord's Supper: Eternal Word in Broken Bread*. Phillipsburg: P & R, 2001.

Lewis, C.S. *The Four Loves*. New York: Harcourt Brace, 1960.

———. *God in the Dock: Essays on Theology and Ethics*. Edited by Walter Hooper. Grand Rapids: Eerdmans, 2014.

———. *Mere Christianity*. London: Fontana, 1963.

———. *The Screwtape Letters*. London: HarperCollins, 1942.

Lindsay, Dennis R. "Todah and Eucharist: The Celebration of the Lord's Supper as a 'Thank Offering' in the Early Church." *Restoration Quarterly* 39 (1997) 83–100.

Lombardi, Joseph. "Filial Gratitude and God's Right to Command." *Journal of Religious Ethics* 19 (1991) 93–118.

Long, Thomas. "Practical Theology on the Quad." In *For Life Abundant: Practical Theology, Theological Education, and Christian Ministry*, edited by Dorothy C. Bass and Craig Dykstra, 243–60. Grand Rapids: Eerdmans, 2008.

Longman, Tremper. *Immanuel in Our Place: Seeing Christ in Old Testament Worship*. Phillipsburg: P & R, 2001.

Lopez, Robert S. "The Carolingian Prelude." In *Medieval Society: 400–1450*, edited by Norman F. Cantor and Michael S. Werthman, 4–32. 2nd ed. New York: Crowell, 1972.

Luther, Martin. "Disputation Against Scholastic Theology." In *Martin Luther's Basic Theological Writings*, edited by Timothy F. Hull, 34–39. Minneapolis: Fortress, 1989.

Lyubomirsky, Sonja. *The How of Happiness: A Scientific Approach to Getting the Life You Want*. New York: Penguin, 2008.

MacIntyre, Alasdair. *After Virtue: A Study in Moral Theory*. London: Duckworth, 1997.

———. *A Short History of Ethics*. New York: Macmillan, 1966.

Macquarrie, John. *A Guide to the Sacraments*. New York: Continuum, 1999.

Malatesta, Carol Z., and Carrol E. Izard, eds. *Emotions in Adult Development*. Beverly Hills: Sage, 1984.

Marion, Jean-Luc. *Being Given: Toward a Phenomenology of Givenness*. Stanford: Stanford University Press, 2002.

———. *The Erotic Phenomenon*. Chicago: University of Chicago Press, 2006.
———. *In Excess: Studies of Saturated Phenomena*. New York: Fordham University Press, 2001.
———. *Idol and Distance: Five Studies*. New York: Fordham University Press, 2001.
———. *On Descartes's Metaphysical Prism: The Constitution and Limits of Onto-Theology in Cartesian Thought*. Chicago: University of Chicago Press, 1999.
Marsak, Leonard, ed. *The Enlightenment*. New York: Wiley & Sons: 1972.
———. "Introduction." In *The Enlightenment*, edited by Leonard Marsak, 3–9. New York: Wiley & Sons: 1972.
Marshall, I. H. *Last Supper and Lord's Supper*. Exeter: Paternoster, 1980.
Martelaere, Aldo de. "Personal Obligations in Personal Relations." In *Gifts and Interests*, edited by Antoon Vandevelde, 209–25. Leuven: Peeters, 2000.
Marx, Karl. *Economic and Philosophic Manuscripts of 1944*. Translated by Martin Milligan. New York: International, 1964.
Mauss, Marcel. *The Gift: The Form and Reason for Exchange in Archaic Societies*. Translated by W. D. Halls. London: Routledge, 1990.
———. "Gift, Gift." In *The Logic of the Gift: Toward an Ethic of Generosity*, edited by Alan D. Schrift, 28–32. New York: Routledge, 1997.
Mays, James L. *Psalms*. Interpretation. Louisville: John Knox, 1994.
McConnell, Terrence. *Gratitude*. Philadelphia: Temple University Press, 1993.
McCraty, Rollin, and Doc Childre. "The Grateful Heart: The Psychophysiology of Appreciation." In *Psychology of Gratitude*, edited by Robert A. Emmons and Michael E. McCullough, 230–55. Oxford: Oxford University Press, 2004.
McCullough, Michael E., et al. "Is Gratitude a Moral Affect?" *Psychological Bulletin* 127 (2001) 249–66.
McCullough, Michael E., and Jo-Ann Tsang. "Parent of the Virtues? The Prosocial Contours of Gratitude." In *Psychology of Gratitude*, edited by Robert Emmons and Michael E. McCullough, 123–43. Oxford: Oxford University Press, 2004.
Meilander, Gilbert. *The Theory and Practice of Virtue*. Notre Dame: University of Notre Dame Press, 1984.
Merleau-Ponty, Maurice. *Phenomenology of Perception*. New York: Humanities, 1962.
Milbank, John. *Being Reconciled: Ontology and Pardon*. London: Routledge, 2003.
———. "Can a Gift Be Given?" *Modern Theology* 11 (1995) 119–61.
———. "Can A Gift Be Given: Prolegomena to a Future Trinitarian Metaphysic." In *Rethinking Metaphysics*, edited by L. Gregory Jones and Stephen E. Fowl, 119–61. Cambridge, MA: Basil Blackwell, 1995.
———. "Gregory of Nyssa: The Force of Identity." In *Christian Origins*, edited by Lewis Ayres and Gareth Jones, 94–116. London: Routledge, 1998.
———. "Introduction." In *Introducing Radical Orthodoxy: Mapping a Post-Secular Theology*, by James K. A Smith, 11–20. Grand Rapids: Eerdmans, 2004.
———. *Theology and Social Theory*. 2nd ed. Oxford: Blackwell, 2006
———. *The Word Made Strange: Theology, Language, Culture*. Oxford: Blackwell, 1997.
Milbank, John, et al. "Introduction." In *Radical Orthodoxy: A New Theology*, edited by John Milbank, et al., 1–20. London: Routledge, 1999.
Milgrom, Jacob. *Leviticus 1–16*. Anchor Bible 3. New Haven: Yale University Press, 1998.
Millar, Patrick D., Jr. "Enthroned on the Praises of Israel: The Praise of God in Old Testament Theology." *Interpretation* 39 (1985) 5–19.

———. *The Religion of Ancient Israel*. Louisville: Westminster John Knox, 2000.

Millar, Patrick Lee. "Finding Oneself with Friends." In *The Cambridge Companion to Aristotle's Nicomachean Ethics*, edited by Ronald Polansky, 319–49. Cambridge: Cambridge University Press, 2014.

Miller-McLemore, Bonnie J. *Christian Theology in Practice: Discovering a Discipline*. Grand Rapids: Eerdmans, 2012.

———. "Cognitive Science and the Question of Theological Method." *The Journal of Pastoral Theology* 20 (2010) 64–92.

———. "The Human Web: Reflections on the State of Pastoral Theology." *Christian Century* (1993) 336–39.

———. *The Wiley-Blackwell Companion to Practical Theology*. Chichester, UK: Blackwell, 2012.

Mitchell, Lynette. *Greeks Bearing Gifts: The Public Use of Private Relationship in the Greek World, 435–323 BC*. Cambridge: Cambridge University Press, 1997.

Mitchell, Mark T. *The Politics of Gratitude: Scale, Place and Community in a Global Age*. Washington, DC: Potomac, 2012.

Moloney, Francis J. *A Body Broken for Broken People: Eucharist in the New Testament*. Blackburn, Australia: Dove, 1997.

Mudge, Lewis S., and James N. Poling. *Formation and Reflection: The Promise of Practical Theology*. Minneapolis: Fortress, 1987.

Mumford, Lewis. "The Monastery and the Clock." In *The City Cultures Reader*, edited by Ian Borden, et al., 121–23. London: Routledge, 2000.

Murray, John. *Principles of Conduct: Aspects of Biblical Ethics*. Grand Rapids: Eerdmans, 1957.

Newman, Elizabeth. "Diagnosing Vice and Prescribing Virtue: Sloth and the Lord's Supper." *Perspectives in Religious Studies* 41 (2014) 137–50.

Nolan, Kirk J. *Reformed Virtue After Barth: Developing Moral Virtue Ethics in the Reformed Tradition*. Louisville: Westminster John Knox, 2014.

Nouwen, Henri. *Adam: God's Beloved*. New York: Orbis, 2011.

———. *Can You Drink the Cup?* Notre Dame: Ave Maria, 1996.

———. *Peacework*. Maryknoll: Orbis, 2005.

———. *Reaching Out: The Three Movements of the Spiritual Life*. New York: Doubleday, 1975.

———. *The Return of the Prodigal Son*. New York: Doubleday, 1992.

———. *Show Me the Way: Daily Lenten Readings*. New York: Crossroad, 1992.

Nygren, Anders. *Agape and Eros*. Philadelphia: Westminster, 1953.

Oden, Thomas C. *Contemporary Theology and Psychotherapy*. Philadelphia: Westminster, 1967.

O'Donovan, Oliver. *Resurrection and Moral Order: An Outline for Evangelical Ethics*. Leicester: InterVarsity, 1986.

———. *The Ways of Judgment*. Grand Rapids: Eerdmans, 2005.

Ogilvy, James. "Greed." In *Wicked Pleasures: Meditations on the Seven "Deadly" Sins*, edited by Robert C. Solomon, 87–115. Lanham, MD: Rowman & Littlefield, 1999.

O'Reilly, Kevin. "The Significance of Worship in the Thought of Thomas Aquinas: Some Reflections." *International Philosophical Quarterly* 53 (2013) 453–62.

Osmer, Richard. *Practical Theology: An Introduction*. Grand Rapids: Eerdmans, 2008.

Pao, David W. *Thanksgiving: An Investigation of a Pauline Theme*. Downers Grove, IL: InterVarsity, 2002.

Pattison, Stephen. *A Critique of Pastoral Care*. London: SCM, 2000.

———. "Straw for Bricks: A Basic Introduction to Theological Reflection." In *The Blackwell Reader in Pastoral and Practical Theology*, edited by James Woodward and Stephen Pattison, 136–45. Oxford: Blackwell, 2000.

Pattison, Stephen, and James Woodward. "Introduction to Pastoral and Practical Theology." In *The Blackwell Reader in Pastoral and Practical Theology*, edited by James Woodward and Stephen Pattison, 1–19. Malden, MA: Blackwell, 2000.

Patton, John. *From Ministry to Theology: Pastoral Action and Reflection*. Nashville: Abingdon, 1990.

Pembroke, Neil. *Renewing Pastoral Practice: Trinitarian Perspectives on Pastoral Care and Counselling*. Burlington, VT: Ashgate, 2006.

Pennington, Jonathan T. "The Sermon on the Mount and the Kingdom of God." Paper presented at IBR-SBL, San Antonio, TX, November 19, 2016.

Peskett, Howard and Vinoth Ramachandra. *The Message of Mission*. Downers Grove, IL: InterVarsity Academic, 2003.

Peterman, G. W. *Paul's Gift from Philippi: Conventions of Gift Exchange and Christian Giving*. Society for New Testament Studies Monograph Series 92. Cambridge: Cambridge University Press, 1997.

———. "'Thankless Thanks': The Epistolary Social Convention in Philippians 4:10–20." *Tyndale Bulletin* 42 (1991) 261–70.

Piper, John. *Future Grace*. Sisters, OR: Multnomah, 1995.

Pitre, Brant. *Jesus and the Last Supper*. Grand Rapids: Eerdmans, 2015.

Plantinga, Cornelius, Jr. "The Concern of the Church in the Socio-Political World: A Calvinist and Reformed Perspective." *Calvin Theological Journal* 18 (1983) 190–205.

———. *Not the Way It's Supposed to Be: A Breviary of Sin*. Grand Rapids: Eerdmans, 1995.

Pohl, Christine D. *Living into Community: Cultivating Practices That Sustain Us*. Grand Rapids: Eerdmans, 2012.

Polansky, Ronald, ed. *The Cambridge Companion to Aristotle's Nicomachean Ethics*. Cambridge: Cambridge University Press, 2014.

Pope, Stephen J. "Aquinas on Almsgiving, Justice, and Charity." *Heythrop Journal* 32 (1991) 167–91.

———. "Virtue Ethics in Thomas Aquinas." In *Virtue*, edited by Charles E. Curran and Lisa A. Fullam, 3–20. Readings in Moral Theology 16. New York: Paulist, 2011.

Porter, Jean. "Virtue Ethics in the Medieval Period." In *The Cambridge Companion to Virtue Ethics*, edited by Daniel C. Russell, 70–91. Cambridge: Cambridge University Press, 2013.

Purves, Andrew. *The Crucifixion of Ministry: Surrendering Our Ambitions to the Service of Christ*. Downers Grove, IL: InterVarsity, 2007.

———. *Reconstructing Pastoral Theology: A Christological Foundation*. Louisville: Westminster John Knox, 2004.

Purvis, Zachary. *Theology and the University in Nineteenth Century Germany*. Oxford: Oxford University Press, 2016.

Rahner, Karl. *The Trinity*. Translated by J. Donceel. London: Burns and Oates, 1970.

Reed, Jeffrey T. "Are Paul's Thanksgivings 'Epistolary'?" *Journal for the Study of the New Testament* 18 (1996) 87–99.

Reinders, Hans. "Being Thankful: Parenting the Mentally Disabled." In *The Blackwell Companion to Christian Ethics*, edited by Stanley Hauerwas and Samuel Wells, 427–40. Reprint, Chichester: Wiley-Blackwell, 2006.
———. *Receiving the Gift of Friendship: Profound Disability, Theological Anthropology, and Ethics*. Grand Rapids: Eerdmans, 2007.
Ricoeur, Paul. *Freud and Philosophy: An Essay on Interpretation*. New Haven, CT: Yale University Press, 1970.
———. "The Golden Rule: Exegetical and Theological Perplexities." *New Testament Studies* 36 (1990) 392–97.
Roberts, Robert C. "The Blessings of Gratitude: A Conceptual Analysis." In *Psychology of Gratitude*, edited by Robert A. Emmons and Michael E. McCullough, 58–79. Oxford: Oxford University Press, 2004.
———. *Spiritual Emotions: A Psychology of Christian Virtues*. Grand Rapids: Eerdmans, 2007.
———. "Virtues and Rules." *Philosophy and Phenomenological Research* 51 (1991) 325–43.
Russell, Daniel C. "Introduction." In *The Cambridge Companion to Virtue Ethics*, edited by Daniel C. Russell, 1–6. Cambridge: Cambridge University Press, 2013.
———. "Virtue Ethics, Happiness, and the Good Life." In *The Cambridge Companion to Virtue Ethics*, edited by Daniel C. Russell, 7–28. Cambridge: Cambridge University Press, 2013.
Sacks, Oliver. *Gratitude*. New York: Knopf, 2015.
Sahlins, Marshall. "The Spirit of a Gift." In *The Logic of the Gift: Toward an Ethic of Generosity*, edited by Alan D. Schrift, 70–99. New York: Routledge, 1997.
———. *Stone Age Economics*. Chicago: Aldine, 1972.
Sayers, Dorothy. *Creed or Chaos*. 1949. Reprint, Manchester, NH: Sophia Institute, 1999.
Schimmel, Solomon. "Gratitude in Judaism." In *Psychology of Gratitude*, edited by Robert A. Emmons and Michael E. McCullough, 37–57. Oxford: Oxford University Press, 2004.
Schlabach, Gerald W. "Peace and War." In *The Blackwell Companion to Christian Ethics*, edited by Stanley Hauerwas and Samuel Wells, 360–74. Reprint, Chichester: Wiley-Blackwell, 2006.
Schlossberg, Herbert. *Idols for Destruction: The Conflict of Christian Faith and American Culture*. 1990. Reprint, Wheaton: Crossway, 1993.
Schoch, Richard W. *The Secrets of Happiness: Three Thousand Years of Searching for the Good Life*. New York: Scribner, 2006.
Schrift, Alan D., ed. *The Logic of the Gift: Toward an Ethic of Generosity*. New York: Routledge, 1997.
Schubert, P. *The Form and Function of the Pauline Thanksgiving*. Berlin: Alfred Topelmann, 1939.
Schuringa, H. David. "Hearing the Word in a Visual Age: A Practical Theological Consideration of Preaching within the Contemporary Urge to Visualization." PhD diss., Theologische Universiteit te Kampen, 1995.
———. "Wagging the Dog: The Church's Crying Need for Reformed Practical Theology." *Calvin Theological Journal* 35 (2000) 151–61.
Schwartz, Daniel. *Aquinas on Friendship*. Oxford: Oxford University Press, 2007.

Seligman, Martin. *Authentic Happiness: Using the New Positive Psychology to Realize Your Potential for Lasting Fulfillment.* New York: Atria, 2002.

Seneca. *De Beneficiis.* Vol. 3 of *Moral Essays.* Translated by John W. Basore. Loeb Classical Library 310. Cambridge, MA: Harvard University Press, 1935.

———. *De Providentia. De Constantia. De Ira.* Vol. 1 of *Moral Essays.* Translated by John W. Basore. Loeb Classical Library 214. Cambridge, MA: Harvard University Press, 1928.

———. *Epistles 66–92.* Translated by Richard M. Gummere. Loeb Classical Library 76. Cambridge, MA: Harvard University Press, 1920.

Shelton, Charles. "Gratitude: Considerations from a Moral Perspective." In *Psychology of Gratitude*, edited by Robert A. Emmons and Michael E. McCullough, 257–81. Oxford: Oxford University Press, 2004.

Silva, Moisés. *Philippians.* Baker Exegetical Commentary on the New Testament. 2nd ed. Grand Rapids: Baker Academic, 2005.

Smedes, Lewis. *Mere Morality: What God Expects from Ordinary People.* Grand Rapids: Eerdmans, 1983.

Smith, Christian, and Melinda Lindquist Denton. *Soul Searching: The Religious and Spiritual Lives of American Teenagers.* New York: Oxford University Press, 2005.

Smith, Christian, and Patricia Snell. *Souls in Transition: The Religious and Spiritual Lives of Emerging Adults.* New York: Oxford University Press, 2009.

Smith, James K. A. *Desiring the Kingdom: Worship, Worldview, and Cultural Formation.* Grand Rapids: Baker Academic, 2009.

———. *Introducing Radical Orthodoxy: Mapping a Post-Secular Theology.* Grand Rapids: Baker, 2004.

———. *Jacques Derrida: Live Theory.* London: Continuum, 2005.

Smith, James K. A., and James Olthuis, eds. *Radical Orthodoxy and the Reformed Tradition: Creation, Covenant, and Participation.* Grand Rapids: Baker, 2004.

Solomon, Robert. *In Defense of Sentimentality.* Oxford: Oxford University Press, 2004.

———. "Introduction." In *Psychology of Gratitude*, edited by Robert A. Emmons and Michael E. McCullough, v–xi. Oxford: Oxford University Press, 2004.

———, ed. *Wicked Pleasures: Meditations on the Seven 'Deadly' Sins.* Lanham, MD: Rowman & Littlefield, 1999.

Sommers, Shula. "Adults Evaluating Their Emotions: A Cross-Cultural Comparison." In *Emotions in Adult Development*, edited by Carel Z. Malatesta and Carrol E. Izard, 313–36. Beverly Hills: Sage, 1984.

Steindl-Rast, David. "Gratitude as Thankfulness and as Gratefulness." In *Psychology of Gratitude*, edited by Robert A. Emmons and Michael E. McCullough, 282–89. Oxford: Oxford University Press, 2004.

Stob, Henry. "The Heidelberg Catechism in Moral Perspective." *The Reformed Journal* 13 (1963) 6–9.

Stott, John R.W. *God's New Society: The Message of Ephesians.* Downer's Grove: InterVarsity, 1979.

Straw, C. E. "Cyprian and Matthew 5:45: The Evolution of Christian Patronage." *Studia Patristica* 18 (1989) 329–39.

Swinton, John. *Raging with Compassion: Pastoral Responses to the Problem of Evil.* Grand Rapids: Eerdmans, 2007.

Swinton, John, and Harriet Mowat. *Practical Theology and Qualitative Research.* London: SCM, 2006.

Sykes, Karen. *Arguing with Anthropology: An Introduction to Critical Theories of the Gift*. London: Routledge, 2005.
Tanner, Kathryn. *Economy of Grace*. Minneapolis: Fortress, 2005.
———. "Economy of Grace." *Word & World* 30 (2010) 174–81.
Taylor, Charles. *A Secular Age*. Cambridge, MA: Belknap, 2007.
Terpstra, Marin. "Social Gifts and the Gift of Sociality: Some Thoughts on Mauss's *The Gift* and Hobbes's *Leviathan*." In *Gifts and Interests*, edited by Antoon Vandevelde, 191–208. Leuven: Peeters, 2000.
Thurneysen, Eduard. *A Theology of Pastoral Care*. Translated by J. A. Worthington and Thomas Wieser. Richmond, VA: John Knox, 1962.
Tillich, Paul. *The Courage to Be*. New Haven, CT: Yale University Press, 1952.
———. *Systematic Theology*. Vol. 1. London: SCM, 1951.
Tracy, David. *The Analogical Imagination: Christian Theology and the Culture of Pluralism*. New York: Crossroad, 1981.
———. *Blessed Rage for Order: The New Pluralism in Theology*. Chicago: University of Chicago Press, 1996.
———. "Practical Theology in the Situation of Global Pluralism." In *Formation and Reflection: The Promise of Practical Theology*, edited by Lewis S. Mudge and James N. Poling, 139–54. Minneapolis: Fortress, 1987.
Turnbull, Stephan K. "Grace and Gift in Luther and Paul." *Word and World* 24 (2004) 305–14.
Vandevelde, Antoon, ed. *Gifts and Interests*. Leuven: Peeters, 2000.
Vanier, Jean. *Community and Growth*. 2nd rev. ed. New York: Paulist, 1989.
———. *Happiness: Aristotle for the New Century*. Translated by Kathryn Spink. 2001. Reprint, New York: Arcade, 2012.
Visser, Margaret. *The Gift of Thanks: The Roots and Rituals of Gratitude*. New York: Houghton Mifflin, 2009.
Volf, Miroslav. *Exclusion and Embrace: A Theological Exploration of Identity, Otherness, and Reconciliation*. Nashville: Abingdon, 1996.
———. *Free of Charge: Giving and Forgiving in a Culture Stripped of Grace*. Grand Rapids: Zondervan, 2005.
Volf, Miroslav, and Dorothy C. Bass, eds. *Practicing Theology: Beliefs and Practices in Christian Life*. Grand Rapids: Eerdmans, 2002.
Volpe, Medi-Ann. *Rethinking Christian Identity: Doctrine and Discipleship*. Chichester: Wiley-Blackwell, 2013.
Von Rod, Gerhard. *Old Testament Theology: The Theology of Israel's Historical Traditions*. Vol. 1. Translated by D. M. G. Stalker. New York: Harper & Row, 1962.
Vos, Pieter. "Christelijke Deugden in de Gemeente." In *Oefenen in Discipelschap: De Gemeente als Groeiplaats van het Goede Leven*, edited by James Kennedy and Pieter Vos, 27–49. Zoetemeer, NL: Uitgeverij Boekencentrum, 2015.
Walker, A. D. M. "Gratefulness and Gratitude." *Proceedings of the Aristotelian Society* 81 (1980–81) 39–55.
———. "Obligations of Gratitude and Political Obligation." *Philosophy and Public Affairs* 18.4 (1989) 359–64.
———. "Political Obligation and the Argument from Gratitude." *Philosophy and Public Affairs* 17 (1988) 191–211.
Walton, Robert. "The Bible and Tradition in Theological Reflection." *British Journal of Theological Education* 13 (2003) 133–51.

Watkins, Philip. "Gratitude and Subjective Well-Being." In *Psychology of Gratitude*, edited by Robert A. Emmons and Michael E. McCullough, 167–92. Oxford: Oxford University Press, 2004.
Webb, Stephen H. "Christian Giving and the Trinity." *Quarterly Review* 22 (2002) 333–46.
———. *The Gifting God: A Trinitarian Ethics of Excess*. Oxford: Oxford University Press, 1998.
———. "Whatever Happened to the Sin of Gluttony? Or Why Christians Do Not Serve Meat with the Eucharist." *Encounter* 58 (1997) 243–50.
Westermann, Claus. *The Praise of God in the Psalms*. Translated by Keith R. Crim and Richard N. Soulen. Atlanta: John Knox, 1965.
White, James F. *Protestant Worship. Traditions in Transition*. Louisville: Westminster John Knox, 1989.
Whitlark, Jason. "Enabling χαρις: Transformation of the Convention of Reciprocity by Philo and in Ephesians." *Perspectives in Religious Studies* 30 (2003) 325–57.
Williams, Rowan. *Being Christian: Baptism, Bible, Eucharist, Prayer*. Grand Rapids: Eerdmans, 2014.
Willimon, William. *Sinning Like a Christian: A New Look at the Seven Deadly Sins*. Nashville: Abingdon, 2005.
Wilson, Jonathan R. *Gospel Virtues: Practicing Faith, Love, and Hope*. Eugene, OR: Wipf & Stock, 1998.
Wilson, Timothy. *Strangers to Ourselves: Discovering the Adaptive Unconscious*. Cambridge: Harvard University Press, 2002.
Winter, Bruce W. "The Public Honoring of Christian Benefactors, Romans 13:3–4 and 1 Peter 2:14–15." *Journal for the Study of the New Testament* 34 (1988) 87–103.
Witherington, Ben, III. *The Gospel of Mark: A Socio-Rhetorical Commentary*. Grand Rapids: Eerdmans, 2001.
Wolterstorff, Nicholas. *Justice in Love*. Grand Rapids: Eerdmans, 2011.
———. *Lament for a Son*. Grand Rapids: Eerdmans, 1987.
———. *Until Justice and Peace Embrace*. Grand Rapids: Eerdmans, 1983.
Wong, Craig. "Household Debt in Canada Hits a Record High—Again." *Macleans*, September 15, 2016. https://www.macleans.ca/economy/household-debt-in-canada-hits-a-record-high-again.
Woodward, James, and Stephen Pattison. *The Blackwell Reader in Pastoral and Practical Theology*. Malden: Blackwell, 2000.
Wright, N. T. *After You Believe: Why Christian Character Matters*. New York: HarperOne, 2010.
———. *Holy Communion for Amateurs*. London: Hodder & Stoughton, 1999.
———. *John for Everyone: Part One*. Louisville: Westminster John Knox, 2004.
———. *The New Testament and the People of God*. Minneapolis: Fortress, 1992.
———. *Small Faith, Great God*. 2nd ed. Downers Grove, IL: InterVarsity, 2010.
Zizioulas, John D. *Being as Communion: Studies in Personhood and the Church*. Crestwood, NY: St. Vladimir's Seminary, 1997.
Zylla, Phil C. "Practices of Acceptance, Understanding and Reciprocity: Caring for Children with Disabilities and their Families." *Pastoral Psychology* 65 (2016) 703–15.
———. *The Roots of Sorrow: A Pastoral Theology of Suffering*. Waco, TX: Baylor University Press, 2012.

———. *Virtue as Consent to Being: A Pastoral-Theological Perspective on Jonathan Edwards's Construct of Virtue.* McMaster Ministry Study Series 2. Eugene, OR: Pickwick, 2011.

www.ingramcontent.com/pod-product-compliance
Lightning Source LLC
Chambersburg PA
CBHW071247230426
43668CB00011B/1620